# Dreams:
# The Dark Speech
# of the Spirit

# Dreams:
# The Dark Speech
# of the Spirit

*A Christian Interpretation*

Morton T. Kelsey

*Doubleday & Company, Inc., Garden City, New York*
1968

# Contents

# Preface

This book deals with a long-forgotten aspect of church teaching and practice, the Christian understanding and interpretation of dreams. For two centuries very little has appeared on this subject; indeed, it has been considered dead and buried in most theological circles. Then came the psychological revolution started by Freud and Jung, and now the discoveries of the recent laboratory research on dreams. It has been the work of these pioneers which led me to take another look at my Christian heritage in the matter of dream interpretation. For ten years I have been interested in this and have been collecting the materials presented here.

Because there are no studies available to the reader that deal with these materials as a whole, I have attempted to present the facts as completely as possible in order to show how much support there is for a Christian approach to dreams. Many of the materials, particularly from the fathers of the church, have never been compiled and studied from this standpoint. It is also necessary to take a fresh look at what the Old and New Testaments have to say on the subject, and at the origins of this understanding. Although at times this treatment may seem repetitive, all of the materials need to be gathered together and considered, and this is exactly what is attempted.

Why have I continued to study dreams from a Christian point of view? Primarily, the consideration of dreams brought my own religious faith and practice to life. It brought substance to my theology, a thinking that had its origins in the Christian philosophy of Baron von Hügel and A. E. Taylor. It brought reality to the spiritual world. I have also seen a like interest in dreams do the same for others who were stranded on the shores of a barren rationalism. In the end, these things have led me to think through again the basic philosophy of Christianity, and particularly the conceptions of how man comes to know God.

During the years of writing this book I have been greatly aided by a close friend, the Reverend John A. Sanford, whose similar interest and wide reading have given me materials and ideas and encouragement. My wife and family, who are great dreamers and have shown me the reality of many aspects of dreams that cannot be found just in the counseling hour, have given me support in a spirit which has made this study possible. Leo B. Froke, who is a psychiatrist, has also been a constant friend and sounding board for many of the ideas presented in these pages. Three Jungian analysts, James and Hilde Kirsch and Max Zeller, have also been of the greatest help in understanding my own dreams and those of others.

In the actual writing of this book I am indebted beyond measure to Paisley Roach, who researched many materials and reworked much of the manuscript with an eye to expression and meaning. Without her help this book could not have reached its present form.

Through the courtesy of Claremont Colleges the facilities of Honnold Library have been available for much of the research of the materials, and I deeply appreciate the help Mrs. Kenneth R. Jackman has given me. The careful and clear translations were made by Gerald F. Penny and Elizabeth Shedd. I am especially grateful to Mrs. Judy Starman, Mrs. Leslie Meyer, and Mrs. Greta Melickian for their long hours of typing and careful checking of the manuscript.

I am also deeply thankful to the many who have come to talk with me of their problems, hopes, and fears, and who have shared their dreams with me. These people have given reality to the meaning of the dream as nothing else could have.

# Dreams:
# The Dark Speech
# of the Spirit

*If there is a prophet among you,
I the Lord make myself known to
him in a vision, I speak with him
in a dream . . . in dark speech.*

NUMBERS 12:6 AND 8

# *one* Why Bother with Dreams?

It is unusual to find a Christian today who pays religious attention to dreams; it is even unusual to find Christians who know what is meant by this. Modern students of theology do not seem to recognize the existence of a religious point of view on the subject, and the ordinary churchgoer, for good reason, is either caught unawares or with a negative attitude by questions about the religious meaning of dreams. In this scientific era of ours he may be quite well informed about the important new research on dreaming. He may even be one of the few who pay attention to their own dreams. But in our Western Christian society today there is no group, practically no voice at all, that would encourage him to understand his dreams as a source of religious insight into life. Instead, most twentieth-century Christians simply assume that the idea of finding religious meaning or reality in dreams is a proven fallacy that went out with the dark ages, and they see no need to think about it again.

This attitude is strange for several reasons. In the first place, the early Christian church viewed the dream as one of the most significant and most important ways in which God revealed his will to man. Dreams were understood to give men access to a reality that was difficult to contact in any other way. Not only do we find this view in the Old Testament, in the New Testament, and in the church fathers up to the time of Aquinas, but it is the attitude of nearly every other major religion of the world. Instead of simply accepting that these people were all off the track, it would be well to hear what they had to say. Some of the most astute observations about dreams were made by the early Christian thinkers, and this evidence has not been systematically presented to the Christian public in our time.

Then there is the important support for this traditional Christian view which comes from two sections of the healing profession, psychiatry and clinical psychology. In the writings and practice of both of them the dream has come in for serious consideration. Here it is seen to reveal the autonomous psychic depth of man known as the unconscious, and to give hints about attitudes and forgotten contents that, when understood, can heal men of various forms of nervous and mental illness. As this science has developed, more and more medical men have come to see the dream as revealing not only the individual psyche, but a collective unconscious, a vast realm of experience that is beyond the individual's ken and which touches realities of a religious and spiritual nature. The work of Dr. C. G. Jung and his followers in particular has revealed the religious implications of the dream, while other medical research, recently reported in the *International Journal of Neuropsychiatry*, is revealing powers of human perception that would have been scoffed at twenty years ago. The influence of these ideas about the dream and the unconscious has also reached far beyond the individual, into fields as diverse as modern drama, anthropology, and all kinds of criticism.

Besides this, the current research on sleep and dreaming has shown that dream experience is universal, and that it occurs in a regular pattern night after night in spite of most people's total amnesia the next morning. The person who is convinced he never dreams is simply not aware of what is going on below the level of consciousness. The studies have demonstrated conclusively that something is going on practically all the time in sleep, while about every ninety minutes a vivid dream occurs, absorbing almost every reaction of the dreamer completely. This work, which we will describe in a later chapter, is in progress at a number of the larger medical schools across the country.[1] It certainly does suggest how limited most Chris-

[1] A comprehensive survey of the material on experimental study of sleep has been compiled by Charles Fisher in his article on the "Psychoanalytic Implications of Recent Research on Sleep and Dreaming," *Journal of the American Psychoanalytic Association*, Vol. 13, No. 2, April 1965, pp. 197–303. A more popular treatment of the work of William Dement is given in the feature article in *The New Yorker* of September 18, 1965. *MD Medical Newsmagazine* for December 1965 also features dreams, dealing with several aspects, including the interesting cover story, "Dreams and History" (Vol. 9, No. 12). There is also

tians have been in their attitude toward dreams and dreaming.

And then finally it must be admitted that men are fascinated by dreams. Ever since there were words to talk about them, these strange happenings in the night have been the subject of wonder and discussion wherever men gathered to talk about their hopes and fears. Literature is full of dreams. And even in this day of their sophisticated rejection, after a few cocktails people begin to talk about the funny dream they had the night before. Whenever I lecture and mention my interest in the serious study of dreams, the questions about them begin to come out, and people invariably show their hunger to talk and to hear more about the meaning of their dreams.

Recently I was visiting the rector of a large and smoothly organized urban parish, a man who admits that he has probably not been bothered by an illogical thought since the first grade. When I mentioned that I was doing some writing on dreams, he could not wait to tell me of the dream that had awakened him a few nights before with the picture of an accident so real that it terrified him. The next day he had learned to his horror of an accident that had claimed the life of a close friend that night. He was still shaken by the experience when I talked with him, and he expressed the hope that someone would write of dreams in religious tradition, for he could find no material relevant to his experience in modern religious writing.

Yet it is easy to forget how many people are still concerned with dreams. The man in the street is still concerned enough about them to keep a big business going in dream books, which can be found in the paperback racks of almost any newsstand or corner drugstore. There are a dozen or more of them in print at any one time,[2] and they are turned to by millions of people even though the basic idea in them is highly questionable. Most of them try to separate out

---

an excellent and very readable summary of the whole subject published by the U. S. Department of Health, Education and Welfare, called *Current Research on Sleep and Dreams*, Public Health Service Publication, No. 1389, Washington, D.C., U. S. Government Printing Office.

[2] Last year one of these volumes was the hardback edition of *Zolar's Encyclopedia and Dictionary of Dreams*, brought out by Doubleday in 1963. One of the most popular little handbooks is the Dell paperback, *Dreams*, which has gone through at least one revision. Although, as we shall indicate later, dream symbols cannot be handled in the arbitrary way these books employ, they at least make a stab at understanding dreams, and the great amount of interest in them is a token of the popular attitude.

specific dream images and assign meanings to them in order to foretell the future or to explain certain life situations, and this is quite contrary to the legitimate study of dreams. These books, however, are interesting because they do show how great the popular interest is in the subject, and how persistent the popular "common-sense" attitude toward dreams continues to be.

## Two different attitudes

In fact, it is easy for us in the twentieth Christian century to forget that there can be two very different attitudes about something like dreams. The church has been immersed in one point of view for nearly two hundred years, and its teaching and practice show little acquaintance with any other. And so before we come to the questions "What is the meaning of the experience of dreaming?" and "What exactly is a dream?", it is well to state these two attitudes and see how basically different they are from each other. According to one of them, dreaming is an essentially meaningless experience, not worth the time of day (or night), while the other sees in it a key to unlock the secrets of human personality and even to find meaning beyond the personal.

The most common attitude in our Western culture is the first one. In this way of thinking, the process of dreaming appears to be merely one more way in which the human nervous system reacts automatically to physical stimulus. A dream is "nothing but" the rehash of yesterday's half-forgotten experiences, thrown up mechanically, without any kind of order, before the sleeping consciousness. It is the feedback that occurs as consciousness rewinds itself for another day's activity. Vivid dreams, according to this point of view, result from some immediate stimulus, like dining late on too much joint and chutney or overdoing the mince pie; or they can be caused by something that happens during sleep, like the siren on a passing fire truck, the creaking of a door, or by letting in too much night air. To be concerned about dreams then is silly; it simply indicates a superstitious mind, or else too much interest in pretty poetry.

This attitude was very nearly universal among the intelligentsia of the eighteenth and nineteenth centuries, and it is still held among those influenced by the positivistic science of this period—in other words, by most of us. It was first suggested 2200 years ago by Aristotle in three little papers on dreaming, although he did not go quite as far as the position I have outlined. It was supported by Cicero a few centuries later, but it had few other exponents in the ancient world.

Then after centuries of unpopularity this view was revived to become the accepted point of view. It might well be correct, but it was accepted without ever being subjected to scientific inquiry. It was considered so obvious and certain that there has been no need to spend time and effort verifying it, or even to spell it out very clearly. In fact, it is hard to find this view fully expressed in written form, although it is assumed in much of the writing in every field of our society. Yet there is nothing in the present careful research on dreaming that particularly supports this point of view. Instead, the actual studies frequently seem to give both analytical and empirical support to the other point of view.

This quite different point of view, which finds dreams highly significant and meaningful, has been held in practically all other cultures. Indeed, wherever peoples have not been touched and influenced by our Western world-view with its belief that man is limited to sense experience and reason, the dream has been viewed as the chief medium through which non-physical (or spiritual) powers and realities spoke to man. Although some dreams were seen as meaningless or unintelligible, it was important for men to consider their dreams, for through them a man might obtain intimations of things to come or guidance and confrontation from greater than human powers. All of the major religions of mankind have held this view, and as we have shown, it has never been entirely displaced by the skeptical view of the scientific community.

Instead, the modern support for this view has come from a strange source. Beginning in 1900, with the publication of Freud's carefully documented *Interpretation of Dreams*, the subject has come in for serious consideration by the medical profession. Their work, now that it is front-page news in our daily papers, makes it rather hard to avoid the significance of dreams.

Freud first saw dreams as the royal road to understanding man's submerged personality, that hidden nine tenths of the human being which we now know as the unconscious. Jung, if his record can be believed, followed then by witnessing dreams that gave hints of the future and which offered suggestions to men superior to their conscious knowledge and attitudes. Most recently, the studies of Dement and others carrying on similar research have demonstrated that dreams are so important to mental health that simply being deprived of them may lead to mental breakdown and even psychosis. These findings, particularly those of Jung, certainly suggest that the dream—which has been valued and interpreted by all religious groups, Christianity included—is worthy of serious religious consideration and may be one very important access to knowledge. It is true that in the past this understanding has sometimes led to an uncritical and superstitious concern with dreams. Still, their Christian interpretation is an ancient, long-held, and carefully considered religious practice. It deserves to be reviewed and evaluated.

The British writer J. B. Priestley has added a modern voice to this ancient understanding. Commenting on the importance of one early experiment with dreams, Priestley concluded:

> We are not—even though we might prefer to be—the slave of chronological time. We are, in this respect, more elaborate, more powerful, perhaps nobler creatures than we lately have taken ourselves to be. . . . Our lives are not contained within passing time, a single track along which we hurry to oblivion. We may not be immortal beings, but we are something better than creatures carried on that single time track to the slaughter house. We have a larger portion of Time—and more and stranger adventures with it—than conventional or positivist thought allows.[3]

As a matter of fact, when we are perfectly honest we find that both of these attitudes toward dreams struggle with each other within most of us. Much of the time we are dominated by the attitude of the Enlightenment, which devalued dreams as meaningless, and we ignore them. Then there are times when we awake from a vivid dream strangely moved and troubled, hardly able to shake off its influence throughout the day. Or we read of Lincoln's premonitory dream of his assassination and wonder what it means that dreams sometimes have reality and significance like that. What meaning do dreams actually have? But first, exactly what *is* a dream?

## What is a dream?

It may seem hardly necessary to define anything so familiar as a dream, but this is just where the fun begins; in defining the familiar one finds how little he knows. Most commonly the dream is under-

[3] Quoted in *MD*, (December 1965) loc. cit., p. 180.

stood as a succession of images present in the mind during sleep. And here, as Nathaniel Kleitman has shown in his recent book on *Sleep and Wakefulness*, we are getting into one of the least-understood of human activities. We cannot even say precisely what is meant by sleep except in terms of a certain kind of consciousness. According to Dr. Kleitman, it is best described as that period in which there is temporary cessation of the waking state. From time to time in this period anything from a single picture or figure to an elaborate story may be vividly perceived, which is in no sense a direct perception of the outer physical world. Normally this happens four or five times every night, and it can also be "watched" or predicted by keeping track of the sleeper's brain waves, his eye movements, and certain other reactions. Indeed, vivid dreams seem to come spontaneously and to be almost as free from our ego control as our perception of the outside physical world.

This is not the only thing that happens in sleep, however. There is a second process closely related to dreaming, which can be recalled best between the periods of vivid dreaming. This is a conceptual activity, or simply "thinking," and it is apparently continuous in the parts of the brain which do not go to sleep. Apparently most of man's brain goes right on working whether he is awake or asleep. Whether he is conscious of it or not, vivid dreaming takes over alternately with conceptual activity, which is constantly at work changing perceptions into thoughts and ideas. The psychologists call these processes "primary-process activity" and "secondary-process mentation," and together they produce the underlying psychic life that seems to be basic to conscious thinking and activity. It is no wonder that psychiatrists like Lawrence Kubie have pictured the mind as a magnificent computer, as if designed expressly to the scientist's specifications.[4]

It is from this level of psychic life that the sharp and discrete religious intuition probably comes. These intuitions, which are so valued and prized by religious people for direction and guidance, are in most cases the end product of this kind of secondary-process mentation turned upon religious contents. The religious intuition is therefore of the same nature as the dream (and also the vision), and shares in the same reality.

A third form of dream activity is the spontaneous image or vision

[4] Lawrence S. Kubie, "Blocks to Creativity," *International Science and Technology*, No. 42, June 1965, pp. 74ff.

that appears to a person in the borderland of wakefulness when one is not sure whether he is awake or asleep. These dreams and visions—they are termed hypnagogic or hypnopompic, depending on whether the dreamer is falling asleep or waking up—are usually flash pictures focused on a single impression, but in some cases whole scenes, even fairly long stories may appear. At times these images coming on the edge of sleep can seem so tangible that the dreamer really does not know whether he is awake or asleep, whether the images belong to the outside world or to the figures of the dream. And this leads us to the last and closely related form of dreaming.

This final form is the waking dream or vision, in which the dream images are intruded into the waking consciousness. The images themselves are apparently no different from those which can be experienced during sleep, except that they reach the field of consciousness during periods of wakefulness. They rise as spontaneously and with as little ego control as the dream, and in most cases the visions are involuntary. There are persons, however, who are able to cultivate the ability to look inward and observe this spontaneous rise of dream images because they wish to experience them. This experience, which we shall simply call fantasy, seems to be very similar to dreaming; in it the same kind of images and stories arise within one as in dreams. In other cultures and other times the experience of visions has been far more common than it is among most people today.[5] In fact, as we shall show, the people of other cultures have not distinguished as clearly between the dream and the vision as we do today.

There is an activity, however, which is common in our culture today that is not always so carefully distinguished. This is the daydream, which is different from fantasy. In daydreams the flow of images is not spontaneous, but is directed by the conscious center of personality, the ego. The daydream can be created and also changed at will; fantasy, like the true dream or vision, cannot—it must be met with and observed. At times the line between fantasy and daydreams may be a fine one, but unless it is maintained, fantasy loses the spontaneous quality that is characteristic of both dreams and visions.

[5] Visions, however, are still fairly common today. Two studies made by the Society for Psychical Research in England show that about 10 per cent of the normal adult population have had such an experience. *Proceedings*, Vol. 10, 1894, pp. 25ff.; *Journal*, Vol. 34, 1948, pp. 187ff.

One other distinction must be kept quite clear because of the popular modern attitude toward visions. Most people are quite suspicious of visions.[6] They probably would not go so far as to find the dream dangerous or pathological. But even though the dream is so closely related to the vision that at times the two cannot be distinguished, visions are feared as a sign of mental disintegration. Most of us automatically assume that any person who experiences a vision must be mentally ill, that any vision must be hallucination. On the contrary, the real visionary experience is quite different from the hallucination in mental illness.

The true visionary experience is seldom mistaken for giving immediate knowledge of the physical world, but only of the "dream" world, or quite indirectly of the physical one. The vision is superimposed on the physical world, or the two may in some way be synchronized, but they can be distinguished just as easily as the dream is usually distinguished from the experience of waking. The hallucination in mental illness, on the other hand, is a definite sign of pathology. Here the same kind of content one finds in dreams arises spontaneously and is attributed directly to the world outside where it does not belong; the "dream" world is mistaken for the physical world of sense experience. The person who is subject to this kind of hallucination has lost his ability to distinguish between these two kinds of experience and so he projects his inner images directly upon the outer world. Because he cannot distinguish between the two he is not able to deal adequately with either the outer world or the inner one. His actions become inappropriate and he is seen as sick. Such hallucination is a common occurrence in several kinds of mental illness where the ego under stress cannot distinguish be-

[6] This is rather different from the attitude of science and the arts. Many scientists show something of pride, almost reverence, for the visionary experiences that have been known to produce basic scientific discoveries. The story is repeated of how one of Poincaré's famous mathematical solutions came to him while he was half-dreaming on a bus ride. Even more famous was Kekulé's discovery of the structure of the benzene ring from a vision in which he suddenly saw six snakes in a ring, each swallowing the tail of the one ahead.

In a manuscript on "Inner Music," in preparation by Francis Leach, a friend of mine, there are several references to well-known composers who told of music coming to them in auditory visions, or even in actual dreams. Among them were Beethoven, Schumann, the American composer Roy Harris, Tartini, whose great work "The Devil's Trill" came as a whole in sleep, and also Wagner, whose remarkable creation of the prelude to Das Rheingold took form in a visionary state. Others like Tschaikovsky, Mozart, and Brahms have described how close they often were to a dream-state during the work of composing. Some of these references are included in our bibliography.

tween experiences that come to consciousness from psychic reality and those that come from the outer world.

As we shall see, it is not possible to discuss dreams without considering the thought process that goes on in sleep, the true vision, and fantasy as well. The four experiences are basically the same in nature. They are intrusions into consciousness of activities over which we have little if any conscious control.[7]

In the past these spontaneous images and thoughts, distinct from outer physical reality, have been valued as a sign of contact with religious reality. Whether the image was presented in sleep or in wakefulness, whether breaking in unexpectedly or sought and cultivated, it was understood to come from a different world, and nearly all religious groups everywhere have considered that the ability to observe and interpret these images was a religious gift. This was essentially the common Christian tradition from biblical times, through the church fathers, and up into the seventeenth century; in isolated instances it has continued to the present time. In this tradition dreams were significant because they revealed something beyond man which gave purpose and meaning, warning where spiritual disaster impended. In Jung's terminology dreams can express the reality of the collective unconscious, the objective psyche. In religious terms, they kept the people in touch with the purpose and direction of spiritual reality.

## A *neglected heritage*

At the beginning of the twentieth century there was almost no educated person in our culture who seriously considered this way of looking at man's experiences. After Freud had broken the ice, with *The Interpretation of Dreams*, the reaction to his work showed how deeply men were concerned about this area of their lives. But even when the thaw set in, and people of all kinds began to show an interest in the study of dreams, there was still one major group in our society with nothing to say about the subject. The Christian clergy, the theologians are still silent, and this is surprising in itself in a group not noted for silence. It is more surprising when we realize how much there is about dreams in the Christian tradition from the Old Testament on. It is also surprising when we consider the atten-

[7] For the sake of simplicity, when we refer to dreams generically from this point on, all four of these related activities will be signified.

tion given to other aspects of man's inner life. There are groups in the church interested in spiritual healing, in speaking in tongues, or preparing for the imminent end of the world, and even in the ritual handling of snakes. But there is no significant group that suggests that Christians should listen to their own dreams or make any particular study of the many dreams in the Bible and in subsequent church history.

In fact, I cannot help recalling the consternation I caused in speaking to one group devoted to glossolalia when I said what I meant about dreams. It seemed to them that the idea of taking dreams seriously was much farther out than the practice of tongue speaking. What does this mean? Is it just dreams that we have neglected, or is it something more?

The trouble is that the dream comes to man neither from the acceptable material world nor from man's well-ordered and controllable reason. To value the spontaneously given content of the dream one must postulate the reality of something in addition to the material world and man's reason. Depth psychology calls this reality the unconscious; the early Christian community called it the spiritual world; and these two different terms may well refer to the same reality, as the Catholic theologian Victor White has suggested in *God and the Unconscious*. Unless men believe that there is such a realm of reality which can be experienced, they will probably not look very hard for meaning beyond the material world.

Indeed, if there is no meaning beyond the physical world, then what place is there for dreams to come from except the meaningless tag ends of yesterday's sensation? Dreams are then simply the commonest example of the human mind or psyche out of commission. They show how irrational its action can be when logical thinking is switched off. Of course, sense experience is also non-rational in the sense that it is not guided or directed by reason; it is just given. But since it is believed that there is a real physical world that is revealed in sense experience, this essential irrationality hardly bothers anyone except a few philosophers. The irrationality of dreams is something else again. So long as we "know" that there is no other world for them to reveal, no world beyond the material one, there is nothing else for dreams to show us but irrationality—our minds at their most irrational, illogical, in fact.

There is no controversy on dreams as there is with glossolalia; the subject simply does not come up for consideration except very rarely. Except for a work by the Spanish Jesuit Pedro Meseguer, *The Secret of Dreams*, published in 1960, and a book published last year in German by a friend, the Reverend John A. Sanford, I have found no serious religious study of the subject since David Simpson's *Discourse on Dreams and Night-Visions* in 1791. It is very difficult for modern man to imagine meaningful psychic reality beyond the grasp of his reason or his physical senses.

Indeed, the greatest thrust of mid-twentieth-century theology is to maintain unequivocally that man has no direct or immediate contact with any non-physical or "supernatural" realm, and so there is no natural religion. This is the point of view of Bultmann, Bonhoeffer, Barth, and Robinson, and a host of lesser lights.[8] These are strange bedfellows, but they all maintain this as almost axiomatic truth. We have more to say about this in our concluding chapter. Interestingly enough, they also all deny the value of depth psychology in human transformation. And this shows as much about the church's real reaction to Freud and Jung as all the furor over Freud's emphasis on sexuality as the prime human motive. Once it is admitted that men are ever changed in the psychologist's office, then the church is faced with a realm of reality that is neither physical nor rational, and which is sometimes revealed in dreams. Once the dream is taken seriously, as something given, with religious significance, then it is inevitable that there is some direct and "natural" contact with reality other than material or rational. Then the door is open and anything can happen, even transformation. Dreams may well be a doorway to religious significance and a new theology, as well as to the unconscious.

## The author's point of view

My own belief in the value of dreams did not start from a consideration of their place in religious history. In fact, until my attention was drawn to them by the late Dr. C. G. Jung of Zurich and his followers, I had skipped over the references to dreams in the Bible, hardly recognizing that they were there. But as I worked with some of the followers of Dr. Jung, I observed that consideration of dreams was one factor in helping emotionally disturbed people

[8] There have been excellent surveys of the "God is dead" movement in *Time* for October 22, 1965, (in the section on Religion), and in the main feature article by Ved Mehta in *The New Yorker* for November 13, 20, and 27, 1965.

become well. I saw more than one person obtain from his dreams the suggestions he needed to return to health. I then began to study the voluminous work of Dr. Jung. In his careful scientific studies, which admittedly are somewhat difficult to read,[9] his accumulated evidence with regard to the value and significance of dreams is overwhelming. I also found support for his evidence in my own experience. It was only after I was convinced from the practical and scientific point of view that dreams had meaning and purpose that I looked back into my Christian heritage. Only then did I find that what seemed so new was not very different from the ancient wisdom of the Christian church. For instance, in the fifth century of our era Synesius of Cyrene, for one, had anticipated many of Jung's twentieth-century conclusions, and his views have been the basis of Eastern Orthodox interest in dreams ever since.

For the last decade I have been closely associated with a group of clinical psychologists and psychiatrists. A religiously oriented psychological clinic was established at the church of which I am rector. I have seen many people able to return to useful functioning and many others able to deal with their paralyzing religious doubts through a basically Jungian therapeutic practice, which involves an understanding of their dreams. In 1959 I visited Jung in Zurich and when I told him of what we were doing, he expressed surprise that any present-day church would become so involved with his therapeutic methods. But he went on to say that the nearest approach to his treatment of patients was the classical Christian direction used in France in the nineteenth century by the directors of conscience there. During these last ten years I have observed a mounting mass of evidence regarding the present-day religious value of dreams when they are seriously considered and symbolically understood.

The understanding of Jung also had a surprising effect upon my own religious belief. I had been brought up in an environment that was predominantly rationalistic and materialistic, and so I had doubted many of the experiences described in the New Testament. Along with the dreams and visions of the New Testament, I had rejected the stories of healing, as well as those of superhuman knowledge and wisdom. Then I discovered that this very careful and highly respected psychiatrist, with a fine record of healing his patients, had encountered many experiences in his patients similar

[9] This fact has kept psychologists as sophisticated as O. Hobart Mowrer and Seward Hiltner, on their own admission, from reading Jung.

to those described in the New Testament, and had made his studies of them available to the public. Re-enforced with such reliable current knowledge, I began to reread the New Testament with a greater open-mindedness, and I was surprised by what I found.

I then preached on certain neglected aspects of this New Testament heritage, and was amazed to find that my parishioners would come to me, tentatively and half afraid, to tell me of significant dreams and visions and other similar experiences in their own lives. It was almost as if they had been waiting for someone to open up the New Testament so that they could take their own experiences seriously. With this background I began a serious study of the dreams and visions of our Christian heritage and their possible value for the present-day Christian.

In my own counseling I have used much the same approach. Besides a regular schedule in the church, for the last three years I have worked as a licensed marriage, family, and child counselor, and also served as management consultant in industry. Particularly with one larger firm I have found how vitally helpful this Jungian and essentially religious point of view can be in the management process as people become convinced of the value of listening to dreams.

During this time I have also been surrounded by tremendous dreamers, and there have been unusual experiences. There was one man who dreamed the name of a publisher interested in my work before even I had access to the information, and who later brought me a dream about the contents of a letter that only I and the distant sender had actually read. In another strange instance a friend found that she had dreamed up the whereabouts of a missing person, a relative whose disappearance had been worrying her family for some time. My study of Jung made it possible to understand experiences like these in a context of religious reality.

Apparently the understanding of dreams formed an essential part of our Christian heritage, and I found that the dream, properly understood, was believed to give religious insight, wisdom, and direction. I began to see that if dreams are accepted as religiously significant, the reality and accessibility of the spiritual, the non-physical world, is made quite probable. This then necessitates a theology that envisions some direct contact with other than physical reality. Within such a framework the gifts of the Spirit mentioned by Paul in I Corinthians 12 no longer appear absurd. Instead, they are one of the crowning evidences of the action of spiritual reality in the life of man, and the dream is one of these evidences, a common and natural one. The sheer givenness of the religiously significant dream removes the current doubt that something other than physical reality can invade consciousness directly. If this is true, then the whole charismatic life of the church needs to be considered more seriously from a practical and theological point of view.

We shall try to demonstrate this rather novel thesis in several ways. First of all we shall give a historical survey of the value that has been placed upon dreams within the Judaic-Christian heritage. We turn first to the Old Testament and Apocrypha and the beliefs of the later Hebrews about dreams and visions. Next we look at the Greeks, those ancients whom we revere for having so far rid themselves of illusion, to see if their beliefs about dreams were significantly different from those of the Hebrews. With this background we take up the dreams and visions of the New Testament. As we then turn to the first centuries of the church's life, we find a surprisingly sophisicated and critical evaluation of dreams by the monumental early fathers of the church. We follow this concern of the church, its earnest regard for this aspect of human life, up through the beginnings of our modern scientific era into the present time. Dreams, although intellectually dispossessed from man's life, are still at work where he lives and moves.

Our interest then leads to the most recent times, to the scientific findings of certain psychological schools and the empirical support that is currently coming from medical research, following the lead of Dr. Dement. We shall then consider the current theological devaluation of dreams, presenting instead an approach in which they have a significant place. From this will be drawn our concluding suggestions as to what attitude toward dreams and visions is possible for modern Christians, religiously possible and advisable. A practical list of ways we can use and understand our dreams winds up our discussion.

It is not my intent to present either a treatise on the practical interpretation of dreams or an exhaustive analysis of the dream and visionary material of the Bible or the early church. My purpose is rather to open a door, first by showing how far we have neglected Christian teaching on this subject, and then by making it clear that this teaching is neither as archaic or illusory as most present-day

Christians seem to believe. Indeed, this material has important implications for current Christian life and theology.

My purpose, in fact, is to raise questions and to point out directions of inquiry rather than to provide test-tube solutions. This book is an attempt to show that there ought to be a modern Christian interpretation of dreams, rather than to show in detail how it can be done.[10] For this, to my way of thinking, is a most productive challenge for the individual Christian who takes the Bible and his own inner being seriously, as well as the life of the historic church.

[10] An important work in this latter direction has been ably done by a close friend and colleague, the Reverend John A. Sanford. His book *God's Forgotten Language* is soon to be published in this country, but not until it had been translated and published in German by the Jung Institute did he find an American publisher willing to consider this material. His work suggests ways in which Christians can use their dream material, and the unique contribution he makes to the religious understanding of dreams merits the attention of every concerned and thoughtful Christian today. The present work is, in fact, complementary to Mr. Sanford's study.

*two*  The Dreams of the
Hebrews and
Other Ancient Peoples

During the last century no book has been studied more carefully
or more critically than the Bible we Christians use. In the process,
opinions about its historical accuracy have ranged all the way from
literal acceptance of every word to complete rejection of its authenticity. But now that this body of literature, particularly the Hebrew
portions, has been analyzed by several generations of scholars, there
is general agreement among those working in the field. Today it is
concluded essentially without question that the Old Testament contains authoritative traditions which date back to at least 1800 B.C.
This book provides a record of the history and travail, religious insights and musings, the moral and ritualistic laws of these people
from that time until the first or second century before Christ.

Nearly every aspect of this tradition has been studied exhaustively
by competent scholars except for the dreams and visions and associated phenomena of the Old Testament and the New. This is
surprising when we consider that visions and dreams, which are
often essential to the narrative, are scattered throughout the Old
Testament from Genesis to Zechariah. Indeed, the Old Testament
presents a clear and consistent theory about the value of dreams and
visions as a medium of revelation. It provides, sometimes implicitly,
sometimes expressed and examined explicitly, one of the oldest and
historically most continuous examples of this belief about dreams
which are available to us today.

Yet the dreams of the Old Testament have been largely ignored by the standard biblical studies of the last hundred years. As *The Interpreter's Bible* so casually puts it, "The development of textual criticism . . . not only destroyed belief in verbal inspiration but also opened the way to an empirical investigation" of things like dates and authorship. As historical facts became more and more interesting, the idea that anything important in the Bible could have been revealed in dreams was gradually lost. In Hastings' *Dictionary of the Bible*,[1] for instance, the subject is introduced gingerly, and then dismissed as quietly and decently as one wishes one could an embarrassing relative. *The Interpreter's Bible* itself contains no serious consideration of the subject throughout its twelve volumes, while *The Interpreter's Dictionary of the Bible* offers just over one page for both dreams and visions out of nearly four thousand pages of other materials. Other commentaries show the same lack of interest.

Since the modern research into dreams suggests that they may have a far greater significance than has been considered during the past few centuries, it would seem advisable to take a fresh look at this tradition in the Old Testament to see what is actually there. Therefore, in spite of the professional prejudices, let us look first at the theory of dreams and visions which it contains and the Hebrew words it uses to describe these experiences. With this key to understanding the materials that follow, we shall then look at the dream experiences in the historical narrative, the prophetic literature, and the "writings." After following the same ideas as they occur in the Apocrypha and in later Jewish tradition, we shall conclude by showing that this very important aspect of their tradition was far from unique among the Hebrews.

## The Hebrew theory of dreams

Throughout the Old Testament we find the belief that Yahweh is concerned with human beings and makes direct contact with them in order to give them direction and guidance. Dream and vision experiences were one medium of this communication. Through this means, which was not subject to ego control, God brought men special knowledge of the world around them, and also knowledge of his divine reality and will. Dreams and visions were an avenue of revelation that Yahweh continued to use because from time to

[1] First published in 1909.

time they were the best, or even the only way he could make connection. Because of their importance, false prophets and charlatans sometimes manufactured false dreams and false interpretations of dreams in order to meet their own needs, or the needs of those who hired them. And so the Bible does not express only reverence for dreams; it also offers critical evaluation of them so that men will not be duped by false religions and false religious leaders.

Cruden's *Complete Concordance* also makes this significant statement:

> As the belief in dreams was generally connected with consultation of idol-priests, or those pretending to deal in magic, the Israelites were warned against dealing with these. But God revealed his will frequently in dreams, and there were those who could explain them.

Thus there is an open attitude toward dreams in the Old Testament, and at the same time a more critical and less superstitious one than is found in any other ancient culture. Dreams and visions are spoken of as actual events, encounters that happen to men and make a difference in their lives. But these experiences can also be simulated, and so they must be examined carefully and by the right people.

The way a people use language reveals a great deal about the way they look at the world about them. In the same way, the Hebrew expressions for dream experiences reveal much of their attitude toward the value of these non-physical intrusions into man's consciousness.

In the first place, there is no clear-cut distinction between the dream and the vision in the Hebrew language; where moderns see a great gulf of separation, the Hebrews did not. Although the two experiences were sometimes distinguished, more often they were seen as aspects of the same basic perception of reality, different sides of the same encounter from beyond the world of sense experience. The word dream (*chalom,* or the verb *chalam*) is related to the Aramaic and Hebrew verb "to be made healthy or strong." The dream is spoken of almost as if this were the form of the experience whose content comes through as a vision. The dream then is the mode or expression of the experience, while the vision is the content, the substance of what is seen or visualized or experienced. Dreams are the normal way to receive such experiences, but the same content can break through in waking moments, and this can happen either out of the blue or as a man turns to this reality for direction. This same overlapping of meaning is also found in the Greek of the New Testament.

We find many examples in which a dream experience is referred to as a vision of the night, as in I Samuel 3:15, Job 20:8, Isaiah 29:7, and Daniel 2:19 and 7:2. There are also several places in which dreams and visions are equated through the characteristic parallelism of Hebrew style (Job 20:8, Numbers 12:6). On the other hand, the visions of Zechariah are simply introduced by the statement: "I saw by night . . .". When the Old Testament speaks of visions, one cannot be sure by modern standards that this does not signify those which occur in the night, and therefore are actually what we would call dreams. And when the Hebrew does speak of a dream, this may carry more the idea of givenness and religious authority that we have come to associate with visions. It is really impossible to discuss the dreams of the Old Testament without describing the visions also. They are of one piece in the Hebrew.

Technically, of course, a vision is simply a visual image, something seen which is not an immediate perception of any outer physical object. The words *chazon, marah,* and their several variations all come from two common Hebrew verbs meaning "to see." But closely associated with visions is the auditory experience that is described as listening to God or speaking with him, in which something beyond one's ordinary self appears to speak to the individual in his own language. Many people know of this experience in dreams when there is a voice and no visual image at all. Sometimes, instead of being the object to which the speaking is directed, the individual becomes the subject through which the speaking is done. This is prophecy if the power speaking is God.

Since it is not too uncommon for people to talk in their sleep, or to perform somnambulistic actions, this idea of prophecy is actually strange only because so few of us believe that there is any reality beyond the physical which could make such contact with the individual. In fact, glossolalia in the New Testament is the same experience except that the individual speaks in an unknown language. While our interest will be limited to instances in which voices were heard in dreams or in connection with visual images, it must not be fogotten that the auditory experience alone, when it comes autonomously, is of the same nature as dreams and visions. We do

not discuss these auditory experiences, primarily because there are
so many examples that this would require a book in itself, but also
because dreams and visions give a clearer picture of the process by
which autonomous materials intrude into our consciousness.

Probably the most common vision described in the Old Testament is the experience of an angel. In spite of the modern fear that
the Bible may be talking nonsense when it describes the appearance
of angels, they were seldom viewed as concretized "pieces" of
spirituality, materializing and then disappearing into thin air. It is
true there are stories in the early chapters of the Old Testament in
which angels appear as actual human beings, but these are greatly
overshadowed by the passages in which they are not viewed in this
way. Later authors left no doubt about their understanding that
the reality of an angelic being arises from someone's visionary
experience. This in no way devalues these experiences. It is simply
stating that it is through visionary experiences that one comes into
relationship with these non-physical entities.

The word for angel, *malak* or messenger, can be used either for
an ordinary human messenger or to indicate a spiritual messenger
of God. There are several dozen passages in which the word is used
in this latter sense, and these passages, where the messenger was
clearly more than human, show four different ways in which angels
were viewed. In the first place, the angel, which is understood to be
acting as God's agent, is actually seen in a visionary experience or
dream, as in Genesis 22:11, Exodus 3:2, Numbers 22:22, Judges
6:11, and Zechariah 1:9. This meaning is similar to the ancient
Greek understanding of dreams in which heroes or gods appeared,
which we shall discuss in the next chapter. In other passages the
angel is viewed as the impersonal instrument of God, carrying out
God's will for weal or woe. In this sense they are more hearkened to
than experienced, as in Exodus 14:19, 23:20, II Samuel 24:16,
II Kings 19:35. Third, the angel occasionally appears as a concrete
physical being, materializing out of spiritual reality, who drinks and
eats and converses with men (Genesis 19:1 and 15). These are
the passages that embarrass the modern reader. Finally, the idea of
an angel dealing with men is used as a substitute for God by those
authors who did not speak of God's dealing directly with man. In
these passages the words for God and angel are practically interchangeable.

The two Hebrew words that are translated by our word "seer"

show clearly how highly the Hebrews valued those who could see visions. They are *chozeh* and *roeh,* which are derived from Hebrew words for perceiving, seeing, the same roots from which the Hebrew words for visions are derived. "The see-er" is an excellent translation for either of these Hebrew words. The see-er is another name for a prophet. He is the one who perceives more than just the space-time world. Samuel was called a seer (I Chronicles 29:29), and it is stated that the prophet was aforetime called a seer. (I Samuel 9:9.) One of the earliest specific references is in II Samuel, in which "the word of the Lord came to the prophet Gad, David's seer." (24:11).

In several places in the books of prophecy, as well as in the books of history, the prophet is clearly identified as a seer. Amos is called a seer (7:12), while Isaiah equates the prophet and the seer (29:10), as does Micah in 3:6–7. The latest of these references may well be the passage in Isaiah 30:10 which speaks of a rebellious people "who say to the seers, 'See not'; and to the prophets, 'Prophesy not to us what is right. . . .'" Many scholars believe that these words were written very close to the time of Jesus' birth. Here and in other places it is clear that the main task of the seer was to see and understand the visionary realities—to know angels and hear God's voice and see visions.

All of these experiences, then—talking with God, angel, dream, vision, prophecy—express the same basic encounter with some reality that is not physical, and the most common of them is the dream experience. The majority of the Old Testament authors took care to express their belief—as Plato did in later times—that man was in contact with two realities, a physical world and a non-physical one which they called spiritual. The contact they described with this second reality was made directly through these experiences.

As we look at the Old Testament record, we shall not try to distinguish the various strands of Hebrew authorship. It is obvious that certain writers were more concerned with dream experience than others, but the same reverence for the non-physical breakthrough is found in all of the different strands. It is even more obvious that this reverence was carefully preserved by the later writers. As these men turned to the job of compiling a complete and consecutive story, they approached the earlier records with skill and understanding. Their history, their very approach to life had been born out of the visions given to them, and these experiences were not only kept alive in memory; it was expected that they would continue.

## The great dreamers—the patriarchs

The first description of a dream in the Old Testament occurs in the same passage with the first of the references to visions. In Genesis 15:1, Yahweh appeared to Abram in a vision (*machazeh*) to assure him of a great future and to tell him that his own off-spring would be the ones to share in it. Abram believed. He made his sacrifice, and then "as the sun was going down, a deep sleep fell on Abram, and lo, a dread and great darkness fell upon him." God spoke again, this time of the tribulation that would come before the vision was fulfilled, and now there appeared "a smoking fire pot and a flaming torch," which passed between the pieces of the sacrifice. This ceremony of covenant which Abram saw in his vision of the night was an ancient magic practice, so convincing that it had become the basic ritual for agreements between men. In practice the contracting parties sacrificed an animal and cut it in half; then, if they were equals, both walked between the pieces of the carcass, demonstrating their willingness to be bound by the agreement or else to suffer the same treatment. Thus in a numinous and mysterious experience that touched a man to the depth, God turned his promise to Abram into the Covenant, the effective contract between God and man.

For Abram this was the verification of the reality of his call from Ur, as genuine an experience of the Holy as one will find in religious literature. Symbolism like this recurs wherever men take note of their religious experiences. Nor was it the only encounter for these people. Hagar, the Egyptian servant, was twice comforted by the angel of God and was helped to bear Abram's child who was to grow up in the wilderness. (16:7 and 21:17.) After Hagar's flight three angels appeared to both Abraham and Sarah (whose names were now changed). These were described as angels, and also as two men accompanying the Lord himself, who became known only when Sarah's thoughts were read. In spite of her down-to-earth disbelief, she was to bear a child. Abraham then learned of their terrible errand, and was able to intercede for his cousin Lot (Genesis 18 and 19). Again, it was through an angel that Abraham's eyes were opened as he was about to sacrifice Isaac. Of that place—where the angel spoke and Abraham looked up to see a ram caught in the thicket and understood the test to which God had put him—it was said, "On Yahweh's mountain there is vision"[2] (22:11ff.). Not only was Abraham a seer in the technical sense, but King Abimelech also learned through a clairvoyant dream the true identity of Sarah, whom he had taken for his concubine (20:3).

While Isaac was not recorded as being much of a dreamer, some of the greatest moments in his younger son's life were marked by dreams. As Jacob fled from the birthright he had stolen, and stopped for the night to sleep on the rocky ground, he dreamed of a ladder from earth to heaven with angels going back and forth. The Lord stood above and reiterated the promise given Abraham in his vision. So deeply moved was Jacob, awakened, that he said, "Surely the Lord is in this place; and I did not know it" (28:11ff.). In accordance with the idea of incubation common in these cultures,[3] he felt that the place in which he had dreamed such a dream was the very "gate of heaven." He vowed that if God would remain with him, that place at Bethel should become a sanctuary, and he would give to God a tithe of all he had. To Jacob this experience was no mere dream, but a religious experience of the most profound kind; one which had the extraordinary result of establishing the idea of tithing, a practice central to the very heart of Judaism.

Jacob spent twenty patient years in his new home with Laban. Then he was given God's help in two dreams to leave his possessive father-in-law peacefully and with wives and wealth. In the first, which he interpreted well, he saw the spotted he-goats mate with the flock and was given God's assurance that he should take the increase and return to the land of his birth (31:10). The second dream was Laban's, in which God warned him on the night before he overtook the fleeing families not to press matters with Jacob, either for good or bad (31:24).

The magnificent passage which then follows, the story of Jacob's wrestling through the night with his unknown adversary to win both a blessing and a name, strongly suggests a dream or vision as its origin (32:24). Jacob had briefly encountered the angels of God

[2] E. A. Speiser, *Genesis* (The Anchor Bible, Vol. I), Garden City, New York, Doubleday & Company, Inc., 1964, pp. 162ff.
[3] Incubation was the practice of sleeping in a temple or holy place specifically to receive a divine dream. We shall say more about this later.

after Laban turned back (32:2), and then he had faced all the practical details of his meeting with Esau. There is a realism about his night in the desert alone, and yet not alone, which recalls other descriptions of the dark night of the soul. Later biblical authors referring to this experience held that Jacob wrestled with an angel (Hosea 12:4).

And Jacob, now become Israel, was an old man before another of his dreams was recorded. For at this point his favorite son arose to stand out among all the patriarchs as both dreamer and interpreter of dreams. In good measure it was just this about Joseph that brought down the hatred of his brothers on his head. Joseph did not dream directly of God, but symbolically of his brothers' sheaves bowing down before his sheaf, and of the sun and moon and eleven stars doing obeisance before him (37:5). And his naïveté in telling his dreams set the scene for the action that followed. Sold into Egypt as a slave, his similar frankness with Potiphar's wife landed him in an Egyptian prison. Here he was consulted by Pharaoh's erring butler and baker about their own dreams, which they could not interpret. "Do not interpretations belong to God?" Joseph asked, and correctly foretold the future (40:5). Again, when Pharaoh himself was troubled by dreams, the butler remembered the interpreter back in prison. This time Joseph's wise interpretations, explaining the fat and lean cows and the full and thin ears of grain, were rewarded directly, and he was placed in a position of authority over Egypt (41:1). These dreams are central to the whole story of Joseph and his brothers.

Finally, when Jacob heard that his son was alive, he believed it only after God again appeared to him in a vision of the night with reassurance (46:2). And Jacob went down to Egypt knowing that God would go with him and in time would bring his people forth. Indeed, if there is any reality in this tradition of the patriarchs, which many modern scholars have come to view with great respect, it is certainly inseparable from the idea that dreams and visions are expressions of man's contact with some reality beyond the physical world.

## Moses and the dark speech of God

While we do not find the same concern with the dream in the account of Moses, this aspect was far from forgotten. The story of the exodus essentially begins with Moses' visionary experience of the burning bush and the angel, a content that recurs with authority in the dreams of people today (Exodus 3:1ff.). Moses was one, however, with whom it was believed that God spoke face to face, and so did not use his dark and parabolic speech of dreams and visions with which he communicated to most men. The passage in Numbers that makes this clear (12:6) gives both a deep insight into the Hebrew reverence for Moses, and at the same time an understanding of their attitude toward dreams. The Lord was about to become angry with those who questioned Moses, and he said, "Hear my words: If there is a prophet among you, I the Lord make myself known to him in a vision, I speak with him in a dream. Not so with my servant Moses; he is entrusted with all my house. With him I speak mouth to mouth, clearly, and not in dark speech; and he beholds the form of the Lord. Why then were you not afraid to speak against my servant Moses?"

There are many references throughout the time of the exodus to the angels of the Lord, who drove back the Red Sea and went before the people of Israel as their protection and guide (Exodus 14:19, 23:20, 32:34, 33:2, Numbers 20:16). The repeated experience of the pillar of cloud also has a visionary quality, and the appearance of the pillar to Miriam and Aaron was undoubtedly a vision (Numbers 12:5).

Perhaps some of us would like to forget that Balaam's ass saw a vision, but this was probably not the first nor the last time an ass has taken the lead. It tallies with the popular belief that animals are sometimes more aware of spiritual realities than their more rationally conscious masters. But Balaam is also interesting for the fact that God's message was given directly to a stranger (as it had been to Abimelech), and because it is allowed that he could be conquered by it. When Balaam, the seer, was approached by the princes of Moab to deliver a curse on Israel, God's word came to him in the night. But apparently there was a chance he had not gotten the message, for he was on his way to Moab when an angel of God appeared first to his ass, and then to Balaam. He was shaken, and he set his face toward the wilderness and delivered the truth that he saw instead of a curse (Numbers 22:21ff.). After this brief contact it is not recorded whether the power of God continued in this way in Balaam's life. After this there were the years of conquest, and except for the intervening discussion in Deuteronomy which we will take up later, not much consideration was given to dream experiences. Even when the commander of the Lord's army appeared to Joshua, the experience was taken at face value.

But following the account of Joshua's period, we come upon the stories of the book of Judges, which continue the spirit of the earlier Biblical narrative. Here angels and signs abound, and the direction of the Lord, which elsewhere had been asked directly, was sought through them, often in experiences that were clearly visionary. Gideon found his destiny when an angel appeared to him (6:11), while the birth of Samson was announced by the appearance of an angel to both Manoah and his wife (13:2). In Judges 7:13 it was a dream that determined Gideon's defeat of the Midianites; in the night the Lord told him to get up and go spy on the enemy camp and he would hear something to strengthen his hand. As Gideon was following these instructions, he overheard an enemy soldier telling his dream of a cake of barley bread that fell on their tent and crushed it. "This can mean no other than the sword of Gideon," the man's comrade interpreted. Hearing these words, Gideon worshiped, and then he set forth to defeat the enemy.

In the next books we find once again a more careful depiction of the reverence for dreams and visions. The story of Samuel opens with the magnificent description of the child's dream, in which the Lord speaks to him and the old priest clearly recognizes the action of God (I Samuel 3:1). In this vision of the night, with so many of the signs of the troublesome dreams that come to people today, it is difficult for the child to distinguish between outer reality and the visionary experience. Then he learns that the house of Eli will be overthrown, and he is afraid to tell the dream. Up to this time, we are told, the word of the Lord had been precious in Israel; there was no open vision, or more literally, "no vision breaking through." This vision-dream of Samuel's opened up a new era, and in several places Samuel is described simply as the seer, the one who sees beyond ordinary things.

## The dreams of the great kings

In some ways even more striking for us is the casual way in which the statement of Saul in his distress is recorded in the text. Samuel is dead, and Saul sees his enemies come upon him, and when he "inquired of the Lord, the Lord did not answer him, either by dreams, or by Urim, or by prophets" (I Samuel 28:6). Saul had lost his guidance, and so he went to the medium of Endor to ask her to bring forth the spirit of Samuel. Confronting the ghost of Samuel—in itself a visionary experience—he asked: "I am in great distress; for the Philistines are warring against me, and God has turned away from me and answers me no more, either by prophets or by dreams; therefore I have summoned you to tell me what I shall do" (28:15). So desperate was Saul's condition that he broke his own law and consulted with a medium. The distress of Saul at not dreaming is paralleled among modern natives who lose their power when they can no longer dream big dreams. It means to them that the gods have left them, and there is a repetition of Saul's tragic state in the adjustment they face.

David was not left in the lurch by his prophets as was Saul. The word of the Lord came to Nathan the prophet in the night with instructions for David that he should not build the temple but should leave it for his heir (II Samuel 7:4, I Chronicles 17:3). In accordance with this vision or dream, Nathan spoke and David obeyed. Later, when the Lord became angry with David's actions and Gad prophesied the people's destruction, David himself saw the angel of the Lord and was given the chance to repent and stay the Lord's hand (II Samuel 24:16 and I Chronicles 21:15).

As for Solomon, though we might wonder about his dreaming, we find that he was as reverent about it as any of his predecessors. The reputed source of his wisdom was a dream at Gibeon in which the Lord appeared to him by night and said: "Ask what I shall give you." And in this experience, which sounds very much like incubation, Solomon asked for an understanding mind and received it. Then he went to Jerusalem to make offerings and hold a feast for all his servants (I Kings 3:5ff). God had come to him and acted; what Solomon did with his wisdom was another part of the story.

After Solomon had finished building the temple, God appeared to him a second time, "as he had appeared to him at Gibeon" (I Kings 9:2). In the same kind of dream experience he was given the promise of God's protection to his house if he would follow only Yahweh. Solomon saw and listened. Although he evidently forgot what he experienced, for him, as for Saul and David, the dream itself was an experience of contact with more than human knowledge. To be deprived of dreams could even be a catastrophe.

But as the kings of Israel got into more and more trouble, the record of their own dreams ceased. Instead, we are told that the word of the Lord came to Elijah and to Elisha, and marvelous things happened. After Elijah had fled from Jezebel's outburst, an angel came and touched him *in sleep* to show that he was taken care of in the wilderness, and he was comforted (I Kings 19:5). His experience of earthquake, fire, and still small voice in the cave there at Horeb also has the quality of a numinous vision (19:11). Again after Ahab's death an angel of the Lord came to Elijah, to direct him in his dealings with the new king in Samaria (II Kings 1:3, 15). The wonderful things that Elijah did were told right up to the end of his life. And then in a tremendous visionary experience of the assumption of the prophet, Elisha fell heir to the same spirit and power (2:12). As Elijah was taken up by a whirlwind, Elisha saw the horses and chariots of fire, just as they were later seen by the young man who served him (6:17). At that time, when they were surrounded by the forces of the Syrian king, Elisha opened the eyes of his servant to the same numinous vision of the spiritual power which was available to him. Wonderful things continued to be told about Elisha.

After his death there was one more experience recorded in the history: when the angel of the Lord went forth and destroyed Sennacherib's famous army before Jerusalem (II Kings 19:35, Isaiah 37:36), and there was the same destroying aspect of angels which David had once seen turned on his own people. With this, the dream experiences in the historical portion of the Old Testament come to an end. But right up to the end of II Chronicles the prophets continued to be seen as seers.[4] These men were important politically and religiously because they were understood to have the power to see beyond the immediate world.

## The prophetic tradition and Deuteronomy

There are not many religious leaders who have had as much impact on the history and religious life of mankind as the prophets who thrived in Israel from the end of this period through the sixth century B.C. These men are universally admired for their insight into the moral nature of God and the religious endeavor, and it was

---

[4] Prophets individually or as a group are referred to as "seers" in I Samuel 9:9, II Samuel 24:11, II Kings 17:13, I Chronicles 21:9, 25:5, 29:29, and II Chronicles 9:29, 12:15, 19:2, 29:30, 33:18–19, and 35:15. There are also many experiences of precognition or extrasensory perception described of various prophets, as in I Samuel 9:20 and II Kings 5:26.

among them that dreams were first openly valued in the Old Testament. Up to this time dream experiences had been recorded and acted upon, and not analyzed. But now the prophets, who all describe the inspiration of some kind of dreamlike experience, began to voice real concern for distinguishing the true dreamer from the false dreamer, the genuine interpreter from the false interpreter, and the true prophet from the false prophet. They considered it one of the specific tasks of the prophet to be open in dreams and visions to intrusions of another realm of reality, and to be able to interpret them correctly.

The writings of these men agree in expressing, in one way or another, the basic idea that when the spirit of God is poured upon men, "your sons and your daughters shall prophesy, your old men shall dream dreams, and your young men shall see visions" (Joel 2:28). In a new time of the outpouring of God's spirit at Pentecost the authors of the New Testament turned back to point to the significance of this passage. But when God is not with his people, the prophets maintain with Saul that "disaster comes upon disaster, rumor follows rumor; they seek a vision from the prophet, but the law perishes from the priest, and counsel from the elders" (Ezekiel 7:26). The same basic thought is contained in Isaiah 29:10 and 32:15, Lamentations 2:9, Jeremiah 31:34, Ezekiel 39:29, and Micah 3:5. Thus if life was not to be all bitter, it was essential that there be men who were open to something beyond the physical, and that there be those who could distinguish the true vision and true dream from the false, the true prophecy from the false. In these passages, dream, vision, and prophecy are obviously inextricably linked together, as we have suggested in our introduction to this chapter.

This concern about the proper understanding of dreams is first expressed in the book of Deuteronomy. Whether this book actually comes from the insights of the seventh- and eighth-century prophets, or whether it is an older tradition to which they turned, makes no difference in its basic importance and authority among Jews and Christians. Deuteronomy expresses the faith given in the wilderness and says explicitly how it shall be kept. And when it came to the prophet and dreamer of dreams in Chapter 13, a legal problem was tackled which had to be stated conditionally.

Legally a prophet or dreamer of dreams is false *if* he says "Let us go after other gods and let us serve them." Even if he shows wonders or correctly foretells the future, he must not be listened to.

It is simply accepted as fact that the prophet or dreamer of dreams has the power to see beyond the present. But if he uses this power to turn Israel away from its God, then his words shall be shunned, and he shall be put to death (13:1–5). Yet it never occurred to the author of Deuteronomy to do away with dreams by simply ignoring them or maintaining that they never have value, the simple solution of our time. Instead, this passage implies that the prophetic function of dreaming and interpreting was so important that to pervert it was a heinous offense and had to be punished by death. In a backhanded way, dreamers were thus treated with real reverence.

This whole matter, of course, was complicated by the fact that the Hebrews lived among non-Hebraic people who had their own priests who had dreams and visions and interpreted them; and these priests used other interesting practices for divining the future. There was clearly a will in Israel that their own people stay away from pagan diviners. This is accepted unconditionally in Deuteronomy 18:9–22, which simply directs that there shall not be found among the people anyone who makes his son or daughter pass through the fire or who practices divination, or any soothsayer, augur, sorcerer, charmer, medium, wizard, or necromancer. While this passage, like the same tradition found in Leviticus 19:26–31, is often taken as a prohibition against dream interpretation, dreams are specifically *not* mentioned in either place, even though the writer practically exhausts the Hebrew words to include all the religious magic of other peoples.

This is a remarkable passage. Among even the Greeks and the Romans, with their highly developed religious forms and ethical practice, there was no attempt to curb the superstitious practices of the common people. But here it is put in unmistakable terms. The Israelites shall have nothing to do with pagan priests who do liver-reading or call forth the spirits of the dead. Practices like these were rife in the Near East at the time Israel's life and culture were developing, and it was undoubtedly meant that the children of Israel should not take dreams to such priests for interpretation. But the remarkable part is the next section, which tells the people what they *should* do.

The passage goes on to establish *in the law* the foundation for prophecy and the visionary experience of the prophet. So that the Lord may speak in a direct way to his people, he will raise up a prophet among them who is strong enough to hear the voice of the

Lord their God, and *see* the fire like that on Sinai. He will put his words in the prophet's mouth. Then it is up to the prophet to speak what is given. The people shall listen and the Lord will deal with those who will not, but for the prophet the penalty again is death if he speaks anything but what is given, or if he speaks in the name of other gods. Thus these passages, which are the only part of the law touching on prophecy or dreams, contain no injunction against listening to visions and dreams, but only against failure to distinguish the word of the Lord. This placed a real responsibility on men who believed that God could actually approach and speak directly to them. They not only had to speak the word of God which would "come to pass or come true"; in effect, the final test for the true prophet of the Lord was to see if his prophecies led the people into closer communion with their God.

## The prophets wrestle with the problem of dreams

No wonder Jeremiah wrestled with the problem of the value of the dream (14:14, 23:16–32, 27:9, 29:8). He had a responsibility. He also had reason to be skeptical about the way dreams and visions were understood. All around him Jeremiah heard men prophesy soothing words in the face of the disaster he saw brewing, and he tried to picture what made these prophets see only what they wanted to see. Like Ezekiel (Chapter 13), he tried to find some method of distinguishing the genuine prophetic dream or vision from those which were self-deluded, "vanities" manufactured out of whole cloth. (And even one's own dreams are hard to check on and so easy to forget.) But Jeremiah came to no real solution of the problem, except to suggest that the dream itself be brought into the open for scrutiny (23:28) and that time be allowed to test the interpretation (28:9).

Isaiah took perhaps a more sophisticated view of the problem (28:15, 29:10, and 30:9). He too made it clear that judgment waited for those who made a covenant with death, and who to save themselves told the people just what they wanted to hear. They were "seers of hell" whose "vision with Sheol" would not last (the literal expressions in 28:15 and 18). They became blind, unconscious. But then he shifted the burden back upon the people, who demanded deceitful things and would not listen to the prophet who told them what he really saw. Indeed, in meeting this problem the

Hebrew prophets went deeper than even the rational Greeks in trying to understand the nature of visionary inspiration and its interpretation, and they showed a more critical attitude.

But there was one further step, which had been hinted at in I Kings. When Ahab demanded the truth of the prophet Micaiah, the king heard the prophecy of his death. Micaiah then told his vision of a spirit that became a lying spirit in the mouth of all the king's other prophets. At this, one of them stepped up "and struck Micaiah on the cheek and said, 'How did the Spirit of the Lord go from me to speak to you?' And Micaiah said, 'Behold, you shall see on that day when you go into an inner chamber to hide yourself'" (I Kings 22:24, II Chronicles 18:23).

This understanding is fully developed in the little-known but deeply significant book of Habakkuk—"the oracle of God which Habakkuk the prophet *saw*"—whose words seem almost to be formed in a vision. When the prophet described the way in which it was received, he said, "I will take my stand to watch, and station myself on the tower, and *look forth to see* what he will say to me" (2:1). It is as if the prophet must go off by himself into his inner watchtower. The vision "comes to one whose feet are on the firm foundation of confident expectation, and who rises even a little above the toil and moil to take a look about him. God's revelation, though available for all, is not actually received by all; man must look forth or be on the alert as a watchman stands attentive." Charles Taylor has written these wise words in his exegesis on these lines in *The Interpreter's Bible.*

And when the vision comes, it is about visions. The vision takes its own time to form and mature. It comes from a place that has its own time schedule, its own will to break through at the right time. And the task of the prophet is to put it forth so that all can know. The prophet's words were: "And the Lord answered me: Write the vision; make it plain upon tablets, so he may run who reads it. For still the vision awaits its time; it hastens to the end— it will not lie. If it seem slow, wait for it; it will surely come, it will not delay. Behold, he whose soul is not upright in him shall fail, but the righteous shall live by his faith." It would be hard to speak more plainly than this about the autonomy of the vision and its reality. And the advice is excellent: write it down, for the vision is easily swallowed up in other matters, and then forgotten.

All of the great Hebrew prophets seemed to derive their messages from some kind of direct confrontation of God himself, or from some type of visionary experience which must be interpreted. Either they see images—as Amos saw the image of a plumb line (7:7), Jeremiah a rod of almond (1:11), Isaiah the Lord upon his throne in full panoply (6:1), or Ezekiel his beautifully specific sequences— or their very being is possessed by God's spirit and they speak as the mouthpiece of God. Psychologically there is little difference between having the visual screen possessed by images, and possession of the motor centers which results in speech. Perhaps in the later prophets there was somewhat more conscious control and awareness during the experience, and perhaps not. They themselves did not distinguish very clearly between the experience of the dream, the vision, the hearing of God's voice, or possession by the spirit. The important thing was not the actual images, but the prophetic ability to see their significance and speak of this. Many people may have seen a rod of almond or a plumb line, but it takes the prophetic personality to see the significance and to speak of it.

At the same time, as the prophets agreed, their experience came when the spirit of God was made available to them, and whether they or anyone else liked it or not. Jeremiah complained almost as strongly about his own compulsion to speak as about the evils he had to speak about. Even centuries later the Jews, according to Jerome, forbade men under thirty to read the beginning of the book of Ezekiel with its marvelous vision of the throne chariot. The most famous of Ezekiel's visions, that of the valley of dry bones (37:1), was described as the action of the hand of God upon him which lifted him up and set him down within his insight. This experience has all the qualities of a dream, like many of the other prophetic experiences, even to the being lifted up and set down in another place. The images of Ezekiel, although little studied in recent years, are well known in song and literature. They are genuine productions of what depth psychology would call the collective unconscious, something from beyond the conscious mind and often beyond the limits of personal experience. Comparable dreams and visions are by no means unknown today; in fact quite recently an experience similar in quality was told to me by a minister who received it. The specific references to visions in Ezekiel are found in 1:1, 7:26, 8:3, 11:24, 12:22, 12:27, 13:7, 13:16, 40:2, and 43:3. These passages, most of them the very ones Biblical critics consider likely to be from Ezekiel's own hand, contain the essential message of the prophet.

Isaiah 1:1 speaks of the vision which came to him, while in 6:1 he simply "sees." The inference, however, is clear that he sees something outside of this space-time continuum, something in the form of a vision. Other specific references to visions in Isaiah are 21:2, 22:1, 28:15 and 18, 29:7 and 11, and 30:10. In these last verses he laments that these visions are to the people as a sealed book, and they wish it so. He also condemns those who turn to some pagan practice of incubation and "sit in tombs, and spend the night in secret places," instead of waiting for the Lord to speak (65:4).

Among the "minor" prophets, Hosea received the word of the Lord, and according to his own record, lived out what might be called a vision (12:10) of guilt. The book of Obadiah simply begins with the words: "The vision of Obadiah." The word of the Lord came to Micah, and he *saw* and passed on the warning to false prophets that "therefore it shall be night to you, without vision, and darkness to you, without divination . . . for there is no answer from God" (3:6). His meaning may well be that, until they begin to see straight, God will no longer answer the prophets in dreams. Finally, after Nahum's graphic vision of what was to befall Nineveh, there is the book of Habakkuk, which we have discussed, and then the visions and dreams and angels described by the prophet Zechariah. His experiences, which happened at the time the Hebrews were returning to Jerusalem to rebuild their city and their temple, gave hope and encouragement to this work. The first six chapters are almost entirely taken up with vision after vision, in which the prophet conversed with an angel and saw images in such detail that long analyses would be required to understand them fully. These experiences began with a dream (Moffatt, for instance, translates it so), which is described in Hebrew simply as what the prophet "saw in the night" (Zechariah 1:8), and the following visions may well have come in the same way. In a later chapter the prophet accused the diviners of seeing lies and telling false dreams (10:2), and Zechariah followed this charge up by predicting a day of cleansing on which "every prophet will be ashamed of his vision when he prophesies" (13:4).

## Dreams in the Hebrew poetic tradition

Alongside of the prophetic understanding of these experiences, there was a similar appreciation of the dream developed in the "writings." This last part of the Old Testament for us to look at includes those portions of scripture which are neither law, history, nor prophecy. Among them, the book of Psalms and the book of Job have probably had as great an influence upon the devotional life of men as anything written outside of the New Testament. Here we find a great variety of literary references to dreams and visions.

Amid the flood of imagery of the Psalms there are three specific references to visions and dreams, and several poetic allusions. Psalm 89:19 sings of God speaking to his holy one in a vision, while the Seventy-third Psalm pictures the dream as a nightmare of revelation from which one awakes despising the image of wickedness (73:20). In Psalm 126:1 the dream is likened to the wish which has been fulfilled and the poet goes on to strengthen this by showing that the Lord "gives to his beloved in sleep" what cannot be had simply by rising early and working late (127:2).

The psalmist frequently speaks of his communion with God in the night without distinguishing very clearly between sleep or wakeful hours in the darkness. Current studies of the practice of incubation in ancient cultures see vestiges of this practice in several of these passages. André Caquot in his study of the dreams of Canaan and Israel in *Les Songes et Leur Interprétation* refers particularly to Psalms 17, 63, and 91.[5] Showing that to pass the night on the ground was a known rite of lamentation in Israel, he cites the ancient verses of Psalm 91: "Happy the man who stays by the Most High in shelter, who lives under the shadow of Almighty God," protected from "the terrors of the night" (91:1, 5, Moffatt translation). Again the psalmist cries out that God tests his soul by night and concludes, "But may our innocent lives enjoy thy favour, may we be satisfied, when we wake to see thy vision" (17:3, 15, Moffatt translation). A Norwegian writer, S. Mowinckel, has shown the close connection of this Psalm to incubation, and also suggests that the same thing is seen in Psalm 63:

> When I remember thee in bed, and muse on thee by night, my soul clings close to thee, thy right hand holds me fast; for thou hast been my help, and shadowed by thy wings I sing thy praise (63:6–8, Moffatt translation).

[5] Sources Orientales, *Les Songes et Leur Interprétation*, Paris, Editions du Seuil, 1959, pp. 116ff. This study presents an excellent bibliography on the biblical study of dreams and incubation.

While there are other references to disturbing nights, as in 22:2 and 32:4, the psalmist also sings that he can lie down to sleep in safety, which the Lord alone gives (3:5 and 4:8). And in the night His song is with the psalmist (42:8), like the maiden in the Song of Solomon (5:2) who tells that she sleeps, but her heart awakes. Certainly in the night season the psalmist found that something came through to him which he knew as the revelation of God.

Throughout the Psalter there are also references to the angels which are messengers of God, destroying the wicked and helping the righteous. The vengeful arm of the Eternal is spoken of in Psalm 35:5–6 and 78:49, but in 34:7, 68:17, 91:11, 103:20, 104:4, and 148:2 the Lord is praised for the protection and power he gives through his angels. These were often-present realities to the psalmist.

In Proverbs there is little concern about dreams, visions, angels, or anything of the sort. This is an intensely "practical" book, this world book. The best it can say for sleep is that we should not indulge in it too much or too often. The skeptical preacher of Ecclesiastes goes a step further, and looks at dreams as another example of vanity (5:3, 7). They mean nothing more than a fool's fears, and their only result is empty words. In the whole history of the Christian church, whenever a text proof has been needed to support the contention that dreams are of no value, it is this passage to which one is referred, with no reference to the far more authoritative books of Genesis, Numbers, I Samuel, or Habakkuk. And yet if we had to weigh each book for its relative value in the Old Testament, Ecclesiastes would certainly show up somewhat on the light side.[6]

## Job and Daniel see dreams and visions

In the magnificent book of Job, in some ways the crowning piece of literature of the Old Testament, we find again a great reverence for dreams as communications from God. And as always, where dreams are taken seriously, the same attitude is shown toward visions.

[6] The problem of interpreting any passage in Ecclesiastes is complicated by the nature of the book. There is a strange interweaving of passages which express the skeptical point of view with those which express the traditional faith. One of the most interesting of the several attempts to solve this critical problem is Morris Jastrow's A Gentle Cynic: Being a Translation of the Book of Koheleth, Commonly Known as Ecclesiastes, Philadelphia, J. B. Lippincott Company, 1919.

Job complained that in addition to all the rest of his difficulties, God frightened him in the night with *dreams* and *visions*. "Then thou dost scare me with dreams and terrify me with visions" (7:14). Eliphaz was also terrified by "thoughts from visions of the night, when deep sleep falls on men" (4:13). Many moderns in the throes of anxiety and neurosis have felt comradeship with Job in these night fears, and had comfort. In Zophar's speech the parallel was carried farther; his understanding told him that the sinner would disappear like the dreams and visions of the night (20:8).

The most important passage about dreams in Job is found in the speech of Elihu, in which he held that God speaks to men in two ways. He speaks once, and then "in a dream, in a vision of the night, when deep sleep falls upon men, while they slumber on their beds, then he opens the ears of men, and terrifies them with warnings" (33:15). God's purpose in so treating men is to lead them back to himself and away from the pit. In this chapter (33:22–24) the destroying and protecting angels are also mentioned, probably as part of the vision. The author of the book of Job believed that God had some things to say which he could put in unmistakable terms in dreams and visions. It would be difficult to express more clearly a valuation of what can occur in man's dreaming. The dream can be an entrance, according to Job, into direct communication with God himself.

A word about Lamentations should be said at this point. This book belongs among the writings in the Hebrew canon of scripture, rather than with the prophets, and indeed the book is a psalm of lamentation. Among the other desolations lamented here—and they are real and terrible ones—is the fact that the vision no longer comes to the prophet. This is as tragic as anything that can happen to the people (2:9).

Those who are not acquainted with the Hebrew Bible may be surprised also to find the book of Daniel considered at this point. The Hebrew, however, separates it clearly from the prophets, and it is more akin to Job and Esther than to the more mundane and concrete histories. One who is interested in dreams and visions can have a field day in Daniel. Here again the two experiences are constantly equated. Daniel is wise and his wisdom comes largely from the very fact that he can interpret dreams and visions (1:17, 5:12). The story has hardly begun before there is a dream, the dream that Nebuchadnezzar had forgotten, but which proceeded to trouble him until he could no longer sleep (2:1). He was about to have the wise men (the dream interpreters) of Babylon killed because none of them could tell him his dream, when Daniel heard about the predicament. And God revealed to him the king's dream in a night vision, and also its interpretation. He was then able to satisfy Nebuchadnezzar by making known the mysteries of the future that God had tried to show the king. From this point on, Daniel's position in the court was assured.

The rest of the book is filled with dreams. Chapter 4 contains the king's vision predicting his madness, while the entire seventh chapter is devoted to Daniel's dream of the four beasts, and the eighth to his vision of the powerful ram and the interpretation given to him as he lies in deep sleep face downward on the ground. It should be noted that up to this point the dreams and visions are spoken of almost in the same breath, without distinction, and they certainly cannot be distinguished by content. From here on, the interest seems to shift to the waking vision. Two further visions given to Daniel (9:21 and 10:5) are elaborated in the final chapter. In the midst of his long forecast Daniel remarks that men of violence will lift themselves up to fulfill the vision, but will fail (11:14). In addition, the story of the handwriting on the wall (5:5) has the unmistakable quality of a group vision, and Daniel is also released by angels from the den of lions, as are Shadrach, Meshach, and Abednego from the fiery furnace (3:28, 6:22). In fact, the book of Daniel is so much concerned with these experiences that it might well be subtitled "A Romance of the Dream." And this is the note on which we close the Old Testament.

## The Apocrypha

But as we step from the Old Testament into the New, we are not exactly stepping across a gap. The Apocrypha continues the spirit of Job and Daniel, and this was the spirit in which Judaism was bathed at the time of Jesus of Nazareth. This fact was easily forgotten after the Apocrypha was excluded from our Bibles; indeed, it was repressed. The books of the Apocrypha are simply those which are found in the Greek translation of the Old Testament, the Septuagint, but which are no longer a part of the Hebrew canon of scriptures. With the rise of Christianity it was necessary to close the list of books in the Hebrew scripture, and those books that may have had a Christian taint, or were perhaps inferior in quality or known to have been of recent vintage, were dropped from the Hebrew Bible.

The Christian church up until the time of the Reformation, however, looked on these books as having almost the same authority as the other books of the Old Testament. In fact, St. Jerome in the fifth century was the first to explain clearly that there was a difference between the Hebrew and Christian Bibles. But today the average Protestant who is not a student of the Bible hardly knows what the Apocrypha is, and so he has no idea how much concern there was with dreams and visions during those centuries just before the birth of Jesus. Six of these neglected books deal in some way with dream experiences, and in three of the major ones dreams are central to the action, as well as in the more complete story of Esther told in the Apocrypha.

In II Esdras, Ezra was lying upon his bed lamenting the sad fate of his country when the angel Uriel was sent to him from the Most High to comfort him (4:1ff.). Three times the angel came to Ezra, who was then chief priest, to interpret signs and to lay certain visionary images before him. Then he told him, "But tomorrow night you must stay here, and the Most High will show you in dreams those visions of what the Most High is going to do in the last days to those who live on the earth" (10:58f., Goodspeed tr.). This apparently was the normal way in which God spoke his message. And Ezra began to behold visions in his dreams which go on for pages and pages. They were interpreted to him sometimes by the angel Uriel, sometimes by God. After that he prophesied to the people.

The book of Tobit is a delightful story in which the angel Raphael directed Tobias on the journey he took to help his father in their exile. At the same time they overcame the demon that afflicted Sarah and destroyed all of her husbands, and so provided a wife for Tobias. But the story does not concretize the angel. Instead, it lets Raphael himself declare that his appearance has been a vision. "All these days," he says, "that I appeared to you, I did not eat or drink, but you beheld a vision. Now give thanks to God, for I must go up to him who sent me, and you must write all that has happened on a scroll" (12:19–20, Goodspeed tr.).

The Greek version of Esther begins with the dream of Mordecai

(11:5ff.),[7] which he saw as a revelation of God's purpose and tried to understand in every detail. As the story then unfolds, with all its political overtones, Mordecai sees his dream fulfilled, and in the end he says, "These things have come from God. For I remember the dream that I had concerning these matters, and none of them has failed to be fulfilled" (10:5).

The Wisdom of Solomon tells of the time when God's all-powerful command brought doom and death that touched even heaven. The author says that apparitions in dreadful dreams then troubled the people, warning them with disturbing fears so that they would not die without knowing why they suffered (18:17ff.). In Ecclesiasticus, the wisdom of Sirach, we do find (34:1–7) an opposite view expressed about most dreams; they are made for fools, simply to pit this against that, face against face and shadow against shadow. And when they are divined, all they do is keep the law from being fulfilled. But even so, the writer cannot dismiss all dreams as delusions or deceptions, for he sees that some come as visitations from the Most High and are meant to be taken seriously. The negative comments of Sirach were also quoted throughout the Middle Ages, and in Roman Catholic circles until this day, whenever men wanted to belittle the value of dreams.

The vision of Heliodorus in II Maccabees (3:22ff.) reminds one of the vision of Paul on the Damascus road. In both cases the person who received the vision was struck down and later raised up. Where Paul was healed by Ananias, Heliodorus, after his vivid and detailed vision, was restored through the agency of the very angels he had seen, who returned to help him because of the prayers of the High Priest. And the narrative ends essentially with the dream of Judas Maccabeus, "a dream that was worthy of belief, a kind of vision," which he told because it gave his men inspiration (15:11, Goodspeed tr.). In this dream he saw the former high priest Onias with another man, who turned out to be Jeremiah and who presented Judas with a golden sword, a gift from God with which to smite his enemies (15:12ff.). And he did. One is reminded of the dreams of Alexander and the high priest Jaddus, which had the opposite result of saving Jerusalem from harm.

As we look over the whole body of these writings, we have to

---

[7] The chapter and verse numbers are those of the King James version, which places all the parts of the Greek story that do not appear in the Hebrew version into a supplement at the end of the book.

conclude that the authors of the Old Testament and the Apocrypha
had a belief about dreams and visions which they considered important. They believed that when men dreamed and saw genuine
visions, they were experiencing the break-through of another world.
This was one way in which God, the Most High or Yahweh, spoke
what he had to say to men. It was the way in which angels appeared
and made contact with people. It was an experience which can
hardly be distinguished from that of the prophetic inspiration. Indeed, whatever else they have to say about them, the Jewish writings
seldom devalued dreams and visions as meaningless. They realized
that too much concern with these experiences could lead to superstition, or to delusion, but still their inherent value was not negated.
They also realized that men could be fooled or even lie about
dreams and visions, and that one must be on guard against this
deception, whether unconscious or consciously purposed. Indeed
these writings leave little doubt what the Hebrew people believed
and taught about the value of dreams and visions, and how basic
they were to the revelation that is found in the Old Testament and
the Apocrypha. It is difficult to understand this book or the spirit in
which it was written unless one clearly understands this belief concerning inspiration, of which its dream theory is an essential part.

## Dreams in later Jewish literature

The reverence for dreams that is found from Genesis through the
Apocrypha continues and even grows in later Jewish literature. In
the opening tract of the Babylonian Talmud—which was reduced to
written form between 200 A.D. and 500 A.D.—there are four chapters
(55–58) on dreams. This book, which is second in authority in
Judaism only after the Bible, consists of the sayings of the famous
rabbis and their interpretations of Holy Writ. Many of the famous
leaders of Israel during this period spoke of the value of dreams and
encouraged the interpretation of them. Rabbi Hisda said that an
uninterpreted dream was like an unread letter. Dreams were specifically described here as a break-through from the beyond, from
the world of the spirit, or from God himself. There were good dreams
and bad dreams, and fasting was one of the best ways of avoiding
the bad ones. However, the bad ones often were more valuable since
they led to repentance and had a more transforming effect.

The Jewish Encyclopedia summarizes an excellent article on dreams in these words: ". . . that the most famous teachers frequently discuss dreams and enunciate doctrines regarding them, shows the strong hold dreams had even on the intellectual leaders of Judaism. Belief in dreams was the rule; doubt concerning them the exception."[8] According to this article the dream interpreters were so highly valued that they were nearly always paid for their services.

We find the same reverence for dreams among the Jewish philosophers. Philo, the great Jewish Hellenist of Alexandria, according to Eusebius, was the author of five books on dreams, three of which have been lost. Two of these, which deal with the dreams of Joseph and others around him, are mentioned in other works by Philo. The same feeling persisted in medieval times, as is shown by the work of Maimonides, the theologian who tried to integrate the thinking of Aristotle into later Judaic theology. This man, who was called the second Moses because of his strong influence on the Judaism of that time, believed that dreams were a kind of prophecy, and expressed this idea carefully in his chief work, *The Guide for the Perplexed.* "The principal and highest function is performed when the senses are at rest and pause in their action, for then [the imaginative faculty] receives to some extent, divine inspiration in the measure as it is predisposed for this influence. This is the nature of those dreams which prove true, and also of prophecy, the difference being one of quantity, not of quality. . . . In a similar manner the action of the imaginative faculty during sleep is the same as at the time when it receives a prophecy, only in the first case it is not fully developed, and has not yet reached its highest degree."[9]

In the Kabbalistic movement, which was once so well known to Christians through the *Zohar*, and which played such a part in the development of European scholarship and thought, there is evidence that dreams continued to be seen as communications of the divine. Dreams, it was said in these writings, are the unripe fruit of prophecy. Again, the later fathers of Hasidism showed a similar point of view. These stories of Hasidism have been collected and retold

[8] *The Jewish Encyclopedia*, New York, Funk and Wagnalls, 1925, Vol. IV, pp. 654ff.
[9] Moses Maimonides, *The Guide for the Perplexed*, trans. M. Friedländer, London, Routledge & Kegan Paul, 1951, p. 225.

so well by Martin Buber. Among them, for instance, is the one about Rabbi Eisik of Cracow, who followed his dreams and was led in the end to a great treasure.

The recently published *Rosenbaums of Zell* brings the thinking of the first of these movements, the Kabbalah, into the history of our own time. This work tells the story in some detail of a rabbinic family in nineteenth-century Germany. It also sets forth a number of their writings, in which it is clear that one of the chief ways in which these rabbis were given illumination was through dreams. One of those described relates to the integration of the Christ figure into Jewish thinking.[10]

There are also described here certain dreams that pictured the extinction of the Jewish community in Germany, which were dreamed over half a century before Hitler came to power and nearly twenty years before the Zionist movement was suggested as a political reality. These were dreams that came to Reb Hile Wechsler, one of the members of this influential family, about 1880. "These dreams happened more than once and were of such a compelling nature that he felt the urge to impart them to the Jewish world— the description of his dreams shows the typical cabbalistic ideology. Whenever he awoke after such dreams a verse out of the Scripture was on his lips which gave him the fitting interpretation. Yet he said he was by nature a rational person and not inclined to indulge in fantasies."[11] The way in which he handled these disturbing dreams also suggests that this was true of the young rabbi. He began by reasoning from the Talmud, and from other source works of his faith, how much importance he could give to the dreams, and how far he could go in seeing them in relation to the practical world. From his dreams, and from this strictly rational approach to them, Reb Hile was led then to encourage a return of the Jewish community to their homeland of Palestine. Thus in a time not only of rationalism but of devaluation of dreams, these deeply religious Jewish rabbis were still listening to their dreams for religious enlightenment and prophetic insight.

This attitude of Jewish leaders and scholars was picked up and lived out in popular Jewish thinking. As late as 1902 the famous

[10] Berthold Strauss, *The Rosenbaums of Zell: A Study of a Family*, London, Hamakrik Book and Binding Co., 1962.
[11] Ibid., p. 38.

dream book *Pitron Halomot* was published in translation in New York City; this was a book written during the period of Turkish occupation of Constantinople by Jacob Almoli. In substance these facts show that the attitude toward dreams which is found imbedded in the Old Testament has lived on in the rabbinic, philosophical, and popular traditions of Israel right up to the present time.

## Dreams in other ancient cultures

As might be expected, an interest in dreams was by no means unique among the Hebrews. The Old Testament springs out of an ancient and highly developed tradition. Long before the Greeks had put a word to papyrus, the Semitic cultures of Asia Minor and the Tigris and Euphrates valleys were recording an extensive and sophisticated literature. One of the ideas common to these writings was the belief that there are spiritual (as well as physical) realities that are beyond the control of human beings, and that one way to learn what they are like and how they are disposed toward men is by listening to dreams and visions. The gods and goddesses, demons and angels—these non-physical realities with which ancient people found themselves surrounded—revealed themselves in dreams. The Gilgamesh epic, dating back at least to 2000 B.C., is one of the finest examples of this Sumerian and Babylonian literature. It relates how this earliest prototype of the great hero came to know himself and later overcame the enemy the gods had put in his way. At each step it was through dreams given by beneficent heavenly powers that he was given direction to reach his goal.[12]

Tablets discovered at the eighteenth-century (B.C.) site of Ugarit tell about one Daniel who was blessed by a son after he had slept in the temple and had a dream in which he communicated with his god. This practice of incubation, for the purpose of receiving such dreams, has been common in many cultures. In the Assyrian empire, which continued Babylonian civilization, records show the same traditional respect for dreams. The Annals of Assurbanipal tell how the goddess Ishtar, after a prayer from the king, revealed herself to one of his seers in a dream with a message of direction and confidence for the king. Dream books were also used in ancient As-

[12] Alexander Heidel, *The Gilgamesh Epic and Old Testament Parallels*, Chicago, The University of Chicago Press, 1949.

syria, and those that were found in the royal library at Nineveh have been translated in the transactions of the American Philosophical Society. Our own Bible confirms the high regard for dreams among these peoples and also the Egyptians.

The Egyptian attitude is also learned through much the same kind of sources, rather than in any single document. For instance, among the papyri there are specific instructions for obtaining either a dream or a vision of certain gods. There is a record that King Thutmes IV, while still a prince, encountered one of the great gods in a dream. This was inscribed on a memorial stone found at the foot of the Sphinx, and while some students believe it to be a later restoration, it agrees equally with what we know of Egyptian belief in the time of Joseph and in modern times.

In fact, there is hardly a culture on earth that has not shared this interest in dreams. *The Dream and Human Societies*, recently published by the University of California Press following an international conference, shows the important place dreams have held from the shamanic culture of Siberia to the Moslem world. Several writers in this volume deal with the reverence throughout Islam for prophetic dreams, those in which the prophet appears.

In *The World of Dreams* Ralph L. Woods has put together a sizable anthology of similar materials from all over the world. From India we find one of the early Upanishads from nearly a thousand years before Christ, which held that in dreams one lies in an intermediate state between the world of the spirit (to which he passes in death) and life in this material world. Thus, the treatise explains, the dreamer is self-illuminated and receives important insights. There are the two chief dream books of the Chinese, the *Meng Shu* and *Meng Chan I Chih*, which were written relatively late; dating from the seventh and sixteenth centuries, they are less concrete and more philosophical than those of other traditions.

Teutonic people considered the wisest counselor the one who was charged with interpreting dreams; this is pictured in sagas like the Heimskringla, the Nibelungenlied, and the Laxdale Saga, where symbolic dreams are brought for interpretation. The same tradition continued in Iceland, for instance with the stories of St. Thorlak, who took great pleasure in telling his own dreams.

All of these cultures manifest the belief that, beside the physical world, there is another significant world of reality that breaks in upon the individual, particularly in dreams.[13] As Mircea Eliade has shown so clearly in his *Myths, Dreams and Mysteries*, this idea occurs among peoples everywhere, except in modern Western culture, where it is so foreign that men find it difficult to comprehend. It persists among modern primitive peoples, as Woods demonstrates by his collection of dream experiences among Bantus, Ashantis, Navajos, Papuans, and others. Jung found the same thing when he visited the Hopi Indians and certain African tribes to study their dream experiences. Laurens van der Post substantiates this with a delightful story of the Bushmen, told in *The Heart of the Hunter*. When he pressed these primitive men of the Kalahari to talk about the beginning of meaning in their lives, he was given only one significant answer: "But you see, it is very difficult, for always there is a dream dreaming us." Among peoples who have not been touched by Western positivism there is an almost universal belief that man is in contact through dreams with something more substantial than his own imaginings.

Many Christians fear the suggestion that anyone but a Christian could have contact with more-than-human spiritual realities. This would mean that Christianity does not have a corner on spiritual truth, on religious perception. But the Bible does not suggest that they should. It suggests, instead, that only through the tradition of these Testaments could the Jew, and later the Christian, come into the right kind of contact, which would lead them to the center and source of spiritual reality. Christianity does not offer any exclusive contact with the spiritual realm, but rather the guidance and power to find one's way through this realm to hope and salvation. It is the universal reality of the spiritual world, in fact, which makes Christianity and its power essential to our lives.

[13] The current interest in such beliefs is shown by the number of eminent scholars from Europe and the Orient who have contributed to *Les Songes et Leur Interprétation*, (op. cit., the second volume of the series called Sources Orientales). Not only is the ancient religious interpretation of dreams discussed, represented by the Egyptians, Babylonians, Persians, Hittites, Canaanites, and Jews, but also the belief in dreams found among the shamanistic people, the Cambodians, the Chinese, Japanese, and Indians, as well as the attitude of Islam. It is interesting to note that, although Christianity was for a large portion of its history one of the significant religions of the very part of the world under discussion, not a word is included about the Christian belief. In spite of this omission, this is one of the best such studies available, indeed the only one that covers some of the material.

Few people, however, take primitive dream experiences or those of the Assyrians or Egyptians too seriously. But when ancient Greece speaks, our roots are stirred, and we moderns listen. Let us turn now to the thinking of the Greeks on the subject of dreams to see how it tallies with that of other peoples.

*three*        # The Greek Attitude Toward the Dream

Perhaps it seems strange in a study of the Christian interpretation of dreams to devote a whole chapter to the ideas of the Greeks. But there is good reason for this. Although the earliest Christian church was born within the Hebrew community, it quickly became a Greek institution, with its main missionary thrust toward the Graeco-Roman world. Its earliest surviving scripture and liturgy were both in Greek, and from the time of these documents Greek ideas were penetrating the new church. As it grew, its nascent theology was deeply influenced by Greek philosophy. Thus the Christianity that survived the ancient world was formed by the commingling of the Greek and Hebrew cultures, while that which was exclusively Jewish hardly stayed alive after the second destruction of Jerusalem in 132 A.D.[1] In order to understand the Christian attitude toward dreams in the New Testament and in the fathers of the church, it is necessary to understand the Greek beliefs about dreams as well as what the Hebrews believed, for their beliefs supported and extended the Hebrew experience and theory.

There is another reason for studying the Greek interest in dreams. Ever since the Renaissance, with its fresh look at ancient cultures, Western man has been rightly astounded at the creativity and intellectual power of the Greek community for several centuries just before the Christian era. During this time, among a relatively small number of people, there flourished a culture that laid the foundation for modern philosophy, modern art, modern drama and lit-

[1] The last Jewish Christian church, in Pella, existed until about 350 A.D.

erature, and also for the scientific thinking of today. In most sophisticated quarters there is a far greater reverence for things Greek than there is for things Hebrew, because the philosophic and aesthetic contributions of the Greeks have been more highly valued than the more specifically religious and ethical contributions of the Hebrews. Once it is realized that the Greeks with very few exceptions viewed the dream much as the Hebrews did—as a vehicle for communication from the divine—and with even greater reverence than the Hebrews, modern Western man may be more likely to take seriously the dream tradition of the Old and New Testaments. He may even find reason to listen with open-mindedness to his own modern dream experiences.

It was among the Greeks, as everyone knows, that man first learned how to develop and use his reason consciously. Among them is found the first careful analysis of reason and the first self-conscious philosophy. There is no question that it was the Greek mind that gave the philosophical, theological, rational foundation for Christianity. For the past several centuries many people have been so taken by the magnitude of the Greek discoveries, particularly their understanding of reason and its use, that they believed the Greeks were a "rational" people par excellence. Students have laid so much stress on the rationality of the Greeks that they have failed to see them as living people.

Recent modern scholarship does not uphold this idealistic picture of Greek rationality. As one studies the documents of ancient Greece objectively, he finds that the Greeks from Homer through Plato and Aristotle, through the poets of the Golden Age, down to the Stoics and Skeptics, were just as concerned with the irrational elements of life as the Hebrews. The Greeks were just as "superstitious," just as moved by the numinous depths of the unknown, as any other early people, the Hebrews included. The fact that they developed rational understanding did not mean that they neglected an interest in the irrational aspects of life, such as dreams, prophecy, oracles, visions, or gods and demons. They were both rational and irrational at the same time. One reason for their greatness was that they avoided no part of the reality of life.[2]

[2] Yet it was at this very point that Greek culture broke down. A principal reason for the rapid conquest of the Greek world by Christianity was the fact that Christianity offered a method of dealing with and relating to these non-rational depths, whereas the later Greek thinking failed to integrate them. Between phi-

The regius professor of Greek at Oxford, E. R. Dodds, has written a very careful study of these neglected aspects of Greek life in a book entitled *The Greeks and the Irrational*. With painstaking documentation he demonstrates quite clearly and definitively that Greek understanding and culture did not erase or conquer the irrational side of life, and that poets and philosophers alike recognized this fact and wrote about it. Jane Harrison in her equally well-documented study, *Prolegomena to the Study of Greek Religion*, gives extensive evidence of the same fact. The Greeks indeed were quite as irrational as the Hebrews, and their *non-rational* ideas and practices reinforced the direction the developing church was already taking. In discussing the dreams of the Greeks we shall rely heavily on the material that Dodds and Miss Harrison have so thoroughly brought to light.

It is much more difficult to study the Greek attitude toward a particular subject than the Hebrew. The Greeks never obliged posterity, as did the Jews, by codifying and canonizing their literature in one book. Any who can read can discover the ancient Hebrew attitude toward practically anything, and so much critical work has been done on the Old Testament that there is now a generally accepted framework of basic agreement. This is not true of Greek culture. There is a wide variety of Greek literature—some of it discovered only in recent years—and there are the most diversified opinions about it. The very multiplicity of Greek literary output is often what keeps us from seeing very clearly how their thinking on specific matters originated. Where the Old Testament, in most cases, weaves its varying ideas around a few cohesive trends of thought, Greek culture instead presents us with a variety of completely unrelated ideas on nearly every subject, including that of dreams.

In fact, this is especially true of dreams, since this concern of the Greeks represents one of the best examples of their attitude

---

losopher and common man a great gulf became fixed. The people's irrational desires and impulses, their sudden whims and fears, became separated from their rational understanding of life. There came to be such a wide chasm between the rational and the irrational that popular thought broke down and disintegrated into a hodgepodge of superstition and necromancy. The early Christian church, undergirding itself with Greek thinking, stepped into the breach to offer an integration of the rational and the irrational. Ironically, Christianity did not have as much to offer to the Hebrews. They had forged out of their travails a religion of adversity that gave its adherents a tool for dealing with the most pressing irrational problems of life. Greek philosophy gave no such tool.

toward the non-rational aspect of life. They manifested the same interest in dreams, and the same belief that they are intrusions of a more-than-human world, that we have found in the Old Testament, but on the whole without the same caution or critical evaluation we have found among the Hebrews. In order to find what pattern there was in the plethora of material, let us look first of all at the popular attitude toward dreams as revealed in early Greek literature. The importance of dreams in the classical period will then be examined, and we shall finally consider the philosophic and "scientific" attitudes toward dreams as revealed in Plato and Aristotle and later thinkers.

## Dreams of the Heroes

Two basically different ideas about dreams can be distinguished in the popular thinking of ancient Greece. The first of these was the archaic point of view, which can be described as an objective view of dreams. According to this idea, which was expressed by the Homeric poets, dreams are supernatural revelations given by the gods or other supernatural figures. Later a second theory was superimposed upon this first one; it was the Orphic idea that during sleep the soul left the body and communed with the gods, returning with important information, either symbolic or direct in nature. These two views became mingled and interwoven in popular thought, which continued to find utmost significance in dreams of both kinds. Both were seen as avenues of contact with "daemonic" reality.

In the poets of Homeric antiquity the references to dreams are many, and almost uniformly they are treated as objective fact. It was a dream-figure sent by Zeus to hunt out Agamemnon and stand over him in the form of wise, old Nestor that roused the Greeks to action before Troy (*Iliad* 2.1ff.). In the same way the sad spirit of Patroclus stood over Achilles after Hector was dead (23:65), and in the *Odyssey* Athene formed an image that came in through the keyhole to bring Penelope a message as she slept (4.795ff.), while the goddess in disguise came to Nausicaa in a dream. (6.14ff.)

These dreams, according to Dodds, usually take "the form of a visit paid to a sleeping man or woman by a single dream-figure (the very word *oneiros* in Homer nearly always means dream-figure, not dream-experience). This dream-figure can be a god, or a ghost, or a pre-existing dream-messenger, or an 'image' (*eidolon*) created specially for the occasion; but whichever it is, it exists objectively in space and is independent of the dreamer. It effects an entry by the keyhole (Homeric bedrooms having neither window nor chimney); it plants itself at the head of the bed to deliver its message; and when that is done, it withdraws by the same route. The dreamer, meanwhile, is almost completely passive. . . ."[3] He knows he is in bed and asleep, and is seeing a dream. In fact, the Greeks of this period did not speak of having a dream, but like the Hebrew experience of seeing an angel, they told of "seeing a dream."

There is no doubt that the Greeks prized these objective dreams with their messages delivered directly to the sleeper. Later on, in the great Periclean age as well as in archaic times these dreams were considered divine, "god-sent." The bearer of the message might be either a god or some person, even a member of the dreamer's family; it made no difference. Many, many examples in Greek literature show this, and also suggest that people generally took such directions seriously and acted upon them. But this was not all. There were also dreams that prescribed some kind of dedication, a plaque, a statue, or even a chapel, which left tangible evidence. Archaeologists have discovered many inscriptions dedicated "in accordance with a dream" or "having seen a dream," and while these do not tell much about the content of the dreams, they leave no questions about the way they were valued. Plato commented on this in the *Laws* (909f.), remarking how frequently such instructions were received in dreams, and the follower of Plato who wrote the *Epinomis* also noted (985) that "many cults of many gods have been founded and will continue to be founded, because of dream-encounters with supernatural beings, omens, oracles, and deathbed visions."

But the Greeks wrote about other dreams besides these objective ones. Even in Homeric times the poets also spoke of symbolic dreams that required interpretation. One of the oldest parts of

---

[3] E. R. Dodds, *The Greeks and the Irrational*, Boston, Beacon Press, 1957, pp. 104f. Dodds has written a masterful study of dreams among the Greek people in his fourth chapter, which he calls "Dream-Pattern and Culture-Pattern."

the *Iliad* (5.149) tells of an interpreter who failed to give his sons the meaning of their dreams when they went off to the Trojan War, while Penelope's dream in Book 19 of the *Odyssey* spoke its own meaning as she slept. In this dream she saw her beautiful geese killed by an eagle and was weeping for them when the eagle swooped down and spoke to her in a human voice, assuring her that Odysseus would return and scatter her unwanted suitors like the dead geese. Certainly, anxiety dreams were also known to these early Greeks, and there is as good a description in the *Iliad* as any modern psychologist listens to. Four times around the walls Hector fled from Achilles, *"as in a dream* one flees and another cannot pursue him—the one cannot stir to escape, nor the other to pursue him—so Achilles could not overtake Hector in running, nor Hector escape him" (22.199).

Hesiod also wrote of more than one idea about dreams. This eighth-century poet, who probably invented the idea of teaching by poetry, described how the muses spoke to him on lonely Mount Helicon; by his own description Hesiod himself then had the powers of a seer. But later on he wrote that night gives birth, without father, to "hateful Doom and black Fate and Death, and she bare Sleep and the tribe of Dreams" (*Theogony* 22ff., 32, and 211ff.).

Although it is often suggested that the objective pattern of dreams in archaic cultures is peculiar to that period, we can legitimately conclude that the early Greeks dreamed much as we do now. The argument, in the first place, that the objective type of dream no longer occurs in our time simply does not hold water. This feeling is probably very common among men who have paid little or no attention to their own dreams, but it is not borne out by the published material, such as the modern dream series found in C. G. Jung's *Psychology and Alchemy*. More likely the fact is simply that all primitive peoples attach greater significance to their objective dreams than to others. Naturally, the early Greek heroes would be heroic in their dreaming, as well as in their more conscious activities. But more than this, they undoubtedly remembered the objective dreams, which seemed clear and easy to understand, when the more symbolic dreams, which had to be interpreted, were often forgotten, as they also are today.

They also had good reason, like Penelope in the *Odyssey*, to ignore what some dreams were saying. Faced with a houseful of suitors who wanted the place of Odysseus and even threatened to kill her son, Penelope could not trust her dream that the eagle would return. She told the "stranger" who brought her news of her husband that

". . . in truth dreams, do arise which are perplexing and hard to understand, which in men's experience do not come true. Two gates there are for unsubstantial dreams, one made of horn and one of ivory. The dreams that pass through the carved ivory delude and bring us tales that turn to naught; those that come forth through polished horn accomplish real things, whenever they are seen. Yet through this gate came not I think my own strange dream."

ODYSSEY 19.559ff.

But like Penelope, these early Greeks knew, as far back as we have any record, that there were different kinds of dreams, some of them imperative, and others, just as today, cloudy and uncertain.

Sometime about the fifth or sixth centuries before Christ, however, a new idea was introduced to the popular Greek mind that resembled quite closely the shamanism of the Northern peoples of Europe and Siberia. Whatever its origin—and Dodds makes a good case for the introduction of this new idea from outside of the culture, from the North—this belief was developed by the Pythagoreans and among the followers of Orphism, and it took much the same turn as the similar belief found in early Hindu thinking. This role of the spiritual leader or shaman brought a realization that the power of the dream comes from within the individual, or at any rate from within certain individuals. It was believed that during sleep the soul left the body and communed with other spirits, took trips, or visited with the gods. Thus the body came to be looked upon as the prison house of the soul, the binding element from which the soul waited to be freed; and the state most favorable for this freedom, other than death, was that of sleep. The poet Pindar was one of the first to express this, and it is later found in the writings of Xenophon and Plato.

At the same time in this period of greatness the temples of Aescylapius became important, because here a dream could be sought from the god. It was believed that the sick person who came to be cured and slept within the temple confines could be visited by the god in a dream, and so receive a healing touch or an omen.[4] From the fifth century on, incubation became of the greatest importance throughout the Greek-speaking world, down to the latest pagan times and into the modern Christian era. In this way the dream with a direct message or omen continued to be sought by numbers of people, among them the great Sophocles, who offered his home as the first shrine of Aescylapius in Athens, apparently at the bidding of a dream.[5]

## Dreams in classic Greek literature

Many of the classics of Greek literature contain references to dreams, and this is scarcely strange. In the great Greek dramas the authors were creating an essence of life as it really was, a picture that struck at the hearts of those who watched, as these plays still do today. It would be surprising if dreams had not appeared as one of the crises providing dramatic suspense.

In Aeschylus' plays, for instance, we find numerous examples in which dreams occur in this way. In his *Persians*, which was the only Greek tragedy we know of based on actual history, the action begins with the striking scene in which the queen mother is warned through a strange dream of Xerxes' impending death (176–230). One of the most dramatic points in his last play, *Choephoroe*, is the scene in which Orestes learns of his mother's dream of giving birth to an asp that suckles her; this is the scene that lays bare before him the tragic role he is to play (523–52). *Prometheus Bound* was raised entirely to the level of the gods except for the character of Io, and here the fateful quality of dreams is brought into the open. As Prometheus rants at his fate among the gods, he stops to recall what he has done for men. They were huddled phantoms in a dream when he first found them, and one of the greatest gifts he brought them was the ability to understand dreams and to distinguish the true ones from the false (442–506). Later, when Io comes to Prometheus in her half-crazed wanderings and wants to know her fate, he insists that she too speak of her sufferings. Io complains of her dreams, the fearful dreams of love that Zeus gave her. She

---

[4] Two works that consider this subject from different points of view are C. Kerényi, *Asklepios: Archetypal Image of the Physician's Existence*, New York, Pantheon Books, Inc., for the Bollingen Foundation, 1959; and Mary Hamilton, *Incubation (or the Cure of Disease in Pagan Temples and Christian Churches)*, London, Simpkin, Marshall, Hamilton, Kent & Co., 1906.

[5] Dodds, op. cit., pp. 193 and 203, notes 85–86.

finally had to tell her father about them, and he asked the oracles again and again how the demand of the gods could be met; in the end they learned that, because of her dreams, she was committed to wander the ends of the earth (645-60).

Aeschylus was living in the great age of which Herodotus wrote, when Pheidippides made his 150-mile run before the battle of Marathon. According to Herodotus, the runner was helped by a vision of the god Pan to reach Sparta and bring aid (5.105), while the turncoat Hippias was dreaming of lying in the arms of his mother. Herodotus told that Hippias hoped to regain power by helping the Persians at Marathon, and was sure his dream was a good omen. But as he was directing the operations of the Persians, Hippias sneezed, coughed, and a tooth flew out of his mouth into the sand, and he could not find it. Then he knew that this was the end of his dream: his only share was to be the tiny spot of land of which his tooth had taken possession (5.107). The Persians took the pass and then were defeated on the plain of Marathon. When there was peace again, the Athenians set up a temple to Pan under the Acropolis, and established sacrifices in accordance with the vision of Pheidippides.

These were also the years in which the great Pindar was writing his odes. In them Pindar expressed the basic Greek reverence for the dream. "Each man's body," he wrote, "follows the call of overmastering death; yet still there is left alive an image of life, for this alone is from the gods. It sleeps while the limbs are active; but while the man sleeps it often shows in dreams a decision of joy or adversity to come" (Fragment 131, 116B). According to the later writers Pindar himself had seen a vision of "the Mother of the Gods" in the form of a stone statue, and had also seen the establishment of a cult of worship because of his vision.[6]

Sophocles, the man of social position and civic prominence who let the world know his devotion to the cult of Aescylapius, wrote into his plays both the fateful character of dreams and the need to see them clearly. In *Electra* the queen dreams that Agamemnon lives again and plants his scepter beside the hearth, and it sprouts a tree that overshadows the whole country. And the queen reacts one way; she makes a fearful offering to propitiate the dead king. But throughout the rest of the play her dream and the righteous

[6] Dodds, op. cit., pp. 117, 135.

interpretation Electra gives it foreshadow what will actually happen. The chorus sings: "If I am not an erring seer . . . Justice, that hath sent the presage, will come, triumphant. . . ." (470)

In one brief comment in *Oedipus the King* Sophocles essentially encompassed the whole relationship of the world of dreams to human action and motivation. In this scene Oedipus, who bears the curse that he was destined to slay his father in order to possess his own mother, is talking with Iocasta, his queen. Iocasta has almost persuaded him that no human being can really "see" or divine what is to be, when a messenger comes to tell the king that Polybus, his supposed father, no longer lives. But Oedipus is not relieved of his fear, and the queen almost taunts him with his foolishness. It is better, she says, to live at random; many men have had dreams like this, "but he to whom these things are as nought bears his life most easily" (876–986). And then this woman walks out and kills herself for "nought"—because the king has discovered that she was his mother, wife to his real father, who had died as the seers said he would, by his son's hand.

Euripides also used dreams to set the theme of several of his plays. *Hecuba* begins with the scene in which the former queen of Troy cries out for someone to interpret her tragic symbols, and these dread visions of Hecuba's sleep set the stage for both this play and *The Trojan Women*. The whole story of *Iphigenia among the Tauri* hangs on those "strange visions the past night brought me [Iphigenia], which I will tell to the air, if there is really any help in that" (42–66). Iphigenia is captive of the primitive Tauri and serves them as priestess, sacrificing the Greek warriors who fall into their hands. She has dreamed of the fall of her father's house, with one pillar left standing which sprouts hair and becomes human. To the empty air she says: "the meaning is that my brother Orestes is dead." And then Orestes and his companion, led by the command of the gods, land on the Tauri shore.

As the real meaning of her dream becomes clear (more like Electra's dream), this heroic daughter of Agamemnon throws herself back upon the fates. "Begone, ye lying dreams," she says, and bravely helps her brother face the visions of his madness. Finally, as they are escaping from the primitive land, the chorus of captive women relates the reason why dreams are no longer so significant as they used to be. The great earth-oracle at Delphi had originally been a dream-oracle, guarded by a great serpent. Apollo vanquished the serpent, and then mortals became less concerned with his oracles, and when he complained to the father god, Zeus simply stopped mother earth from sending dreams to them (1234–83). Without the protection of the serpent, it would seem, the authority of the gods was endangered if mortals could understand dreams.

Throughout his history Herodotus continued the tradition of the divine origin of dreams. A world traveler, he brought back tales and history from all over the known world, found visions and dreams from as far off as Persia and Egypt that were significant enough to relate. One story he brought back from his African travels was about the variation of incubation found among the Nasamonians in Western Africa. According to Herodotus' description this nomadic people would return to the graves of their ancestors for divination; after praying, they lay down to sleep there, and dreams came to them which guided their conduct (4.172). In several cases he told how the great figures of history were warned of impending disaster by the dreams that they or those around them received; he also told of omens of great deeds that came in dreams.[7]

By the time of Aristophanes the great age of Greek enlightenment had reached its height and, as Dodds shows so clearly, the reaction had set in. Intellectual leaders in Athens were prosecuted and punished, book burnings took place, and many suffered for their opinions. The comedies of Aristophanes poked fun—none too gentle fun—at some of the most serious matters of Greek life. There was an increasing reliance on dreams, and the diviners, who were always good for a laugh, were mentioned in several of his comedies. For instance, The Wasps opens with a discussion between two drowsy slaves who have each had a dream; instead of hiring an interpreter, they decide to save the money and just tell the whole tale to the audience.

The story of The Wasps has to do with an old man who wants to spend all his time standing in the Court and judging. Everything has been done to cure him; he has even been taken to sleep the night in Aescylapius' temple. And Athens laughed at this first literary

[7] See particularly 1:34ff., 107ff., 209ff.; 2.139; 3.64ff., 124f.; 4.172; 5.56; 6.105ff., 118, 131; 7.12ff.

It is interesting to find, as Kenneth Rexroth details in a recent issue of the *Saturday Review*, (December 2, 1967), that modern scholars have had to change their idea of Herodotus as a superstitious romancer. Instead, his facts check out, and he has come to be regarded as the truly scientific historian of the cultures of his time.

notice of incubation in the temples of Aescylapius. But while Athens laughed, the people themselves continued to seek for the divine dream, and the philosophers sought to understand what was going on.

## Plato and the dream

Whatever else we may say about Greek philosophy, it unquestionably reached maturity in the fourth century with the work of Plato. There is hardly a sector of human thought that has not been influenced in some way by his reasoning, for Plato's was one of the greatest minds the world has yet produced. While he tried to find a rational way of approaching men's experience, he did not attempt to rationalize any part of it out of existence. On the contrary, he placed a high value on men's experiences of the non-rational side of life, including dreams and the way men looked at them.

In the century before Plato there were skeptics who denied the objective value of dreams. Heraclitus, who earned the name of "the Weeping Philosopher," saw that in dreams each of us retires to a world of his own, and for him this denied what should be the rule—"to follow what we have in common." The poet-philosopher Xenophanes apparently also denied the validity of divine dreams, since he rejected any form of divination. But there was also the great physical philosopher Democritus, who tried to understand an actual physical mechanism by which objective dream experiences could occur. His theory was that there are images—and he even used the Homeric word *eidola*—continually emanating from persons and objects that penetrate the pores of a dreamer's body and cause him to see happenings at a distance, even in another person's mind. This older and respected contemporary of Socrates became known as "the Laughing Philosopher," and it has been suggested that many of his interesting and useful theories were forgotten in modern times simply because he did not seem serious enough to be weighty.

While perhaps Plato did not put the same stress on dreams as some of his contemporaries, he did give attention to their influence on people's actions.[8] In the passages of the *Crito* and the *Phaedo*

---

[8] Very few of us are aware of these passages; although there are several, they have seldom been discussed by the scholars. The graduate course on Plato that I took in one of the leading universities in the East called no attention to this aspect of Plato's philosophy.

when he depicted the last days of Socrates, Plato carefully set down the great master's concern with two of his own dreams. It is not even clear whether Plato was expressing his own opinions or those of his master. The first of these, which has been discussed at length by one Jungian analyst because it is so revealing, occurs in the *Crito* when Socrates was discussing the ship from Delphi whose coming meant death for him:

> *Socrates:* But I do not think that the ship will be here until tomorrow; this I infer from a vision which I had last night, or rather only just now, when you fortunately allowed me to sleep.
> *Crito:* And what was the nature of the vision?
> *Socrates:* There appeared to me the likeness of a woman, fair and comely, clothed in bright raiment, who called to me and said: 'O Socrates,
>  The third day hence to fertile Phthia shalt thou come.'
> *Crito:* What a singular dream, Socrates!
> *Socrates:* There can be no doubt about the meaning, Crito, I think.
> *Crito:* Yes; the meaning is only too clear. But oh! my beloved Socrates, let me entreat you once more to take my advice and escape.
>
> CRITO 44

In the *Phaedo*, Cebes and Socrates were talking about the fact that so many people had noted how Socrates turned poet during his last days in prison. He was turning Aesop's fables into verse, and had even composed a hymn in honor of Apollo. The poet Evenus teased Socrates, wondering if the philosopher were trying to equal him. To this Socrates replied:

> Tell him, Cebes, he replied, what is the truth—that I had no idea of rivalling him or his poems; to do so, as I knew, would be no easy task. But I wanted to see whether I could satisfy my conscience on a scruple which I felt about the meaning of certain dreams. In the course of my life I have often had intimations in dreams 'that I should make music.' The same dream came to me sometimes in one form, and sometimes in another, but always saying the same or nearly the same words: 'Set to work and make music,' said the dream. And hitherto I had imagined that this was only intended to exhort and encourage me in the study of philosophy, which has been the pursuit of my life, and is the noblest and best of

music. The dream was bidding me do what I was already doing, in the same way that the competitor in a race is bidden by the spectators to run when he is already running. But I was not certain of this; for the dream might have meant music in the popular sense of the word, and being under sentence of death, and the festival giving me a respite, I thought that it would be safer for me to satisfy the scruple, and, in obedience to the dream, to compose a few verses before I departed. And first I made a hymn in honour of the god of the festival, and then considering that a poet, if he is really to be a poet, should not only put together words, but should invent stories, and that I have no invention, I took some fables of Aesop, which I had ready at hand and knew by heart—the first that occurred to me—and turned them into verse.

PHAEDO 6of.

In both of these instances it is clear that Socrates takes his dreams quite seriously, and Plato takes Socrates quite seriously. One does not talk of trivia in the last days under sentence of death, at least not this man, and it is certainly with reverence that Plato treats these incidents. Both men saw meaning in dreams. Not only did Socrates take careful note of them, but he took pains to understand and interpret them, and tried to live the suggestions that they gave. He wanted to satisfy a certain anxiety, a matter of conscience arising from his dreams, and so he spent part of his last days in an unusual activity that a recurring dream had suggested.

In the *Republic* it is simply accepted that God communicates with men by dreams and waking visions. "He changes not, and does not deceive others, waking or dreaming, either by phantasms or by sign or by word," Plato remarked in Book II, when he was discussing whether the poets had given an adequate picture of God in their portrayal of certain actions of the gods. He brought up particularly Homer's story of the false dream Zeus sent to Agamemnon, and concluded, "Then, although we are admirers of Homer, we shall not admire the lying dream which Zeus sends to Agamemnon" (*Republic* II, 382). He believed that one should not speak of divine things in this way; when the gods spoke, they spoke the truth, and one of the ways was by dreams and visions.

In the ninth book of the *Republic* Plato wrote further on dreams. There he showed a clear understanding of the fact that dreams can often reveal the dark, instinctual side of man. And as Dodds has

pointed out, he no longer saw the clear-cut dialogue between the
soul and "the passions of the body" which his earlier works depicted;
in the *Republic* this had become an internal dialogue between two
parts of the soul itself. Plato knew that dreams could be an expression of the bestial side of man's nature, the id of Freud. Yet he also
realized that if a man's life is in harmony and well balanced, he
can approach the timeless unknown and find truth in dreams. By
using his reason to keep the "appetites" from simply taking over in
sleep, he can leave the other side of his nature free to contemplate
the unknown, past, present, and future, and so come most nearly
to truth in his dreams. The passage is as follows (italics are mine):

I do not think that we have adequately determined the
nature and number of the appetites, and until this is accomplished our inquiry will always be confused.

Well, he said, it is not too late to supply the omission.

Very true, I said; and observe the point which I want to
understand: Certain of the unnecessary pleasures and appetites
I conceive to be unlawful; everyone appears to have them,
but in some persons they are controlled by the laws and by
the better desires with the help of reason, and either they
are wholly banished or they become few and weak; while
in others they are stronger, and there are more of them.

Which appetites do you mean?

I mean those which wake when the rest of the soul—the
reasoning and human and ruling power—is asleep; then the
wild beast within us, gorged with meat or drink, starts up
and having shaken off sleep goes forth to satisfy his desires;
and you know that there is no action which at such a time,
when he has parted company with all shame and sense, a
man may not be ready to commit; for he does not, in his
imagination, shrink from incest with his mother, or from any
unnatural union with man, or god, or beast, or from par-
ricide, or the eating of forbidden food. And in a word,
no action is too irrational or indecent for him.

Most true, he said.

But when a man's pulse is healthy and temperate, and when
before going to sleep he has awakened his rational powers, and
fed them on noble thoughts and inquiries, collecting himself
in meditation; after having first indulged his appetites neither
too much nor too little, but just enough to lay them to
sleep, and prevent them and their enjoyments and pains from
interfering with the higher principle—which he leaves in the

solitude of pure abstraction, *free to contemplate and aspire to the knowledge of the unknown, whether in past, present, or future*; when again he has allayed the passionate element, so that he does not go to sleep with his spirit still excited by anger against anyone—I say, when, after pacifying the two irrational principles, he rouses up the third, in which resides reason, before he takes his rest, then, as you know, he attains truth most nearly, and is least likely to be the sport of fantastic and lawless visions.

I quite agree.

In saying this I have been running into a digression; but the point which I desire to note is that in all of us, even the most highly respectable, there is a lawless wild-beast nature, which peers out in sleep.

REPUBLIC 571f.

Plato gave hints here that he saw something besides a negative or bestial side in man's irrationality, and in other passages these suggestions were developed. In much the same way that C. G. Jung came to this realization in the present century, Plato had come to see that some of man's highest intuitions and understandings arise from his non-rational side, from his dream life. Man's greatest gifts are given to him when something more than human breaks through his rationally constructed autonomy and gives him a divine *mania*. "Our greatest blessings come to us by way of *mania*, insofar as *mania* is heaven-sent," Plato wrote in the *Phaedrus* (244),[9] and he went on to show that this mania or inspiration is of four kinds. The first of them is prophecy, which was originally called by the name *mania*, and this the ancients testify is "superior to a sane mind, for the one is only of human, but the other of divine origin." The others are catharsis (or healing), poetry, which is inspired by the muses, and the greatest, the inspiration of love.

As Josef Pieper shows in *Love and Inspiration*, his excellent study of the *Phaedrus*,[10] the cathartic or healing mania is sometimes given through dreams. In the tradition of the temples of Aescylapius, he points out, they were the perfect example of being possessed by divine madness, since a dream is something that simply happens to the dreamer, in which he is passive. It is not at all

[9] Hackforth's translation, as quoted by Josef Pieper; see note 10.
[10] Josef Pieper, *Love and Inspiration: A Study of Plato's Phaedrus*, London, Faber & Faber, 1965, p. 61.

dependent upon his conscious rational personality, but in this case was the seed in which the dreamer found a new reaction to himself and to the world around him.

In the *Symposium* (203) Socrates reports what he was told by the prophetess Diotima, that "God mingles not with man; but through Love all the intercourse and converse of gods with men, whether they be awake or *asleep*, is carried on. The wisdom which understands this is spiritual; all other wisdom, such as that of arts and handicrafts, is mean and vulgar. Now these spirits or intermediate powers are many and diverse, and one of them is Love."

It is even more obvious that Plato believed that prophecy was received through dreams and visions. His explanation in the *Phaedrus* was not only confirmed by his reverence for the dreams of Socrates, but it was expanded at length in the *Timaeus*. Here Plato took some pains to demonstrate this belief. Because man might be led night and day only by phantoms and visions, instead of caring for rational consciousness, God contrived to place these images in the lower regions, giving them as reflections on the smooth surface of the liver, which has both a bright and sweet and a bitter quality.[11] Thus the liver is the seat of divination, because at times it is stirred by some gentle inspiration that makes use of its natural sweetness, correcting all things and enabling it to practice divination in sleep.

This, Plato goes on, "is a proof that God has given the art of divination not to the wisdom, but to the foolishness of man. No man, when in his wits, attains prophetic truth and inspiration; but when he receives the inspired word, either his intelligence is enthralled in sleep, or he is demented by some distemper or possession." If he wants to understand what was said in a dream or know the meaning of a vision, he must first recover his wits and be able to judge; but that is not prophecy. There are men customarily appointed interpreters or judges of inspiration, but it is ignorant to call them prophets, for they are "only the expositors of dark sayings and visions . . . [the] interpreters of prophecy" (*Timaeus* 71f.).

One does not take this much trouble to explain something in

---

11 This explanation tallies closely with the understanding that Euripides expressed in *Iphigenia among the Tauri* that Apollo's oracle at Delphi had originally been a dream-oracle, but once the great serpent (the bitter side) had been vanquished, dreams sent by the gods had to be closed off. Farnell in the Encyclopaedia Britannica shows that incubation was originally practiced at Delphi (11th Ed., Vol. 20, p. 143).

which he does not believe, nor return to it again and again, as, for instance, Plato did in the *Meno* (99f.), the *Symposium* (203), and in *Ion* (533ff.). Certainly he valued the force of man's reason as few people did in that day or any other, but he also believed that for the highest reaches of life and understanding something more than man's reason is necessary. For prophetic understanding and healing, poetic insight, and even to know love or beauty, there must be intrusions of the divine, the more-than-human realm of reality that sets aside man's ordinary, rational consciousness. And these intrusions often take place in dreams, as Pieper shows in his thorough reading of the Greek sources.[12] At the same time Plato recognized that dreams also come from the lower, often repressed elements of man's nature, which at times he described almost in Freudian terms, save for the explicitness of "the unconscious." Indeed, the greatness of Plato was that he saw man as a whole and did not try to fit him or his dream life into one simply understood and easily comprehended point of view.[13]

[12] In this study Pieper (op. cit.) comes to much the same conclusions as we have reached.
[13] Even when he was concerned more strictly with formal or rational matters, Plato did not deny this deeper side of man's life. In the Laws (909f.) he recognized the reality of dreams and visions that lead or drive men to worship, but he denied people the right to establish private temples or shrines whenever they had such visitations, or found remedy for sickness or difficulty before an altar. As he had already shown (738), the traditional gods and temples were originally established because of visions (apparitions) or some other inspiration of heaven, but intellect was needed to decide rightly about establishing further shrines.

Plato was also well aware of the illusory quality of dreams and visions. This is particularly clear in the *Theaetetus* where Socrates is beginning to demonstrate the impossibility of "knowing" knowledge (155ff.). The discussion is introduced with the telling preface that only the initiated are to be listening:

> Socrates: Take a look round, then, and see that none of the uninitiated are listening. Now by the uninitiated I mean the people who think that nothing *is* save what they can grasp in their hands, and who will not allow that action or generation or anything invisible can have real existence.
> Theaetetus: Indeed, Socrates, they are themselves a very hard and metallic sort of men.
> Socrates: Yes, my boy, outer barbarians.

Far from proving, then, that dreams are illusions while the world of sense experience is entirely real, Socrates sees something quite different. Dreams are true to the dreamer, and they even cast doubt upon the reality of sense experience, since it is impossible to be sure that one who relates a fact is not awake and telling a dream, or even dreaming and telling a dream.

## *The new thinking of Aristotle*

Aristotle, however, took a very different approach to the subject of dreams, which he dealt with directly in three little books: *On Sleep and Waking, On Dreams*, and *On Prophecy in Sleep*. His thinking on the subject was completely new. Seldom, in fact, do we find such daring originality buttressed by such careful and consistent thinking. Aristotle broke with the time-honored tradition about dreams, which had been nearly universal until his time, and so he gave us a totally different point of view from which the more ancient view can be observed and assessed. Although it had very little popularity in the ancient world, one aspect of his thinking was revived at the end of the Middle Ages, and, fragmented or not, this point of view took over until it became almost unquestioned authority for Western culture in modern times as well as for the entire Moslem world. His thinking is so modern, however, its arguments so commonplace to most of us, that it is difficult not to be swept off our feet when they are brought out into the open again.

According to Aristotle man is in contact only with the world of sense experience, which he comes to understand through his reason. Since there is no experienceable non-physical world from which dreams may emerge, they cannot be seen as anything but residual impressions left upon the soul by the previous day's activities. In the *Metaphysics*, where he uses the dream experience as one example of the category of the non-existent ($\triangle$.29, 1024b), Aristotle shows clearly that his theory of knowledge is a naïve realism that has no place for the reality of psychic phenomena. Therefore most dreams are nothing more than random re-experiencing—as if something accidentally flips the switch on our mental tape recorder and there are bits of playback. They have practically no significance. But since this, for the most part, was merely Aristotle's way of providing some rational understanding of dreams, it did not occur to him to deny them all significance.

On the contrary, Aristotle believed that the soul was more sensitive during sleep and was, therefore, able to pick up sensations from outside that it would not ordinarily be able to perceive. This quality enabled it to appear prophetic or clairvoyant at times. Likewise he believed that during sleep the soul was more aware of bodily sensations of which one was unconscious during waking hours, and so dreams might contain hints about the body's functioning that normal conscious thinking could not provide. This kind of prophetic knowledge, however, could be explained by good, natural reasons. He also reasoned that some dreams may bring about their own fulfillment by suggesting a course of action to the dreamer which he later pursues, and thus the prophetic result comes about naturally. Other dreams of the future, he concluded, are probably coincidental.

Aristotle's main contention was that dreams are not sent by the gods, that they are natural rather than divine phenomena. He did not come to this conclusion on empirical grounds, however, but by the following reasoning. He believed that the gods are the very epitome of rationality. If the gods sent dreams to people, they would send them only to intelligent and rational people. Instead, the fact is that simple people seem to receive significant and prophetic dreams as often as intelligent individuals. Aristotle was quite sure that the gods would not get their wires so crossed, and he had all the proof he needed in the fact that important dreams are not restricted to the intelligentsia; therefore the gods can have nothing to do with imparting them. His reasoning, of course, was based upon the assumption that rationality is the essential quality of the gods and the only aspect of human life that they can appreciate. Jung has pointed out quite another possibility in *The Development of Personality*, where he stresses the fact that all gifts are not of the intellect, and that the godlike forces of the unconscious are not always intelligent. Still, Aristotle did observe at one point that some dreams have a demonic quality and that in a certain sense nature is demonic. But it is difficult to say exactly what he meant by this. Perhaps he wanted to suggest that there is still something of the unknown and the mysterious in both nature and dreams.

There was no similar rational analysis of dreams and dreaming in ancient literature, and even in the nineteenth century A.D. those who tried their hand at it added little to what Aristotle wrote in the fourth century before Christ. His ideas were gradually accepted during the Renaissance, largely through the church and the efforts of Aquinas, until an exaggerated Aristotelian attitude became the dominant one in Western culture. Yet there is one basic difference between Aristotle and his modern followers. It never occurred to Aristotle to ignore or belittle dreaming or dream interpretation; his idea was rather to bring it under rational scrutiny and analysis.[14] He simply wanted to remove the superstition and quackery that so often surrounds the consideration of dreams. In his time the concern with dreams was already increasing. And whether Aristotle went too far or not, it is our purpose to discover in the rest of these pages.

## The reconciliation in Hippocratic medicine

It is easy to trace the source of Aristotle's ideas about the relation of dreams to the body. His father was a physician of the Hippocratic tradition at the court of the king of Macedonia. Although Aristotle mentions the great father of Greek medicine, Hippocrates of Kos, only once, he was clearly influenced by this school of medicine and may well have started on his scientific studies as a result of this background. There is a large body of Hippocratic writings that date back to the fourth century B.C. Although it is impossible to determine which, if any of them, came from the hand of Hippocrates, these writings form the unquestioned base for Greek and Roman medicine. In them we find a far more appreciative view of the value of dreams than is found in Aristotle.

An analysis of dreams is found in the book *On Regimen*, in which the author began his study (in Book IV) by a careful attempt to understand the process of dreaming and relate this to the traditional understanding of its meaning and value. He wrote:

> He who has learnt aright about the signs that come in sleep will find that they have an important influence upon all things. For when the body is awake the soul is its servant, and is never her own mistress, but divides her attention among many things, assigning a part of it to each faculty of the body—to hearing, to sight, to touch, to walking, and to acts of the whole body; but the mind never enjoys independence. But when the body is at rest, the soul, being set in motion and awake, administers her own household, and of herself performs all the acts of the body. For the body when asleep has no perception; but the soul when awake has cognizance of all things—sees what is visible, hears what is audible, walks, touches, feels pain, ponders. In a word, all

[14] Pedro Meseguer, in the work we have mentioned, *The Secret of Dreams*, centers his discussion around a very appreciative account of Aristotle's theory of dreams (London, Burns & Oates, 1960).

the functions of body and of soul are performed by the soul during sleep. Whoever, therefore, knows how to interpret these acts aright knows a great part of wisdom.

Now such dreams as are divine, and foretell to cities or to private persons things evil or things good, have interpreters in those who possess the art of dealing with such things. But all the physical symptoms foretold by the soul, excess, of surfeit or of depletion, of things natural, or change to unaccustomed things, these also the diviners interpret, sometimes with, sometimes without success.

The author then goes on to show how dreams can be interpreted to help in understanding one's physical health. His basic idea is that some dreams, by expressing the outer world simply as it is, show that the dreamer is in good relationship with it, and suggest that his body is in good health. But when dreams show change contrary to the acts of the day, especially violent change, it is a sign that the soul of the individual is in turmoil and his body either is or will be affected. The underlying assumption is that psyche and body are in close harmony and that one greatly influences the other, which is precisely the understanding of modern psychosomatic medicine.

While the direct interpretations do sound funny—for instance, to diagnose circulatory disease from a dream about rivers in flood, or to prescribe purging because a patient dreams of a fiery, hot star— actually they are not so far out compared with the latest thinking in medicine and psychology.[15] This follower of Hippocrates might not sound foolish at all discussing diabetes or arthritis or heart disease with a group of internists and psychiatrists today, trying to picture the interplay of psyche and body that makes for disease or health. At the same time this Hippocratic physician did not hesitate to mention his belief that some dreams are given directly by the gods.

[15] Or, compared with the "strange dream" and the extensive medical results that are reported in detail in *Life* for September 29, 1967. This was the dream of Jack Dreyfus, Jr., founder of the Dreyfus Fund, which led to the diagnosis of his own medical problem, and then to the initiation of new research at Johns Hopkins and Harvard that offers great hope for certain kinds of mental illness. Dreyfus' dream was simply that he had somehow been *electrically* frozen into immobility. From this fact the connections established themselves one after another until, one day, he spoke to his physician about the possibility of abnormal electrical activity in his brain, and the doctor surprisingly agreed with his idea and the suggestion he made for medication. This has led to the establishment of the Dreyfus Foundation and research into the idea that came from a dream.

In fact, on the island of Kos, where medical science had its beginnings, Aescylapius was also present in temple and ritual. As
Carl Kerényi has shown in *Asklepios*, his careful study of the
mythological origins of Greek medicine, incubation simply represented one side of the healing tradition. On the one hand, the
physician studied and knew his patient, and told him what to do; on
the other, the elements within the patient himself were given first
chance to bring about a cure. In incubation, with its emphasis on
dreams, the individual mystery of healing was preserved; although
the physician might be called on to administer treatment suggested
by a dream, he had no part in the process of incubation itself. For
example, one early plaque dedicated by a grateful patient shows him
lying on a bed being licked by a serpent, while in the foreground is
a picture of the dream he is having of being operated on by the
god. As Kerényi suggests, the divine dream undoubtedly played a
large part in the amazing development of Greek medicine. And the
two approaches continued to live side by side; about 250 B.C. a new
temple for incubation was built at Kos, and in the following century it was replaced by an even larger one, serving this original
center of Hippocratic medicine. It is not surprising that the same
relationship continued as the concern with dreams increased in the
later Hellenistic world.

## Increasing concern with dreams

In these later pagan times the growing concern with dreams was
part of a generally increasing reliance upon the irrational, the supernatural experience of life. One aspect of this was the spread of
Aescylapian healing, which was carried to many places throughout
the Greek-speaking world. Pergamum in Asia Minor became one
of the chief centers to which people came to be healed by the god.
Here the great physician Galen also grew up, and here he studied
medicine because Aescylapius had appeared to his father in a dream
with instructions for the boy. Galen, who is revered today as the
father of modern scientific medicine, was influenced throughout his
life by dreams.

His various works describe not only an operation he performed on
himself at the bidding of a dream that he apparently had in the
temple of Aescylapius, but also the fact that he treated many patients
successfully by remedies revealed in dreams, and saw others cured by

healing in the temple.[16] One of these was Marcus Aurelius, who was the physician's friend; the emperor spent an incubation period in the shrine at Pergamum and later thanked the god for remedies against his blood-spitting and dizziness. During the last half of his life Galen practiced in Rome, where Aescylapius had long before been established. According to Ovid the god was brought to Rome with great ceremony, and in the *Metamorphoses* it was described how dreams had made this possible. Traces of the temple carving and the head of the god can still be seen on the walls of the Tiberine Island in Rome.

In other matters dream books were widely used. These works on interpretation grew out of the "tables of correspondences," which Aristophanes undoubtedly refers to in *The Wasps* when the slave asks: "Shan't I give two obols and get us one of those clever interpreters of dreams?" A generation or so later a grandson of Aristides the Just was earning his living by using one of these forerunners of the dream book. After that a long list of men are known to have written on dream interpretation, whose works are all lost. The only example of this ancient study which has survived to modern times is the *Interpretation of Dreams* by Artemidorus of Daldis, from the second century of our era. Interestingly enough, my search for a copy produced no modern translation from the Greek, but only the one made in 1644 and printed with a commentary in 1690, which is in the rare-book room at Harvard.

Artemidorus' work, which is clearly in the Hellenistic tradition, was originally composed of five little handbooks on the meaning of common dream symbols, based on deduction from what he had observed to happen in people's lives. They were meant to be practical, and each one hammered away at the point that dream symbols have different meanings in different situations and for different persons. He followed the older classification of dreams that directly foretell the future and others that, in his estimation, are always symbolic. But Artemidorus was not concerned with arguing whether dreams were sent by the gods or not, since it was his view that all dreams have their fulfillment, each in its own time and manner. Most dreams are simply not to be construed directly, and his purpose

---

[16] Descriptions of dreams are scattered all through Galen's works, which were the first textbooks of modern medicine. These references are discussed in detail by Joseph Walsh, M.D., "Galen's Writings and Influences Inspiring Them," *Annals of Medical History*, January 1934, Vol. 6 (New Series), No. 1, pp. 2ff.

was to establish a few rules to help in the difficult and complex matter of understanding them, and to support this with specific applications.

During these centuries there was scarcely any disagreement with the understanding that dreams are significant. Writers like Vergil, Horace, Lucretius, and others who were greatly influenced by Greece all showed interest in them. Even the philosopher Cratippus, who was otherwise a follower of Aristotle, felt that the divine mind acted directly upon men when their bodies were asleep. Pliny the Elder wrote that, while some dreams are the result of an upset constitution, others are caused by divine intervention. Like the later Dio Cassius (who also wrote an account of the dreams that foretold that Alexander Severus would become emperor), Pliny was inspired to write history because of a dream. Pliny the Younger recorded his consultation with Suetonius about interpreting dreams, while in The Golden Ass, with all of its ribald humor, Apuleius presented graphically the Platonic theory of their religious importance.

Cicero, in fact, was the only later writer of any significance who balked at the popular conviction that some dreams might be prophetic. He was so annoyed with the idea that he wrote On Divinations, in which he let his brother Quintus argue the facts and the ideas of the great philosophers, including his own friends. The Stoic idea of a natural knowledge of the future, Quintus finally held, gives support to the more primitive theory that dreams of the future are divine gifts. Cicero's reply then tore the theory to shreds, using basically the thinking of Aristotle, and concluding:

> Therefore, let divination by dreams be jeered off the stage, along with the other tricks of the soothsayers. . . .
>
> Now sleep is esteemed a refuge from the anxieties and burdens of life, but actually very many apprehensions and fears are born of it. Dreams, indeed, of themselves, would carry less weight and would be more lightly regarded were it not for the fact that they have been taken under the wing of philosophy, and not by incompetent bunglers, but by men of the highest degree of intellectual power—men who are able to distinguish between consistency and inconsistency and who are looked upon as models of all the philosophical virtues.[17]

[17] De Divinatione, II.72, as quoted by Meseguer, op. cit., who presents an appreciative treatment of Cicero's dream theory, pp. 26ff.

Cicero was obviously striking at the common belief in sooth-saying and fortunetelling. But his Aristotelian position made it impossible for him to see why human life needed *any* direct contact with spiritual elements, any intrusion of the non-physical or super-natural that sometimes could bring knowledge of the future. He saw no reason for it. It is interesting that one of his earlier works was to become the basis for most of the medieval interest and belief in dreams.

It is also interesting that when the historians of these ancient times came to Cicero, they set down quite a different picture.

## Dreams in the ancient histories

Plutarch wrote of Cicero that there had been deep reasons for his support of Caesar:

> . . . for it seems, while Pompey and Caesar were yet alive, Cicero *in his sleep*, had fancied himself engaged in calling some of the sons of the senators into the capitol, Jupiter, according to the dream, being about to declare one of them the chief ruler of Rome. The citizens, running up with curi-osity, stood about the temple, and the youths, sitting in their purple-bordered robes, kept silence. On a sudden the doors opened, and the youths, arising one by one in order, passed round the god, who reviewed them all, and, to their sorrow, dismissed them; but when this one was passing by, the god stretched forth his right hand and said, "O ye Romans, this young man, when he shall be lord of Rome, shall put an end to all your civil wars." It is said that Cicero formed from his dream a distinct image of the youth, and retained it afterwards perfectly, but did not know who it was.
>
> The next day, going down into the Campus Martius, he met the boys returning from their gymnastic exercises, and the first was he, just as he had appeared to him in his dream. Being astonished at it, he asked him who were his parents. And it proved to be this young Caesar. . . .
>
> (CICERO 44.2ff.)

Plutarch did not discuss Cicero's later belittling of dreams, but he did compare the orator with the deeply serious Demosthenes, re-marking that Cicero's wit often ran away with his understanding. Unlike Demosthenes, he often used mockery to destroy an adversary. Even when it came to dying, the two were opposites. Cicero met death trying to hide from his murderers, while Demosthenes turned down an offer to treat with his enemy, and instead took his own life. He had dreamed the night before that he was acting in a tragedy and acquitted himself as well as he could, but there was a contest in which he was the loser because the props had not been provided for his part on stage.

Indeed, except for Thucydides, none of these ancient historians looked upon dreams the way Aristotle and Cicero did. Thucydides wrote his magnificent account of the Peloponnesian War without making a single reference to a dream; he became not just the "father of history," but of the modern materialistic interpretation of history. But otherwise all the great historians recorded the important dreams that were associated with so many major events. Like Herodotus and Xenophon before them, Plutarch, Tacitus, Josephus, Philo, Suetonius—all set down these experiences again and again as an essential part of the record.[18] If this seems strange, we must remember that the life of Lincoln furnishes an example of just such a dream before his assassination, which is recorded by the historians who knew him best.

Suetonius, for instance, included the dreams of Nero, which tell so much of the inner life and destiny of this tragic man. It was after the murder of his mother that Nero began to dream. In one recurring vision he saw himself steering a ship, saw the rudder forced from his hand, and then found himself being dragged by his wife into some dark place of torment. Two successive dreams were told

---

[18] For instance, in the *Anabasis*, III.1.11 and IV.3.8, Xenophon recorded dreams that occurred at times when decisions had to be made. In Plutarch's *Lives* the following references to crucial dreams are found: Agesilaus 6.4f.; Agis and Cleomenes 7.2ff.; Alcibiades 39.1ff.; Alexander 2.2f., 18.3, 24.2ff., 26.2f.; Antony 16.3f.; Aristides 11.5f.; Marcus Brutus 20.5f., 36.1ff., 41.4, 48.1; Caesar 42.1f., 63.3ff., 69.4f.; Caius Gracchus 1.6; Cicero 2.2, 44.2ff.; Cimon 13.2f.; Coriolanus 24.1ff.; Crassus 12.3; Demetrius 4.2ff., 29.1f.; Demosthenes 29.2ff.; Dion 2.1ff., 55.1f.; Eumenes 6.5f.; Lucullus 10.2f., 12.1f., 23.3ff.; Lysander 20.5f.; Pelopidas 21.1ff.; Pericles 3.2, 13.8; Pompey 23.1f., 32.4f., 68.2ff., 73.3ff.; Pyrrhus 11.2f., 29.1ff.; Sulla 9.4, 28.4ff., 37.1f.; Themistocles 26.2f.; Timoleon 8.1f.

Typical references in Josephus are found in *The Life* 208f.; *Against Apion* I.207ff.; *Antiquities of the Jews* XI.8.4f., XVI.6.4, and XIX.8.2; and in Suetonius' *Lives of the Caesars* II.xciv.4f. (Catalus) and VI.xlvi (Nero). One of Philo's longest treatises was his work *On Dreams*; Books 2 and 3, which are extant, are interesting examples of Philo's symbolic interpretation, first, of dreams partly due to divine agency, and then of those of a human level. The first category is represented by the dreams of Jacob, and the second by those of Joseph. Three other books on dreams by Philo are mentioned which are wholly lost.

by Josephus which were believed to have saved the city of Jerusalem from destruction in 332 B.C. Alexander the Great had taken Gaza, and his armies looked forward to sacking Jerusalem, but Jaddus the high priest was told in a dream to open the city and go out in all his robes to meet the conqueror. When Alexander saw this man robed in purple and gold, he did a thing so strange that his commanders thought he was mad. He went up alone and knelt before Jaddus. Then he revealed that before leaving Macedonia he had had a dream in which this man, in the very same garments, appeared and gave him conduct to cross over into Asia. Therefore, when Alexander saw the man of his dream, he had knelt down to worship God.

Plutarch in particular left a record of the way the great men of ancient Greece and Rome regarded their dreams. One of the earliest dreams he related was that of Alcibiades just before he was assassinated. Alcibiades dreamed that he was dressed in the clothes of his mistress, who held him in her arms and painted his face like a woman's. A few days later he died alone in Timandra's arms, and she did indeed take her own garments to wrap and prepare his body for burial.

Many of the experiences Plutarch recounted had to do with war and violence, and the direct effect of dreams on history. Jupiter took a hand in one of Aristides' campaigns by appearing in a fascinating dream that told specifically where to prepare for battle, and also led to a lasting alliance, as well as the discovery of a very ancient Eleusinian temple. Lucullus once saved the city he was besieging because he dreamed of a man saying to him, "Go a little further, Lucullus, for Autolycus is coming to see you." The next day, as he was driving the enemy to their boats, he discovered a statue abandoned on the beach. When he was told that it was Autolycus, the founder of the city, then Lucullus remembered the advice of Sulla, that "nothing is to be treated as so certain and worth relying on as an intimation given in dreams." And, instead of leveling the town, he honored Autolycus by turning his city into one of the first urban redevelopment projects in history.

Often these accounts by Plutarch showed how much a dream revealed about a man and what was to happen in his life. Before his final battle Pyrrhus was elated by seeing in his sleep that thunderbolts fell on the city he was about to attack, setting it all on fire; but his adviser interpreted the vision as a warning of the gods not to tread upon the place that has been struck by lightning and so is sacred to them. As it turned out, even the women had trussed up their skirts and pitched in to defend the city, and Pyrrhus and most of his army fell in the battle. Centuries later when Antony dreamed of lightning just before learning of Caesar's plot to kill him, it was his own right hand he saw struck by a thunderbolt. As Plutarch suggested, Antony's downfall was never on this side of the fence; it was his "character to be better in calamities than at any other time." And for Antony, Cleopatra was waiting.

Plutarch also told of Pompey's dream of the theater on the night before his great battle with Caesar. But Pompey dreamed of being a spectator, and of hearing the people make a great noise over him as he made his formal entry into the theater. Then he saw himself go forward with his retinue, carrying the many spoils of war, and these he placed as adornments in a temple to Venus the Victorious. When Pompey woke he could not help being encouraged by his vision. But then he remembered that Caesar's family name was derived from the goddess Venus, and he realized in terror that he might be adorning the temple only for Caesar's role on stage. If Caesar won the battle, the temple of Venus the Victorious would be rightfully his, decorated with everything that should have been Pompey's. Then the day came, and Caesar sliced through Pompey's army like cheese and walked into his camp simply aghast at the splendor—the tables loaded, the wine ready to pour, the garlands and hangings, and rich embroidery underfoot.

Meanwhile Pompey had fled, and spent the night in a fisherman's cottage near the coast. But a dream was already making known his presence there. Offshore there was a large merchant vessel waiting for the morning tide. As Pompey seized a rowboat on the river to row out to sea, the captain was telling a vision he had seen in his sleep. Pompey, whom he knew by sight, had appeared—not as he usually appeared in Rome, but a dejected and miserable man who sat down and talked with the dreamer. Just then one of the crew shouted that they were being hailed by a small boat, and the captain saw the miserable and dejected Pompey of his dream and took him aboard. And so Pompey was started on his journey toward Egypt and death, by a dream.

These ancient people revered dreams. Both the classical Greeks and the later Hellenistic people looked to them for messages, sometimes prophetic messages, from a non-human source. Only a few of the most skeptical cast doubts upon them as revelations of something beyond men, and even these skeptics believed that dreams were, at the least, important indications of the physical state of a man's life. How different this is from the proper attitude of the nineteenth century. The majority of the Greeks did not use their reason and logic to eliminate dreams or other non-rational experiences from life. The Greeks used these faculties, as far as they were able, to develop all their gifts. With this understanding of the attitude of Greek culture, let us now turn to look at the attitude toward dreams found in the Greek New Testament of the Christian Church.

# four

# The Dreams and Visions of the New Testament

"How much there is in the Bible about dreams. There are, I think, some sixteen chapters in the Old Testament and four or five in the New in which dreams are mentioned; and there are many other passages scattered throughout the book which refer to visions. If we believe the Bible, we must accept the fact that, in the old days, God and his angels came to men in their sleep and made themselves known in dreams." These words are not the comment of the biblical critic, but of a President of the United States. Abraham Lincoln was discussing a disturbing dream he had had, talking with a group of friends just before his assassination. He went on to say that after the dream in which he saw his own body lying in state in the White House, he had opened up his Bible, and "strange as it may appear, it was the twenty-eighth chapter of Genesis, which relates the wonderful dream Jacob had. I turned to other passages, and seemed to encounter a dream or a vision wherever I looked. I kept on turning the leaves of the old book, and everywhere my eyes fell upon passages recording matters strangely in keeping with my own thoughts—supernatural visitations, dreams, visions, and so forth."[1]

[1] Quoted from Lloyd Lewis, *Myths after Lincoln*, New York, Grosset & Dunlap, 1957, pp. 294f. This story comes from Ward Hill Lamon, the biographer who did the least to romanticize Lincoln. In fact, Lamon's biography was so down to earth and factual that it did not sell well. The public wanted a more perfect

These observations of Lincoln about the dreams of the Bible are very much to the point. They are also quite right in associating the dreams so closely with the visions and supernatural visitations, for these are all of one piece. Particularly in the New Testament, they can hardly be separated. In the Greek of the New Testament there were many different ways of describing the fact that one had had a vision or a dream; but the important thing was the content that came before consciousness, rather than the exact state in which it came. No hard and fast lines were drawn between the state of dreaming as we understand it and the state of trance or the ecstatic consciousness in which a vision was received. Sometimes two or three quite different names were used to speak of a single experience, and at times it is difficult to be sure which state was signified by the writer. All of them—dream, vision, and trance—were valued to such a degree that there was no urgent need to distinguish one from another. And this basic attitude was shared by later Judaism as well as the Hellenistic world.

## "Basic Greek"

Since it is difficult to understand what the Greek New Testament means by these experiences without knowing the words that were used, we shall look carefully at a little basic Greek. There were twelve different words and expressions, each of them a different way of saying that one had come into contact with some reality other than that perceived through the senses.

These experiences must all be understood if we are to describe and discuss the dreams and visions of the New Testament, for there is no place to make the break. These authors, instead of defining visions and trances and "appearances" strictly, used now one and then another of these words to picture the occurrence of something real that was like a dream, but could happen to some people when they were not exactly asleep. The words all refer to experiences that are alike in this way. They describe how something very real and important came before the consciousness of one or even several individuals which did not originate in the external,

---

figure than this friend and bodyguard of Lincoln told about. He had planned a second volume, but it was never finished. Even so, Lamon's work is one of the best historical sources we have for the life of Lincoln.

physical world, and which could not have been created by the conscious will. These people believed that there was an inner, a psychic world of non-material reality—a spiritual world, they called it—from which these experiences could emerge. Let us look at these expressions and try to see what the New Testament is actually saying.

## 1. DREAM: ὄναρ

*Onar* is a common word for "dream," used in much the same sense as we use that noun to mean any content that comes in sleep and is remembered. Precisely, it is a vision seen in sleep as opposed to waking. This word is used in Matthew to tell of the divine visitations to Joseph and the wise men and the warning about Jesus to Pilate's wife (Matthew 1:20; 2:12, 13, 19, 22; 27:19). *Onar* was in common use from the time of Homer on, and was frequently used to describe experiences in which the spiritual world spoke.

## 2. VISION SEEN IN SLEEP: ἐνύπνιον

*Enupnion* signifies a thing or vision seen in sleep. It is derived from the common word for sleep, *hupnos*, and means literally "in sleep," or the events or happenings that occur during sleep. This word was also common in Greek literature, but in the New Testament it is found only in Acts 2:17 and Jude 8. It stresses the givenness, almost surprise quality, of what is received in sleep.

## 3. VISION: ὅραμα

There are three words in Greek that were used for our word "vision." All of them are related to the verb *horao*, which can mean either to see or notice in the sense of outer perception, or to see something that is not physical, a vision.

*Horama*, vision, is the most common of these words. It occurs twelve times, eleven of them in the book of Acts (Matthew 17:9; Acts 7:31; 9:10, 12; 10:3, 17, 19; 11:5; 12:9; 16:9, 10; 18:9). It is especially interesting because it can refer to visions of the night or sleeping experiences, as well as to waking visions. Thus it covers both the dream as we know it and the vision. *Horama* is used to translate the Hebrew words for both dream and vision, and since it can refer to the state in which one receives a vision, it may also refer to the dreaming state. Significantly enough, this word does not make the distinction we so carefully make either between dreams and visions, or between physical and non-physical perceptions.

### 4. VISION: ὅρασις

The second of these, *horasis*, can signify the eye as the organ of sight, an appearance of any kind, even a spectacle, but there are also two instances where it means a supernatural vision (Acts 2:17 and Revelation 9:17). While the word is related to *horama*, it refers to the supernatural content received rather than to the act or psychological process of seeing it. It has to do with the appearance conferred on things, and here again the distinction between the perception of the physical and the non-physical is lacking in the Greek. Both "seeings" are genuine perception.

### 5. VISION: ὀπτασία

*Optasia* is still another word for the supernatural vision derived from *horao*, one that refers almost exclusively to this kind of seeing. Derived from the aorist passive tense of the verb, it has the sense of self-disclosure, of "letting oneself be seen." It is found four times in the New Testament (Luke 1:22, 24:23, Acts 26:19, II Corinthians 12:1), and can refer either to the content of the visionary experience or to the state of being in which one receives it. Specifically, the idea is a self-revealing of the divine; the Deity permits a human being to see either his own divine being or something else usually hidden from human sight.

### 6. TRANCE, ECSTATIC STATE: ἔκστασις

*Ekstasis* is the word from which the English word "ecstasy" is derived. It means literally standing aside from oneself, being displaced or over against oneself, and ordinarily there is a sense of amazement, confusion, even of extreme terror. It was used to describe the astonishment of those who saw the mighty works of Jesus (Mark 5:42, Luke 5:26), the awe of the disciples at the empty tomb (Mark 16:8), and the reaction of the crowd to Peter's first healing (Acts 3:10). The meaning is that one has been shaken out of his ordinary attitudes, and thus it can denote a state in which a man's ordinary consciousness has been suspended by God's action so that some new perception will get through to him. This was the word for Peter's state when he fell asleep on the rooftop in Joppa and God spoke to him (Acts 10:10, 11:5), as well as Paul's experience when he was praying in the temple and the Lord spoke (Acts 22:17). Thus *ekstasis* may refer to either sleeping or waking experiences, and psychologically both the dreams of sleep and the imagery that occurs on the border of wakefulness, hypnagogic or hypnopompic imagery, fit the condition that *ekstasis* describes. It is misleading to use the word "trance" as a direct translation.

### 7. To Become in the Spirit: γίνομαι ἐν πνεύματι

The whole revelation of John is introduced by the phrase *ginomai en pneumati*, which is quite similar in meaning to *ekstasis* (Revelation 1:10). This expression, "to become in the spirit," signified a state in which one could see visions and be informed or spoken to directly by the spirit. It is translated by Goodspeed as "to fall into a trance," and by Moffat as "to be rapt in the Spirit." In other places there are related phrases used, as in the temptation story when Jesus was "led or driven by the spirit" (Matthew 4:1, Mark 1:12, Luke 4:1), and when Elizabeth was "filled with the Spirit" and suddenly knew that Mary was to bear the Christ (Luke 1:41).

### 8. To Stand By: ἐφίστημι, παρίστημι, ἵστημι

Sometimes the New Testament refers simply to the fact that some reality stands by (*ephistemi, paristemi*) in the night (Acts 23:11, 27:23), or is made to stand (*histemi*) in the day (Luke 1:11, Acts 10:30, 16:9). This may be the Lord, or it may be described as an angel, or even as a man who appears and commands attention in order to bring some message. It was thus that the author of Acts described the vision that led Paul to go into Greece.

### 9. Angel: ἄγγελος

*Angelos* or angel, which occurs so often in the New Testament, can mean either an actual physical envoy, a messenger, or a divine being sent by God. The passages are almost always clear; something very real appears which is seen and usually heard, but the experience is not concretized. The angel is a visionary reality, one of great importance and power. It inspires the emotional reaction of awe and fear that is always present when one comes into contact with the numinous or holy; and the angel's first action is often reassurance, to calm the fear of the person who is having the experience. In many places after a transaction with an angel has been described, the author later refers back to the vision that has been experienced. In fact, there is hardly a reference in the New Testament in which angels can be seen as anything but visionary contents, beings without physical reality which are still powerful and very real and significant.

### 10. Demons, the Devil: δαίμων, δαιμόνιον; διάβολος, Σατᾶν

Then, there are the demons (*daimon, daimonion*) and the devil (*Satan, diabolos,* and several other colorful names). Throughout the New Testament men appear to have direct knowledge of these realities, both as they possess other people and directly in dreams and visions. One reason Paul encourages discerning of spirits is so that the evil ones may be confronted and rejected. But they are no more seen as concrete physical beings than the angels. Demons are non-physical entities that can be experienced just as one experiences a vision or a dream. Experiences of demons are essentially visions of negative spiritual realities; they were beings without physical aspects who were still real and powerful enough to get hold of a person's physical body or psyche and cause him trouble.

### 11. To See, to Perceive: βλέπω, εἴδω, ὁράω

Twice in Revelation (1:2, 1:11) the vision is referred to as the action of seeing, using the common Greek verbs *blepo* and *eido*. Here it is simply stated that John recorded "whatsoever things he saw," as the voice he heard in the Spirit instructed him. Again, in the story of the transfiguration, the vision was referred to as "what they had seen," using the verbs *eido* and *horao* (Mark 9:9, Luke 9:36). These were words with an ordinary range of meaning like our word "see" which were familiar expressions in the New Testament for the seeing of visions; this usage was also common in Greek literature.[2] Obviously visionary contents were considered just as easy to perceive and observe, just as much given and as valid, as the perceptions one has of the outer physical world.

## 12. DISCLOSURE OR REVELATION: ἀποκάλυψις

The common Greek word for disclosure, uncovering, or revealing, *apokalupsis* was also used for the divine uncovering. Like the English word "reveal," or un-veil, *apo-kalupto* means simply to uncover. Just as physical things and the secrets of the human heart can be uncovered and brought out of hiding, so can non-physical things, divine things, be unveiled. What is brought to light is then seen as a revelation.

Throughout the New Testament this word is used to signify things disclosed by God or by the Spirit, either in some direct way, or through dreams and visions or human reasoning and intuition. But there was really little distinction made between revelation that was imparted by God in thoughts and understanding, and the disclosures that were given in images in dreams and visions. This word *apokalupsis* is not the same as the English word apocalypse, with its specialized theological meaning. We have trouble separating revelation from its eschatological meaning, referring only to things to come, the final things in the ultimate divine purpose. The Greek word instead refers simply to any disclosure in the realm of spirit which was formerly hidden. This meaning is found clearly in Romans 16:25, I Corinthians 14:6 and 26, II Corinthians 12:1 and 7, and Galatians 2:2. In II Corinthians the word is linked closely with visions. Its use throughout the New Testament shows the belief of these writers that man could be given special knowledge of a non-physical world, that the veil which so often covers this world could be rolled back and one could see what was there. The dream and the vision were two ways in which this revealing took place.

These earliest Christians believed that the meaning and purpose of the outer world originated in this inner, spiritual world and was deeply influenced by it. They believed that God speaks and works through this inner world, using such non-material media as dreams and trances, visions, and appearances of angels. To them this was

[2] *Eidolon*, meaning phantasm and also idol, is derived from *eido*.

one of the regular ways in which God works, one which is complementary to his action through the material world and through history. They saw that through the death and resurrection of Christ there was a spirit of creative power, a new life that was available to men and could come from this invisible world. Christianity, then, offered not a devaluation of the importance of dreams or visions, but a new way of understanding them, and a new, supremely significant content for them to manifest.

It is unfortunate that the visions and trances and even the dreams of the Bible have come to be regarded as purely religious and supernatural. These experiences are still quite common. And while they do sometimes manifest a "more than natural" content, they are still natural experiences that can be observed and analyzed. They come from the world that is natural for man to encounter. In fact, the authors of the New Testament had a far more sophisticated view of these experiences than people seem to realize. They had a consistent theory about man in which dreams and visions had a definite place. Man, they saw, was in contact with both a physical world and a non-physical one, both of them necessary to him. Neither could be avoided if man was really to live, if he was to live with reality as it is. Dreams and visions, then, were important because this was one way in which the non-physical world intruded directly into man's psyche. This was basically a Platonic point of view.

Of course, this seems strange to us today. It is difficult to shake ourselves free of the assumption of our culture that man has contact with only one kind of reality. But if we are to grasp what they really believed, we must listen to these writers who felt the importance, as well as the difficulty, of describing the various encounters with non-physical reality. Stripped of all these experiences, the meaning of the New Testament is difficult indeed to grasp. Let us turn to the record itself and see how frequent they are.

## Dreams and visions in the four Gospels

The account of the life of Jesus of Nazareth begins in Luke with the story of the birth of John the Baptist. His father, Zechariah, was doing his division of duty in the temple when he saw an angel of the Lord standing by the altar. Zechariah was afraid, but the angel reassured him and then told him that his wife was to have a child and they were to call his name John. When he left the temple, he was dumb, and it was apparent to the people waiting for him that he had had a vision (*optasian*) (Luke 1:11–22).

We have two accounts of the annunciation. In Luke the angel Gabriel was sent to Mary and she too had to be told not to fear; she would conceive by the power of the Holy Spirit, and was to call her son's name Jesus. She also learned that her kinswoman Elizabeth had conceived in her old age, and Mary departed to see her. When she arrived, Elizabeth was filled with the Spirit and given knowledge that Mary was to bear the Savior (Luke 1:26–45). What Mary learned through the angel, Elizabeth was taught by being filled with the Holy Spirit (*eplesthe pneumatos hagiou*). In Matthew, when Joseph found that Mary was pregnant, he was about to put her away when an angel of the Lord came to him in a dream (*onar*) to tell him the story and inform him that the child's name was to be Jesus (Matthew 1:20). Here the annunciation is given in a dream, and thus far the story of the coming of the Christ child has woven together the different experiences of visions of angels with a dream and information by the Spirit.

In Luke's account the birth of Jesus was literally surrounded by angels. There was first the angel who stood by the shepherds in a great light. They too were afraid, and the angel quieted their fears, and then gave them the good news that they were to go to Bethlehem and find the child. And then there was a whole army, a multitude of heavenly host praising God (Luke 2:9). Certainly the intent of Luke was to convey a tremendous spiritual experience, an experience like the vision (*optasia*) of angels at the tomb in 24:23. These were both visionary experiences, real but not physical, in both cases seen by a group. Matthew's account tells first how the wise men were warned in a dream (*onar*) to avoid Herod, and then that an angel appeared in the same way to warn Joseph, and the family fled to Egypt. They remained there until Joseph was informed once more in a dream (*onar*) that Herod was dead. Finally, in a third dream (*onar*) he was instructed not to go into Judea, where Herod's son was ruler (Matthew 2:12–23). And Luke adds that when Jesus was circumcised on the eighth day, he was called by the name the angel had given before his conception (2:21). Here again dreams and visions that are certainly central to the story are used alternately by Matthew and Luke to describe experiences of non-human intervention in the life of Jesus. This, of course, is one of the embarrassments that cause modern scholars to cast doubts upon the historical validity of the whole birth narrative.

While there is no record of dreams as such in the life of Jesus, there were visionary experiences that surrounded all the important events of his life. The first, the experience at Jesus' baptism, is described in the same way by all three synoptic writers. The Spirit was seen descending upon him in the appearance of a dove, and at the same time a voice was heard from heaven speaking about God's pleasure in Jesus (Matthew 3:16, Mark 1:9, Luke 3:21). Thus the vision was both seen and heard, probably by more than a few people according to the Gospel of John, where the experience was first reported by John the Baptist (1:29). Then this Gospel later described what happened when Jesus saw he must reveal himself. "Father, glorify thy name," Jesus asked, and when a voice came out of heaven saying, "I have glorified it, and will glorify it again," some of the crowd heard thunder, and others the voice of an angel speaking to Jesus (12:28). This experience, so similar to the baptism, was shared by the whole group, though each man described what he heard in his own way.

After his baptism Jesus was led or driven into the wilderness by the Spirit (*pneuma*) to be tempted by the devil (Matthew 4:1, Mark 1:12, Luke 4:1). This of necessity was a visionary experience. Jesus was guided, not to confront any outer manifestation of evil, but to meet face to face the inner power of evil, to confront its primary source in an experience as real as any physical encounter. And after he had withstood the vision of demonic power, the angels came and ministered to him and he was restored. As Jung has commented in *Psychological Types*, the tremendous significance of the temptation narrative lies in the fact that it was a vision, and not a psychotic error about worldly power. Jung knew what was meant by such an experience; his own encounter with the power of darkness is described in Chapter VI of his *Memories, Dreams, Reflections*.

All through his ministry Jesus dealt with the demons he saw troubling people. He healed many of the sick by casting out demons and all kinds of evil spirits. These stories, telling of people who were released from the power of Satan and made well, occur twenty-seven times in the Gospels.[3] While there are no specific descriptions of seeing the demons or spirits, several times there were auditory visions in which Jesus spoke with them. Once the demons begged to enter a herd of swine and he gave them leave (Matthew 8:31, Mark 5:9, Luke 8:31), and others he rebuked for trying to reveal who he was (Mark 1:25, 34; 3:11; Luke 4:33, 41). These were clearly realities without physical bodies, who were trying to take over and possess a human person and were quite capable of doing so.

In his teaching Jesus showed that he also believed in the reality of non-material beings that were good or angelic. In John 1:51 he gave Nathanael the expectation of seeing the heavens opened (much as Jacob once dreamed) and seeing the angels of God ascend and descend on the Son of Man. He taught that the angels of children always behold the face of his Father in heaven (Matthew 18:10), and also that the poor man Lazarus was carried to Abraham's bosom by the angels (Luke 16:22). Explaining that men do not marry after death, he compared them to angels and showed that in resurrected life they become equal to the angels (Matthew 22:30, Mark 12:25, Luke 20:36).

Again and again he explained how the Son of Man would come in his glory, and all the angels with him, but he made it clear that not even the angels know when this will be (Matthew 16:27; 24:31, 36; Mark 8:38; Luke 12:9). In both parable and direct statements he taught that angels are reapers who will gather the chosen of God and rejoice in them and acknowledge them (Matthew 13:49, Mark 13:27, Luke 15:10, 12:9). Sometimes he contrasted the angels with the devil, or even with the devil and *his* angels, as in the parables of the sower and the sheep and the goats (Matthew 13:39; 25:31, 41). When the guard of the high priest came upon them in the garden of Gethsemane, Jesus turned to the disciple who had drawn his sword and told him, "Put your sword back. . . . Do you think that I cannot appeal to my Father, and he will at once send me more than twelve legions of angels?" There can be no doubt what this term meant to Jesus; angels were actual entities that did

[3] These references occur in Matthew 4:24, 7:22, 8:16, 8:28ff., 9:32ff., 10:1, 10:8, 12:22ff., 15:22, and 17:18; Mark 1:23ff., 1:32, 1:34, 1:39, 3:11, 3:15, 3:22ff., 5:2ff., 6:7, 6:13, 7:25ff., 9:17ff., 9:38, 16:9, and 16:17; Luke 4:33ff., 6:18, 7:21, 8:2, 8:27ff., 9:1, 9:39ff., 9:49, 10:17ff., 11:14ff., 13:11ff., and 13:32.

not belong to the physical world, but had power to benefit men's lives, to help men in ways that were set against the destructive power of demons and the devil. In Jesus' references to these opposing realities there is no hint of naïveté, no concretizing of that which is so clearly non-material.

Before Jesus went up to Jerusalem, one of the most amazing experiences occurred, which was shared by the inner circle of disciples. They were on the Mount of Transfiguration when Moses and Elijah appeared to them, and the three disciples saw Jesus filled with radiant light. According to Luke they stayed awake in spite of being heavy with sleep, undoubtedly experiencing something like a collective *ekstasis*. Coming down from the mountain, Jesus then told them to tell no one of the vision (*horama*, Matthew 17:9; "what they had seen," *eidon*, Mark 9:9; *horao*, Luke 9:36). Later at Gethsemane, when the disciples had gone to sleep and Jesus was going through the very depth of agony, an angel appeared to him to give him strength (Luke 22:43). After this there was one last dream that was recorded; as Pilate was sitting to judge Jesus, Pilate's wife sent word to her husband to have nothing to do with that righteous man because she had suffered much in a dream (*onar*) concerning him (Matthew 27:19).

In all the accounts of the resurrection we hear of angels. Luke describes the two men in dazzling apparel who spoke to the women inside the tomb (24:4), and then tells how the vision (*optasian*) was later described to Jesus on the road to Emmaus before the disciples recognized him (24:23). In each of the narratives this appearance of angels in the tomb has an important place (Matthew 28:2, Mark 16:5, John 20:12). Those who were there certainly experienced something more than just an empty tomb; they found something that moved them greatly. These men and women had a vision of *non*-physical reality. Something numinous from the world of spirit appeared to them and they were ministered to by the Spirit.

## The dreams and visions of the apostles in Acts

If this is true of the Gospels, it is even more so with Acts, and here the experiences are even more interrelated. Beginning with what happened at Pentecost, every major event in Acts is marked by a dream, a vision, or the appearance of an angel, and it is usually upon this experience that the coming events are determined.

It was on Pentecost, Acts tells, that the apostles were given the power to pick up the pieces of their lives and begin the organized life of a church with thousands of new converts. As these men were filled with the Spirit and spoke in other tongues ("tongues of ecstasy," according to the translators of the New English Bible), tongues of fire were seen (horao) resting upon each of them, and the crowd who gathered heard words spoken in each of their many different languages (Acts 2:3). This was immediately understood by the apostles as a fulfillment of the prophecy of Joel, and Peter quoted the prediction that God would pour out his Spirit and their young men would see visions and their old men dream dreams (Joel 2:28). According to Acts this prophecy was fulfilled on Pentecost, and a vision was lived out. Certainly these men and women, who were a joke to the pagans and treated like criminals by their own people, were empowered by something from beyond the physical world. The experience of tongues was a break-through of non-physical reality if it was anything at all; it opened them to new experiences, and also a new understanding of dreams and visions.

Twice when the apostles made their escape from jail it was with the help of an angel (Acts 5:19 and 12:7). The first time, when the whole group had been arrested after healing great numbers of people, an angel simply opened the prison and told them to go back to the temple and tell more about this way of life; and at daybreak they were doing so. Later, when Peter was arrested alone, an angel appeared in a bright light to take him from where he was chained between two jailers. In this account the apostles showed clearly their understanding that angels were visionary beings who seldom had power to act in the physical sense. When the angel told Peter to get dressed and follow, Peter "did not know that what was done by the angel was real, but thought he was seeing a vision (horama)," which was his usual understanding of angels (Acts 12:9). And when he reached the house of the apostles, the maid recognized him, but his friends kept him standing outside knocking while they insisted it must be his angel she had seen (12:15).

Meanwhile Stephen, who had been appointed to his ministry by the apostles, was accused before the council, and filled with the Spirit (pneuma), he spoke wisdom to them which hit home (Acts 6:10). Stephen told them to look to their own history; it was an angel, he recited, who appeared to Moses at the burning bush, an angel who made Moses their deliverer and gave them the divine law through him (7:30, 35, 38, 53). Stephen all but told them that such powers were still available through the Spirit, and his brief story ends with a theophany. With the heavens open and his eyes full of what he saw (*eido*), he died asking forgiveness for those who took part in his death, and among them was Saul (7:55–8:1).

In the story of Philip, who was also appointed like Stephen, we see the direct interchangeableness of angels with the Spirit. An angel of the Lord directed Philip to go down toward Gaza, and on the road the Spirit prompted him to join the chariot of an Ethiopian eunuch, a pilgrim to Jerusalem whom he converted right there by the roadside. Later the Spirit caught Philip up so that the eunuch saw him no more, and he went on about his preaching in the towns (8:26–40). It is clear in this account that Luke considered the experience of an angel essentially the same as prompting by the Spirit. And from this point on the interrelation is unavoidable.

For at this point the unexpected happened. On the way to Damascus Saul was converted, who not only had no expectation of this, but who was going there with the strongest intention of persecuting the Christians. Again the experience is first described objectively, as it was seen to happen and as the group shared in it. A light from heaven struck Paul to the ground blind and he heard a voice that said to him, "I am Jesus, whom you are persecuting"; those around him heard and were speechless (9:3).

Then when Paul described this to Agrippa in Acts 26:12ff., he spoke of "the heavenly vision (*optasia*)," and outlined to the king the ways in which he had been obedient to it. He also wrote in II Corinthians 12:1, "I must boast; there is nothing to be gained by it, but I will go on to visions (*optasias*) and revelations (*apokalupseis*) of the Lord. I know a man in Christ who fourteen years ago was caught up to the third heaven—whether in the body or out of the body I do not know, God knows."[4] For three days

---

[4] In Galatians Paul told how it pleased God by his grace (*charitos*) "to reveal (*apokalupsai*) his Son in me" (1:16); and in Ephesians he spoke of how the mystery of Christ was made known to him by revelation "as it has now been revealed (*apokalupsthe*) to his holy apostles and prophets by the Spirit (*en pneumati*)" (3:5). When Paul told the tribune in Jerusalem about his experience, he also mentioned the trance (*ekstasei*) in which the Lord had again appeared to him as he was praying in the temple (Acts 22:17).

Paul was blind, and then the Lord spoke again in a vision (*horama*), and told Ananias to go and lay his hands on a man named Saul so that he would recover his sight. When Ananias objected that he knew too much about this Saul, the Lord convinced him (9:10), and thus Paul was started on his way as a chosen instrument for the Lord.

In the conversion of Cornelius by Peter there occurred a wonderful mixture of God's speaking through a trance, a dream, a vision, an angel, and by the Spirit. The chain of events began with Cornelius' vision (*horama*) of an angel while he was praying, apparently in the way he had learned from the Jews. The angel let this Gentile know that his charity and devotion had been noticed, and that now he was to send to the next town for a man by the name of Peter. Then, knowing very well that Peter was stiff-necked about Jewish law and particularly about eating with Gentiles, the Lord sent him a dream-trance, in which He showed him a "thing" full of unclean animals that He told him to kill and eat. Peter knew that he had dreamed and was trying to figure out the wonderful symbolism of his vision (also, *horama*) when the men from Cornelius arrived. Before they could knock, Peter was informed by the Spirit that they were outside and that he was to go with them without hesitation. The next day he preached to the whole household of Cornelius, and as the Spirit fell on them they spoke in tongues, and Peter had them baptized on the spot. There was no avoiding it, for these people had received the Spirit just as he had in the beginning; then they begged him to stay on with them for several days (Acts 10).

Back in Jerusalem, when the circumcision party attacked Peter for this, he told them point by point what had happened. After hearing about his dream-trance and the angel and all the rest, they were convinced that he had done the right thing in bringing Gentiles into the new church, and they glorified God. Thus even the conservatives in Jerusalem were convinced when the knew that there had been dreams and visions and ecstatic gifts of the Spirit (Acts 11:1–18). And because of this they accepted a new turning point—one that was certainly important to us.

The first missionary project was also inspired by the Spirit when a prophet of Jerusalem came to Antioch. He foretold by the Spirit that there was to be a great famine in the land during the time of Claudius, and so the brethren in Antioch determined to send down relief to the Christians in Judea (11:28). The church there was also being attacked by Herod, and about this time Peter had his second experience of being taken from prison by an angel (12:6). And the next thing told is the rather gruesome way Herod died, which was confirmed by Josephus.[5] Herod had just made a rousing speech and was letting the people boost his stock instead of giving the glory to God, when an angel of the Lord smote him, and he was eaten by worms and died (12:20).

In Antioch, as Paul started out on his travels, the Holy Spirit was giving instruction (13:2), and Paul made several decisions that have been important to history. Probably the most important was his decision to cross from Asia into Europe, taking Christianity there into the heart of the Greek world. Since he was forbidden by the Spirit to speak the word in Asia, and the Spirit of Jesus did not permit his party to go into Bithynia, they passed by Mysia and went down to Troas. Here "a vision (*horama*) appeared to Paul in the night: a man of Macedonia was standing beseeching him and saying, 'Come over to Macedonia and help us'" (16:6). Here the same message is given in experiences of the Spirit, and then in a dream or vision of the night which was exactly like the objective dreams of the Greeks in Homeric times. These were both experiences to which Paul listened with care. Western Christianity, in fact, owes a great deal to this particular dream, and to the fact that Paul quickly interpreted it and then acted upon it. It is interesting that at this point the "we" passages begin, and so this story may well be an eyewitness account.

But when Paul came to Corinth, he was discouraged. The agreeable indifference of Athens had left its mark, and now the Jews were attacking him again. At this point "the Lord said to Paul one night in a vision, 'Do not be afraid, but speak and do not be silent; for I am with you, and no man shall attack you to harm you; for I have many people in this city.'" Paul obeyed, and stayed there to work and preach for a year and a half (18:9). Need we point out that his reverence for this kind of experience has had rather far-reaching results. The time he spent in Corinth accounts, at the least, for two thirds of the letters that he left us. Besides the letters to the Corinthians, while he was with these people he wrote his great epistle to the Romans, and also Thessalonians and probably Galatians.

[5] *The Antiquities*, XIX.8:2, where the symbolism is slightly different.

Paul's decision to go to Jerusalem is described first as his being resolved in the Spirit (19:21), and later as being bound in the Spirit (20:22). But through the Spirit the disciples at Tyre told him not to go (21:4). I rather suspect that Paul himself had muddled the Spirit somehow about going to Jerusalem. He told the elders at Miletus that the Holy Spirit kept testifying to him (probably through dreams) that imprisonment and afflictions awaited him (20:23), and after he was arrested in Jerusalem, he recalled how he had once been warned in a trance (*ekstasis*) that the people there would not accept his testimony about the Lord (22:17). Paul might have been wiser to give more consideration to this advice from the Spirit (20:23) or the Lord (22:17). As is the way of the Spirit, however, his mistake was repaired; even though he had failed in Jerusalem, the Lord stood by him again in the night, in a vision or a dream, and directed him to go to Rome (23:11).

The last of Paul's dreams that was recorded occurred once more at a crucial moment. The boat taking him to Rome was adrift before the storm, and the men were frightened and desperate. Then Paul had an experience that gave them all courage. "For this very night there stood by me an angel of the God to whom I belong and whom I worship, and he said, 'Do not be afraid, Paul; you must stand before Caesar; and lo, God has granted you all those who sail with you.' So take heart, men, for I have faith in God that it will be exactly as I have been told" (Acts 27:23ff.). Acts ends with the fact that Paul finally arrived at Rome, and stayed there for two whole years, teaching and preaching quite openly. These final, factual chapters again are keyed by a series of experiences, at first described only generically as experiences of the Spirit, which then become as specific as a typical Homeric dream experience.

## The Epistles, Revelation, and the visionary experience

In much the same way the influence of visionary experiences runs through the rest of the New Testament. While there is only one more mention of dreams as such, all the rest of it is shot through with the idea that the Spirit is directly active in the lives of those who are committed to Christ. There are references to visionary experiences like angels and demons, and many discussions of the inner spiritual man, but it is when Paul comes to his own visions that he is explicit about the nature of these experiences. And then the New Testament closes with an entire book devoted to describing the visions that one man experienced when he was in the Spirit. These books are specifically concerned with demonstrating that the Spirit deeply influences the lives of committed people by the guidance of direct and definite information, as well as by the gradual shaping of their lives.

In addition to the visions and revelation granted to men directly, the New Testament believes that men have seen the reality of the non-physical world incarnated in Jesus Christ, and so they can look to him as their revelation (*apokalupsis*) (Galatians 1:12, I Peter 1:13, Romans 16:25). He is the disclosure of the nature of non-physical reality. This, of course, is stressed in the Epistles, but not to the exclusion of other ways of knowing. Unlike some modern theologians, there is little suggestion in the New Testament that the revelation of Jesus Christ has put an end to direct revelation in dreams or visions. Rather, the latter is heightened.

To begin with, Paul told enough about himself in his letters to corroborate the accounts given in Acts of his visions and revelations. In fact, he referred to them several times, twice at some length (II Corinthians 12:1-7, Galatians 1:11-16; also I Corinthians 9:1, 15:8, and probably Ephesians 3:1). Since he was concerned with two things here—first, to make it clear that the knowledge and insight he was discussing could be imparted directly by God, and second, to show that this could make a real difference in one's outer life—he did not need to describe them in detail. It is from Acts that we know some of the specific content, and whether it came in dreams or in broad daylight.

But it is in Paul's letters that we learn his view of them. His visions and revelations (some of them undoubtedly in dreams) have given him insight into the world of the spirit, and also guidance and direction in the outer physical world. In three places he referred quite definitely to the visionary experience on the Damascus Road, and implied that he could speak much more of such experiences. In them he has been taught by God himself through the Spirit, and not by man.

Then in I Corinthians 12 Paul enumerated the gifts that are to come to the person who is in the Spirit. The individual who is possessed by the Spirit or in contact with the Spirit is given the wisdom and understanding and power the Spirit possesses. He has superhuman knowledge and faith; he can distinguish spirits, and has miraculous powers and the ability to heal and to prophesy, the gift of tongues and the power to interpret tongues. The abundant literature on the subject shows that the Spirit was viewed as a *personality* to which the individual could relate or by which he could be possessed.[6] Thus the experience of the Spirit was comparable to that of experiencing an angel, and as we have seen, the two were often interchangeable in meaning. In the terms of our Western culture there is simply no other way to describe these experiences except as dreamlike experiences or visions. These people believed that they were in direct contact with a reality that was anything but physical, the Spirit, which saved them from other non-physical realities that were evil and could destroy them. Nothing else could rescue them from the principalities and powers of that dark world. This is the basic message of Paul and the other New Testament authors.

It is true that the authors of the Epistles were not much more explicit than the authors of the Gospels as to *how* man received this knowledge of non-physical realities. Aside from Paul's references to his visions, the lone mention of dreams in Jude 8 is about the only indication of the process by which men either became entangled with demonic forces or woke up to the life of the Spirit within them. Here the author warned Christians to beware the "dreamers" who treat their bodies, as well as the powers above them, dishonorably. The word he used (which is related to *enupnion*) refers to the thing or vision seen in sleep, and is translated by Moffat as "visionaries." While the use may be metaphorical, the passage certainly suggests that these men are being led into evil by their particular dreamings or spurious visions.

Finally, the book of Revelation, which is also known as the Apocalypse, was written to record the visions that came to John on the island of Patmos. This book is filled with images of angels and other non-physical realities that have a dreamlike quality, and were presented to the author in a trancelike state. He described the fact that he "became" or was "carried away in the Spirit" (*en pneumati*) and then simply saw and heard the visionary beings who spoke and moved before him, as in a dream. Volumes have

[6] See W. F. Arndt and F. W. Gingrich, *A Greek-English Lexicon of the New Testament*, Chicago, University of Chicago Press, 1952, pp. 683ff.

been written about the symbols and images found in this work, and there will probably be many more before its interpreters run out of meaning.

The greatest modern student of apocalyptism, R. H. Charles, has written that the knowledge of both the prophet and the apocalyptic writer "came through visions, trances, and through spiritual, and yet not unconscious communion with God—the highest form of inspiration."[7] It is hard to deny this understanding if we take seriously the belief the early church demonstrated when they canonized the Book of Revelation.

Yet *The Interpreter's Bible* insists that "the claim made in many apocalypses that the predictions came through visionary experiences is a literary device to give greater effectiveness to these writings. That this device is effective is shown by the ready acceptance of the claim by modern students of apocalyptism. . . . Do these purportedly divine visions correctly interpret the past and present and accurately predict the future? Are their depictions of the universe in which we live in conformity with our present astrophysical knowledge? Are their doctrines of God, of Satan, of Christ, of angels and demons, of two ages, of righteousness, and of rewards and punishments in harmony with our best Christian teaching? If our answers are in the negative, then the divine origin of these visions is subject to question." The introductory study of Revelation then goes on to question the use of literary and traditional sources in this work, and also the skill and artistry that the author displayed and even the fact that, if he followed the apocalyptic tradition, he probably signed the name of "John" as a pseudonym. It is never once suggested that the book might be the record of one man's inner spiritual journey, and the form of the images a revelation of his inner spiritual life. As for Paul's visions, *The Interpreter's Bible* quite agrees with what Paul has to say. They just don't discuss it.

The trouble is that Paul and the other New Testament writers are talking about something that seems to be almost entirely strange to us today. They viewed man as beset by a world of dark and evil forces—demons, elemental spirits, Satan, a god working error, thrones and dominions, and various others—and they believed that he had direct communication with these powers, and also with God

[7] R. H. Charles, A *Critical History of the Doctrine of a Future Life* (New York, A. & C. Black, 1913, p. 174), quoted in *The Interpreter's Bible*, Vol. 12, p. 350.

and his angels and the Spirit. In my book *Tongue Speaking* I have made a very careful listing of all these non-physical realities in the New Testament to show the concern these authors had with these things. Outside of Revelation (which would have extended the list too far) there are hundreds of these references, which clearly reveal the belief that man had some kind of direct contact with these realities. As the eminent Dominican scholar Victor White has pointed out with such care in *God and the Unconscious*, these descriptions of a "spiritual world" in Christian tradition are actually very similar to the "complexes" and "archetypes" that are described today by Dr. C. G. Jung and others; the two sets of descriptions, in fact, seem to refer to the same basic reality. As we know, a "complex" can be most clearly seen in the images of dreams and waking fantasies (or visions). And it is probable from the record that this is also the way these realities were seen in New Testament times. We shall have more to say about this in a later chapter.

## A broad look at the biblical record on dreams

If we look back to the attitude of the entire Bible toward dreams and visions, we find that there are certain similarities and differences between the Old Testament and the New. There was no less reverence for these spontaneous intrusions into man's consciousness in one or the other. Neither one made any particular distinction between visions that come in the daytime and visions of the night that come in dreams. Equally, they were the way par excellence by which God speaks to man. As Napier says in *The Interpreter's Dictionary of the Bible*, "Among the earlier classical prophets, the vision is a conventional (in prophetism's understanding) means of Yahweh's communication to the prophet of the meaning of immediate events in Israel's immediate history. The vision is at one with the disclosure of the Word of Yahweh." This attitude was accepted as the unquestioned base for the New Testament.

In the Old Testament, however, there was deliberation about the meaning of visions and dreams which did not occur in the New Testament. There was greater fear among the Hebrews as they entered the Near Eastern world of diviners and necromancers and Baal priests than there was on the part of the Christian community. The Old Testament discussed the meaning of the dream and the vision and their place in the life of the people, as in Numbers 12 and in Job, Jeremiah, Deuteronomy, and Ecclesiastes. In the New Testament these experiences were simply accepted as one of the ways in which God speaks to his people, a method that is used when it applies. The Christian world had to wait for the later fathers of the church before the same kind of self-conscious deliberation about dreams and visions developed within the church literature. The New Testament simply assumed the general valuation and conclusions of contemporary Judaism, which had gone a step beyond the attitude of the Old Testament and were more closely related to the Hellenistic inheritance from Greek culture and literature. Out of the Old Testament a tradition had developed that ignored some of its more skeptical passages, and on this base the New Testament was founded.

We do not find the push to distinguish true and false dreams in the New Testament, partly because dreams and visions were not discussed, and partly because a new solution had been found for this problem. Spiritual reality was seen dualistically. This brilliant Persian solution to the problem of evil had left its impact upon later Judaism. Now in the New Testament the good dreams and visions were attributed to God, the Spirit, or angels, while the lying, the negative, or bad ones were seen as the result of demonic activity or infiltration rather than the creation of the false prophet. It is for this reason that the gift of discernment of spirits mentioned by St. Paul is so important. The individual must now be able to distinguish and differentiate the influences that come to him and to others in a non-sensory way. The dream or vision itself is real; but it is now good or bad depending upon which aspect of spiritual reality has given it.

All of this is more or less assumed in the New Testament. It is never clearly or consciously stated in so many words. As we shall see in the next chapters, the church fathers did wrestle with this problem, and as they came to discuss the dream itself as a separate entity, this point of view was stated very clearly. Many of the fathers believed that man was particularly susceptible to demonic influences in sleep, and that it was here that these forces had free rein in our lives.

As the church then moved from the apostolic age on, there was no basic change in the attitude of reverence toward dreams and dreamlike experiences. I have found practically no criticism of the

New Testament understanding of dreams. Instead, they are finally ignored. I have not even run into a dispensationalist suggestion that God used to speak through dreams and no longer does. The subject is simply not mentioned at all in most biblical criticism.

In summary, then, we find that the early Christians valued dream experiences as a contact with another realm of reality beyond the physical. This reverent understanding was in no way an isolated tradition, but arose from earlier cultures and continued to develop as the new Christian culture developed. It came to these first Christians both from their Jewish heritage, and from the tradition of the highly civilized, rational Greeks. It is difficult to eliminate this strand of New Testament belief without striking at the whole belief that there is a non-physical, a spiritual world that exists and influences the lives of men in intuitions, in healings, prophetic inspiration, and tongues, as well as in dreams and visions. According to both biblical and Hellenistic traditions this world is most clearly and widely known in its influence upon men through the agency of the dream or the vision. Let us turn to the understanding of the fathers of the church about this intrusion of another world of reality into man's conscious mind.

*five*   The Dreams and Visions
of the First Christians

The literary activity that produced the New Testament certainly did not run dry when Christianity began to spread. Instead, those first Christians found they had something to write about, and the range and scope of their writing increased. Soon there was a body of literature that began to fill volumes and that has never stopped growing. There have been changes in its general leanings, however, and in some ways this literature was as important as the New Testament in shaping the foundations of the Christian Church. It is nearly impossible to understand later Christianity if one does not know the things these writers considered and discussed. One of the things that mattered to these men who were the fathers of the church was the significance of dreams and visions.

How much they had to say about dreams and visions, however, is something that cannot even be guessed from any ordinary survey of their works. It is certainly not revealed in what is generally written in the church today. And the English editions of the fathers which have been used in the church during the past century show some remarkable omissions. There are thirty-eight thick volumes of ante-Nicene, Nicene, and post-Nicene fathers which seem to have been rather carelessly indexed in relation to dreams and similar subjects.

Not only is the indexing of these subjects hit and miss in the English editions, but when there was a choice of materials, the editors often left out those which referred to dream-vision experiences. I first discovered this when I looked for certain works on dreams which had been mentioned by writers of a later period. The very significant writings of Synesius of Cyrene, the early-fifth-century bishop of Ptolemais, have been omitted entirely. Out of John Cassian's twenty-four *Conferences* twenty-two are included in the post-Nicene fathers; only two are missing, the twelfth and the twenty-second *On Nocturnal Illusions*. The theological poems of Gregory of Nazianzen with his dream experiences are not included, nor are many similar passages in Gregory of Nyssa and Jerome. In translating the works of Gregory the Great, the two in which he discussed dreams at some length, *The Dialogues* and *The Morals*, have been omitted without any mention of their content. There is no reference at all to Augustine's *De Genesi ad Litteram*, in which he took the entire Twelfth Book to explain his understanding of dreams and visions. Several of these could not be found in English anywhere, and I had to have them translated from Latin in order to read them.

In fact, there has been no serious study of the thinking of the church fathers on the subject of dreams for at least two centuries, and almost none of the earlier studies have been translated into English. My own study of these materials has occupied me on and off for ten years. In addition, the Reverend John Sanford has undertaken the laborious task of reading these volumes one by one with an eye to these and other similar experiences. His list of the references supplements my own, and I am deeply indebted to him for his help.[1]

As we consider these materials, we discuss first the Apostolic Fathers and the New Testament apocrypha that come out of the same period. We then look at a different kind of literature, the apologies that developed around the middle of the second century and forged out the theological foundation of the later church. These writers were followed next by the important school at Alexandria and finally by the Latin fathers, whom we discuss more or less in chronological order, taking up the references to dreams in each of them in the general context of their Christian theory.

## The Apostolic Fathers

The first of these Christian authors, the Apostolic Fathers, were men who probably had contact with the apostles themselves. For

---

[1] The excellent new translations of the fathers being brought out by the Roman Catholic foundation, Fathers of the Church, Inc., have also been helpful.

the most part their works were addressed to the faithful, to strengthen and inspire or to instruct them, and now and then these writings were given the rank of scripture. Some were even included for a time in the canon of holy books. At the same time, for about the first three centuries of the church's life, there was also a stream of apocryphal gospels and acts and epistles that the church almost uniformly rejected because these were fanciful rather than historical accounts of events surrounding the lives of Jesus and the apostles.

One of the most popular books of this time was the *Shepherd of Hermas,* an inspirational work written to the church in Rome early in the second century. This book, which was regarded as scripture by many Christians of that time, begins with a vision that the author experiences as he falls asleep and is carried away by the Spirit. This "vision of sleep" is followed by many others like it, and then after certain commandments and parallels are explained, one final dream-vision concludes the work, which is much like *Pilgrim's Progress.* Like Bunyan's masterpiece, its writing has the quality of a genuine visionary experience and is of great value when understood symbolically. In Jung's *Psychological Types* there is a lengthy and brilliant analysis of Hermas as an example of the creative process of individuation taking place in a dream-vision.[2] Here Jung gives evidence of the authenticity and value of this work that is so strange to the modern world.

It was this unquestionable dream quality that gave the *Shepherd of Hermas* its authority in the long period in which it was so popular; what the author had to say came to him out of a dream-vision experience and so had more value than a consciously conceived writing. The fact that it was read for three centuries in several languages shows the value attributed to dreams in this period.

One particularly important vision was described in the *Martyrdom of Polycarp,* written about the same time. As Polycarp was praying not long before his martyrdom, he was informed through a symbolic vision of what was to happen. He saw the pillow under his head catch fire and realized that this image of destruction signified his own impending capture and death.

[2] C. G. Jung, *Psychological Types,* London, Routledge & Kegan Paul Ltd., 1953, pp. 275ff. The Jungian medical doctor M. Esther Harding has written an interesting analysis of *Pilgrim's Progress,* entitled *Journey Into Self,* (New York, David McKay Company, Inc., 1956), which shows the depth and significance expressed by the imagery in this kind of work.

In both of these works one finds the same feeling about dreams and visions which we have found expressed in Acts, in the Epistles, and also in the Revelation of John.[3]

## The New Testament Apocrypha

Among the apocryphal writings that began to appear in this period are some interesting materials based on dreams. These writers were attempting to carry on the tradition of the canonical New Testament, and it is interesting to see how closely these materials are related to those which were accepted as genuine visions of the holy. In the *Acts of the Holy Apostle Thomas* the Lord came to Thomas in India in a dream to give him instructions as to what he was to do. Later, at the time of his death, a beautiful young man also appeared to Thomas and his friends in a dream to give them comfort and instruction in the last days of the apostle's life; this experience is described in the *Consummation of Thomas, the Apostle*. The *Apocalypse of Moses* tells a further story of the garden of Eden, in which Eve was warned in a dream about the murder of Abel by his brother, and knew in advance what would happen to her son. And in the *Testament of Abraham*, Isaac dreamed in symbolic images of Abraham's coming death, while at the same time Abraham himself was being prepared by the Archangel Michael to understand and interpret the dream that Isaac would tell him.

The *Acts of Xantippe and Polyxena* was written as a religious novel and was the forerunner of the religious romances of the third century of our era. In this romance dreams were used to show the heroine that she should be baptized, and several times there were visions of a beautiful young man who brought important information. This work also described a dream through which Peter was sent on a mission into Greece. In the *Clementine Homilies*, which were probably written late in the second century, there is a delightful passage in which Peter and a certain Simon carry on a lengthy discussion about dreams. There is no doubt, they decide, that God sends dreams that present true visions, and these dreams can come to evil men as well as to good ones; but they feel that to the best of

[3] These materials are found in *The Ante-Nicene Fathers*, ed. Alexander Roberts and James Donaldson, Grand Rapids, Michigan, Wm. B. Eerdmans Publishing Company, 1951:
*The Pastor of Hermas*, Vol. 2, pp. 9ff.
*Epistle Concerning the Martyrdom of the Holy Polycarp*, V, Vol. 1, p. 40.

men God will reveal himself through intelligence rather than through dreams. Indeed, the conclusion is that, unless a dream answers the specific questions of men, it has not brought the dreamer into face-to-face contact with God. Finally, the *Clementine Recognitions* described how the demons gain power over men; when men forgo moderation, they are open for demons to strike them in dreams.[4]

For almost three centuries of the church's life, these scattered references are the only apocryphal writings on dreams or visions that have come down to us. In this material the emphasis on dreams did not increase; if anything, it declined, as the apocryphal writers instead saw God speaking and working in more miraculous ways than through the medium of the dream.

## Post-Apostolic times

About 150 A.D. a new kind of Christian writing appeared. Christianity was faced with two opponents, one from the outside, the other from within. As Christians became the scapegoats of the Roman Empire, it was necessary to show the world how false and ludicrous the opinions of the government and the general populace were. And as divisions and pagan ideas threatened the church from within, it became equally necessary to take a studied and intellectual look at the meaning of Christian experience, to establish and hold what orthodox Christians had found. In this period men came to the fore who were equipped for the job.

Many of the writers at this time had become Christian after thorough training in Greek rhetoric and philosophy, and they took the rational and intellectual approach for which they had been educated. Their writings were some of them polemic in nature, others philosophic in the Greek tradition. But whether their aim was to contradict theological error, or to give Christianity a place in the cultural heritage of the ancient world, these works on the whole

[4] *The Ante-Nicene Fathers*, op. cit.:
*Acts of the Holy Apostle Thomas*, Vol. 8, p. 542;
*Consummation of Thomas, the Apostle*, Vol. 8, p. 550;
*Apocalypse of Moses*, Vol. 8, p. 565;
*Testament of Abraham*, IV and VII, Vol. 10, pp. 187 and 189;
*Acts of Xantippe and Polyxena*, XVff. and XXIIff., Vol. 10, pp. 209ff. and 212ff.;
*Clementine Homilies*, XIVff., Vol. 8, pp. 322ff.;
*Clementine Recognitions*, IV.15ff., Vol. 10, pp. 136ff.

were reasonable, careful, telling. They were produced by some of the finest minds of those centuries, these men who forged out the foundations of Christianity that have stood as the basic faith of Christians from that time until now.

The authors of the New Testament themselves had not been particularly well versed in Greek philosophy, and they probably would have found it difficult to defend their world view in the academies of the ancient world. This view that was expressed in the New Testament was simply not much discussed by Matthew, Mark, or any of the others, and the same thing was also true of the Apostolic Fathers. But as these new Christian apologists emerged, we find Christians conscious of their place in the ancient world and speaking intelligently to that world. Justin Martyr, Irenaeus, Tertullian, Clement, Origen, Athanasius, Augustine, Gregory of Nyssa, Synesius, and Chrysostom were intellectuals, educated to their place in the world. Although it is possible to look with some condescension on the first Christian writers as philosophically naïve, this attitude is out of place with regard to these later writers. A knowledge of our historic Christian roots makes this fact perfectly apparent.

These church fathers wrote as philosophers who held a world view quite different from that of the twentieth century. Their view was quite consciously based on the thinking of Plato,[5] which they found compatible with both the biblical tradition and their own Christian experience, and these they merged to produce the first serious theology the world had known. With this consistent point of view they stood against pagan religion, against the skepticism of the ancient world (of which there was more than we sometimes think), and against the heretical ideas that grew up within the Christian church. Unquestionably, if they had had the chance, they would also have defended this point of view against the Aristotelian thinking that is so basic to our present Christian culture, and which leaves little place for the break-through of the divine, or more than human, into human life.

When I began to examine the fathers to discover their attitude toward dreams, I did not really expect to find an attitude very

[5] Only a few attempts were made in the ancient world to relate the church to Aristotelian thinking, and these ended in heresy. Most Arianism had an Aristotelian base. See Adolf Harnack, *History of Dogma*, London, Williams & Norgate, 1912, Vol. III, p. 46; Vol. IV, pp. 48, 65, and 74ff.

different from our own in the twentieth Christian century. It is true that my own experience was different; through depth psychology I had come to see the value and significance of dreams, but I also knew their importance to the ancient pagan world, which we have discussed at some length in the last chapters. These men had been trying to separate from that world, and these first theologians would naturally have taken the opposite attitude toward dreams. I expected to find them condemning the pagans for being interested in dreams, or at least warning Christians to be cautious about such dangerous superstition.

Instead I found that when these men spoke of dreams, it was almost always to express a positive view. One essential element of their theological thinking was the belief that God still spoke directly through the medium of dreams and visions. Even the warnings about lying dreams (or demons) were far less frequent than in the Old Testament. As a matter of fact, these great fathers of the church did not have to say a great deal to support the coherent and well-integrated theory they held regarding the place of dreams in human life, for there was no great breach between Christians and sophisticated non-Christians about this.

On the whole, these fathers of the church accepted the dream theory of the later Greeks and the world view in which it has meaning very much as these had been expressed by Plato and the Greek dramatists. As we have shown, the Greeks maintained the reality of a world of gods and spirits and strange intimations, which existed alongside of the physical world and was revealed in dreams and visions. Like the fathers, they saw the significance of the non-physical world for man, and thus that dreams are revelations of the greatest consequence for men. In fact, the later Greeks sometimes went overboard about this,[6] while the fathers were simply more careful and guarded in their statements. Those who are familiar with the writings of Dr. C. G. Jung will find themselves in a strangely congenial atmosphere here. With slight changes in terminology, it would appear that Dr. Jung and the fathers are talking about the same reality. Of course, they both considered that man has an eternal destiny in that world which is revealed by dreams. In

[6] E. R. Dodds demonstrates this graphically in the story of Aelius Aristides and his interpretations of his dreams. He also offers excellent detail of the Hellenistic world-view in the early Christian era, particularly as seen by Plotinus and Porphyry. Dodds, *Pagan and Christian in an Age of Anxiety*, Cambridge, The University Press, 1965, pp. 39ff. and 72ff.

the case of the fathers it is practically impossible to understand their theory of the spiritual world and revelation unless we understand their theory of dreams and associated experiences.

## The Apologists

The first of these men who were able to interpret Christianity to the pagan world was Justin Martyr, who was perhaps the first Christian philosopher. Justin was born a pagan and searched the philosophies of the day until he found in Jesus of Nazareth what he felt Plato had been seeking. He wrote in Rome in the first half of the second century, and was martyred for his belief in 165 A.D. Dreams, Justin mentioned in passing, are sent by spirits, and he used this idea to show his belief that souls do not cease after death; in dreams we already have direct spiritual communication with non-physical realities, and beings who are capable of such communication need not cease with the death of the body. He believed that dreams are sent by evil spirits to hold us in bondage, as well as by God. For Justin Martyr dreams had intrinsic meaning and importance because they give hint of man's participation in a more-than-physical world.

Irenaeus, who carried on the tradition of Justin, fought mainly against the gnostic speculation that was so popular among second-century intellectuals. He was a native of Smyrna and became the bishop of Lyons in the last half of the second century. Christianity had spread far from the old centers of Greek culture, and Irenaeus worried about speaking Celtic and letting his Greek become rusty. Like Justin, he assumed that dreams are revelations of a spiritual world. In his principal work, *Against Heresies,* Irenaeus commented appreciatively and intelligently on the dream of Peter in Acts 10; he believed that the dream itself was a proof of the authenticity of Peter's experience. Again, he stressed the authenticity of Paul's dream at Troas, drawing attention like a modern biblical critic to the introduction of the "we" passages at this point. He also inferred from the dreams of Joseph in Matthew that Joseph's dreaming showed how close he was to the real God, and in another context he suggested that the fact that an angel came to Joseph was additional evidence of his close relationship to God.

Irenaeus also used his understanding of dreams to refute the idea of reincarnation or transmigration of souls. Since the soul can receive knowledge directly and communicate it to the body after a dream has occurred, there is no reason that the body should make us forget a former life of the soul if it had one. In still another place he explained that although God is himself invisible to the eye directly, he gives us visions and dreams through which he conveys the likeness of his nature and his glory. Thus God manifests himself not only through mighty works, but through the use of both visual and auditory visions as well. Again, the revelatory nature of dreams is simply assumed.

Another Christian philosopher in this period was Tatian the Assyrian, who was a close follower of Justin for part of his life. In the *Address to the Greeks*, his only complete work that remains, Tatian wrote a long passage on demons in which he explained that the way demons make their presence known to people is through dreams. Since none of these men left works of a more personal nature, we can only guess that their own experience with dreams was probably the same as the experience of Christians who came before and after them.[7]

## The School at Alexandria

Two of the keenest minds the early church produced were Clement and Origen in Alexandria. Clement had been pagan; he was probably Greek, and he was certainly widely traveled and highly educated. His bibliography of Greek references in one manuscript took fourteen pages to list. In the Alexandrian school where he settled down at the end of the second century he probed into the whole subject of reason and faith. Origen, who was his pupil, was even more famous. His was considered one of the greatest minds, pagan or Christian, of the third century; he was a voluminous writer and is credited with establishing theology as a science. Both of these men stated clearly the great significance they saw in dreams.

In discussing the nature and meaning of sleep, Clement urged:

> Let us not, then, who are sons of the true light, close the door against this light; but turning in on ourselves, illumining

[7] The references above are found in *The Ante-Nicene Fathers*, op. cit.:
Justin Martyr, *The First Apology*, XIV and XVIII, Vol. 1, pp. 167 and 169;
Irenaeus, *Against Heresies*, III.12.7 and 15, III.14.1, IV.23.1, III.9.2, II.33.1–4, and IV.20.8–12, Vol. 1, pp. 432, 436, 437, 494, 409f., 490ff.;
Tatian, *Address to the Greeks*, XVIII, Vol. II, p. 73.

the eyes of the hidden man, and gazing on the truth itself, and receiving its streams, let us clearly and intelligibly reveal such dreams as are true.

True dreams, Clement believed, come from the depth of the soul, which is always active. He argued that they reveal spiritual reality, the intercourse of the soul with God, and this idea was used by many of the fathers as evidence for the immortality of the soul. As the following words show, he saw sleep as a time of special receptivity to spiritual reality, a time of special clarity in discovering the soul's destiny:

> Thus also such dreams as are true, in the view of him who reflects rightly, are the thoughts of a sober soul, undistracted for the time by the affections of the body, and counselling with itself in the best manner. . . . Wherefore always contemplating God, and by perpetual converse with Him inoculating the body with wakefulness, it raises man to equality with angelic grace, and from the practice of wakefulness it grasps the eternity of life.

In the *Stromata*, or *Miscellanies*, Clement made two other interesting references to dreams. Since God gives truth symbolically rather than directly, therefore truth should not be communicated to one who has not at least "been purified in a dream." In another section of the same work he described at some length the life of the soul at night in sleep. He believed that "the soul, released from the perceptions of sense, turns in on itself, and has a truer hold of intelligence." Thus are the mysteries celebrated at night. He also believed that man can so purify himself that the passions may not even perturb us in dreams.

Almost from the beginning of his writings, which made the Alexandrians famous all over the world, Origen left no doubt about his thinking on dreams. In his great answer to the pagans, *Against Celsus*, he defended the visions of the Bible, saying:

> . . . We, nevertheless, so far as we can, shall support our position, maintaining that, as it is a matter of belief that in a dream impressions have been brought before the minds of many, some relating to divine things, and others to future events of this life, and this either with clearness or in an enigmatic manner,—a fact which is manifest to all who accept the doctrine of providence: so how is it absurd to say that

the mind which could receive impressions in a *dream* should be impressed also in a waking vision, for the benefit either of him on whom the impressions are made, or of those who are to hear the account of them from him?

And having satisfied his parallel between dreams and visions, Origen then went on to discuss the nature of dreams. He could hardly have introduced his subject with a more concise and adequate statement of the attitude of the ancient world toward dreams.

The discussion that follows has a modern ring to it. Origen saw the dream, not as physical perception, but as the presentation of symbols that reveal the nature of the non-physical world. He believed that in Jacob's dream of the ladder reaching to heaven Jacob was presented with a vision of the nature of heaven as valuable and as valid as Plato's discussion of this realm. The image of the ladder, he suggested, was comparable to the degrees of "planets" through which the soul, according to Plato, must pass in going from earth to heaven, and he concluded by referring the reader to Philo's discussion of this vision. Origen clearly was stating here that the understanding of Plato and the vision of Jacob were in agreement with each other.

Writing to the famous Africanus, Origen rejected this friend's doubts as to the value of the story of Susanna in the Apocrypha. Africanus was offended by the idea that Daniel had been "seized by the Spirit," and Origen pointed out that God had seized the spirits of many of the saints and had in so doing "favored [them] with divine dreams and angelic appearances and [direct] inspirations." The opening verses of Hebrews, he went on, support the conclusion that God speaks in these ways by the prophets, just as he spoke to Jacob through a dream and then by the direct appearance of the angel who wrestled with Jacob at Jabbok. Another most emphatic statement occurs in *Contra Celsus*, in which Origen declared that many Christians had been converted from their pagan ways by this kind of direct break-through into their lives in waking visions and dreams of the night. He made it clear that many such instances were known of this sort of conversion. Later, in refuting one of Celsus' diatribes against the Jews, Origen remarked, however, that all dreams are not of this quality; some persons may "dream dreams, owing to obscure phantoms presenting themselves." Thus one must distinguish between dreams from God and those originating from phantoms.

When Celsus ridiculed the dreams that occurred in the story of Jesus' birth, Origen countered his statements by saying:

> . . . and that in a dream certain persons may have certain things pointed out to them to do, is an event of frequent occurrence to many individuals,—the impression on the mind being produced either by an angel or by some other thing. Where, then, is the absurdity in believing that He who had once become incarnate, should be led also by human guidance to keep out of the way of dangers?

And a few paragraphs later he pointed out that when Peter had to be broken from his narrow Judaism, he was given a vision that made it possible for him to take the message of Christianity to Cornelius.[8]

Clearly for Origen the dream, the waking vision, and divine inspiration were all of one piece. Through these methods God reveals himself to men and gives them a symbolic knowledge of the nature of the spiritual world and of heaven. The dream-vision is an essential part of the method of God's revelation. The content of these revelations put the believer on a par or higher than the best of pagan philosophy when properly understood. Yet at the same time Origen urged caution, for evil spirits can also break through into the lives of men by the same avenue God uses.

## Tertullian offers wide evidence about dreams

The first great Latin apologist was the famed and fiery Tertullian, who flourished at the beginning of the third century and was roughly contemporary with Origen. Few writers of the time turned out more lucid and admirable prose than this controversial church leader, whose background was that of a cultivated North African. His father was a military man and a pagan, and Tertullian was converted to Christianity after studying law in Rome. While his immediate influence on the church was somewhat diminished by his adherence to the Montanist sect, his works were read and studied with great care by later Christians, particularly Cyprian and Augustine, and

[8] The passages from Clement and Origen come from *The Ante-Nicene Fathers*, op. cit., Vol. 2, pp. 258f., 458, and 435; Vol. 4, pp. 416f., 583, 389f., 415., 546, 426, and 429, as follows:
Clement of Alexandria, *The Instructor*, II.9; *The Stromata, or Miscellanies*, V.9 and IV.22.
Origen, *Against Celsus*, I.48, VI.21–23; *A Letter from Origen to Africanus*, 10; *Against Celsus*, I.46, V.9, I.66, and II.1.

through them his thinking became one of the foundation stones of our Christian theology.

There are many references to dreams scattered throughout the writings of Tertullian, particularly in his *Apology*, in the *Treatise on the Resurrection of the Flesh*, in the *Defense against Marcion*, in his work on the Trinity entitled *Against Praxeas*, and in his introduction to the *Martyrdom of Saints Perpetua and Felicitas*. We shall not discuss them separately, however, because Tertullian obliged us by writing an excellent and concise statement of his theory of dreams and their relation to the Christian doctrine of revelation in his major work, *On the Soul*. These conclusions of Tertullian expressed the general Christian belief of the third century, which remained the general attitude of thinking Western Christians for the next twelve hundred years, until the thinking of Aquinas began to take over in Western Europe. We shall therefore analyze Tertullian's discussion of dreams at some length, since it is one of the most authoritative discussions in the church's literature. It also compares favorably with modern psychological discussions of the subject.

Tertullian devoted eight chapters of this work (A *Treatise on the Soul*, or *De Anima*) to his study of sleep and dreams. Like the modern psychologists who are studying dreaming, he believed that everyone dreams (as we now know they do), and as evidence of this fact he called attention to the movements of sleeping infants. What he had to say came from his own observations as well as the opinions of both the Christian and pagan community. He began by ridiculing the "vulgar" idea that the soul leaves the body in sleep, as if it were taking off on a holiday. Rather, he found dreaming an indication that the soul is perpetually active, and this he saw as the best evidence of its immortality. But there is in sleep an *ekstasis*, a standing aside, in which the soul has power to act but is like a gladiator deprived of his arms. This *ekstasis* (the same word is used for Peter's trance in Acts 10, and also for the experience of God in Dionysian religion) is something the soul is given, a givenness that overwhelms it in the same way sense experience does in the waking states. To emphasize this he suggested that we can hardly be crowned for imaginary martyrdom in our dreams any more than we are condemned for visionary acts of sin.

Thus like Plato Tertullian saw that dreaming is akin to madness, a madness in which the soul, instead of being given something reasonably sensed, is overwhelmed by something other than sense experience. This is closely related to the idea of some depth psychologists that psychosis is the living out of one's dream life without orientation to the physical world. We might translate Tertullian's meaning into modern terms by saying that in sleep the unconscious makes its autonomous impression on the center of consciousness in the form of the dream.

Tertullian turned his ridicule then on the Epicureans for denying the validity of dreams, and for support he surveyed the whole literature on dream significance and interpretation, citing names like Homer, Herodotus, Heracleides, Strabo, and Callisthenes, as well as the Romans Vitellius and Cicero. He also referred to others whom he did not quote, including five portly volumes written by Hermippus of Berytus. He discussed the use of dreams in divination and also gave the names of the authors who had treated this subject. There is no question that Tertullian was well informed on the extensive literature of dreams that was current in the ancient world. He was making this perfectly evident; he wanted it known that he knew what he was talking about. He mentioned the people of Telmessus, who maintained that dreams are always meaningful (quite like modern analysts) and believed that it was only their own weakness that kept them from understanding a dream. He specifically suggested that dreams have various levels of interpretation, and finally he asked: "Now, who is such a stranger to human experience as not sometimes to have perceived some truth in dreams?"

Proceeding then to analyze the cause of dreams, Tertullian found that they occur from four sources. There are dreams caused by demons; indeed, they inflict most of them, although these dreams "sometimes turn out true and favorable to us." There are also dreams that come from God, and according to Tertullian "almost the greater part of mankind get their knowledge of God from dreams." Third, there are natural dreams that the soul apparently creates for itself from "an intense application to special circumstances." And in the final category are dreams that come from none of these but must be ascribed "to what is purely and simply the ecstatic state and its peculiar conditions"; in other words, the unconscious, the state of standing aside from consciousness. He called attention to the fact that he was omitting any category based on "ingenious conjecture" about the effect of physical activities, and criticized Plato and others for holding that the physical body, the liver, fasting, or the like have any particular effect on dreaming. He saw dreams basically as psychic phenomena common to all men, which can be understood only through careful consideration of men's experiences. Indeed, his total discussion is an example of skillful understanding of the human psyche.

In another passage Tertullian definitely stated that he was describing not only his own private opinions about dreams, but the body of thinking on the subject accepted by Christians generally. It would appear that dreaming was considered the normal way to receive visions from God. This theology of dreams was stated explicitly by Tertullian in his introduction to the *Martyrdom of Saints Perpetua and Felicitas*. He considered dreams one of the gifts from God, a *charisma*. After referring to the prophecy of Joel that when God pours out his Spirit, men would dream dreams and see visions, he went on:

> And thus we—who both acknowledge and reverence, even as we do the prophecies, modern visions as equally promised to us, and consider the other powers of the Holy Spirit as an agency of the Church for which also He was sent, administering all gifts in all, even as the Lord distributed to every one as will needfully collect them in writing, and commemorate them in reading to God's glory; that so no weakness or despondency of faith may suppose that the divine grace abode only among the ancients, whether in respect of the condescension that raised up martyrs, or that gave revelations.

Indeed, this was so much accepted that in the narrative that follows it is only the simple statement of St. Perpetua that she awoke which gives away the fact that these visions were received in sleep as dreams. How many other early Christians' visions were received in this way without the acknowledgment of awakening would be difficult to tell.

In any case, this book, which once had wide circulation, is an example of the practical Christian understanding of dreams. Some critics also ascribe the conclusion of the narrative and its circulation to Tertullian, for these martyrs were fellow North Africans. The dreams, however, were told by Perpetua. After she had been imprisoned her brother suggested that, since she was there because of her faith, she might ask God for a vision that would show her the outcome. She did ask for such a sign, and saw the vision of a golden ladder that reached up to heaven. Attached to it were daggers and hooks to slash the careless who did not keep looking up, and at its foot was a dragon. Seeing herself mount the ladder with the others, she then woke, knowing that they must die. She also saw in a dream the figure of a friend who had died, a man who had had cancer of the face. She saw him suffering, but after she had prayed for him, he again appeared to her in another night vision, restored and happy.

In her fourth dream Perpetua saw herself changed into a man in order to fight with the devil and overcome him, and knew she would be able to withstand her martyrdom. Because of this dream she also realized that her agony and suffering were caused, not by men, but by the power of Satan. Thus these early Christians were able to hold their persecutors in charity, knowing them to be dominated by Satan and his hosts. These dreams, comprising the central and largest portion of the narrative, reflect directly the popular Christian view of dreams of which Tertullian wrote learnedly.[9]

## Theologians who wrote of their own dreams

In the years that followed we find the tradition set by Tertullian and Origen continued in North Africa with Cyprian, in Alexandria with a succession of church leaders, and in Rome with Hippolytus, and later with Arnobius and Lactantius. Apparently the whole church acted upon the belief that God directs individuals and the destiny of the church by imparting knowledge and wisdom directly through dreams and visions, and this was expressed as it had been in the book of Acts. In fact, the history of this period by Eusebius reads almost like a sequel to that book. All of these writers accepted the general Christian attitude that Tertullian had so ably presented.

It is difficult for us in the modern Western world to relive those times in which it was important *to know* one's belief. Thascius Cyprian was bishop of Carthage in 250 A.D. when a new wave of Christian persecution began under the emperor Decius. After a

[9] The principal references to dreams in Tertullian's works are found in *The Ante-Nicene Fathers*, op. cit., Vol. III, pp. 37, 558, 343, 609f., 699ff., and 221ff., as follows:
*The Apology*, XXIII; *On the Resurrection of the Flesh*, XVIII; *The Five Books Against Marcion*, III.25; *Against Praxeas*, XIV; *The Passion of the Holy Martyrs Perpetua and Felicitas*; and *A Treatise on the Soul*, XLII–XLIX.

period of relative freedom many Christians looked only for an easy out and recanted, and then the problem arose as to how these lapsed Christians might be received into fellowship again. Many of Cyprian's writings were related to this question, for which he was well prepared by his education as a professional rhetorician. The fire of his words contributed to his own death as a martyr, while his unquestioned orthodoxy made him one of the foundation stones of the Latin church. Even so, the modern editors of his works found it necessary to explain the kind of direct encounter with God that he described in many places. In one letter objecting to some of the most devastating critics of Christianity, he wrote to Florentius Pupianus that he knew the truth of which he spoke because of direct manifestations to him in dreams and visions. Supporting his position by referring to the dreams of the patriarch Joseph, he remarked, "Although I know that to some men dreams seem ridiculous and visions foolish, yet assuredly it is to such as would rather believe in opposition to the priest, than believe the priest." To the church at large he demonstrated that God continued to chide even young men and bring them to their senses in visions of the night, just like Job.

In another letter he wrote that God guides the very councils of the church by "many and manifest visions." He commended the reader Celerinus because his conversion to the church had come through a vision of the night. Cyprian concluded that this gave him greater honor, as Eusebius also testified when he described the good character of this same Celerinus in his *Ecclesiastical History*. In Cyprian's *Treatise on Mortality* he related the vision of a man at the approach of death, a vision that gave certitude to those who were with him and heard the dying man describe "a youth, venerable in honor and majesty, lofty in stature and shining in aspect," who appeared and stood by him. Cyprian's own experience before he was beheaded was described in the restrained and factual *Life and Passion of Cyprian* by Pontius. Told in the martyr's own words, ". . . ere yet I was sunk in the repose of slumber . . ." he saw a vision of "a young man of unusual stature" who told him what was to happen and so prepared him to go on.

But when the editors of the fathers came to Cyprian, they could not quite take so much outspoken emphasis on direct encounters with God. They felt the need to support the inclusion of so much detail about dreams and visions that had guided and inspired

Cyprian's life, and so they appended the following note to the original discussion of his narrative and letters:

> It is easy to speak with ridicule of such instances as Dean Milman here treats so philosophically. But, lest believers should be charged with exceptional credulity, let us recall what the father of English Deism (Lord Herbert) relates of his own experiences, in the conclusion of his Autobiography: "I had no sooner spoken these words (of prayer to the Deist's deity) but a loud though yet a gentle noise came from the heavens, for it was like nothing on earth, which did so comfort and cheer me, that I took my petition as granted, and that I had the sign I demanded. . . . This, how strange soever it may seem, I protest, before the eternal God, is true. . . ."[10]

In the third century Alexandria was still the seat of Christian learning, and there Gregory Thaumaturgus (or "wonder-worker") and Dionysius continued the traditions of learning that the great school at that city had established. These men were the disciples of Origen who prepared the way for Athanasius and his remarkable formulation of Christian orthodoxy. Both of them were led by dreams. It was told of Gregory, who was born of a wealthy family and studied Roman law, that his declaration of faith came to him in a beautiful dream, as a revelation from the blessed John by the mediation of Mary.[11] In a letter quoted by Eusebius, Dionysius related the vision that had confirmed him in his determination to know both the pagan and heretical Christian worlds; in it a voice spoke to him, telling him that he need fear nothing, because he stood on secure ground.

Another pupil of the school at Alexandria was Julius Africanus, later the bishop of Emmaus according to some traditions. In his writings there is a story of dreams as fanciful as the nineteenth-century editors thought it was, which therefore leaves little doubt about the attitude of third-century Christians on the subject. Africanus described how, before the birth of Christ, the king of Persia sought wisdom through incubation, and how, sleeping in the holy place, he was given a dream that revealed the coming of the Christ. In Jerusalem Narcissus, while still bishop, named his own successor because of a night vision that he believed was divine

---

[10] *The Ante-Nicene Fathers*, op. cit., Vol. 5, p. 266.

[11] S. Gregorii Nysseni: *De Vita S. Gregorii Thaumaturgi*, J. P. Migne, *Patrologiae Graecae*, Paris, 1862, Vol. 46, Col. 911–13.

instruction. The man thus selected was Alexander of Cappadocia, who died in 251 A.D. during the Decian persecutions, and whose letters remain among the works of the fathers. In 300 A.D. the bishop of Alexandria was the much-revered Peter, the last to die in the persecutions of Maximinus and who was later sainted. In *The Genuine Acts of Peter* the story was told of how his way had been determined by a vision of the night in which a radiant boy of twelve, clothed in a divided tunic, stood before him and told him that he should beware of Arius and his heresy. Later, the next prelate of Alexandria, the Alexander who succeeded to the see in 312 A.D., used this same dream to support his arguments when he was writing against the Arians.[12]

## Dreams in Rome

Meanwhile Rome had its first schismatic "pope" when the controversial Hippolytus was made a bishop there in 215 A.D. He believed that Callistus, the regular bishop in Rome, was quite naïve in his theology and also questionable in his life, and some of the most influential Christians followed Hippolytus. In the end the two churches were reconciled after the persecutions of Maximin when both leaders were dead. Although Hippolytus was famous enough to have a statue erected to him in Rome, little was known about him until a century ago. When some of his major writings turned up then, it was discovered that his works as much as any other had given the laws and liturgy of the Eastern church their permanent form.

Hippolytus' works contained various studies, including the last of the apologies written in Greek. In his discussion of evil in the *Treatise on Christ and Anti-Christ*, dealing largely with dreams and visions in the Bible, Hippolytus showed that the prophets had

---

[12] The material in this section comes from *The Ante-Nicene Fathers*, op cit., Vol. 5, pp. 375, 290, 338, 312, 473f., 271f.; Vol. 6, pp. 79, 128f., 263, and 291:
Cyprian, *Epistles* LXVIII.10, IX.4, LIII.5, XXXIII.1; *Treatise VII On Mortality*, 19f.;
Pontius, the Deacon, *The Life and Passion of Cyprian, Bishop and Martyr*, 12f.; Introductory Notice to Dionysius, Bishop of Alexandria; Julius Africanus, *Events in Persia*;
*The Genuine Acts of Peter* (Bishop of Alexandria); Alexander, Bishop of Alexandria, *Epistle on the Arian Heresy*, 1.1.

been instructed about the future through visions, some of which were in sleep. "Wherefore," he concluded, "prophets were with good reason called from the very first 'seers.'" There also remain extensive fragments of his commentaries on Daniel, in which he discussed these divine dreams at length, clearly considering them as revelations of the future. In one last work, attributed to Hippolytus but felt by many to be someone else's summary of his genuine writings, we find the same ideas on dreams and visions expressed at even greater length.

In the Latin church the same traditions were continued by Arnobius and his pupil Lactantius. Arnobius was a pagan rhetorician teaching in a Roman colony near Carthage when, according to Jerome, he was led by a dream to seek Christianity. He died a martyr in the Diocletian persecutions in 303 A.D. His only work that has survived, however, was less sanguine about dreams than any of the other ante-Nicene writings. This book was written when Arnobius was a new convert and better informed about pagan ideas than Christian ones. By attacking heathen mythology and the follies of paganism, however, he preserved many choice stories about the gods for future ages. His discussion of the meaning of dreams quoted Plato's *Theaetetus* and warned against diviners and interpreters who devise heathen myths. While the Latin is not clear, he seemed to suggest that Christ would appear directly "to unpolluted minds" rather than in "airy dreams."

We know little about the personal life of his pupil, who was also a teacher of rhetoric, except that he was close to the imperial family. Constantine the Great selected Lactantius as tutor for his son, and his *Divine Institutes* was written in part to instruct the emperor. In it he referred again and again to dreams from the gods, whom he considered the same as demons. He included a chapter on "The Use of Reason in Religion; and of Dreams, Auguries, Oracles, and Similar Portents," in which he cited examples to show that through dreams a knowledge of the future is occasionally given to pagans as well as to Christians. Interestingly enough, his example of a logical fallacy is that of a man who has dreamed that he ought not believe in dreams. In both this book and the *Epitome* Lactantius discussed at length the prophecies that had been fulfilled in the Christ, showing that visions had been brought before the prophets' eyes by the divine Spirit.

In still another work Lactantius suggested that the same Spirit could still instruct men in the same way. This was when he came to Constantine's dream before the battle of the Milvian Bridge. In telling it—somewhat differently from Eusebius' version, which will come to our attention in the next chapter—he added a dream-vision of Constantine's brother-in-law Licinius, in which an angel of the Lord provided him with the prayer that encouraged his men to overcome Daia and so join the emperor. The victory thus won was followed by the Edict of Milan, which freed the Christians from persecution.

Thus, while we encounter two different attitudes in Arnobius and Lactantius, it is clear that these men knew how to receive a divine dream when they encountered it in reality. It would be centuries before rationalism such as Gibbon's influenced our judgment so deeply that we ignored these experiences entirely. Yet there is no more reason to overlook the carefully written account of a dream in Lactantius or Eusebius than to discredit other parts of their story.[13]

[13] These materials are found in The Ante-Nicene Fathers, op. cit., Vol. 5, pp. 204ff., 177ff., 242ff.; Vol. 6, pp. 406ff., 418, 436, 426; Vol. 7, pp. 51f., 73, 240f., 318ff., as follows:

Hippolytus, Treatise on Christ and Anti-Christ, 2ff.; Fragment from the Commentary on Daniel, I–III;
A Discourse by the Most Blessed Hippolytus, Bishop and Martyr, on the End of the World, and on Anti-Christ, and on the Second Coming of our Lord Jesus Christ, Iff.;
Introductory Notice to Arnobius;
Arnobius, Against the Heathen, I.24, II.7, I.46;
Lactantius, The Divine Institutes, II.8, III.6; The Epitome of the Divine Institutes, XLVff.; and Of the Manner in Which the Persecutors Died, XLIVff.

# six

# The Dreams of the Victorious Christian Church

To the Christians who survived persecution under Diocletian and Galerius nothing was more important than freedom from these sufferings. It is even hard for most of us to imagine a Christian adherence that involved such risks. But with the victory of Constantine and the Edict of Milan in 313, persecution of the church almost ceased, and this freedom opened up a new era in the church's life. There was a burst of activity within the church that brought a flow of new literary work. Great Christian leaders arose to solve a host of religious problems. Athanasius laid the foundation for all subsequent Christian thinking, while Augustine in his voluminous writings set the general direction of the Western church for the next thousand years. Under Chrysostom and the great Cappadocians the mold was also formed for all Eastern Christianity down to the present day. Not one of these great leaders ignored the subject of dreams. Rather, we find each of them taking the trouble to show, often many times, that the dream is one significant way in which God reveals himself to man.

Indeed, this new era of Western civilization was opened by the dream-vision that came to Constantine before his battle for Rome. Constantine was not the likeliest candidate to become emperor of the entire Roman world. He had been passed over for the rank of Caesar, and probably only saved his life by fleeing the court to join his father's army in Britain. When his father was dead, and

Constantine had patiently gained recognition, his chance finally came for the bold, almost desperate move against Maxentius at the Milvian Bridge. The pagan world regarded the outcome of this battle as directed by divine providence.

> When the Senate erected a triumphal arch to his honor in A.D. 315, Constantine, in the dedication thereon, ascribed his victory not only to the greatness of his imperial genius, but also to the "inspiration of the godhead."[1]

The pagan story of foreboding owls whose appearance on the city walls of Rome announced the doom of Maxentius, along with other current writings, expressed the same general feeling. A few years later the court orator Nazarius added still further that at the Milvian Bridge the dead Caesar Constantius had personally come to his son's assistance at the head of a heavenly army.

## The Christian account

The first account that mentioned the insignia carried by Constantine's army, the Christian sign called the labarum, was written by Lactantius, who was probably closer to Constantine than any other Christian writer. This brief account was included as part of a historical work published soon after the events. In it Lactantius told of the dream of the emperor:

> Constantine was directed in a dream to cause *the heavenly sign* to be delineated on the shields of his soldiers, and so to proceed to battle. He did as he had been commanded, and he marked on their shields the letter X, with a perpendicular line drawn through it and turned round thus at the top, being the cipher of Christ. Having this sign, his troops stood to arms.[2]

Eusebius also told the story of Constantine's victory, in two places. In the *Church History*, which he wrote about 315 A.D., he described only how Constantine had asked in prayer to Jesus Christ

[1] Hans Lietzmann, *A History of the Early Church*, Cleveland, The World Publishing Company, 1961, Vol. III, p. 75.
[2] *Lactantius, Of the Manner in Which the Persecutors Died*, XLIV, *The Ante-Nicene Fathers*, op. cit., VII, p. 318. Unless otherwise noted, further references to the fathers are found in *A Select Library of the Nicene and Post-Nicene Fathers*, published by Wm. B. Eerdmans Publishing Company, Grand Rapids, Michigan, various dates.

for the protection of God before the battle, in which Maxentius was defeated "in a remarkable manner." He added that Constantine ordered a cross placed in the hand of the statue erected to him, with an inscription stating that he owed the victory to this symbol.[3]

Some twenty years later, after Constantine's death, Eusebius added the details that the emperor had told him as a friend. Constantine had affirmed that before his decision to fight for the liberation of Rome he had reflected on his need for powerful aid against Maxentius and had meditated on the attitude of his own father toward the one, supreme God. Eusebius then told of the young Caesar's prayer and what happened:

> Accordingly he called on him with earnest prayer and supplications that he would reveal to him who he was, and stretch forth his right hand to help him in his present difficulties. And while he was thus praying with fervent entreaty, a most marvelous sign appeared to him from heaven, the account of which it might have been hard to believe had it been related by any other person. But since the victorious emperor himself long afterwards declared it to the writer of this history, when he was honored with his acquaintance and society, and confirmed his statement by an oath, who could hesitate to accredit the relation especially since the testimony of after-time has established its truth? He said that about noon, when the day was already beginning to decline, he saw with his own eyes the trophy of a cross of light in the heavens, above the sun, and bearing the inscription, CONQUER BY THIS. At this sight he himself was struck with amazement, and his whole army also, which followed him on this expedition, and witnessed the miracle.
>
> He said, moreover, that he doubted within himself what the import of this apparition could be. And while he continued to ponder and reason on its meaning, night suddenly came on; then in his sleep the Christ of God appeared to him with the same sign which he had seen in the heavens, and commanded him to make a likeness of that sign which he had seen in the heavens, and to use it as a safeguard in all engagements with his enemies.
>
> At dawn of day he arose, and communicated the marvel to his friends: and then, calling together the workers in gold and precious stones, he sat in the midst of them, and described to them the figure of the sign he had seen, bidding

[3] Eusebius, *Church History*, IX.9.

them represent it in gold and precious stones. And this representation I myself have had an opportunity of seeing.[4]

Eusebius then went on to describe the sign, the labarum, which became the insignia of the Christian emperors, and also told of Constantine's determination to follow the divine vision in his own life. This story has stuck in the craw of modern rationalistic historians, particularly religious historians. Lietzmann dealt with it merely as an example of legend building. The late nineteenth-century translators of the fathers were scandalized, and the French Catholic church historian Duchesne dismissed the event with these words:

> As to the visions, by day and by night, we have no reason to doubt Eusebius when he tells us that they were related to him by Constantine: but it is difficult for the historian to appreciate the exact value of such testimony, and speaking generally, to investigate with any profit into such personal matters. Leaving, therefore, to mystery the things which belong to mystery, we will confine ourselves here to stating facts known as facts, and to acknowledging that Constantine undertook the war against Maxentius, and in particular the encounter at the Milvian Bridge, in firm conviction that he was under the protection of the Christian God, and from that time he always spoke and acted, in religious matters, as a convinced believer. The monogram of Christ, painted upon the shields of his soldiers, displayed at the top of the military standards, (labarum), soon stamped upon the coins, and reproduced in a thousand different ways, gave an unmistakable expression of the opinions of the emperor.[5]

Indeed, the eminent religious historians today do not seem to question how Constantine became so conscious of the need for Christian conviction. Perhaps they believe that he understood all the excellent theological reasoning that runs through their own minds.

## The attitude of the church historians

While this was certainly not the only dream told in the ecclesiastical histories of the time, these works show almost as much

[4] Eusebius, *The Life of Constantine*, I, 28–30.
[5] Monsignor Louis Duchesne, *Early History of the Christian Church*, London, John Murray, 1931, Vol. II, pp. 47f.

reticence about telling dream experiences as people do today. These experiences were actually relied on very little in presenting the history and activity of the early church. Two others of these historians, Socrates and Sozomen, followed Eusebius' account of Constantine's vision of conversion. Both of them also told how Constantine's mother, St. Helena, visited Jerusalem on the inspiration of a dream and so was led to discover the true cross. Sozomen countered the idea that her information had instead been given by a Jew with these words:

> But it seems more accordant with truth to suppose that God revealed the fact by means of signs and dreams; for I do not think that human information is requisite when God thinks it best to make manifest the same.[6]

Both writers then described the churches that the emperor ordered built in Jerusalem to commemorate this discovery.

In general, these authors were no more concerned with dreams and visions than the secular writers of the period, perhaps even less than the slightly earlier Tacitus and Suetonius. Only two or three further references occur in each of their histories. In one place Eusebius told of a gnostic sect who boasted that certain demons sent them dreams and lent them protection, and in another he recounted briefly the divine vision given to Dionysius of Alexandria, which we have already discussed. The third story was about Natalius, a confessor, who became involved in heresy even though he was warned about it in visions. But when the heretics elected him bishop and gave him a salary of 250 denarii a month, Natalius was so afflicted through the whole night that he went early in the morning to the legitimate bishop to ask forgiveness and to be taken back into the fold—a story very similar to one we shall hear from Jerome's own hand about himself.[7]

Socrates added two stories, one of the Empress Dominica, who was warned in dreams of the death of her child as she and the Emperor Valens withstood Basil the Great. The other was the dream of Justina's father, in which he saw the imperial purple brought forth out of his right side; when he told it, the emperor had him assassinated, but then married Justina, who bore him a son, the Emperor Valentinian, and a daughter, who married The-

---

[6] Socrates, *Ecclesiastical History*, I.2 and 17; Sozomen, *Ecclesiastical History*, I.3; II.1.

[7] Eusebius, *Church History*, IV.7; VII.7; and V.28.

odosius the Great. Socrates also mentioned the fact that Ignatius of Antioch had a vision of angels who sang hymns in alternate chants, and so introduced the mode of antiphonal singing.[8] In the later writings of Theodoret it was mentioned that John Chrysostom had been shown in a dream where he would be buried, and that the Emperor Theodosius, while still only a general, dreamed of being invested with the imperial robe and crown by Bishop Meletius of Antioch.[9]

Sozomen did include several stories about dreams and visions connected with the imperial city of Constantinople. He told how Constantine was directed by God in a dream to abandon the rebuilding of Troy and seek another spot for his capital city; obedient to the dream, the emperor was then led by the hand of God to Byzantium, where he constructed a city whose wonders the historians described. Sozomen went on to tell that in one of its Christian temples, his own friend Aquilinus received a divine vision in the night, by which he was healed of an illness, and later was instructed about the power of the cross in another such vision. In telling how Gregory of Nazianzen took over in Constantinople at the end of the Arian controversy, Sozomen added a delightful story about the healing of a pregnant woman in Gregory's church, concluding that in the church of Constantinople "the power of God was there manifested, and was helpful both in waking visions and in dreams, often for the relief of many diseases and for those afflicted by some sudden transmutation in their affairs."[10]

Constantine himself placed an inscription over the gateway of his city, which said "that Christ had helped him on account of his constant and devout reverence for the 'divine'; Christ had quenched the fire of the tyrant, and granted him the rulership of the entire world."[11] Indeed, there is no more reason to discredit the historians who told of God's guidance of Constantine in dreams and visions than there is to discredit Carl Sandburg, who repeats the stories of Lincoln's dreams. There is no reason, that is, unless one is stuck with a theory of reality that denies the possibility of divine knowledge in dreams. As far as Constantine's morals are concerned, those who suggest that what he did to his family precluded

[8] Socrates, *Ecclesiastical History*, IV.26 and 30; VI.8.
[9] Theodoret, *Ecclesiastical History*, V.35 and 6.
[10] Sozomen, *Ecclesiastical History*, II.3; and VII.5.
[11] Lietzmann, op. cit., pp. 8off.

anything from God simply forget that David also ordered the death of his own son, while the fact that Henry VIII ordered the death of his wife did not keep him from having quite a religious influence in the Protestant world.

## An example today

If these Christian stories about Constantine seem simply incredible, however, it will be well to consider some facts about a modern Christian warrior, General George Patton, who followed much the same pattern, with the same brilliance and many of the same faults. Patton was a deeply religious man, who half expected and feared a "call" that might send him into the ministry; yet he often abused his position and power. According to the reserved young teacher, Joe Rosevich, who was his personal secretary for over three years, Patton's superb military intuitions often came in sleep, undoubtedly from dreams.

One of these nocturnal inspirations has been described in detail in Ladislas Farago's definitive biography of this great general. It occurred one December night in 1944, during the fateful Battle of the Bulge. Rosevich answered a 4 A.M. summons to the office in Luxembourg, and arrived to find Patton ready to dictate, still in his rumpled pajamas, with part of his uniform hastily thrown over them. Quickly, point by point, he laid out the order for an attack to be mounted at the very time the Germans themselves were jumping off to attack. They "were stopped cold in their frozen tracks," Rosevich recalls, and thus Patton avoided a further threat to his beleaguered army.

A few days later, when success was assured, Patton discussed with his secretary the way his inspiration for the operation had come that night. At 3 A.M. he had opened his eyes with a start—as on so many other occasions, for no apparent reason. He had not, in fact, known that the German attack was coming; he was simply wide awake, the idea that it was going to happen and that he knew what to do about it fully formed in his mind. It was in this way, he went on, that every one of his inspired ideas had come. It could be "inspiration or insomnia," Patton suggested. But his secretary had so often responded to calls in the night that he knew very well how close the general was to his dreams, and how ready to act when inspiration came in them.[12]

Whatever trouble we have in understanding the source of Constantine's uncanny genius, there are many of us old enough to remember George Patton, and to realize how probable this account is, and how much help it offers in understanding the genius of this man in the face of Nazi aggression.

It is interesting to find that similar stories also circulated around the life of another religious emperor, Julian the Apostate. The Roman historian Ammianus Marcellinus recorded that as this last pagan emperor faced his struggle for power, he was visited in a dream by "the genius of the Roman Empire." In this way Julian was prepared, while his opponent Constantius was beset with evil visions and premonitions, even in broad daylight. After Julian's success this spirit came once more to him. This was just before his fatal battle with the Persians. This time his vision left the tent sorrowful, with head veiled. The Emperor went out into the night and a star fell with a streak of light from the sky. Next day Julian was killed, according to Ammianus, whose meticulous accuracy and intimacy with the court at this time made him famed as the reliable historian of this last period of opposition to Christianity.[13]

## The struggle for orthodoxy and the view of dreams

As warfare ceased against the Christian church, it began within, in the struggle against heresy, primarily in the great Arian conflict. In this struggle the man who stood almost singlehanded in support of orthodoxy against government interference and dissensions was Athanasius. As bishop of Alexandria from 328 to 373, he showed a courage and brilliance that laid the foundations of later orthodoxy. Three times he went into exile, and three times he returned. Nearly all historians of this period show admiration for this great man, this monumental figure whose writings are authoritative for the theologians of all churches, Protestant, Catholic, and Orthodox alike.

In an early work, *Against the Heathen*, and in a late work,

---

[12] Ladislas Farago, *Patton: Ordeal and Triumph*, New York, Dell Publishing Company, 1965, p. 254.
[13] Lietzmann, op. cit., pp. 234 and 286f.

*The Life of St. Antony*, Athanasius showed that he shared the early Christian attitude toward dreams and visions as revelations of an unseen world. At the same time he was careful, even wary, in interpreting them. In his sermon for Easter in the year 341 he admonished his people to beware of those who use dreams and false prophecies to lead men astray, and referred to the specific statement in Deuteronomy 13. Again, in the *History of the Arians* he referred to the dream-vision of Daniel in which the prophet saw the Antichrist (7:25), showing how the interpretation applied specifically to the Emperor Constantius. Because he believed in dreams and supernatural experiences, Athanasius did not hesitate to refer to the dream material of the Bible as authoritative.[14]

The mature genius of Athanasius was already evident in the first part of his great masterpiece of Christian apology, *Against the Heathen*, written when he was only twenty-one. Early in this work he insisted on the importance of the dream as a means of revelation:

> Often when the body is quiet, and at rest and asleep, man moves inwardly, and beholds what is outside himself, travelling to other countries, walking about, meeting his acquaintances, and often by these means divining and forecasting the actions of the day. But to what can this be due save to the rational soul, in which man thinks of and perceives things beyond himself? . . .
>
> For if even when united and coupled with the body it is not shut in or commensurate with the small dimensions of the body, but often, when the body lies in bed, not moving, but in death-like sleep, the soul keeps awake by virtue of its own power, and transcends the natural power of the body, and as though travelling away from the body while remaining in it, imagines and beholds things above the earth, and often even holds converse with the saints and angels who are above earthly and bodily existence, and approaches them in the confidence of the purity of its intelligence; shall it not all the more, when separated from the body at the time appointed by God Who coupled them together, have its knowledge of immortality more clear?[15]

Sometime after his exile in the Egyptian desert, in his maturest years, Athanasius wrote his *Life of St. Antony*, which reveals his

---

[14] Athanasius, *Festal Letter*, XIII.7; *History of the Arians*, VIII.75.
[15] Athanasius, *Against the Heathen*, II.31.5 and 33.3.

admiration for this charismatic old hermit. It also shows that Athanasius continued to appreciate man's capacity to see more than the physical world. Antony's converse with angels and demons, his extrasensory knowledge, his healing power, and other gifts are described at length. Thus this work reveals much that does not come out in Athanasius' more polemic writings. Revelation of the spiritual world was one matter upon which Arians and Trinitarians were not divided, and this great theologian's concern with the pressing conflicts of theology and practical church polity kept him from developing his ideas on this subject. Although a later age has looked at his account of Antony's life with raised eyebrows, a careful reading of the document with the insights of depth psychology shows that there is an objective reality to this account.

Athanasius' view of the angelic and demonic betrays little tendency to concretize these beings materialistically. They are seen as psychic in origin, but real nonetheless. These encounters with non-physical reality, which most men have only in dreams, were given to Antony both in direct daytime visions and also in the night, when many of them unquestionably refer to visions in dreams. Athanasius recorded the life of Antony with a mature psychological understanding, showing that the state of a man's soul and his fearfulness have a profound effect upon the kind of experience he has and the outcome of it. Just as Antony could have converse with these realities in his waking hours, ordinary men can and do meet them in sleep.

Athanasius quoted with approval Antony's statements:

> And if even once we have a desire to know the future, let us be pure in mind, for I believe that if a soul is perfectly pure and in its natural state, it is able, being clear-sighted, to see more and further than the demons—for it has the Lord who reveals to it—like the soul of Elisha, which saw what was done by Gehazi, and beheld the hosts standing on its side.[16]

One cannot understand the power and vitality of Athanasius if he excises the *Life of St. Antony* from his important works. His interest in Antony shows his own religious aspiration and his belief that the soul can be given direct communication with the non-physical, the spiritual world, without the mediation of reason or sense ex-

[16] Athanasius, *Life of St. Antony*, 34.

perience. Dreams are one form of this communication. This writing, coming from the later part of this great man's life, shows the conviction of his inner life that he had expressed very clearly and simply in one of his earliest writings.

## The same view of dreams among the orthodox leaders

Following Athanasius in the Greek church were four men who established the trinitarian thinking of the Eastern church once and for all. These four doctors of the Greek church, who forged the structure of orthodox faith, had much in common. The three great Cappadocians—Basil the Great, Gregory of Nazianzen, and Gregory of Nyssa—were the theologians, while Chrysostom was the great preacher who popularized the ideas of these men and made them current in the popular mind. All four men had an ascetic interest. All four have been sainted by the church. All four were from cultured Christian families, had been educated in the best pagan tradition of the time, and were only baptized as adults after an inner conviction of the reality of Christian experience. All four were bishops of the church during the last half of the fourth century; two of them were brothers, and two were close friends. In the writings of all of them one finds the conviction that God speaks through the medium of dream-vision experiences. Since not all of their writings are accessible in English, one must plow through the Latin or Greek of Migne in order to find many of their teachings on this subject.

We turn first of all to Gregory of Nyssa, whose major philosophical work, *On the Making of Man*, deals directly with the meaning and place of sleep and dreams in man's life. Since this work was written to supplement the *Hexaemeron* of his brother Basil, it undoubtedly reflects the ideas accepted by all three Cappadocians on the subject of dreams. Tillemont has described this Gregory as "the master, doctor, peacemaker, and arbiter of the churches." He was moved by the brilliant theological tradition of Origen, which Gregory Thaumaturgus had introduced to Asia Minor, and he carried on the best of that tradition.

According to Gregory of Nyssa, when man is asleep, the senses and the reason rest and the less rational parts of the soul appear to take over. Reason is not, however, extinguished, but smoulders like a fire "heaped with chaff," and then breaks forth with insights that modern dream research calls "secondary mentation." As Plato had previously suggested, and as Jung later confirmed, in the sleeping state the mind has

> . . . by its subtlety of nature . . . some advantage, in ability to behold things, over mere corporeal grossness; yet it cannot make its meaning clear by direct methods, so that the information of the matter in hand should be plain and evident, but its declaration of the future is ambiguous and doubtful,— what those who interpret such things call an "enigma."

Gregory then referred to the dreams around Daniel and the patriarch Joseph, concluding that the interpretation of dreams is indeed a gift from God. And he went on:

> As then, while all men are guided by their own minds, there are some few who are deemed worthy of evident Divine communication; so, while the imagination of sleep naturally occurs in a like and equivalent manner for all, some, not all, share by means of their dreams in some more Divine manifestation. . . .

His reasoning was that there is a natural foreknowledge that comes in an unknown way through the non-rational part of the soul —the "unconscious," according to modern depth psychology—and it is through this part of the soul that God communicates himself directly.

Gregory then enumerated the other meanings that dreams can have, offering quite a complete outline of the subject. He suggested that dreams can provide mere reminiscences of daily occupations and events. Or, they can reflect the condition of the body, its hunger or thirst, or the emotional condition of the personality. Dreams can also be understood in medical practice as giving clues to the sickness of the body. Again anticipating depth psychology, he wrote:

> Moreover, most men's dreams are conformed to the state of their character: the brave man's fancies are of one kind, the coward's of another; the wanton man's dreams of one kind, the continent man's of another; the liberal man and the avaricious man are subject to different fancies; while these

fancies are nowhere framed by the intellect, but by the less rational disposition of the soul, which forms even in dreams the semblances of those things to which each is accustomed by the practice of his waking hours.[17]

Indeed, far from stating a superstitious belief, Gregory laid out quite well the principle upon which today's analytical study of dreams is based.

In addition to these philosophical reflections on the religious and secular meaning of dreams, Gregory also told, in a sermon entitled "In Praise of the Forty Martyrs," of a dream that occurred while he was attending a celebration in honor of the soldiers who had withstood a last, brief outburst of persecution. In the dream these men of Licinius' army, Christians who had died in the freezing waters of a pond rather than deny their faith, came upon him with rods and lashes for his Christian lethargy. When Gregory awoke, he was shaken to the depth by his lack of Christian devotion. Thus, he told, he was started on the serious practice of his Christian way. In the same sermon he also told of a soldier attending the memorial celebration who was healed by the appearance in a dream of one of these martyrs.[18] Again, in his *Life of St. Gregory Thaumaturgus* he told of the dream-vision in which the earlier Gregory had beheld the Virgin Mary and John, who discoursed before him, answered his questions on the Trinity, and gave him thoughts which he then put forth in his well-known creed, *A Declaration of Faith.*[19]

It is clear that philosophically, practically, and personally Gregory of Nyssa believed the dream could be a revelation of depths beyond the human ego. Interestingly enough, however, like many of the Latin fathers, he did not mention the relation of false dreams and demons, although this matter was discussed by his brother Basil.

Basil the Great left as great an impact on the church as any of the Eastern fathers. Because of his outstanding mind he was able to stand against the best of the Aristotelian, Arian thinkers. His personal courage in confronting the Arian Emperor Valens, and his willingness to suffer for orthodoxy, gave conviction to those under

---

[17] Gregory of Nyssa, *On the Making of Man*, XIII; quotations from paragraphs 10, 12, and 17. (This chapter is included in the appendix.)

[18] S. Gregorii Nysseni, *In Quadraginta Martyres*, J.-P. Migne, *Patrologiae Graecae*, Paris, 1862, Vol. 46, Col. 783–86.

[19] *De Vita S. Gregorii Thaumaturgi*, Migne, op. cit., Col. 911–13. Also told in *The Ante-Nicene Fathers*, Vol. 6, p. 7.

his banner. His personal asceticism and his writings on this subject deeply moved his own age and laid the foundations for later Greek monasticism. Here he showed the influence of another great theologian, Origen.

In his commentary on Isaiah Basil indicated that the scriptures were intended by God to be somewhat difficult to comprehend. First, they were meant to exercise our minds and keep them occupied and away from lower things, and second, they were designed to take longer to understand because the things we have to work over longer stay with us longer. And for much the same reason, therefore, dreams are obscure and involved so that they require our sagacity and mental agility in no slight degree. He concluded:

> The enigmas in dreams have a close affinity to those things which are signified in an allegoric or hidden sense in the Scriptures. Thus both Joseph and Daniel, through the gift of prophecy, used to interpret dreams, since the force of reason by itself is not powerful enough for getting at truth.[20]

That Basil believed in continuing to consider dreams is indicated by the letter he wrote to a woman in which he interpreted the dream she had sent him. He suggested to her that her dream meant she was to spend more time in "spiritual contemplation and cultivating that mental vision by which God is wont to be seen." In introducing The Hexaemeron, his exposition on cosmology based on the opening chapters of Genesis, he referred with approval to "the testimony of God Himself" in Numbers 6 that only Moses came to know the Lord face to face, while he spoke to all others in a vision or a dream. Twice in his treatise On the Spirit he referred to the fact that the Spirit spoke through dreams to the patriarchs Joseph and Jacob.[21]

In spite of his theoretical agreement that dreams are sources of revelation, Basil found them a cause of embarrassment. In his early asceticism he learned that they spoke of levels of the human psyche that he could not control by his rational mind, and so he warned Gregory of Nazianzen that it is better not to sleep too hard, because this opens the mind to wild fancies. It was hard for Basil to

---

[20] S. Basilii Magni, Commentarium in Isaiam Prophetam, Prooemium 6f., J.-P. Migne, Patrologiae Graecae, Paris, 1888, Vol. 30, Col. 127–30.
[21] Saint Basil the Great, Letter CCLXXXIII, To a widow; The Hexaemeron, Homily I.1; On the Spirit, V.12 and XXVI.62.

bear the fact—now commonly accepted by modern psychology—that dreams do compensate for one's conscious attitude. Even worse was Basil's experience with his former friend Eustathius. This turncoat ascetic and his friends told dreams and interpretations against Basil that put him in a very bad light. In making his reply, Basil had to admit that some dreams do come from God, but warned that every dream is not a prophecy. They can be false and demonic, he added, and "bring strife and division and destruction of love." He complained about the gossipy nature of the non-Christian dream interpreters and warned Christians to stay away from them. He concluded the defense of his reputation from Eustathius' attack with these words:

> Let them therefore not give occasion to the devil to attack their souls in sleep; nor make their imaginations of more authority than the instruction of salvation.[22]

It is surprising that this is the first time we come upon an expression of such negative feelings about the misuse of dreams, that up to Basil there had not been this concern about pagan or unorthodox interpreters in the writings of the fathers.

Gregory of Nazianzen was one of the most attractive of these fourth-century figures. Willing to give himself to the doctrines laid down by Origen and Athanasius, and to use all his energy and eloquence to support them, he was able to put Christian love first. His letters reveal the depth of his personal relationships, and in the orations his honest understanding and teaching have been preserved, summing up the thinking of the orthodox leaders in its clearest and most palatable form. Alone among the Greek fathers Gregory shared the title of "Divine" or "Theologian" with John of the Gospels. He was a close friend of Basil the Great and spent much time in ascetic practice at Basil's retreat. Against his own wishes, he first took the small see of Sasima to help his friend. Later he was asked to come to Constantinople, where he rallied the orthodox forces with his educated mind and his personal purity. The building of the great center of orthodoxy, the Church of the Resurrection, in the Eastern capital was the work of Gregory. But when his person caused embarrassment as president of the Second Ecumenical Council in 381, he resigned both as patriarch of Con-

---

[22] Saint Basil the Great, Letter II, Basil to Gregory, 6; Letter CCX, To the notables of Neo-Caesarea, 6.

stantinople and as president of the council and went into retirement from the world until his death.

Had not Gregory left us his theological poems, we would not realize the important part that dreams played in his life. Since these poems tell about Gregory himself, they tell things that did not have a place in his arguments against heretics. They reveal a theory and practice on dreams that was integrated in one consistent theological pattern. He told in the second book of these poems:

> And God summoned me from boyhood in my nocturnal
> dreams, and I arrived at the very goals of wisdom.[23]

The very themes of Gregory's life, his purity, his devotion to the Trinity, were given and reinforced by his dreams. In the story of one of them he told how chastity embraced him as two maidens who came to him with warmth and affection. When he asked who they were, they replied: Temperance and Virginity. Then they asked him to mix his mind with theirs, his torch with their torch, so that they might place him near the light of the immortal Trinity. This vision of the night led him to renounce the "severe yoke of marriage" and give himself to the ascetic way.[23] In another place he told that this nocturnal vision was the hidden spark that set his whole life aflame for God.[23]

Again, Gregory told of a dream in which he saw himself sitting on a throne in humble fashion. From this spot he was speaking and people came from all sides to hear his words. Then they began to argue what he should say,

> But from my mouth there poured forth
> That the Trinity alone ought to be adored. . . .[24]

In other places he referred again to the fact that Chastity embraced him through his dreams,[24] and that he was promised by his mother to God, to whom he was bound by "the dangers and the favors of the night."[24]

In one place in his poems he counseled caution in interpreting dreams, in these words:

[23] S. Gregorii Theologi, Carminum, Liber II, 994–95, XCVIII; 930–33, lines 229–84; 990–91, XCII, lines 5–6; J.-P. Migne, Patrologiae Graecae, Paris, 1862, Vol. 37, Cols. 1449–50, 1367–74, and 1445–46.
[24] Carminum, Liber II, 844–45, lines 7–29; 992–93, lines 4–5; 822–23, lines 805–10; Migne, op cit., Cols. 1255–56, 1447–48, and 1225–26.

*Devote not your trust too much to the mockery of dreams,*
*Nor let yourself be terrified by everything;*
*Do not become inflated by joyful visions,*
*For frequently a demon prepares these snares for you.*[25]

Yet in his funeral oration on Basil, Gregory praised the visions of Jacob and Joseph to show that his friend had been greater than these dreamers.[26]

The records of this attractive life, which was crucial for Christian orthodoxy, leave no doubt that one very important fount of his religious conviction was his experience of God through dreams, and there is nothing in his theoretical writings to suggest that it should not be so with other men.

During the period of these great fathers there were many lesser lights in the Greek church. While it is impossible to discuss them all, St. Cyril of Jerusalem was one who produced some of the standard fourth-century expositions of the faith. In a letter he wrote to the Emperor Constantius, Cyril described a public vision that occurred in Jerusalem in 351. On the morning of Whitsunday, the seventh of May, about 9 A.M., people flocked out to see the bright cross that hung in the sky, brighter than the sun, stretching from Golgotha to Mount Olivet and remaining there for several hours. He regarded this sign as a good occasion for announcing the beginning of his episcopate to the Emperor.[27] Here was an experience as objective and powerful to that time as the experiences of the flying saucer today, one similar to that attested by Constantine.

## John the Golden-mouth

To the Greek church the writings of St. John Chrysostom, John the Golden-mouth, have authority approaching that of the scriptures themselves. The great Cappadocians were primarily concerned with establishing the Nicene faith. Chrysostom went on from there and preached in his inimitable fashion on every subject, bringing the implications of this faith to bear on every aspect of the life in Constantinople of the late fourth and early fifth century. Chrysostom

[25] *Carminum,* Liber I, 608–9, lines 209–12; Migne, op. cit., Cols. 943–44.
[26] Gregory Nazianzen, Oration XLIII, *The Panegyric on S. Basil,* 71f.
[27] *Nicene and Post-Nicene Fathers,* Second Series, Grand Rapids, Michigan, Wm. B. Eerdmans Publishing Company (no date), Vol. VII, pp. ivf.

lived what he spoke, and imposed a Christian discipline on his
clergy and the court. This brought the enmity of the Emperor's
wife Eudoxia. He was banished and recalled and then banished
again.

Even in exile the banished bishop continued as a power. The
Empress finally sent him on foot to one of the farthest and most
inhospitable spots in the Empire, and as he neared the end of his
journey he died. In all this he maintained the finest Christian perspective. No wonder his age revered him as a saint and brought his
body back to Constantinople to rest with the Emperors and patriarchs. His works were balanced, careful, and irenic. His liturgy and
his homilies became the model of later Greek piety and religion.
His commentaries on scripture anticipated modern methods of exegesis; they were far more historical and critical than allegorical.

While there is no systematic treatment of dreams in the works of
Chrysostom, he had enough to say about them, and in enough
different ways, to indicate that he shared the current sophisticated
attitude toward dreams as a source of revelation. Perhaps even more
significant, he made no suggestion at any point that the Christian
should not take his dreams seriously. There is not even a reference
anywhere in his writings to the biblical passages that urged caution
in the use of dreams. He simply expressed his ideas about their
value when an appropriate handle appeared in one of his homilies.
For instance, in the discussion of Pentecost in the homilies on Acts
he stated specifically:

> To some the grace was imparted through dreams, to others
> it was openly poured forth. For indeed by dreams the prophets
> saw, and received revelations.[28]

According to Chrysostom dreams are sent to those whose wills are
compliant to God, for they do not need visions or the more
startling divine manifestations, and he mentioned Joseph, the father
of Jesus, and Peter and Paul as examples of this truth.[29]

A dream is no small thing, he concluded. Rather, it can be a
revelation and sure sign from God, as we know not only from the
New Testament, but from the dreams of Abimelech and Joseph as
well. And like those of Daniel, dreams can be given for the common
good, as well as for personal direction. To show this he discussed at

[28] St. Chrysostom, *Commentary on Acts*, V.1.
[29] Ibid., XXXIV.6; *Homilies on Matthew*, IV.1of., 18; V.5.

length the dreams surrounding the birth of Jesus.[30] In other discussions he also mentioned twice the consolation that Paul had received from God in dreams and how these experiences encouraged him to go on.[30]

Chrysostom took care to explain that we are not responsible for our dreams; one is not disgraced by the things he may see in them, or guilty for what he may do there. These images are given, and do not reveal an external physical reality. They do, however, reveal spiritual reality for men, who can even be buffeted so much by angels in dreams that they are as terrified as if a hostile human being were coming at them. The dream may also reveal the state of man's soul, his bad conscience, and bad character. They can even deter him from acting on his immoral desires.[31]

As Chrysostom came to each dream experience in the parts of the Bible he commented on, he took them up one by one, trying to understand them directly. He wrote page after page on the way in which God revealed himself to Abraham and then to Joseph in dreams and visions of the night.[32] He took particular pains to understand the nature of the *ekstasis* of Peter's dream on the rooftop in Joppa, which he considered was one way of perceiving spiritual reality.[32] In all of the discussions of Paul's experiences and the dreams around the life of Jesus, there is no hint that these experiences did not happen in the present, just as they did in those times. Only once, in talking about Jesus' baptism, did he suggest that such visions did not occur as often in his own time. He concluded that God gives them when they are needed—"evermore at the beginnings of all wonderful and spiritual transactions"—but that faith could take the place of these more obvious break-throughs of the divine into human life.[32]

Sir Thomas Browne once mentioned how often Chrysostom himself dreamed of Paul, remarking that it was no wonder, since Paul was so much on the saint's mind,[33] but I have not been able to lo-

---

[30] Ibid., IV.18; LXXXVI.1; LIII.6; VIII.4; IX.5; XII.3; *Commentary on Acts*, XXXIX.2; XLIX.1f.

[31] *Homilies on Romans*, XXIV (Ver. 14); XII (Ver. 13); *Homilies on Matthew*, LIII.6.

[32] S. Joannis Chrysostomi, *Homiliae in Genesin*, XXXVI and LXIII, J.-P. Migne, *Patrologiae Graecae*, Paris, 1863, Vol. 53, Cols. 332–35; Vol. 54, Cols. 541–49. *Commentary on Acts*, XXII; *Homilies on Second Corinthians*, XXVI.1ff.; *Homilies on Matthew*, XII.3.

[33] *The Works of Sir Thomas Browne*, ed. by Charles Sayle, Edinburgh, John Grant, 1912, Vol. III, p. 553.

cate these personal references. Yet in other places Chrysostom left
no doubt how these great fathers of orthodoxy viewed the tantaliz-
ing phenomena of sleep; dreams were one possible and often used
means of revelation from the world of spirit.

## An original thinker

About the same time in the early fifth century, Synesius of
Cyrene came into the church, with his Neo-Platonic education
under the famous Hypatia. He also brought a wife, because of whom
he had become Christian at about the age of thirty-five. Soon
after, he was asked to become bishop of Ptolemais. He agreed, on
condition that he might continue to hold certain of his heterodox
opinions; his conditions were accepted, and Synesius became one of
the most noticed bishops of his time. It was no wonder; he was a
handsome man, whom one church historian called "as original as
he was attractive."[34] Brought up in North Africa with great wealth,
his cultivated interests ranged over everything from geometry and
astronomy to farming. The book he wrote on dreams represents the
culmination of early Christian thinking on the subject.

In many ways this work of Synesius' is the most thoughtful and
sophisticated consideration of dreams to be found until we come to
the modern studies of Freud and Jung. Although almost forgotten
in the West, it was highly valued throughout the centuries in the
Eastern Empire, and as late as the fourteenth century it was the
subject of a detailed and careful commentary written by Nicephorus Gregoras, one of the intellectual leaders of his time. He
remarked on its difficulty and obscurity, which he was trying to
make clearer for ordinary men.

The real difficulty (aside from the ancient terminology) was that
Synesius wrote a very complex study of dreams. He was not trying
to simplify the subject; instead, he was laying the foundation both
philosophically and psychologically for the value of dreams. Augustine Fitzgerald, who has provided a very scholarly translation of this
and some of Synesius' shorter works, remarks that no one in the
ancient world made a finer attempt to understand the nature of
the human psyche.

Synesius believed that the entire universe was a unity, and there-

[34] Duchesne, op. cit., Vol. III (1938), p. 203.

fore the dream expressed its meaning as well as, and for certain reasons better than, any other experience of it. The dream, according to Synesius, arises from the faculty of the imagination which lies halfway between reason and the world around us (or rational consciousness and sense experience). It participates in both of these entities, but is not tied down to space and time as is the experience of our senses. His description of the imagination was quite close to Jung's empirical description of the collective unconscious. In sleep the imagination is free; untrammeled by space and time, it can converse with the gods, explore unknown universes, and discover the stars. He concluded that:

> One man learns . . . while awake, another while asleep. But in the waking state man is the teacher, whereas it is God who makes the dreamer fruitful with His own courage, so that learning and attaining are one and the same. Now to make fruitful is even more than to teach.[35]

Having laid out a sound reason for discussing dreams, Synesius then enumerated the blessings to be gained from studying them. For the pure soul who receives impressions clearly, a proper study of dreams gives knowledge of the future with all that this implies. Important information is also provided about bodily malfunction and how it can be corrected. Far more important, this undertaking brings the soul to consider immaterial things, and so, even though it was begun merely to provide knowledge of the future, it turns the soul to God and develops a love of him. Synesius also told how dreams had helped him in his writings and in his other endeavors, and how they often gave hope to men who had been oppressed by the difficulties of life.

He made fun of people who relied on the popular dream books, insisting that only by constantly checking dreams with experience could they be understood. Their essential nature is personal, and they must be understood by the dreamer in terms of his own life. Some of them seem to be direct revelations of God, but there are also many dreams that are obscure and difficult to interpret. He suggested that anyone who is serious in studying them should keep a record so that he knows his sleeping life as well as his waking one. He even saw the connection between mythology and dreams and

[35] Augustine Fitzgerald, *The Essays and Hymns of Synesius of Cyrene*, London, Oxford University Press, 1930, p. 332 (from *Concerning Dreams*).

explained his belief that the myth is based upon the dream; a true interest in mythology helps a man find the more vital meaning in his own dreams. Finally, Synesius showed the reason for his belief that dreams give hints about eternal life. As the sleeping state is to the waking one, so the life of the soul after death is to the dream life, and thus this state gives some idea of the kind of life that is led by the soul after death.

This work was such an important summary of the church's thinking that we include a condensation of it in the appendix. Synesius' importance is recognized and commented on by psychologists of the Jungian school. His enthusiasm for his subject is clear, as in the following:

> For whatsoever things of use and of sweetness those hopes, which nourish the race of men, hold out to him, and as many things as fear controls—things ominous and withal gainful—all these things are found in dreams, nor by any other thing are we so enticed towards hope. And the element of hope is so abundant and so salutary in its nature that, as acute thinkers maintain, men would not even be willing to continue life, if it were only to be such as they had at the beginning . . . these hopes have such force that he who is bound in fetters, whenever he permits the will of his heart to hope, is straightway unbound. . . . And when it spontaneously presents hope to us, as happens in our sleeping state, then we have in the promise of our dreams a pledge from the divinity.[36]

This was the same thinking that was expressed by the great doctors of orthodoxy.

## The doctors in the West

The four men who became recognized as the doctors of the Western church were Ambrose, Augustine, Jerome, and Gregory the Great, each of them quite different. Ambrose and Gregory, who came from wealthy and influential families, were in high civil positions when they turned to the church, while Augustine and Jerome were the scholars, with an interest in classical literature. Each of these men taught that dreams and visions were one of God's methods of revelation to man, and we shall find this expressed in both per-

[36] Ibid., pp. 345f.

sonal and theological terms in their writing. We shall also consider three other writers in this period who touched significantly on the same subject—Macrobius, Sulpicius Severus, and John Cassian.

There have been few personalities in Western Christianity as attractive as Ambrose, the bishop of Milan in the last part of the fourth century. Born about the year 340, he was educated for a civil career and rose rapidly to become governor of Northern Italy in the time when Milan was the seat of Western imperial power. He was still being instructed for baptism when the people of Milan chose him for their bishop by popular outcry. Believing that this was a call from God, he submitted, gave his wealth to the poor and the church, and studied theology, interpreting the conclusions of Eastern orthodox thinking for the West. He stood firm against the encroachments of civil authority, and once even called the Emperor Theodosius to public repentance for what he had done. Through actions like this Ambrose set the pattern for Western church-state relationship. His works on ethics, theology, and asceticism became standard for the Latin church, and many of his hymns are still sung.

Ambrose's own experience left no question of the depth of his belief about dreams. In his most famous letter, the letter to Theodosius calling for his repentance, he declared that God in a dream forbade him to celebrate communion before the Emperor unless he repented. These are his dramatic words:

> I am writing with my own hand that which you alone may read. . . . I have been warned, not by man, nor through man, but plainly by Himself that this is forbidden me. For when I was anxious, in the very night in which I was preparing to set out, you appeared to me in a dream to have come into the Church, and I was not permitted to offer the sacrifice. . . . Our God gives warnings in many ways, by heavenly signs, by the precepts of the prophets; by the visions even of sinners He wills that we should understand, that we should entreat Him to take away all disturbances . . . that the faith and peace of the Church . . . may continue.[37]

Ambrose was deeply moved by the death of his brother Satyrus, who had also resigned an official post in order to be with Ambrose and relieve him of his secular affairs. Out of his grief Ambrose wrote the two exquisite books in which he contemplated his brother's

[37] St. Ambrose, Letter LI, 14.

death and then his own belief in the resurrection. At the close of Book I he compared the former nights of painful separation with his present joy in dreams that brought him the reality of his brother's presence. He wrote:

> I grasp thee whether in the gloomy night or in the clear light, when thou vouchsafest to revisit and console me sorrowing. And now the very nights which used to seem irksome in thy lifetime, because they denied us the power of looking on each other; and sleep itself, lately, the odious interrupter of our converse, have commenced to be sweet, because they restore thee to me. They, then, are not wretched, but blessed, whose mutual presence fails not, whose care for each other is not lessened, whose mutual esteem is increased. For sleep is a likeness and image of death.
>
> But if, in the quiet of night, our souls still cleaving to the chains of the body, and as it were bound within the prison bars of the limbs, yet are able to see higher and separate things, how much more do they see these, when in their pure and heavenly senses they suffer from no hindrances of bodily weakness. And so when, as a certain evening was drawing on, I was complaining that thou didst not revisit me when at rest, thou wast wholly present always. So that, as I lay with my limbs bathed in sleep, while I was (in mind) awake for thee, thou wast alive to me, I could say, "What is death, my brother?"[38]

In another famous letter Ambrose described how the bodies of the two martyred saints Gervasius and Protasius were discovered and brought to the place he consecrated to them in his new church. This event made a great stir in Milan, and a man long-blind was healed during the dedication. Ambrose, however, played down the part his own experience had played; he mentioned only that before the discovery a prophetic spirit had entered his heart. It was Augustine, describing the period after his baptism in Milan, who told that the place where the saints' bodies had been hidden was revealed to Ambrose in a dream.[39]

In his more theological writings Ambrose supported the idea that the Holy Spirit speaks through dreams. He showed that an angel who speaks through a dream is functioning at the direction of the

[38] St. Ambrose, *On the Decease of Satyrus,* Book I, 72f.
[39] St. Ambrose, Letter XXII; St. Augustine, *The Confessions,* IX (VII) 16; *The City of God,* XXII.8.

Holy Spirit, since angelic powers are subject to and moved by the Spirit. The Holy Spirit not only confirmed his presence to Joseph in a dream, but directed Paul through visions and intuitions, and spoke particularly clearly to Peter in his dream-trance experience on the rooftop in Joppa. Ambrose discussed at length the experiences in Acts 10, saying, "How clearly did the Holy Spirit express His own power!" Not long before his death he also wrote a letter of instruction to a certain group of Christians who had been without a bishop for a long time, recommending to them the way Peter had prayed for his revelation in Joppa.[40] In all these discussions he treated the dream and the vision as being of equal authority.

In a book on the duties of the clergy Ambrose referred to the wisdom and prudence of Solomon, Joseph, and Daniel as exemplified by their ability to interpret dreams. Inferring that his own clergy might do the same, he remarked that "confidence was put in [Daniel] in all things, because he had frequently interpreted things, and had shown that he had declared the truth."[41] His long discussion of the dreams in his commentary on Joseph begins with the words "Finally divine grace bloomed forth in the body. Since he dreamed . . ." The prophetic nature of Joseph's dreams was revealed not only in the events of the patriarch's own life, but also in certain events in the life of Jesus. Thus, Ambrose showed, these dreams represented the fact that the life of Joseph in the Old Testament was symbolic of the Christ to come. The eleven sheaves, for instance, symbolized not only the eleven brothers, but also the eleven disciples who adored Jesus. In the second book of *On the Decease of Satyrus* he followed much the same thinking in considering Jacob's dream at Bethel and his encounter with the angel at Jabbok.[41] In none of his works was any reference made to the biblical passages that are critical of dreams.

Ambrose believed that dreams and visions were one means that people had of contact with those who had died, and of knowing and experiencing things beyond the ordinary senses. He also believed that the Holy Spirit used dreams to instruct and warn men when they needed such admonition, and that a part of wisdom was the prudent intepretation of these experiences from God.

[40] St. Ambrose, *On the Holy Spirit*, II.V.37; II.X.101–6; *Letter LXIII*, 16.
[41] St. Ambrose, *Duties of the Clergy*, II.X.54f.; II.XVI.82ff.; *De Joseph Patriarcha*, II.7f.; III.9ff., 485–88; J.-P. Migne, *Patrologiae Latinae*, Paris, 1882, Vol. 14, Cols. 675–78; *On the Decease of Satyrus*, Book II (*On Belief in the Resurrection*), 100.

## Between two worlds

If any one man stands between this era and the modern world, it is Augustine. There is good reason for his influence, not only on Western Catholicism, but perhaps even more on Luther, Calvin, and the entire Protestant world. Within his own experience, Augustine was able to stand between several pairs of worlds, particularly the spiritual and the worldly. His youth was spent carelessly, or sometimes almost carefully, doing what he should not and absorbing gnostic Manicheism. At the same time he became an excellent teacher of rhetoric, and so came to Milan, where Ambrose was bishop. Here he was touched by Neo-Platonism and, turning toward Christianity, he sought out personal contact with Ambrose.

It was then he had his great religious experience, which brought him to baptism. And in the next half century Augustine went on, almost singlehanded, to prepare the intellectual foundation for Western Christian thinking for another thousand years. Until Aquinas became accepted, Augustine was *the* Western theologian.

Not only do we find in him a deeply religious, a mystical longing and experience, but here was one of the most inquiring minds of the time. His philosophical ability and the penetrating psychological insight his studies show would make him important entirely apart from his Christian connections. The study of dreams is for him a significant tool in understanding both the psychology of man and his relations with God and the spiritual world.

Augustine's psychology and epistemology were based upon a sophisticated psychophysical dualism in which he saw two essentially different kinds of reality—the purely corporeal or physical, and the non-corporeal or "mental," which is spiritual in nature. This is essentially the theory that Lovejoy supports in his classical study of modern epistemology, *The Revolt Against Dualism*. It is again essentially the theory of the objective psyche proposed by Dr. C. G. Jung and his followers to explain the experiences of their medical and psychological practice.

Augustine's study of perception was as sophisticated as any in the ancient world. He saw reality as consisting of outer physical objects to which we react with our bodies, and then of the impressions of this sense experience, impressions that are "mental" in nature. We then have the inner perception of this sense experience, and finally the mental species in its remembered form. It is the action of the ego (called the will by Augustine) that unites these perceptions to the object. In one place he calls the faculty of imagination the bridge that mediates the object to consciousness, thus presenting almost the same thinking as that worked out by Synesius of Cyrene. Augustine saw man as possessing an outward eye that receives and mediates sense impressions, and an inward eye that observes and deals with these collected and stored "mental" realities that are called memory.

In addition to the realities that come from outer perception and from inner perception of "memories," autonomous spiritual realities (angels and demons) can present themselves directly to the inner eye. These are of the same nature as the stored "mental" or psychic realities that are perceived inwardly. Augustine writes that men in sleep or trance can experience contents that come from memory "or by some other hidden force through certain spiritual commixtures of a similarly spiritual substance."[42] These autonomous realities are non-physical; yet they can either assume a corporeal appearance and be experienced through the outward eye, or be presented directly to consciousness through the inner eye in dreams, visions, and trances. Thus through dreams man is presented with a whole storehouse of unconscious memories and spontaneous contents; he is given access to a world that the fathers called the realm of the spirit, which Jung has seen as the "objective psyche." Man has no control over this world; the contents of a dream or vision are as objective, as much "given" to the inner eye as sense experience is to the outer eye.[43]

[42] St. Augustine, *On the Trinity*, XI.4.7.

[43] The references to Augustine's psychology of perception and parapsychological experiences are scattered throughout his writings. Most important theoretically are his discussions on the nature of man in his book *On the Trinity*, where he sees in man's inner diversity and unity an archetype of the nature of God. Discussions are found in this work in Book II, 5.9, 6.11, 13.23, and 18.34; Book III, 1.4 through 11.26; Book IV, 17.22, 21.30ff.; Book VIII, 7.11; Book XI, 4.7, 5.8f., 8.13 through 11.18; Book XII, 15.24; Book XV, 12.21f., 13.22. In addition in Book III of Augustine's *Literal Commentary on Genesis* he presents a complete discussion of his psychology, together with his theory of angels, and in Book XII he discusses ideas about different kinds of visions in relation to modes of revelation. (*De Genesi ad Litteram*, J.-P. Migne, *Patrologiae Latinae*, Paris, 1887, Vol. 34.) Shorter discussions are found in Letter IX, To Nebridius, and Letter CLIX, To Evodius. There is even one reference to the relation between dreams and providence in his earliest Christian work, *The Soliloquies*, II.10ff. This belief is found from the earliest to the latest of his works, and it is essential to his teaching.

Augustine admitted that it was easier to describe what the angels and demons do than to explain what they are. In discussing the dreams that people have of the dead, he stated that it is not the dead person himself who appears (just as one doesn't expect the living person to know when one dreams of him), but "by angelical operations, then, I should think it is effected, whether permitted from above, or commanded, that they seem in dreams to say something. . . ."[44] Just as angels have direct contact with man's psyche and present their messages before the inner eye, so also do demons.

> They persuade [men], however, in marvelous and unseen ways, entering by means of that subtlety of their own bodies into the bodies of men who are unaware, and through certain imaginary visions mingling themselves with men's thoughts. whether they are awake or asleep.[45]

Augustine, as we can see, considered these experiences equally important whether they came in a waking vision or a dream.

When asked by his lifelong friend, the bishop Evodius, how man can have such strange experiences of telepathy and clairvoyance, or precognition, Augustine replied that ordinary experience is strange and difficult enough to explain, and such things as this happen, but they are beyond man's power to explain. It should also be noted that, although Augustine believed that these visionary experiences are important sources of knowledge, the highest experience of God transcends even these means. Dreams and visions do not reveal the nature of God, but they are given by him. They are examples of his providential care, his gifts. Referring to a dream that had brought conviction about life after death, he wrote of this vision: "By whom was he taught this but by the merciful, providential care of God?" It is also clear that Augustine found the operation of the inner eye and its lack of dependence upon the physical body to be excellent grounds for belief in the persistence of man's psyche after death.[46]

In addition to presenting a theory of dreams and visions, Augustine also discussed many examples of providential dreams in the course of his writings. One of the most important of them was the famous dream of his mother Monica, in which she saw herself standing on a measuring device while a young man whose face

[44] On Care to Be Had for the Dead, 12.
[45] The Divination of Demons, V.9, New York, Fathers of the Church, Inc., 1955, Vol. 27, p. 430.
[46] Letter CLIX, To Evodius, 2ff.; The City of God, XI.2.

shone with a smile approached her. She was crying, and when he asked why, she told of her sorrow that her son turned away from Christ. He told her to look, and suddenly she saw Augustine standing on the same rule with her and she was comforted. Realizing the significance of the symbolism, she was able to go on praying for him with patience and hope; her dreams and visions are also mentioned in several other places in *The Confessions*.[47]

Fascinating stories of a number of parapsychological dreams, as well as stories and discussions of other influential dreams, are found in various places in Augustine's writings. Particularly in the correspondence with Evodius there are accounts of dream experiences as uncanny as any in the modern literature on psychical research, or even in the Bible. Some of this material is included in the appendix, and there are other references in a letter to Alypius and in *The City of God*,[48] as well as in material already referred to. It is no wonder Augustine was led to study these experiences so thoroughly, and with such faith in his Christian calling.

## *Jerome, the scholar*

While Jerome was not the most charming of the fathers, he certainly made his talents known, and his influence on the church was great. An irascible disposition and a caustic pen kept him in trouble with both friends and enemies. But at the same time he spared no effort on his writings, which gave real support to orthodox Christianity against the threat of Arianism and did much to popularize asceticism and monasticism. His monumental gift to the church was his translation of the Bible into the Latin Vulgate.

Born into a wealthy Christian family about the same time as Augustine, in the last great age of the Western Empire, Jerome grew up in the great port of Aquileia at the head of the Adriatic. There he studied the pagan masters and began his own literary work. He studied in Rome, traveled, collected a library, and gathered a congenial group of friends who were interested in becoming monks. It was then that his life was completely altered by a dream. Jerome had been torn between the classics and the Bible, which seemed to him rough and crude in comparison with Cicero and Plautus.

---

[47] *The Confessions*, III.19, V.17, VI.23, VIII.30.
[48] Letters IX and CLIX; Letter CCXXVII; *The City of God*, IV.26 and XXII.23.

He would fast, keep vigil, but only to read the masters. In Antioch he became very sick, and this experience happened, as he wrote dramatically in one of his most famous letters:

> Suddenly I was caught up in the spirit and dragged before the judgment seat of the Judge; and here the light was so bright, and those who stood around were so radiant, that I cast myself upon the ground and did not dare to look up. Asked who and what I was I replied: "I am a Christian." But he who presided said: "Thou liest, thou art a follower of Cicero and not of Christ. For 'where thy treasure is, there will thy heart be also.'" Instantly I became dumb, and amid the strokes of the lash—for He had ordered me to be scourged—I was tortured more severely still by the fire of conscience, considering with myself that verse, "In the grave who shall give thee thanks?" Yet for all that I began to cry and to bewail myself, saying: "Have mercy upon me, O Lord: have mercy upon me." Amid the sound of the scourges this cry still made itself heard. At last the bystanders, falling down before the knees of Him who presided, prayed that He would have pity on my youth, and that he would give me space to repent of my error. He might still, they urged, inflict torture on me, should I ever again read the works of the Gentiles. . . .
>
> Accordingly I made an oath and called upon His name, saying: "Lord, if ever again I possess worldly books, or if ever again I read such, I have denied Thee." Dismissed, then, on taking this oath, I returned to the upper world, and, to the surprise of all, I opened upon them eyes so drenched with tears that my distress served to convince even the incredulous. And that this was no sleep nor idle dream, such as those by which we are often mocked, I call to witness the tribunal before which I lay, and the terrible judgment which I feared. . . . I profess that my shoulders were black and blue, that I felt the bruises long after I awoke from my sleep, and that thenceforth I read the books of God with a zeal greater than I had previously given to the books of men.[49]

Soon after this Jerome went into the desert as a hermit. He continued to study, and after a few years went to Constantinople under Gregory of Nazianzen. Then began his varied career as scholar,

[49] St. Jerome, Letter XXII, To Eustochium, 30.

biblical consultant in Rome, and, until his death, head of his monastic community in Bethlehem.

Jerome's studies also gave him good reason to value dreams and visions. In commenting on Jeremiah 23:25ff., he shared Jeremiah's concern, indicating that dreaming is a kind of prophesying that God can use as one vehicle of revelation to a soul. It can be a valuable revelation from God if a man's life is turned toward him. But dreams can become idolatrous (like prophecy in the name of Baal) when they are sought and interpreted for their own sake by one who is serving his own self-interest instead of God. The value of the dream depends upon the person who seeks it and the person who interprets it. Sometimes God sends dreams to the unrighteous, like those of Nebuchadnezzar and Pharaoh, so that the servants of God may manifest their wisdom. Thus it is the duty of those who have the word of the Lord to explain dreams.[50]

This word could not be sought, however, by pagan practices like incubation. In commenting on Isaiah 65:4, Jerome went along with the prophet and condemned people who "sit in the graves and the temples of idols where they are accustomed to stretch out on the skins of sacrificial animals in order to know the future by dreams, abominations which are still practised today in the temples of Aescylapius."[50] Later, however, in the discussion of Galatians, he brought up specifically the dream in Acts 16 in which Paul "was given the true light (*lucam vero*)."[50]

Jerome made no distinction at all between the vision and the dream. In his discussions of the dream of Joseph about Mary's conception one would not know whether the vision had been received awake or asleep. God speaks through sleep as well as through visions. He also referred to Peter's dream in Joppa as a revelation of God with symbolic meaning, and in another place called attention to the prophecy of Joel as proof that the Spirit had been poured out upon men. He discussed again and again what Ezekiel had to say about visions. For instance, Ezekiel 8:2 shows that "the visions make it possible to know the sacred things," while the next verse reveals that the prophet, because he was "brought in visions of God to Jerusalem," was carried there "not in the body,

---

[50] S. Eusebii Hieronymi, *Commentariorum in Jeremiam Prophetam*, IV.23; *Commentariorum in Isaiam Prophetam*, 65; *Commentariorum in Epistolam ad Galatos*, 1; J.-P. Migne, *Patrologiae Latinae*, Vol. 24, Paris, 1863, Cols. 858–61 and 656–57; Vol. 26, Paris, 1884, Col. 353.

but in the spirit." Thus the dream-vision is seen as transcending time and space. There are also pages and pages about the dreams in Daniel.[51]

In the life of St. Hilarion Jerome gave a picture very similar to that of St. Antony by Athanasius. He wrote of the same concern with demons that come in the night, and although he did not use the word "dream," the whole character of the book suggests that this was what he was speaking of.[52] But when he got into his sharpest conflict, the controversy with his former friend Rufinus, Jerome revealed a great deal more about the attention these men paid to dreams.

In the heat of this fight, involving subtle charges of heresy, Rufinus questioned Jerome's sincerity by suggesting that he had not been faithful to the oath given in his great conversion dream; he must have reverted to secular reading to remember so much. Jerome came back with a defense of his religious calling, and also of his memory, and then he attacked Rufinus for letting himself be misled by someone else's dream. This was a reference to the dream of one of Rufinus' friends, who had dreamed of him as a ship crossing the seas to Rome with answers to many puzzling questions. Rufinus had introduced his own *Apology* by telling this vision and how it had compelled him to begin the book to which Jerome objected so much. Jerome then told more of his own dreams, which would make an interesting study for an analyst. He told of dreaming of himself as a young man in a toga about to make a speech before his teacher of rhetoric, and of waking up happy that it was not so. He also told about dreams of his own death, and of "flying over lands, and sailing through the air, and crossing over mountains and seas!"[53] Indeed, Jerome, in his anger, revealed almost as much about the way these great Christians regarded their own dreams and the depth of their own experience as others who wrote out of love.

Yet in the end he fixed the ground firmly that would justify a

---

[51] St. Jerome, Letter LVII, To Pammachius, 6; *The Perpetual Virginity of Blessed Mary*, 4, 5, and 7; Letter CXXV, To Rusticus, 2; Letter XLI, To Marcella, 1; Also, S. Eusebii Hieronymi, *Commentariorum in Ezechielem Prophetam*, III, VIII.2ff; *Commentariorum in Danielem Prophetam*, II.1ff.; J.-P. Migne, *Patrologiae Latinae*, Paris, 1884, Vol. 25, Cols. 77ff. and 498ff.
[52] *The Life of St. Hilarion*, 6ff.
[53] *The Apology Against the Books of Rufinus*, I.30f., III.32; Rufinus, *Apology*, I.11.

growing fear of these experiences. In translating Leviticus 19:26 and Deuteronomy 18:10 with one word different from other passages, a direct mis-translation as we shall show, Jerome turned the law: "You shall not practise augury or witchcraft (i.e., soothsaying)" into the prohibition: "You shall not practise augury nor observe dreams." Thus by the authority of the Vulgate, dreams were classed with soothsaying, the practice of listening to them with other superstitious ideas.

## A contrast to Jerome

During these years another Westerner was writing who was to have an increasing influence on Western thinking for centuries. This was Macrobius, whose *Commentary on the Dream of Scipio* became one of the main philosophical handbooks of the Middle Ages, and also the most important and best-known dream book in medieval Europe. We know next to nothing about this man, except that he lived when Jerome did and that, although he may even have been a Christian, he based three popular works entirely on Cicero and the wisdom of classical Greece and Rome. He was one of the first of a group of summarizers who tried to gather together this wisdom for the people of the fourth, fifth, and sixth centuries. In his influence on medieval thought he stands right up with Boethius and Isidore of Seville.

Macrobius' *Commentary* presented a very simplified version of Platonism, in many ways inaccurate and far from the mark; yet it evidently made people who read it think they understood Plato. In fact, most of the Middle Ages got its knowledge of Plato and Platonic thought either from Chalcidius, who is practically forgotten today, or from the writing of this fourth-century summarizer. There are hundreds of manuscript copies of his *Commentary* still in existence, and it had run through thirty-seven printed editions before 1700.[54] No wonder the thought of Plato carried so little weight in the Renaissance; what Plato Macrobius offered was made into an understandable, oversimplified, and otherworldly base for medieval philosophy in the West. In it philosophy and a rather rigid dream interpretation were bound to one another.

The *Commentary* opened with several chapters in which Macro-

[54] William Harris Stahl, *Macrobius: Commentary on the Dream of Scipio*, New York, Columbia University Press, 1952, pp. 9ff., 60ff.

bius expounded and reiterated, in clear and concise Latin, the popular dream theory of his time, thus preserving for later ages what was essentially the theory of Artemidorus. He classified dreams as of five types. The first type is the enigmatic dream (*oneiros* or *somnium*), which conveys its message in strange shapes, veiled with ambiguity. This is the common dream, with many varieties. Next is the dream that foretells the future in a true way, the prophetic vision within a dream (*horama* or *visio*). Slightly different from this is the oracular dream (*chrematismos* or *oraculum*), "in which a parent, or a pious or revered man, or a priest, or even a god clearly reveals what will or will not transpire, and what action to take or to avoid." The fourth type of dream is the nightmare (*enupnion* or *insomnium*), which "may be caused by mental or physical distress, or anxiety about the future." These dreams arise from the conditions of the day before. Finally, there is the apparition (*phantasma* or *visum*), which "comes upon one in the moment between wakefulness and slumber. . . . [One] imagines he sees specters rushing at him or wandering vaguely about . . . either delightful or disturbing." To this class belongs the incubus with its sense of weight. The last two types, according to Macrobius, were "not worth interpreting, since they have no prophetic significance."[55]

This classification tells a great deal about the dream theory of the secular fourth century. It is interesting to see how much agreement there was between this theory and that of later church fathers. Macrobius also considered that the soul, when asleep and disengaged from bodily functions, was better able to perceive truth, but he discussed this only in Homer's symbolism about "the gates of horn and of ivory." Until the medieval Platonism was challenged in the twelfth century, this dream theory was treated by most civilized Westerners as simply accepted and common knowledge.

St. Martin of Tours was also contemporary with Jerome, and the man who wrote his biography was a good friend of both Jerome and Augustine. This was Sulpicius Severus, a Christian who was a highly educated lawyer. He practiced this profession until his wife's premature death about 392, when he entered the priesthood. While he had already gained a wide reputation, Sulpicius is remembered

[55] Ibid., pp. 87ff.

today mainly for his close friendship with Martin. Like his other work, his famous life of the saint was written in such polished and carefully styled Latin that he has been called "the Christian Sallust."

In this book he told about two dreams that were important in the life of this famed ascetic who had so much to do with spreading both Christianity and education in Gaul. Once when the weather became extreme Martin gave away his clothing until he had only his cloak, which he cut in two to cover a naked beggar. That night in his sleep St. Martin had a vision of Christ dressed in the part of the cloak he had given the poor man, and he heard Jesus saying to the angels, "Martin, who is still but a catechumen, clothed me with this robe." Later Martin was warned in a dream to visit his parents, who were still pagans. Obedient to the instruction, he set out to visit them, was able to convert his mother, and this was the last time he was to see his parents.[56]

In one of his undisputed letters Sulpicius also told of his own vision experience about the time Martin was dying. He spoke of the "light and uncertain" morning sleep—the kind of sleep when visions do occur—in which Martin appeared, clearly recognizable and "in the character of a bishop, clothed in a white robe, with a countenance as of fire." Martin then ascended into the air, followed by one of his disciples who had died not long before. Sulpicius then described with awe how he was still rejoicing over the vision when two monks brought the news of Martin's death, and how he was moved both by grief and by the knowledge that God shares the numinous depth of reality and his deepest mysteries in this way.[57]

John Cassian also wrote an interesting discussion of dreams about this time, in relation to nocturnal emissions. This section is available only in Latin, however; the nineteenth century was too prudish to translate and publish it. Since nocturnal emissions were considered polluting, the question arose as to whether the voluptuous dreams that often accompanied them would make a monk unworthy to receive the Eucharist. The monk with whom Cassian discussed this concluded that if a person's life is exemplary, then these dreams are sent by the enemy, the devil, and do not affect the moral quality of the dreamer. Even the best of men may be invaded with

[56] Sulpicius Severus, *The Life of Saint Martin*, III, Vf.
[57] Letter II, To the Deacon Aurelius.

this kind of dream. They are nocturnal illusions sent by the evil one.[58] Within two hundred years the last great doctor of the church, Gregory the Great, would find even more to fear in dreams than this.

## The beginning of darkness

Between the time of Augustine, Ambrose, and Jerome and that of Gregory, a great deal had happened in Italy. Rome had fallen, the Western Empire no longer existed as such, and the church had forgotten persecution. Italy had been overrun by Goths and Lombards, and then partly conquered again by the Emperor at Constantinople, whose regent resided in Ravenna. Education and culture had declined, and the dark ages were beginning. The influence of these conditions was quite apparent in Gregory the Great, who belongs more to the Middle Ages than to classical times.

Gregory, who was born in 540, was an educated Roman gentleman, but no more. He knew only his own language, had little philosophical or literary background. He came from a senatorial family and was an excellent and conscientious administrator in trying times, but without intellectual sophistication in any sense. Around him were the growing ignorance and superstition of a dying culture, and so Gregory was both more superstitious about dreams and more fearful of these experiences that held such interest for the common man. He admitted their validity on one hand, and warned in strong words of their danger on the other. For the first time in the church fathers the warning passages of Leviticus 19, Ecclesiastes 5, and Ecclesiasticus 34 were emphasized again and again. Jerome's anger and unconscious fear had done their work.

In two places Gregory described the six sources of dreams in almost identical words. The first was in the *Morals*, his discussion of the book of Job, and then in the *Dialogues*, where he was so concise and to the point that we quote him in full:

> It is important to realize, Peter, that dreams come to the soul in six ways. They are generated either by a full stomach or by an empty one, or by illusions, or by our thoughts combined with illusions, or by revelations, or by our thoughts

[58] Joannis Cassiani, *Collatio* XXII, *De Nocturnis Illusionibus*, J.-P. Migne, *Patrologiae Latinae*, Paris, 1874, Vol. 49, Cols. 1217-42.

combined with revelations. The first two ways we all know from personal experience. The other four we find mentioned in the Bible. If dreams did not frequently come from the illusions of the Devil, the wise man surely would not have said, "For dreams have led many astray, and those who believed in them have perished," (Ecclesiasticus 34:7, Douay), or "You shall not divine nor observe dreams." (Leviticus 19:26, Douay)* From these words we can readily gather how detestible dreams are, seeing that they are put into a class with divination. And if, at times, dreams did not proceed from our thoughts as well as from diabolical illusions, the wise man would not have said dreams come with many cares. (Ecclesiastes 5:2) And if dreams did not arise at times from the mystery of a revelation, Joseph would not have seen himself in a dream preferred to his brethren, nor would the angel have warned the spouse of Mary to take the child and flee into Egypt. Again, if at times dreams did not proceed from the thoughts in our minds as well as from revelation, the

---

* Not in the Confraternity-Douay version or the new Jerusalem translation. The Bible Gregory read was the Latin translation by Jerome, the Vulgate, on which the scholarly, long-used, and often-consulted Douay version was based. In it, as we have noted, the Hebrew word for soothsaying was given two very different meanings by Jerome. In three places he mis-translated the Hebrew. In II Chronicles 33:6 his incorrect rendition is still in use in the Confraternity-Douay version of the Bible.

This word (anan) occurs ten times in the Old Testament. In most cases in the current versions it is simply translated "soothsayer or soothsaying," although the words witch, sorcerer, magic, and diviner are also variously used, as well as "observer of times" in the King James version.

In Deuteronomy 18:14, II Kings 21:6, Isaiah 2:6 and 57:3, and in Jeremiah 27:9 where the word is used alongside of prophet, diviner, dreamer and sorcerer, Jerome translated it quite correctly as augur or augury (auguror, augur) which included the ideas of interpreting the hum of insects, the whisper of leaves, the flight of birds, and of divining by lightning and by the entrails of sacred birds and animals. In Micah 5:11 he translated it as "evil-doing" (maleficium). And in Judges 9:37, where it designates one of the places from which Abimelech's soldiers are approaching, generally called the "Diviners' Oak" in current translations, he rendered the Hebrew compound by the phrase "the oak which looks backward," (quae respicit quercuum).

But when Jerome came to the statement of the law in Leviticus 19:26 and Deuteronomy 18:10, and the direct negative valuation of these practices in II Chronicles 33:6, he changed the meaning of the word anan. He replaced the verb to practise augury or soothsaying (auguror) by the phrase "to observe dreams" (observo somnia). This direct mis-translation was in authoritative use throughout the Middle Ages, and it has not even yet been completely eliminated. (S. Eusebius Hieronymus, DIVINAE BIBLIOTHECAE: PARS PRIMA, J.-P. Migne, Patrologiae Latinae, Paris, 1889, Vol. 28, Cols. 361, 479, 567, 815, 830, 890, 944, 1105, and 1466.)

Prophet Daniel, in interpreting the dream of Nabuchodonosor, would not have started on the basis of a thought, saying, "Thou, O king, didst begin to think in thy bed what should come to pass hereafter: and he that reveals mysteries showed thee what shall come to pass." And a little later, "Thou O king, sawest, and behold there was as it were a great statue: this statue, which was great and high, tall of stature, stood before thee," and so on. (Daniel 2:29, 31) Daniel, therefore, in reverently indicating that the dream was to be fulfilled and in telling from what thoughts it arose, shows clearly that dreams often rise from our thoughts and from revelation.

Seeing, then, that dreams may arise from such a variety of causes, one ought to be very reluctant to put one's faith in them, since it is hard to tell from what source they come. The saints, however, can distinguish true revelations from the voices and images of illusions through an inner sensitivity. They can always recognize when they receive communications from the good Spirit and when they are face to face with illusions. If the mind is not on its guard against these, it will be entangled in countless vanities by the master of deceit, who is clever enough to foretell many things that are true in order finally to capture the soul by but one falsehood.[59]

In the *Dialogues* Gregory had already shown how "God strengthens timid souls with timely revelations in order to keep them from all fear at the moment of death." He gave several examples of men who were given warning of their death and reception into heaven by the revelation of dreams. He also told how Benedict, the abbot, once agreed to come on a certain day to lay out the site for a new monastery and, instead, came to one of his followers in a dream to give the instructions. In one instance he told how a very holy monk had all physical temptation taken away in a vision, and there were other examples of external events associated with dreams, quite different from the more psychic understanding of such happenings among the earlier fathers. Flowers were seen in a dream and their actual odor later appeared about the man's grave; after a dream of fire before the altar the very spot in the floor was found charred. In other stories a recalcitrant monk saw "with his own eyes the invisible dragon that had been leading him

---

[59] St. Gregory the Great, *Dialogues*, IV.50, New York, Fathers of the Church, Inc., 1959, pp. 261f. Also, *Morals: On the Book of Job*, VIII, 42f., Oxford, John Henry Parker, 1844, pp. 448ff.

astray," while still another died and was found lying outside the grave several times until the abbot forgave him by placing the consecrated Host on his breast.[60]

On the other hand, Gregory's letters to Theoctista, the Emperor's sister, reveal how he tried to get rid of "all phantasms of the body" and to find God through faith rather than in visions of him. It is hard to blame Gregory for wanting to forget the "legion of demons" and "tumults of thoughts" that pestered him. But in his *Pastoral Rule* he took a vision like Jacob's dream of the ladder to heaven to mean that those of high estate must be related to "the bed of the carnal." And in the same work he emphasized that Balaam's ass saw "an angel which the human mind sees not." He was also careful to point out to Theoctista how little Peter relied on the power of his vision in Joppa. To one of his bishops he inveighed against soothsayers and diviners of any kind, showing clearly his fear of pagan culture.[61]

Gregory was torn between two attitudes and experiences, and as "teacher of the Middle Ages" he passed on the same split. For six centuries the value of dreams was accepted with increasing credulity, and then with Aquinas, as we shall show in the next chapter, dreams were placed in an Aristotelian context and so nearly filed away that their value is ignored and even forgotten by the Christian church.

## The Dreams of Islam

Shortly after the death of Gregory the dream as a medium of revelation was given great emphasis in the new religion of Islam. This new spirituality, with roots in Christianity and Greek culture as well as in the Arab world, placed the dream in as central a position as any other culture. That same influence still exists in Islam today. But until Western scholars realized how much fascinating material this tradition had produced, and began to pore over its texts, most of us knew very little about the influence the dream has had in Mohammedan society. At a recent scholarly and scientific meeting on the dream, held in France, six of the twenty-five papers chosen for publication in book form pertained

[60] *Dialogues*, I.4, II.22ff., IV.47ff., op. cit., pp. 16f., 89ff., 258ff., 262f.
[61] Gregory the Great, *Register of the Epistles*, I.5, XI.45, IX.65; *The Book of Pastoral Rule*, II.5, III.12.

to the dream lore of Islam. It is significant that none of the studies in this volume, *The Dream and Human Societies,* related to the specific place of dreams in the Christian tradition.

Islam begins with the dream, for much of the Koran was delivered to the Prophet Mohammed in dreams or in a trancelike state. The Prophet's function was simply to record whatever was given. The first of Mohammed's revelations came to him at the cave on Hira, a hill not far from Mecca. There in the month of Ramadan, toward the end of the month, he fell asleep and heard a voice telling him to read, and he replied that he could not. He awoke from the dream and went outside the cave, where he saw a vision of the angel Gabriel, who told him that he had been selected as Allah's messenger. Later, after he returned home, his wife took him to a wise old man who taught him that the heavenly messenger he had seen was the same who had brought God's message to Moses. From this time until his death the Prophet's dreams formed one of the most important avenues of his inspiration.[62]

After the time of the Prophet major revelation through the dream or any other method was closed in Islam, but still anyone who dreamed of the Prophet was to view his dream as a true one. In addition the emphasis laid upon dreams by the Prophet led to a flowering of dream study in the popular culture and a proliferation of dream books such as is found in practically no other culture. This study was considered a scientific endeavor rather than a religious one, and it expanded and adapted the ideas of Artemidorus, whose book was soon translated into Arabic. Besides the catalogues of thousands and thousands of dream images, detailed methods of interpreting dreams were developed. These were careful and supposedly rational methods, rather than the prophetic interpretation found in the Old and New Testaments and the church fathers. This distinction, which is so fundamental to the understanding of dreams, also marks the real difference between the approach to dreams in Islam and the way they were valued in classical Christianity.[63]

[62] Surahs 96 and 97; also, introduction to *The Meaning of the Glorious Koran* (M. M. Pickthall), New York, Mentor Books, 1960, p. x.
[63] We do not attempt to do justice to this whole subject, which has been treated intensively by the several authors in *The Dream and Human Societies,* G. E. von Grunebaum and Roger Caillois, eds. (Berkeley, University of California Press, 1966), and in their prior publications.

Some of the most recent studies in this field, however, deal with the religious use of dreams among the Shiites and Sufis. In these sects of Islam, where prophecy was regarded as continuous rather than ceasing with the Prophet, the dream was considered the way par excellence through which the individual found entrance into *'ālam al-mithāl*, that stage of ontological reality lying between physical reality and the "world of intelligibles." Some of the great Arab thinkers were followers of these sects and left records of their own initiatory dreams, working out whole philosophies about the dream-vision and its relation to this realm. The closest Christian material is found in the dream analysis of Synesius of Cyrene and the visions of Swedenborg. This material becomes all the more significant and interesting as the parallels are seen in the studies of Freud, C. G. Jung, and other depth psychologists, concerning the reality of an objective psyche and its manifestation in dreams and in free or active fantasy. The mystical Sufi tradition, far from being an archaeological curiosity, is still very much alive in modern Islam. A similar tradition was also alive in Christianity through the Middle Ages, and there was far more intercourse between the two than we have usually realized. Let us turn now to this period in Western Christianity.

# seven

# Modern Christianity and the Dream

There is a long jump between the understanding of the fathers and the modern attitude toward dreams and visions, so long that it is hard to believe they have both been attitudes held by Christians. Yet by the end of the Middle Ages Thomas Aquinas was already putting into words a new thinking about God that would make it easy for the church to avoid most of these experiences. Later on, when skepticism about supernatural dreams and visions began to grow, the lack of a religious approach left only superstition to oppose the growing doubt. In the end the attitude of the skeptic became so generally accepted in Western culture that sensible people were embarrassed to hold any other belief. This attitude has not developed, however, as the careful decision of rational men; instead, it has grown more like an unconscious split in Western personality.

Indeed, it is surprising how little is known of what lies behind our modern ideas about the dream. Even the most specialized encyclopedias fail to list the men who wrote in this area of medieval thinking, and it has been almost by accident that I discovered the materials that show what was happening. Leads about the church's thinking have turned up in scholarly works on Chaucer and on ancient Greece, in one of Jung's careful footnotes, in fact almost anywhere but in writings about the church. Gradually a picture began to form.

On one hand was the speculative thinking that was so important in the church in this period, and here dreams were actually considered seriously up into the eighteenth century. Still, what was there to say about them that had not already been said? These writers were bound by the traditions of the church; and since the ancients, without scientific methods, had pretty well exhausted the speculative possibilities of dream evaluation, one had only to select the correct classifications and the theory that was right.

But then the church had to deal with both the experiences described in the Bible and the prohibition against observing dreams which Jerome had written into the Old Testament law. There were the actual visions and dreams experienced by people, and these raised problems. Most of the time the church took care to let people know that these came from any place but God, and that there was little need for them. There were individuals like Joan of Arc who were led to amazing efforts by the visions they had, and everyone knows what happened to her as a result. There were also the saints like Francis of Assisi, who had a vision at the very time the miracle of his stigmata was occurring, and St. Francis came near to condemnation before he was beatified. Even Luther often fought it out with the devil before tackling a problem in the outside world; in fact, Luther's famous inkwell was thrown at a vision of the devil. Many others, from St. Teresa to Jakob Boehme and John Bunyan, found their lives directed and changed by dreams and visions.

These experiences were hard for the church to accept unless they simply reinforced accepted doctrine. If, instead, the authority of the church seemed to be questioned, they were looked at with real suspicion. The medieval church feared any questioning of its authority, and confidence in a direct contact with God through dreams was just such a threat. The church thus gradually came to a position about such experiences which made it unnecessary (even unseemly) for most of us to take notice of them at all. All necessary truth about God had been laid down and men didn't need direct contact with him any more. As we look at this period, let us see how this way of thinking happened to come about in the church, and also how different it was from classical Christianity and how far it has influenced our own thinking and attitudes.

Let us look first of all at the medieval theory of dreams, considering two rather important works on this theory and also some bits of evidence showing how universal it was. We then turn to the influence of Aristotle through Aquinas, whose formulations led the church in the end to abandon any emphasis on the value of dream experience. Finally, following briefly the seesaw of opinion that occurred after that, let us consider some examples of significant dreams right down to modern times, which show that although the dream has been rejected in theory, it has remained important in practice.

## Medieval speculation

For several centuries after the time of the fathers there is almost no record of the thinking in the West about dreams and visions. These were the "dark ages" in Western Europe, when records of any kind were few and most people had not been either Christian or literate for very long. In the Eastern half of the Roman Empire, where Greek culture continued to flourish, there was no interruption in the traditions of the fathers. The same kind of dream experience the fathers had spoken of continued to be described by the spiritual leaders of the Eastern church, and the same thinking persisted.[1] In the fourteenth century, for instance, one learned Greek commentary was written on the theories of Synesius. But in the West, while here and there we find a dream remembered and recorded, there was little serious Christian thinking on any subject, dreams included. When the writings of Tertullian, Augustine, Cassian, Gregory, and others came into currency again in the West, what they had to say about most matters including dreams was seized upon and carefully studied and compared and elaborated. In both Catholic and Protestant traditions dreams were given serious study within the church almost into the modern era.

This would be difficult to discover from any of the standard sources, however. Most of them steer very clear of the subject and do not even mention the quite sophisticated thinking that preceded our own very definite ideas. My search for some of this material started from an important footnote in Jung's *Psychology*

[1] These experiences were a part of the lives of practically every one of the Orthodox spiritual leaders and were described with wonder and excitement. This is shown by G. P. Fedotov in *A Treasury of Russian Spirituality* (New York, Sheed & Ward, Inc., 1948), and it is also discussed in *Writings from the Philokalia on Prayer of the Heart* (London, Faber & Faber Ltd., 1954), and other works, as well as finding a place in Russian literature right down to the twentieth century, as in the brilliant stories of Nikolai Leskov, for instance (*Selected Tales*, New York, Farrar, Straus & Cudahy, Inc., 1961).

*and Religion: West and East,*[2] in which he quoted two writers who had summarized the thinking of the Middle Ages on dreams. One was a Jesuit priest, Benedict Pererius, and the other, Gaspar Peucer, was the son-in-law of the Protestant reformer Melancthon. Jung had cited a passage from each of their works in order to support his point that, while the medieval writings did not deny the possibility of God's spirit being poured out in dreams, neither did they exactly encourage this idea, because it was a practical threat to church authority.

Both of these men were writing on the subject of divination about the end of the sixteenth century. The theology of Thomas Aquinas has been formulated long before, but the full meaning of his neglect of the dream did not catch on very quickly. Until it did there was quite a different Christian attitude at work in most of the medieval church, and it would seem that the actual biblical and patristic tradition on dreams played a greater part in the growth of our modern culture than we are accustomed to believing. This possibility is rather interesting, and the discovery of Pererius' book shows that it is quite likely the fact.

Since this work has apparently never been translated from the medieval Latin before, except for Jung's quotations, the complete text of Part II concerning dreams is included in the appendix. The original work, written in 1598, which can be found in the rare book room at Harvard University, is entitled *De Magia: Concerning the Investigation of Dreams and Concerning Astrological Divination. Three Books. Against the False and Superstitious Arts.* It was ably translated for me by Elizabeth Shedd of Palo Alto, who is an expert in medieval Latin.

Pererius, who was concerned with the possibility of God's speaking to man through dreams, was also down to earth. His purpose was to establish that Christians had something to gain from considering their dreams, but he saw that certain people were too careful about examining every dream "anxiously and superstitiously." Nor could any one explanation account for all dreams, especially when some of them seemed to give such clear and sensible direction to life while others were so cloudy and obscure. And so he began his inquiry by asking: "Can one have any faith in dreams?"

For his answer Pererius turned to the authorities. He carefully

[2] C. G. Jung, *Collected Works,* Vol. 11, pp. 19ff.

considered the teachings of the Stoics and Epicureans, and then of the Bible and the fathers. He quoted Gregory I, Synesius, Augustine, Cassian, and Justin Martyr as his authorities. He discussed learnedly the theories of Plato, Aristotle, Porphyry, and Hippocrates, citing passages from Homer and Vergil and reciting the experiences of famous men. On this evidence he then determined that there were four causes of dreams. They were caused first of all by the body and its physical condition. Second, they were caused by the emotional life of the soul, its anger, its fear, its affections. They were also caused by the craft and cunning of the devil and his evil spirits, and these dreams, which were often obscene and impure, could sometimes foretell the future without any good reason. And finally there were divine dreams, which posed the important question of how to recognize them.

> As it occurs to me now (Pererius pointed out), one can determine whether a dream has been sent by God in two ways. First, certainly, the excellence of the thing signified in the dream: if things, of which certain knowledge can only reach man by the will and grant of God, become known to a man through a dream, they are of such kinds as are called "future contingencies" in the schools of theologians. Indeed they are the heart's secrets which, enclosed within the soul's deepest recesses, completely conceal themselves from all intellectual perception of mortals; and, finally they are the principal mysteries of our faith, made manifest to no one except by the instruction of God. A dream, therefore, which contains this sort of knowledge and revelation may be considered divine.
>
> Second, the divinely inspired dream is powerfully conveyed by a certain interior illumination and stirring of souls whereby God thus enlightens the mind, influences the will and convinces man of the trustworthiness and validity of this dream in order that he may clearly recognize that God is its author and freely decide that without any doubt he both wants and ought to believe in it.

At this point Pererius quoted Gregory, and then added:

> Thus, just as the natural light of the mind makes us clearly perceive the truth of first principles and embrace it with our approval immediately before the introduction of any proof, so indeed, when dreams have been given by God, the divine

light flooding into our souls has effect with the result that we recognize these dreams as being both true and divine and are confirmed in our faith.

Pererius then went on in scholastic style to discuss why God should use dreams, why he gives them to the uneducated, why they are obscure, and who should inquire into and interpret dreams. He concluded that the Bible is full of examples of divine dreams, and that God reveals himself in this way because the soul is freer and less analytic when it is withdrawn from the body and thus released from sense experience. In addition, God uses dreams to demonstrate his ability to reach men when no other force can, and to give evidence of the soul's immortality. Pererius believed, contrary to the ideas of Aristotle, that God does give his revelations to the uneducated just to show that worldly men can be cut off by their learning from the higher pursuits, and to show that piety is more important than knowledge.

Although one should not base the whole of his life upon a study of dreams, those sent by God can awaken a man to the direction and purpose, even the dangers of his life. Most important is finding the proper interpreter, and here Pererius held that

> . . . the shrewdest appraiser of human dreams, the most apt and accurate interpreter, will be naturally he who is most thoroughly versed in human affairs and likewise one who, as an extremely experienced man, has attained to a complete and perfect knowledge, confirmed by many tests of human character, interests, customs and persuasions, which also assume great variety in different men; one who, as it were, grasps the very pulse of man's social and individual activity.
>
> Yet again, it is up to him to explicate divine dreams who stands in readiness to apprehend them, since it is clear that no one can interpret them unless he be divinely inspired and instructed. "For no one has known," says Paul . . . "what is of God except the spirit of God." But this is especially so since the symbols of divine dreams are ordained through the plan and will of God alone and for this reason can be made known to men only through the revelation of God.

For a good interpreter of dreams, then, find a man who has had plenty of experience and is also open to the voice of God, and he probably has the makings of either a good psychologist or religious counselor in depth. Whatever else one may say of this scholastic

Jesuit, one certainly cannot call him naïve or unlearned. While he was not as original or as consistent as Synesius or Augustine, his approach to dreams was certainly more sophisticated than that of Gregory the Great, or, for that matter, of most moderns, except for Freud and Jung. It is an interesting commentary on our current valuation of the dream that in 1967 his book has to be translated from medieval Latin to be read.

## A Protestant takes the same approach

Gaspar Peucer's work, written a few years earlier, was also in Latin, but a French edition was published in 1584. It is called *Les Devins, ou commentaire des principales sortes de divination*. While Peucer wrote from a Calvinistic and humanistic background, he covered much the same ground as Pererius, so as to suggest that both men followed a generally accepted and well-known body of opinions about dreams.

Peucer included a more specific consideration of Macrobius' theories of dreams, and his discussion of the various kinds—*fantasme, somme, songe, vision,* and *oracle*[3]—probably came directly from Macrobius, who classified dreams as apparitions, nightmares or "mere" dreams, enigmatic dreams, prophetic visions, and oracular dreams. Peucer then went on to the causes of dreams, holding that there are natural causes that come from the body and the emotions, and spiritual causes from God, the holy angels, and demons. He made an unsatisfactory attempt to relate dreams to the physiology of the brain, whose function had recently become the subject of serious attention, and there was also an attempt to understand sleep in terms of the medical doctrine of humors. But the more Peucer tried to be knowledgeable about the science of his time and to relate dreams to these findings, the more absurd he seems. He believed like Pererius, however, that dreams that come from natural causes should be studied by the physician.

He also believed that demons were responsible for many deceiving dreams, such as those that occurred in ancient pagan temples

[3] The general significance of these words is obvious, except for *somme*, which means a nap, a brief sleep, or in this context a dream-content that does not persist but vanishes because it simply represents some irritation or condition of the day which has popped up to disturb one's sleep briefly; and *songe*, a dream as we know it, or more particularly, a dream-content expressed in symbolic language.

during incubation and "telles sont en tous temps les visions des anabaptistes, Enthousiastes & semblables frénétiques, bodillans en cachette après leurs nouvelles révélations (such as the visions of the Anabaptists, those fanatics who act as if they were deranged, always stalking stealthily after their new revelations)." He too discussed the dreams of the famous men of antiquity at some length. In addition he discussed visions, which he considered of the same category as dreams, drawing attention to some interesting group visions that occurred in his time. These he believed occurred most often in the air around fighting armies.

Peucer was more restrictive in his conclusions than Pererius, and he found that except for particularly holy people investigation of dreams is dangerous. He based this on the understanding that,

> Those dreams are of God which the sacred scriptures affirm to be sent from on high, not to everyone promiscuously, nor to those who strive after and expect revelations of their own opinion, but to the Holy Patriarchs and Prophets by the will and judgment of God. . . . [Such dreams are concerned] not with light matters, or with trifles and ephemeral things, but with Christ, the governance of the Church, with empires and their well ordering, and other remarkable events; and to these God always adds sure testimonies, such as the gift of interpretation and other things, by which it is clear that they are not rashly to be objected to, nor are they of natural origin, but are divinely inspired.

Here in effect is the intellectual snobbery of Aristotle, although not yet backed by the careful thinking necessary to support Aristotle's position. There was still a place for God to communicate with men, if they were saints at any rate, through divine dreams and visions.

## Confirmation from many sources

These works by Pererius and Peucer give an idea of the attitude toward dreams which came out of the Middle Ages, and here and there we find bits of confirmation like pieces of the puzzle. In the eighth century the Venerable Bede wrote in his ecclesiastical history of England about the monk Caedmon, who, like Solomon, was given a gift from God in a dream. Unlike Solomon, Caedmon had been tongue-tied in company, and during his dream he received the

ability to write and to sing poetry.[4] All through the Middle Ages
the delightful story of Theophilus of Adana and the salvation he
received in a dream was kept alive. This saint had been tempted
and had promised his soul in writing to the devil. But he repented,
and when the Virgin appeared to him in a vision, he saw that he
wanted no part of the deal. His prayers were answered that night;
he received back his bond in a dream, and awoke to find the
paper lying on his breast. This story circulated in one Latin translation after another until it was set down in final form by the Bol-
landist fathers in the *Acta Sanctorum*.[5]

Some time about the twelfth century an anonymous work *On the
Spirit and the Soul*[6] became so popular that it was included in the
works of various saints; it elaborated at length on the different ways
divine visions were received. Using Macrobius' classification of
dreams, this writer concluded that prophetic *visions* (L. *visione*, or
class of dreams) could be either corporeal, spiritual, or intellectual,
depending on whether they came through the senses, the imagination, or direct intuition. In the same period John of Salisbury followed much the same classification in discussing dreams in the
*Polycraticus*, while the great Jewish theologian Maimonides also
dealt with them as a source of prophecy in his chief work, *The
Guide for the Perplexed*.[7] Even the remarkably secular *Roman de
la Rose*, which was still enormously popular in the sixteenth century,
admitted that the dream was a way in which God could give revelation to men. Besides a careful account of dream theory, the entire
story of this poem was conceived as a dream.

The obscure cleric who captured the imagination of fourteenth-
century England in *Piers the Ploughman* also used dreams again
and again to get his message across. This poet, William Langland,
shared the ideas that were to be summarized so well by Pererius
and Peucer, and he wrote on the assumption that they were
true. His story showed that for him the vision of a dream was a
significant religious truth that could be seen and interpreted. In the
next century the writings of Chaucer gave a popular yet detailed and

---

[4] Baedae, *Opera Historica* (The Venerable Bede, *Ecclesiastical History of the
English Nation*), Book IV.24.
[5] Philip Mason Palmer and Robert Pattison More, *The Sources of the Faust
Tradition*, New York, Oxford University Press, 1936, pp. 58ff.
[6] Pseudo-Augustine, *De spiritu et anima*, published in Migne, *Patrologiae Latinae*, Vol. 40, Paris, 1887, among the works of Augustine.
[7] Moses Maimonides, op. cit., pp. 225ff. and 234ff.

knowledgeable picture of the clerical interest and reverence for dreams. In the *Canterbury Tales*, dream material contributed to many of the stories, and here the influence of Macrobius in Christian thinking was quite apparent. In fact, we do not find a clear separation at this time between secular and religious writing.[8] But meanwhile, inside the church something else was happening.

## A new teaching

With Thomas Aquinas a new teaching had arisen within the church which would one day take over the Christian approach to dreams. This happened because ideas from the Arab world—both directly and through Byzantium—had begun to penetrate the West, and Aquinas found himself in a very difficult position as a teacher. He found himself with two masters—the biblical and church tradition, and Aristotle—and these two masters said very different things about dreams and revelation. Aristotle said that dreams had no divine significance, and the church said they did. So Aquinas solved the problem exactly as the church does at the present time, by simply avoiding it as far as he could. In all the thousands of pages of the *Summa Theologica* he found room for only one side of the question. And this was surprising in view of his treatment of most other aspects of human life.

In his long section on prophecy and revelation in the *Summa*, (II,II.Q-171–74), he carefully discussed the dreams and visions of the Old Testament prophets and the kinds of images that came to them. He examined the relation of dreams to knowledge of the future, to angels and demons, to the beatific vision, and to ecstasy. Yet the closest he came to a conclusion about dreams and revelation was to say that:

> . . . abstraction from the senses takes place in the prophets without subverting the order of nature, as is the case with those who are possessed or out of their senses; but is due to some well-ordered cause . . . for instance, sleep . . .
>
> II,II.Q-173.3

[8] Two of the most interesting works that touch on the medieval thinking about dreams are by Walter Clyde Curry, *Chaucer and the Mediaeval Sciences*, New York, Barnes & Noble, Inc., 1960, and William Harris Stahl, *Macrobius: Commentary on the Dream of Scipio*, New York, Columbia University Press, 1952.

and to suggest that dreams were a lower form of prophecy (II,II.Q-174.3). The reason he did not come to any conclusion on the subject was that dreams did not really fit into his system, and so he put them back into the hopper.

This is quite clear in other places where Aquinas discussed dreams from the Old Testament. In the section on divination he considered the references in Genesis, Job, and Daniel that show that it is all right to practice divination by dreams. But then he explained that this was only lawful when the dream came from divine revelation or natural causes, and not if it came from demons or false opinion, and so the whole question boiled down to determining the causes of dreams. These were inward, coming from the soul and its imagining and from the body, or outward, as from the influence of the atmosphere, heavenly bodies, God, angels, or demons. For instance, Numbers 12:6 showed that the way God approached men was to use the ministry of angels, and these, Aquinas explained elsewhere, were nothing more than thoughts—*intelligentia intelligibilia*, or "thinking thoughts."[9] But one could never be quite sure which dreams came from demons and which from angels or any of the other causes. So Aquinas simply left the subject up in the air, without attempting to differentiate between them, leaving the implication that the whole matter should be avoided (II,II.Q-95.6).

Twice more he struggled to make sense of Numbers 12:6: "If there be among you a prophet of the Lord, I will appear to him in a vision, or I will speak to him in a dream." But Aquinas could not fit this into the philosophical system of Aristotle, and so in the end "the Philosopher" won and the Bible lost. In the end Aquinas actually went contrary to the Bible and the fathers in this matter of revelation (II,I.Q-113.3 and III.Q-7.8).

At the outset it was undoubtedly Aquinas' purpose simply to open the storehouse of Greek thought to Western Christians. But the Islamic medicine and astronomy and philosophy that were beginning to flood Europe were couched in Aristotle's terms rather than in the original Greek thought. There seemed to be no choice but to translate Christianity and the Bible point by point into the language of Aristotle. It did not seem to bother Aquinas that this

[9] The scholarly Dominican priest Victor White goes into this question carefully, as well as other aspects of Aquinas' theory of reality, in his work *God and the Unconscious* (Cleveland, World Publishing Company, 1961), in Chapters 10, 6, and 7.

created a theology based upon only half of the Christian story, or that a large part of the New Testament was played down. He simply ignored not only the dreams, but the experiences of angels and demons, the healings, tongue speaking, and miracles in general in most of the New Testament, particularly in the Book of Acts.

Indeed, there is no place for dreams either in the philosophic system of Aristotle or in the theology of Aquinas. According to both of these men we receive knowledge only through sense experience, and the only thing peculiar about dreams is that we become more sensitive to sense experience at night. To settle this Aquinas quoted Aristotle:

> *Impressions made by day are evanescent. The night air is calmer, when silence reigns, hence bodily impressions are made in sleep, when slight internal movements are felt more than in wakefulness, and such movements produce in the imagination images from which the future may be foreseen.*
>
> I.Q-86.4

Because of his philosophic background it was impossible for Aquinas to believe that the human psyche could communicate directly with any reality that was not physical, not just an angelic or demonic abstraction, a "thinking thought."

He criticized his predecessor Augustine just because he did believe in dreams and in the ability of the soul to experience spiritual reality directly:

> As Augustine says (Confessions xii), the soul has a certain power of forecasting, so that by its very nature it can know the future; hence when withdrawn from corporeal sense,* and, as it were, concentrated on itself, it shares in the knowledge of the future. Such an opinion would be reasonable if we were to admit that the soul receives knowledge by participating [in] the ideas as the Platonists maintained, because in that case the soul by its nature would know the universal causes of all effects, and would only be impeded in its knowledge by the body; and hence when withdrawn from the corporeal senses it would know the future. But since it is connatural to our intellect to know things, not thus, but by receiving its knowledge from the senses, it is not natural for the soul to know the future when withdrawn from the senses.
>
> I.Q-86.4

* As in dreams.

Aquinas then concluded that dreams were really not significant or sure, because he believed that we have no direct, immediate contact with spiritual reality. A rather important conclusion, with all sorts of implications for modern theology.

It is just at this point that the theologians today find it so difficult to accept what Jung is saying. It is precisely Jung's contention that in dreams and visions we do have direct participation in non-physical reality, and that dreams demonstrate this fact if one will observe them carefully. To follow Jung's understanding one must break with Aquinas at this point, for Jung accepts dreams as a direct participation in the collective unconscious or the objective psyche— a world of spiritual reality. Aquinas, on the other hand, put the matter very clearly: there is no direct participation in whatever reality lies beyond the physical, and so dreams cannot have any special religious significance.

Aquinas was very consistent. Whenever he discussed dreams or divination the same basic approach was apparent. In discussing whether man can know God directly he stated the same conclusions and criticized Augustine once more:

> But our soul, as long as we live in this life, has its being in corporeal matter; hence naturally it knows only what has a form in matter, or what can be known by such a form. Now it is evident that the divine essence cannot be known through the nature of material things. . . . This can be seen in the fact that the more our soul is abstracted from corporeal things, the more it is capable of receiving abstract intelligible things. Hence in dreams and alienations of the bodily senses divine revelations and foresight of future events are perceived the more clearly. It is not possible, therefore, that the soul in this mortal life should be raised up to the supreme of intelligible objects, that is, to the divine essence.
>
> I.Q-12.11
>
> . . . we cannot know of God *what He is*, and thus are united to Him as one unknown.
>
> I.Q-12.13

What is "divine revelation" then? In his discussion of prophetic dreams Aquinas carefully completed his clarification. It is the same as that which comes in the natural order by which species are represented to the mind, first to the senses, then the imagination, and finally to the passive intellect. He concluded that:

. . . prophetic revelation is conveyed sometimes by the mere infusion of light, sometimes by imprinting species anew, or by a new co-ordination of species.

II,II.Q-173.2

But nothing new can be added. The only difference from everyday worldly experience was one of degree and the addition of divine light by which any matter could be judged.

In another place he followed Aristotle's explanation of dreams on the basis of the vapors that arise from the body (I.Q-84.8). And finally in the Supplement those who completed the *Summa* made it clear that dreams are an inferior kind of experience because sleep is only half life, as Aristotle said in the *Ethics* (Supplement to III.Q-82.3).

For both Aristotle and Aquinas there was an ethical reason for avoiding dreams and other direct intrusions into the human psyche. Both men believed that if there were such happenings it would cast doubt upon man's free will, and so on the possibility of ethical behavior. They did not believe in freedom as a many-point scale, but saw it only as an either-or proposition. Modern psychological study points out that man can be free and yet not be as free as he thinks he is. Neurosis is a perfect example of a partial loss of freedom, and psychosis exhibits a very nearly total loss. Man's psyche and intellect may not, in fact, be as free as he wishes. His task may well be to seek freedom through greater consciousness, but none of this would abrogate ethical responsibility.[10]

In the end Aquinas' life contradicted what he had written. He did come into direct relationship with God, and ceased to write and dictate. When he was urged to go on, he replied: "I can do no more; such things have been revealed to me that all I have written seems as straw, and I now await the end of my life."[11] But

[10] In *Science and Sanity* Alfred Korzybski has shown the inadequacy of dealing with this matter simply as black and white. This book is integral to the whole movement in general semantics, which sees that man must be freed from Aristotle's categories. In fact, today's science has only been possible as this release has been accomplished. Korzybski's approach was not a completely intellectual one, but arose directly from the facts that modern science was developing. Anyone who wishes to understand the point of view of today's science must understand this idea, which Korzybski developed so fully. (*Science and Sanity: An Introduction to Non-Aristotelian Systems and General Semantics*, Lakeville, Conn., The International Non-Aristotelian Library Publishing Company, 1958.)

[11] *Great Books of the Western World*, Vol. 19 (*Thomas Aquinas*), Chicago, Encyclopaedia Britannica, Inc., 1952, p. vi.

this is not what the Western world knows of Aquinas. Our view of dreams might well be different today if the church had paid attention to his experience.[12] Instead, Catholic and Protestant alike have taken the treatment of dreams in his writings seriously, and the influence of his works has grown in the church until, as a practical matter, there is room for no other view. This did not happen overnight, however.

## Seesaw of opinions

It took many years, in fact, before Aquinas' views were revered as they are now. All through these centuries in which modern culture was developing, the opinions and experiences of thoughtful men seesawed back and forth, until the last century, when Aquinas became the basic theologian of the Roman Catholic Church.[13] By then his teaching was also the *de facto* view of practically the entire body of Protestant believers. Students like Pererius and Peucer were forgotten as if they had never written, for there was really no need to get behind the view Aquinas presented, which was so congenial to the developing rationalism and materialism of our time. As we look at the writings of this next period, we see how well his views were tailored to fit the thinking that was being shaped.

Among those who sided with Aquinas was John Calvin, that most rationalistic of Protestant theologians. In the *Institutes* Calvin made no room for revelation of God through images of any kind, which certainly excludes dreams, since they are nothing at all if not imagery. Yet Calvin also shared the ideas of his time about the

[12] According to Raissa Maritain, the wife of Jacques Maritain, this was far from being the only such experience connected with Aquinas. Knowledge of his death was given in a vision to his old teacher, Albert, who was in Ratisbon at the time and told those around him that he had seen his beloved disciple go.

The monk who wrote Aquinas' biography was also given a vision of his marvelous gifts in a dream, while Aquinas himself was once instructed in the night by the apostles Peter and Paul, and dictated a passage that had been troubling him as if he were reading it from a book. Raissa Maritain, *St. Thomas Aquinas: The Angel of the Schools*, New York, Sheed & Ward, Inc., 1955, pp. 76f., 85f., 115.

[13] This was made official by Pope Leo XIII in 1879. In *Aquinas* (Baltimore, Penguin Books, 1961, pp. 235ff.) F. C. Copleston traces the story of the adoption of his ideas, and in my book *Tongue Speaking* (Garden City, New York, Doubleday & Company, 1964, pp. 186ff.), I have outlined the position of the Protestant churches.

value of dreams. In his *Commentaries on the Book of Daniel,* written about the same time that Peucer and Pererius were writing, he defended the idea that God speaks in dreams as carefully as if he had no question about it.[14] In this work his explanation about the relation of people's beliefs to their understanding of divine symbolism in dreams was as careful and lucid as one expects from Calvin. There were two inconsistent ideas in him, one of the intellectual scholar, the other of the man and the Christian. The trouble is that most of us know the basic ideas of the *Institutes,* but hardly anyone remembers what Calvin wrote about the dreams in Daniel.

Fifty years later Jeremy Taylor, whose writings had such popular influence in seventeenth-century England, preached at some length about dreams. Among other things he told his congregation that:

> Dreams follow the temper of the body, and commonly proceed from trouble or disease, business or care, an active head and a restless mind, from fear or hope, from wine or passion, from fullness or emptiness, from fantastic remembrances, or from some common demon, good or bad: they are without rule and without reason, they are as contingent, as if a man should study to make a prophecy, and by saying ten thousand things may hit upon one true, which was therefore not foreknown, though it was forespoken, and they have no certainty, because they have no natural causality nor proportion to those effects, which many times they are said to foresignify. . . .[15]

In short, he concluded, don't expect anything from dreams, and it is interesting that the good divine, in reaching this conclusion, quoted Artemidorus rather than the Bible or any of the fathers.

But about the same time one of England's great physicians was reaching quite a different conclusion. Although Sir Thomas Browne was not a clergyman, his writing on personal religion places him more on the side of religion than otherwise. In his delightful and mature essay on dreams he discussed much of the material we have been over, concluding that Aristotle did not know what he was talking about and that there are dreams that come directly from angels and demons.

[14] Ralph L. Woods, ed., *The World of Dreams,* New York, Random House, Inc., 1947, pp. 149ff.
[15] Woods, op. cit., pp. 152ff.

> If there bee Guardian spirits, they may not bee unactively about us in sleepe, but may sometimes order our dreams, and many strange hints, instigations, or discoveries, which are so amazing unto us, may arise from such foundations.

As a physician Browne saw that dreams may well reveal the inner man, and in the following remarkable passage he suggested the insight that would one day come to Freud and Jung and be developed:

> However dreames may bee fallacious concerning outward events, yet may they bee truly significant at home, and whereby wee may more sensibly understand ourselves. Men act in sleepe with some conformity unto their awaked senses, and consolations and discouragements may be drawne from dreames, which intimately tell us ourselves. . . .

Thus the author of the *Religio Medici* counseled the individual not to ignore his dreams, adding a most modern note: "That some have never dreamed is as improbable, as that some have never laughed."[16]

John Wesley, the founder of Methodism, was another Englishman who saw that dreams have a value that defies rational explanation. In one of his sermons preached about the middle of the eighteenth century Wesley called attention in several ways to their mysterious nature, and to the fact that God does sometimes reveal himself "in dreams and visions of the night." He also outlined their causes in much the same way that they have been discussed ever since Tertullian. While he did not directly tell his people to pay attention to dreams, his thinking clearly suggests that he was open to his own dream experiences. Wesley concluded that dreams are like digressions or parenthetical expressions, which need no proof of being related to the rest of life.[17]

An even more positive view was expressed by one other English clergyman before the nineteenth century began. In 1791 David Simpson, who was Wesley's close friend, published the work that he called *Discourse on Dreams and Night Visions;* in it he wrote:

> Dreams are of great consequence in the government of the world, of equal authority with the Bible. . . . And has not

[16] *The Works of Sir Thomas Browne*, ed. by Charles Sayle, Edinburgh, John Grant, 1912, Vol. III, pp. 552f.
[17] Woods, op. cit., pp. 157ff.

the experience that many men have of significant dreams and night visions a more powerful effect on their minds than the most pure and refined concepts?[18]

Yet how many of us have even heard of Simpson's work? The eminent philosophic writer L. L. Whyte, who calls attention to it, also notes that Simpson was not alone in holding the ideas he developed. At the time, they were shared by the physicist G. C. Lichtenberg in Germany, by the physician von Herder, and others, and from that time on more and more scientists began to take an interest in the world of the dream. But within the church there seemed to be nothing to say about it. Simpson's work is the last serious religious discussion of dreams until we get to modern times.

## God's forgotten speech

With the Freudian explosion of interest in dreams one might think that the church would take a fresh look at its rich tradition on the subject. Instead, in the last half century there has been almost no serious attempt to consider the dream religiously. Only four works by orthodox clergymen which even touch on this subject have come to my attention, and only one of these was actually an effort to search out the Christian point of view on dreams.

The earliest of them was Canon Burnett Streeter's work *Reality*, published in 1927, which set out to prove that religion was scientifically acceptable, and as a corollary, that biblical dreams were Freudianly acceptable. His thought was that normal persons may become so preoccupied with a religious challenge that they find it represented symbolically in their dreams. According to his theory this was what happened to Peter at Joppa (Acts 10). Peter's dream-trance was merely his primitive way of dealing with his conflict over having to eat with Gentiles. The condescension in Canon Streeter's conclusion is apparent; it is interesting how easily he looks down on men like Augustine and Origen and Athanasius as he says:

> In the modern world the mental balance of a seer of visions is suspect and, in general, not without good reason. The primitive mind thinks in pictures, and in pictures it reasons and resolves, but the intellectual tradition of Europe for the

18 Quoted by Lancelot Law Whyte in *The Unconscious before Freud*, New York, Basic Books, Inc., 1960, p. 115.

last four centuries has trained the race in conceptual thinking. In the half-waking life of dreams symbolic thinking is still universal; but in the full waking consciousness it is usually only the less vigorous minds, or vigorous minds when temporarily unstrung, that reach important conclusions along this route. But at earlier stages of human culture, this rule did not hold; visions were often moments of supreme illumination for the most vigorous intellects and most creative wills.[19]

I had hoped for something better in John Baillie's very recent discussion of the theology of sleep, but this eminent Scotch divine, too, fell for only the narrowest of modern depth psychology. He took as his example the passage from *Pilgrim's Progress* in which Christiana listens to Mercy's dream and shows her that it is true, and that "God speaks once, yea twice, yet man perceiveth it not, in a dream, in a vision of the night. . . . We need not when a-bed, lie awake to talk with God; He can visit us while we sleep, and cause us to hear His voice." To which Baillie replied:

> Of course, the great change that has overtaken the theology of sleep is that the ancients believed dreams to be premonitory of the unborn future, whereas we moderns regard them rather as uprisings from the half-buried past.[20]

And then his discussion turned to ways of controlling our dreams, of getting only good dreams by thinking proper thoughts before retiring. In Baillie's theology there was simply no way for God to break into man's life in dreams. It was not a question of whether they were meaningless, or the products of pure chance; he simply did not believe that God could speak the unexpected, anything that man could not anticipate, in a dream. A change had indeed overtaken the church since the time of Peucer and Pererius.

This was also apparent in another work, written about 1960 by the Spanish Jesuit Pedro Meseguer and published in English as *The Secret of Dreams*. This is an excellent little book, which covers the subject as it had not been approached in the church for many, many years. It provides scientific and psychological information that

[19] Burnett Hillman Streeter, *Reality*, New York, The Macmillan Company, 1927, p. 331.
[20] John Baillie, *Christian Devotion*, New York, Charles Scribner's Sons, 1962, p. 106. Baillie's standard work on the knowledge of God (*Our Knowledge of God*, New York, Charles Scribner's Sons, 1939) is fully consistent with this point of view.

are needed, but the religious conclusions are strictly limited by Father Meseguer's Thomistic background. For instance, he holds that

> The prospective function [in dreams] . . . is nothing but an aspect of all the functions. . . . The unconscious, when it looks into the future, is only continuing the work of the conscious.[21]

In his book it is simply not "done" to look for the supernatural or direct contact with God in dreams. These are questions that Father Meseguer discusses only in the context of established theology.[22]

One work has been written, however, that recognizes in dreams the striving of the individual soul to find God. This is a book by the Reverend John A. Sanford, an Episcopal priest in this country who wrote for American readers in terms of the experience of people like you and me. But his book is only now being published in this country, after being translated and brought out in German[23] by the Jung Foundation in Zurich, Switzerland. It demonstrates, both theoretically and through experiences, that dreams do speak out of a realm that is different from the ordinary world, but in a way that helps the individual relate to his everyday life. It was written to describe the mysterious power that dreams can have in our lives, and develops much the same theological and psychological understanding as my own. This book, called *God's Forgotten Language*, opens up a new understanding of dreaming for religious people, and it deserves far more consideration than can be given to it here.

## Modern Christian dreams

Modern Christians do still dream. And when they are aware of the deeper springs of life, they occasionally take their dreams seriously. The best way to be sure of this is to produce the dreams of Christians, the experience, in fact, of three ministers and one Roman

[21] Pedro Meseguer, S.J., *The Secret of Dreams*, London, Burns & Oates, 1960, p. 203.
[22] Hugh Lynn Cayce, son of the famous psychic Edgar Cayce, has written two appreciative accounts of the place of dreams in the religious life. One is his *Venture Inward*, and the other *Dreams: The Language of the Unconscious*, written with Shane Miller and Tom Clark. The insights on dreams are excellent, but they are not developed in relation to historical Christianity or the ministry today.
[23] John A. Sanford, *Gottes Vergessene Sprache*, Zurich, Rascher Verlag, 1966.

Catholic saint from different parts of this period that has been so hostile to dreams and dreamers.

The first of these was John Newton, one of the most revered and unusual men in the English church, who lived at the beginning of the nineteenth century. He was a man to whom other ministers came for guidance, and he also wrote a number of the hymns we sing today. But John Newton did not grow up like this, but as a seaman and slave trader. Early in his autobiography he told the story of a dream that had warned him of the danger of this way and had given him a sense of God's providence. Twenty years later, when he was about to enter the ministry, he wrote:

> The most remarkable check and alarm I received (and, for what I know, the last) was by a dream. Those who acknowledge Scripture will allow that there have been monitory and supernatural dreams, evident communications from heaven, either directing or foretelling future events: and those who are acquainted with the history and experience of the people of God, are well assured that such intimations have not been totally withheld in any period down to the present times. . . .
>
> For my own part, I can say, without scruple, "The dream is certain, and the interpretation thereof sure." I am sure I dreamed to the following effect; and I cannot doubt, from what I have seen since, that it had a direct and easy application to my own circumstances, to the dangers in which I was about to plunge myself, and to the unmerited deliverance and mercy which God would be pleased to afford me in the time of my distress.

His account, which he had told and retold, continued as fresh as if it had happened yesterday:

> The scene presented to my imagination was the harbor of Venice, where we had lately been. I thought it was night, and my watch upon the deck; and that, as I was walking to and fro by myself, a person came to me, (I do not remember from whence,) and brought me a ring, with an express charge to keep it carefully: assuring me, that while I preserved that ring I should be happy and successful; but if I lost or parted with it, I must expect nothing but trouble and misery. I accepted the present and the terms willingly, not in the least doubting my own care to preserve it, and highly satisfied to have my happiness in my own keeping.

I was engaged in these thoughts, when a second person came to me, and observing the ring on my finger, took occasion to ask me some questions concerning it. I readily told him its virtues; and his answer expressed a surprise at my weakness, in expecting such effects from a ring. I think he reasoned with me some time upon the impossibility of the thing; and at length urged me, in direct terms, to throw it away. At first I was shocked at the proposal; but his insinuations prevailed. I began to reason and doubt myself.

At last I plucked it off my finger, and dropped it over the ship's side into the water; which it had no sooner touched, than I saw, the same instant, a terrible fire burst out from a range of the mountains, (a part of the Alps), which appeared at some distance behind the city of Venice. I saw the hills as distinct as if awake, and they were all in flames. I perceived, too late, my folly; and my tempter with an air of insult, informed me, that all the mercy God had in reserve for me was comprised in that ring which I had wilfully thrown away. I understood that I must now go with him to the burning mountains, and that all the flames I saw were kindled upon my account. I trembled, and was in a great agony; so that it was surprising I did not then awake: but my dream continued.

And when I thought myself upon the point of a constrained departure, and stood, self-condemned, without plea or hope, suddenly, either a third person, or the same who brought the ring at first, came to me (I am not certain which) and demanded the cause of my grief. I told him the plain case, confessing that I had ruined myself wilfully, and deserved no pity. He blamed my rashness, and asked if I should be wiser supposing I had my ring again?

I could hardly answer to this; for I thought it was gone beyond recall. I believe, indeed, I had not time to answer, before I saw this unexpected friend go down under the water, just in the spot where I had dropped it; and he soon returned, bringing the ring with him. The moment he came on board the flames in the mountains were extinguished, and my seducer left me. Then was "the prey taken from the hand of the mighty, and the lawful captive delivered." My fears were at an end, and with joy and gratitude I approached my kind deliverer to receive the ring again; but he refused to return it, and spoke to this effect:

"If you should be intrusted with this ring again, you would very soon bring yourself into the same distress: you are not able to keep it; but I will preserve it for you, and, whenever it is needful, will produce it in your behalf."

Upon this I awoke, in a state of mind not easy to be described: I could hardly eat or sleep, or transact my necessary business for two or three days. But the impression soon wore off, and in a little time I totally forgot it; and I think it hardly occurred to my mind again till several years afterward. It will appear, in the course of these papers, that a time came when I found myself in circumstances very nearly resembling those suggested by this extraordinary dream, when I stood helpless and hopeless upon the brink of an awful eternity; and I doubt not that, had the eyes of my mind been then opened, I should have seen my grand enemy, who had seduced me wilfully to renounce and cast away my religious profession, and to involve myself in the most complicated crimes, pleased with my agonies, and waiting for a permission to seize and bear away my soul to his place of torment. I should, perhaps, have seen likewise, that Jesus, whom I had persecuted and defied, rebuking the adversary, challenging me for his own, as a brand plucked out of the fire, and saying, "Deliver him from going down to the pit: I have found a ransom."

However, though I saw not these things, I found the benefit: I obtained mercy. The Lord answered for me in my day of distress; and blessed be his name, He who restored the ring, (or what was signified by it,) vouchsafes to keep it. O what an unspeakable comfort is this, that I am not in my own keeping!—"The Lord is my Shepherd." I have been enabled to trust my all in his hands; and I know in whom I have believed. . . . But for this, many a time and often (if possible) I should have ruined myself since my first deliverance; nay, I should fall, and stumble, and perish still.[24]

## How Christ came to church

The second of these dreamers was the great Baptist minister in Boston at the end of the nineteenth century, Dr. A. J. Gordon, and the dream he described was an experience that affected his entire ministry and life. The spiritual autobiography he wrote revolved around the dream and described what had happened since

[24] *The Life of the Rev. John Newton,* Oradell, New Jersey, American Tract Society, no date, pp. 28ff.

that day "when the truth of the in-residence of the Spirit and of his presiding in the church of God became a living conviction. . . ."[25] His story began with these words:

It was Saturday night, when wearied from the work of preparing Sunday's sermon, that I fell asleep and the dream came. I was in the pulpit before a full congregation, just ready to begin my sermon, when a stranger entered and passed slowly up the left aisle of the church looking first to the one side and then to the other as though silently asking with his eyes that some one would give him a seat. He had proceeded nearly half-way up the aisle when a gentleman stepped out and offered him a place in his pew, which was quietly accepted. Excepting the face and features of the stranger everything in the scene is distinctly remembered—the number of the pew, the Christian man who offered its hospitality, the exact seat which was occupied. Only the countenance of the visitor could never be recalled.

That his face wore a peculiarly serious look, as of one who had known some great sorrow, is clearly impressed on my mind. His bearing too was exceeding humble, his dress poor and plain, and from the beginning to the end of the service he gave the most respectful attention to the preacher. Immediately as I began my sermon my attention became riveted on this hearer. If I would avert my eyes from him for a moment they would instinctively return to him, so that he held my attention rather than I held his till the discourse was ended.

To myself I said constantly, "Who can that stranger be?" and then I mentally resolved to find out by going to him and making his acquaintance as soon as the service should be over. But after the benediction had been given the departing congregation filed into the aisles and before I could reach him the visitor had left the house.

The gentleman with whom he had sat remained behind however; and approaching him with great eagerness I asked: "Can you tell me who that stranger was who sat in your pew this morning?"

In the most matter-of-course way he replied: "Why, do you not know that man? It was Jesus of Nazareth."

With a sense of the keenest disappointment I said: "My dear sir, why did you let him go without introducing me to him? I was so desirous to speak with him."

25 A. J. Gordon, *How Christ Came to Church: A Spiritual Autobiography*, New York, Fleming H. Revell Company, 1895, p. 63.

And with the same nonchalant air the gentleman replied: "Oh, do not be troubled. He has been here to-day, and no doubt he will come again."

And now came an indescribable rush of emotion. As when a strong current is suddenly checked, the stream rolls back upon itself and is choked in its own foam, so the intense curiosity which had been going out toward the mysterious hearer now returned upon the preacher: and the Lord himself "whose I am and whom I serve" had been listening to me to-day. What was I saying? Was I preaching on some popular theme in order to catch the ear of the public? Well, thank God it was of himself I was speaking. However imperfectly done, it was Christ and him crucified whom I was holding up this morning. But in what spirit did I preach? Was it "Christ crucified preached in a crucified style?" or did the preacher magnify himself while exalting Christ? So anxious and painful did these questionings become that I was about to ask the brother with whom he had sat if the Lord had said anything to him concerning the sermon, but a sense of propriety and self-respect at once checked the suggestion.

Then immediately other questions began with equal vehemence to crowd into the mind. "What did he think of our sanctuary, its gothic arches, its stained windows, its costly and powerful organ? How was he impressed with the music and the order of the worship?" It did not seem at that moment as though I could ever again care or have the smallest curiosity as to what men might say of preaching, worship, or church, if I could only know that he had not been displeased, that he would not withhold his feet from coming again because he had been grieved at what he might have seen or heard.

We speak of "a momentous occasion." This, though in sleep, was recognized as such by the dreamer—a lifetime, almost an eternity of interest crowded into a single solemn moment. One present for an hour who could tell me all I have so longed to know; who could point out to me the imperfections of my service; who could reveal to me my real self, to whom, perhaps, I am most a stranger; who could correct the errors in our worship to which long usage and accepted tradition may have rendered us insensible. While I had been preaching for a half-hour He had been here and listening who could have told me all this and infinitely more —and my eyes had been holden that I knew him not; and now he had gone. "Yet a little while I am with you and then I go unto him that sent me."

One thought, however, lingered in my mind with something of comfort and more of awe. *"He has been here to-day,
and no doubt he will come again"*; and mentally repeating
these words as one regretfully meditating on a vanished vision,
"I awoke, and it was a dream." No, it was not a dream. It
was a vision of the deepest reality, a miniature of an actual
ministry, verifying the statement often repeated that sometimes we are most awake toward God when we are asleep
toward the world.[26]

## A *Saint receives certainty*

Thérèse of Lisieux was canonized in 1925. She died in 1897,
at the age of twenty-four, and she had the dream that we quote
just a year before her death. Her own story was written, as a letter
of obedience, to Sister Marie of the Sacred Heart. As she tells, when
she awoke from the dream, the effect was immediate; her life had
become serene, her belief a certainty. Since the dream was understood to come from Jesus, the part of her letter that follows was
addressed directly to him:

Jesus, my well-beloved, how considerate you are in your
treatment of my worthless soul; storms all around me, and
suddenly the sunshine of your grace peeps out! Easter Day
had come and gone, the day of your splendid triumph, and
it was a Saturday in May; my soul was still storm-tossed. I
remember thinking about the wonderful dreams which certain
souls have been privileged to experience, and how consoling
an experience it would be; but I didn't pray for anything of
the kind. When I went to bed, my sky was still overcast, and
I told myself that dreams weren't for unimportant souls like
mine; it was a storm that rocked me to sleep. Next day was
Sunday, the second Sunday of May, and I'm not sure it wasn't
actually the anniversary of the day when our Lady did me the
grace to smile on me. As the first rays of dawn came, I went
to sleep again, and dreamed.

I was standing in a sort of gallery where several other
people were present, but our Mother was the only person
near me. Suddenly, without seeing how they got there, I was
conscious of the presence of three Carmelite sisters in their
mantles and big veils. I had the impression that they'd come
there to see our Mother; what was borne in upon me with

certainty was that they came from heaven. I found myself crying out (but of course it was only in the silence of my heart): "O, how I would love to see the face of one of these Carmelites!" Upon which, as if granting my request, the tallest of the three saintly figures moved towards me, and, as I sank to my knees, lifted her veil, lifted it right up, I mean, and threw it over me. I recognized her without the slightest difficulty; the face was that of our Venerable Mother Anne of Jesus, who brought the reformed Carmelite order into France. There was a kind of ethereal beauty about her features, which were not radiant but transfused with light—the light seemed to come from her without being communicated to her, so that the heavenly face was fully visible to me in spite of the veil which surrounded both of us. I can't describe what elation filled my heart; an experience like that can't be put down on paper. Months have passed by now since I had this reassuring dream, but the memory of it is as fresh as ever, as delightful as ever. I can still see the look on Mother Anne's face, her loving smile; I can still feel the touch of the kisses she gave me. And now, treated with all this tenderness, I plucked up my courage: "Please, Mother," I said, "tell me whether God means to leave me much longer on earth? Or will he come and fetch me soon?" And, she, with a most gracious smile, answered: "Yes, soon; very soon, I promise you." Then I added: "Mother, answer me one other question; does God really ask no more of me than these unimportant little sacrifices I offer him, these desires to do something better? Is he really content with me as I am?" That brought into the Saint's face an expression far more loving than I'd seen there yet; and the embrace she gave me was all the answer I needed. But she did speak too: "God asks no more," she said. "He is content with you, well content." And so she embraced me as lovingly as ever mother embraced her child, and then I saw her withdraw. In the midst of all that happiness, I remembered my sisters, and some favours I wanted to ask for them; but it was too late, I'd woken up. And now the storm no longer raged, all my sky was calm and serene. I didn't merely believe, I felt certain that there was a heaven, and that the souls who were its citizens looked after me, thought of me as their child. What gave more strength to this impression was the fact that, up till then, Mother Anne of Jesus meant nothing to me; I'd never asked for her prayers or even thought about her except on the rare occasions when her name came up in conversation. So when I realized how she loved me, and how much I meant to her, my heart melted towards her in love and gratitude; and for that matter towards all the Blessed in heaven.

Jesus, my Beloved, this was only a prelude to greater graces still with which you'd determined to enrich me. . . .[27]

## A baptism by the road

The last of these dreamers is active in the ministry today, and is a friend of mine who prefers that his name is not used. The experiences that he wrote out for me began about 1952.

As you know, I had almost too much intellectual faith when I was ordained, and not much else got through to me until I had been at ————— for about three years. Then the tailspin began, with real doubt and conflict. At the height of my neurosis I had the following dream, which certainly set the stage for things to happen.

There was suddenly a little, old church next to the one we had recently constructed, and I went into the old building to have the regular Sunday service. I was appalled to find that an old dead tree had fallen across the chancel of the little church, almost cutting it in two. But apparently I intended to go on with the services. I had to hunt for my vestments, which were behind some discarded furniture, and then I had trouble putting them on. When I finally found a Prayerbook, I could not find the right place in it. Everything was confusion. When the offering was about to be taken, I woke, certain that the ushers could not get through the church to receive it because the dead branches were so thick in their way.

This was when I began to know real anxiety. On a Sunday not long after this dream I actually made the mistake of skipping over the entire consecration prayer in my 8:00 o'clock Communion service, and did not discover what I had done until I found the Host lying unbroken on the patten. About this time I found myself dreaming of hostile creatures who were pursuing and trying to destroy me.

Then I began to give some attention to my own problems. As I worked on them the anxieties became more bearable. The quality of my dreams changed. As I faced my own doubts and dealt with them, the dreams of pursuit almost disappeared. . . .

---

[27] Thérèse of Lisieux, *Autobiography of a Saint*, trans. by Ronald Knox, London, Fontana Books, 1960, pp. 182f.

During the next few years this young minister found he could work with problems he had faced only superficially before. His ministry was changing as he took his dreams seriously from a religious point of view and found that his life changed. I omit the few experiences he included from this period. He went on:

> This time I dreamed that I was driving in the country in my car when I found that I was being pursued again by a witch. Suddenly the demonic thing was astride the hood and I saw that it was no use trying to escape. I stopped the car and faced the creature. She was still coming at me when it suddenly occurred to me that I did not have to be destroyed by a creature like that. I got out, bent on tearing her to pieces. But there beside the road was a bucket of water, and I picked it up and threw it. Three times I doused the witch, "In the name of the Father, and of the Son, and of the Holy Ghost." As I did this she began to shrink, and then she dissolved and disappeared.
>
> A few days later I dreamed that I was in the church. It was Whitsunday, and I was celebrating the Communion service with great joy, wearing a gloriously beautiful red chasuble. The church was filled, and there was a sense of an unearthly presence surrounding me. As I think you know very well, this dream marked the end of that kind of religious doubts. I really think that, finally, I got the message that God was trying to put across.

In fact, dreams have helped this man find a renewed religious belief and creativity. He not only carries the duties of a large and growing church, but finds time to guide and counsel with the many, many people who seek him out.

All four of these were persons who were still close to their spiritual roots. They listened and found that God still speaks in dreams. They had a sure conviction, and because they knew their dreams to be of the same substance and significance as the deepest religious experience, they were able to find meaning that the rationalism and materialism of our time denies. Why, we may well ask, are we so little able to ignore the world view that surrounds us? In our time is there no context of religious experience into which the dream might fit? Let us turn next to the psychological understanding of dreams and see what it offers.

*eight*                    Psychologists
                     Explore the Dream

In 1900 Sigmund Freud published *The Interpretation of Dreams*, which mapped out a way of exploring the relation of the dream to the unconscious side of man's mental life. It is difficult to stress enough the great importance of this contribution, although Freud himself recognized it and more than once remarked that the publication of his book had been timed to coincide with the beginning of a new era. Of course he was neither the first to discover the unconscious nor the first to see the significance of dreams from a scientific point of view. But he was the first modern scientist to connect the two; he was the first to make an empirical study of any length on the subject, and the first to write about it with clarity, indeed with such convincing power that his opinions could not be ignored.

This is an impressive list of firsts, and interestingly enough, the literary world was quick to perceive his significance. Among his own profession, however, Freud met with little but contempt. It took eight years to sell out the first six-hundred-copy edition of his book. While it was difficult to ignore him, the ideas he offered could be laughed at, and for a long time laughter would be a good defense against the contribution he offered.

Even so, there had been medical men who valued dreams in almost every age from Hippocrates down. Men like Daniel Tuke, Wilhelm Wundt, Bernheim, and many others whose names are hardly remembered[1] had been seeking to explain the dream because they saw it was significant from a medical point of view. But these men failed to see that dreams had any particular relation to consciousness. They often failed to see the dream as a psychic reality, and instead they tried to tie it to the physical functioning of the brain. This was a good idea, but it was still only an idea, which has yet to be demonstrated.

There were also thinkers in other fields who had discovered the unconscious, and some of them had written clearly about this. Literature from its inception seemed to understand that human personality has deeper levels of being and a deeper purposiveness than is revealed in our conscious awareness. Shakespeare and Goethe both reveal a knowledge of this deeper level of personality, as do other literary figures. Indeed, it appears that the greater the stature of the author, the greater his understanding and knowledge of this realm of being. From the philosophical side, during the nineteenth century C. G. Carus and Eduard von Hartmann had both written extensively about the unconscious, the former in a work he called simply *Psyche,* and the latter in his massive *Philosophy of the Unconscious.* There was no lack of thinking about this shadowy side of human personality, but it remained entirely speculative until a definite relation to dreams began to be established. Those who are interested in this period of growing curiosity about the structure of the human psyche will find an excellent study in the work by L. L. Whyte, *The Unconscious Before Freud.*[2]

[1] In the century or so before Freud there was wide medical interest in dreaming; among the doctors writing on the subject were David Hartley, John Abercrombie, Wilhelm Griesinger, Robert MacNish, A. J. B. de Boismont, S. Weir Mitchell, and August Forel, to name only a few. In France the purely scientific interest in dreams began particularly early and has continued to grow, as also happened later in the rest of Europe and in America. See Woods, op. cit., pp. 397ff.; also Meseguer, op. cit., pp. 39ff.

[2] The great philosophers from Descartes on added little to the understanding of dreams. They were almost totally absorbed in the study of consciousness, and while most of them had opinions about dreams which were mentioned in passing, none of them treated the subject on its own merits. Their opinions were divided between those who saw the dream as meaningless or merely a reflection of the organic state of the body, and those who saw it as signifying more. Among the followers of Aristotle and Cicero there were Thomas Hobbes, Pierre Bayle, Leibnitz, Kant, Nietzsche, and Santayana. On the other hand, Locke, Voltaire, Goethe, Schopenhauer, Schelling, Emerson, and Bergson could not dismiss the dream so lightly. In 1901 Bergson wrote:
"If telepathy influences our dreams, it probably has the best opportunity to mani-

## Freud makes contact with the unconscious

Freud above all was the first to show a practical application for delving into unconscious material and the meaning of dreams. For Freud, before anything else, was a physician whose interest was in making sick people well. He had received his training in neurology under Charcot in Paris, and following the lead of the French school, he had made use of hypnotism. But he was disappointed in its lasting effect in healing mental disturbances, and so he searched for some other means of making an impact upon the personalities of his patients that would enable them to come to terms with what disturbed them and get well. He found this tool in dream analysis. What he found, in essence, was that understanding the elements of dreams enabled a man to see what was going on in the part of himself of which he was not aware, to come to terms with himself, and so recover from neurosis. To Freud dreams were interesting not only theoretically, but from a practical point of view as well.

Writing with a clarity, simplicity, and logical force that few philosophers or literary men share, Freud first presented his ideas to the world in *The Interpretation of Dreams*. Fifteen years later he gave a series of lecture courses at the University of Vienna, covering his entire theory of neurosis, mental illness, and dreams, which were then put into book form as *A General Introduction to Psychoanalysis*. These amazingly clear discussions reveal the logical development of Freud's theories.

---

fest itself during very deep sleep. But, I repeat, I can make no pronouncement on this point. I have gone forward with you as far as possible. I stop at the threshold of the mystery. To explore the innermost depths of the unconscious, to work in what I have called earlier the substratum of consciousness, that will be the main task of psychology in the century that is dawning. I do not doubt that wonderful discoveries await it there, as important perhaps as were in the preceding centuries the discoveries in the physical and natural sciences." Henri Bergson, *The World of Dreams*, New York, Philosophical Library, Inc., 1958, p. 57.

This was the period in which interest in psychic research and the occult began to grow, as Henry Holt, Frederick Van Eeden, and F. W. H. Myers, to mention but a few of the best-known, pursued the subject, which most philosophers had come to ignore. Long forgotten were the significant insights of the previous century, developed by scientists and literary men like Lichtenberg, Herder, G. H. von Schubert, C. Nodier, and Henri Amiel, which often anticipated the investigations of Freud.

He began with the idea that our errors, our lapses of memory, and our slips of the tongue reveal a purpose within us that is contrary to our conscious goals and direction and often completely out of touch with our conscious thought. This was the same purpose he saw revealed in dreams. What errors betray in a small way, he realized, is continually being portrayed by dreams in a never-ending and inexhaustible panorama. Therefore, if one could come to a way of interpreting dreams, he would then be able to know those factors within men which were in conflict with their conscious attitudes and thus were causing their disruptive neuroses. But the trouble was that we had no way to understand dreams. And so he set out to erect a theory that would enable men to understand their dreams, and by this method, the method of psychoanalysis, to deal with what troubled them from within themselves, and to find health.

In very general terms, the theory went like this. The unconscious wishes to speak clearly in dreams and express its desires and meaning. But it is impeded from this by the conscious attitudes of the dreamer. Much of the dream material is obnoxious to the conscious personality unless it is distorted, and so there exists within the personality a censoring capacity that is responsible for the form a dream takes. The "censor," according to Freud, supervises several interesting processes, all of them unconscious and helping to conceal the real meaning of the dream from the ego:

First the original dream thoughts are condensed; then they are turned into images, and some of the objectionable ideas or wishes are replaced by associations for the dreamer. The unconscious may even produce an opposite meaning by making transpositions or substitutions before the original ideas are translated into images. And finally, when the dream does pass the censor, there are often very important gaps in the way it is seen or remembered.

Thus Freud made the important point that latent dream-content may be quite different from the final, manifest dream. It is necessary, he showed, to distinguish carefully between the original dream thought and the actual dream that occurs after the distortions he described as censorship. He believed that it was because of this process that so few people had ever understood dreams. The original, sexual, wish-fulfilling nature of the unconscious was disguised so effectively that we did not realize the real, primitive roots of personality. It must be noted here that this theory was based upon Freud's own dreams and upon his listening to the dreams of the repressed people of Vienna who formed the greater part of his practice. It enabled him to get at the material that was bothering them, and many people found new life and new understanding of themselves through his method.

There was also a growing group of medical men who began to take Freud seriously, and among them were two groups. Many, of course, became firm adherents to his theory, and the first group formed around Freud. But there were others who thoroughly appreciated his monumental genius, who saw the importance of the points he brought out, and yet could not go along with his total theory of the unconscious or of dreams.

To them Freud's dream theory seemed artificial and contrived. It did not appear to them that human personality was actually contriving to deceive itself so artfully. These men also doubted the validity of reducing the unconscious primarily to sexuality, or to the pleasure principle and the death wish. It seemed to them that out of the unconscious there arose other instinctive forces besides sex. Adler, for instance, broke away from Freud because he believed that the will to power was the basic human drive. These men also believed that from dreams and other unconscious experiences men do receive guidance and wisdom that has something to offer the conscious mind, as well as unacceptable thoughts and incubuses that would keep consciousness constantly on guard. Jung particularly felt that Freud had dogmatized too much. His separation came because he felt that there was not as yet enough evidence upon which to erect a full system and, besides this, that Freud had left out certain important data in order to keep his system neat and simple.

## The development of Jung's thinking

It is true that Jung could not accept Freud's systematic doctrine of sexuality, but there was a far more important and fundamental reason for the break. Freud was a rationalist, and rationalist he remained, while Jung was an empiricist through and through. Freud assumed that the unconscious thinks rationally and wishes to communicate in this way through dreams, and that it is only impeded by a censorship working quietly in the rational mind to distort these essentially rational communications.

Jung, on the contrary, suggested that the unconscious does not think rationally to begin with, but rather symbolically, metaphorically, in images. And this, rather than purposeful distortion, accounts for the difficulty we have in understanding dreams. The difficulty is that we have either forgotten or have never known how to think symbolically. The task of dream interpretation, according to Jung, is that of learning a strange language with many nuances, of learning to understand the symbolic communications of the unconscious, the language of art, literature, mythology, and folklore. He saw no attempt on the part of the unconscious to deceive or distort. It is simply using the best method of communication available to it. And this we need to learn to understand.

About 1912 Jung set down his independent ideas in a book published in English as *The Psychology of the Unconscious*. In this work—which he later rewrote and which is now published as *Symbols of Transformation*—Jung introduced his study with a discussion of man's two ways of thinking, analytical thought and symbolic thought.[3] He showed that in one kind of thinking we are active, in the other passive. In one we lead; in the other we are led. One is the thinking of logic and science, the other the thinking of imagination, of poetry, art, and religion, and also of dreams. In its analytical function the conscious mind uses known facts; it sorts and directs them toward a particular order. In symbolic thinking the function is quite different, for here the mind is flooded by new images, symbols of something that has been *un*known, or has been laid aside and forgotten.

Jung went on in this work to demonstrate the importance of this latter kind of thinking in approaching the unconscious. Taking for his material the dreams and fantasies of a young woman whom he knew only from these bits of writing (and much later from her doctors), he showed quite accurately how the unconscious was leading her to serious mental disorder. Yet at the same time it outlined for her a picture of new life and greater wholeness if she had only had the help to understand and act upon these directions. They were directions that Jung recognized because they had appeared over and over again in the myths and religious stories and works of art of every kind of people. It was clear how important such dream experiences were to the religions of mankind and how much attention had once been paid to them.

At the same time Jung was coming to know a similar realm of experience in himself. He saw that if he were to allow his patients'

[3] C. G. Jung, *Collected Works*, Vol. 5, pp. 16ff.

dream experiences to speak for themselves as facts, then he had to treat his own dreams in the same way. As he did, it became evident how little was actually known about the contents of the unconscious and the almost incredible realm that was opened. Dealing with these contents, Jung wrote, "brought home to me the crucial insight that there are things in the psyche which I do not produce, but which produce themselves and have their own life."[4] From this fact came the certainty that reality, and frequently the best of reality, is found in these depths. This is also reality that demands a religious attitude from man, and it is found only when one allows himself to be led by the thinking of the unconscious, symbolic thinking that can be found in fantasy and dream, and myth and story.

It is almost impossible to put too much stress on symbolic imagination, for this way of thinking has been almost entirely ignored in the development of modern Western culture. It is of primary importance to religious people; it puts into their hands a method through which they can come to know and understand the religious depths of themselves and perhaps get intimations of God speaking through these depths. This method of meditative, devotional, imaginative thinking is an approach to experience at which Christians ought to be adept.

For Jung this way of thinking was vital to an understanding of human personality. It offered a basic approach to the unconscious which allocated to the psyche all the complexity and the amazing depth that were often found in it. It offered the only view of men that satisfactorily reflected the empirical facts. Therefore Jung made it his business to listen to dreams and other productions of the unconscious in a way that practically no other psychologist has attempted. He also spent most of his life describing and integrating what he learned. His approach is one that has something constructive to offer Christianity, something that is hard to find elsewhere.

## Listening to the psyche

From the beginning Jung seemed to know that he was to listen to the psyche and hear what it had to tell him. Now and then he encountered some very strange experiences that made him know the different quality of the contents with which he was dealing. One of

[4] C. G. Jung, *Memories, Dreams, Reflections*, New York, Pantheon Books, Inc., 1963, p. 183.

these, which occurred early in his career, was the vision that a para-
noid patient in Zurich tried to show him. The man, who had been
hospitalized for years, called Jung into the corridor one day to instruct him how to squint and move his head in order to see the
phallus of the sun and how it moved from side to side; this, explained the patient, was the origin of the wind. Jung noted this
experience in 1906; then in 1910 he was reading one of Albrecht
Dieterich's works when he came across words from an ancient
papyrus that had recently been published, to which his patient had
had no possible access, and realized that he was reading almost
exactly the same vision. It told how to see "hanging down from the
disc of the sun something that looks like a tube," which is "the
origin of the ministering wind."[5] It did not take many experiences of
this kind to convince Jung of the need for a religious point of view
in dealing with unconscious contents.

Indeed, he gave an essentially different value to the unconscious
than other psychologists. About 1930 he wrote:

> In this respect I go several steps further than Freud. For
> me the unconscious is not just a receptacle for all unclean
> spirits and other odious legacies from the dead past. . . . It is
> in very truth the eternally living, creative, germinal layer in
> each of us, and though it may make use of age-old symbolical
> images it nevertheless intends them to be understood in a
> new way.[6]

But new understanding does not spring full-fledged like Minerva
from the head of Zeus; "a living effect," he went on, "is achieved
only when the products of the unconscious are brought into serious
relationship with the conscious mind." Above all, the unconscious
does not need to be further dissociated from consciousness; too
many people are already suffering from inner incompatibility, from
an inability to make out with unconscious drives and still get on
with their conscious aims. The first thing needed was to hear what
the unconscious really had to say, and so Jung listened to the
dream as "one of the purest products of unconscious constellation."[7]
For fifty years he studied and wrote about dreams.

He did not try to get around the fact that most dreams are

[5] C. G. Jung, *Collected Works*, Vol. 8, pp. 150f.
[6] C. G. Jung, *Collected Works*, Vol. 4, p. 330.
[7] Ibid., p. 148.

attempting to say something that is *not* in accord with conscious wishes and intentions. Instead, he suggested, they are agents for an independent function in the psyche, and in this sense they act autonomously. In this way they also act very differently from daydreams, whose subject matter and direction is already present in consciousness, simply waiting to gather other elements around it. Daydreaming may be built around anything from wishful thinking about Hawaii or a new car to things of the spirit, and this has its place, but it is not the same as dreaming. The dream chooses its own time to speak, and we are not asked what topics will be brought up or what they will mean to us, or even what objects will be chosen to represent this meaning, for consciousness does not make the rules. Dreams operate autonomously in this realm, if not beyond it.

## The language of dreams

Since this is the case, the language of dreams does present a real challenge to man's understanding. In the first place, dreams are like cartoons or parables. They signify something beyond themselves. They attempt to tell a meaning, or many meanings, by means of images, in much the same way that the cartoon artist expresses his meaning by the use of symbols. The cartoonist uses an image because it is well enough known to readers to evoke the memories, feelings, ideas that go with a whole situation. The dream does essentially the same thing as best it can, by switching on the picture of an experience that at least once was associated with a group of memories and feelings and ideas.

Jung sometimes illustrated this to his American listeners by referring to our political cartoons. His favorite was a prize-winning depiction of the Democratic party in 1927 that showed a donkey being ridden by a Southern belle and stubbornly balking at the sight of a derby hat that lay in its path. It certainly does not take much knowledge of American history to see in this picture a meaningful representation of the political situation in that year—with the Southern states still in the saddle, the Democratic party was resisting being represented by Al Smith, the big-city politician who had tossed his celebrated brown derby into the ring. And basically this is the way most dreams speak. But just as a foreigner might have some trouble with the idea of someone leaving his hat in the road, or a girl in ruffles and pantaloons riding a donkey, so the language of dreams is very often puzzling to the conscious mind.

Except for the different level of meaning, however, this is very similar to the parable, the form in which Jesus so often spoke. He told the story of the prodigal son, of the good Samaritan, of the foolish virgins, not to conceal his meaning, but to express it. Furthermore, these same themes that Jesus brought out in the form of stories still come out in the dreams of people today. People dream of finding the great pearl, of coming across one beaten by thieves and caring for him, of seeing a person raised from the dead, or of watching a fire that does not go out. These are all images that have been told me from their dreams by people with whom I have counseled, and there are many other examples from psychological practice. This indeed is the greatness of Jesus' parables. They touch the deepest level in man, the substance of his life, and it is interesting that this is how Jung described the level from which extremely significant dreams arise. He also called attention to the fact that, like Jesus' examples, these dreams do not always have to operate upon the conscious mind in order to bring about an effect upon the personality.[8]

Most dreams do tell a story, generally with definite dramatic form, although the plot may vary from the simplest to the most exceedingly complex. They are often just like plays, staged either before one's eyes or with the dreamer cast in an active role, and sometimes with a great variety of characters, both known and unknown. In what way, then, can the action and the people in these inner dramas be understood? If they are not to be taken concretely, but only symbolically, then what does one do with a dream about his mother-in-law? or, say, a truly frightening nightmare in which he sees a friend die in an automobile accident? I am well aware of the temptation to take such dreams all too concretely, but this brings us to the second major point about this mysterious language.

Primarily *my* dreams speak to *me*, to my own inner, psychic life, and each of the figures in them represents some part of *my being*. As Jung was careful to show, a dream is a way of self-reflection, and

> One should never forget that one dreams in the first place, and almost to the exclusion of all else, of oneself. . . . The

8 C. G. Jung, *Collected Works*, Vol. 8, p. 294.

"other" person we dream of is not our friend and neighbor, but the other in us, of whom we prefer to say: "I thank thee, Lord, that I am not as this publican and sinner."[9]

The fact that strange, unexplained phenomena are at times associated with dreams only reinforces this conclusion. Such psychic events as clairvoyant dreams and extrasensory perception are simply given, and they must be understood in this way in order to be valued in their religious meaning. They come to such persons and at such times, apparently, as are chosen by the same mysterious power that speaks to the person's own needs in his dreams. Jung suggested briefly how important it is to see oneself in the dream:

> No one who does not know himself can know others. And in each of us there is another whom we do not know. He speaks to us in dreams and tells us how differently he sees us from the way we see ourselves. When, therefore, we find ourselves in a difficult situation to which there is no solution, he can sometimes kindle a light that radically alters our attitude—the very attitude that led us into the difficult situation.[10]

Behind this is one of Jung's most basic ideas. Our unconscious life, he held, is made up of almost innumerable complexes, bundles of ideas and related thoughts and feelings that function with almost a life of their own. These complexes, then, are the parts of ourselves that are pictured in dreams, represented by the various characters and situations of the inner drama. For example, a man dreams of a religious figure, let us say of Paul. If the action that involves Paul is to have meaning for him, the dreamer must ask himself: What does this figure represent in my life? What part of me is actually like Paul? What stands out about Paul in my dream, and what does this mean to me? When the dreamer knows what this image represents to him, then the action of the dream can show how that part of himself is related to the other elements as they appeared. If the dream-figure is a familiar one, like a mother-in-law or friend, then the questions are the same; the only difference is that they may be more difficult and complicated to answer. In either case the problem is to understand the meaning that the

[9] C. G. Jung, *Collected Works*, Vol. 10, p. 151f.
[10] Ibid., p. 153.

unconscious has presented for one's knowledge and guidance, and this is anything but simple.

Dealing with dreams is not simple, because right away it involves the individual in a realm of experience beyond himself. Jung was one psychologist who realized that dreams could not be reduced only to personal factors. Symbols from mythology and from the history of religion continually appear in them, so often that it is difficult to ignore the presence of deeper, universal meanings. Very few dreams seem to be entirely free of these elements. But even more important is the fact that "big" or "meaningful" dreams do occur which seem to carry little or no personal significance for the dreamer, but still produce a most powerful impression. As Jung pointed out, these dreams are generally difficult to interpret. Although they make a terrific impact, often with forms of poetic force and beauty, they do not produce many associations from the dreamer's own experience. One must turn to myth and parable and fairy tale to find the symbols and some illustration of their meaning.

Such dreams are no longer concerned with immediate, personal experience, but with the *ideae principales* of which Augustine spoke, "which are themselves not formed . . . but are contained in the divine understanding."[11] These dreams reveal powerful realities that have their being in man's unconscious, realities that he needs to touch and know because they lead the soul of man and through it often determine his whole approach to life. These are the realities that Jung called archetypes, which are probably at the core of all our dreaming. Certainly they account for the vast number and variety of figures that we dream about.

## The dramatis personae of dreams

Jung found these archetypal forms represented over and over again in the characters that people our dreams, and out of this vast dramatis personae he isolated several of the important images and carefully described them. The most significant of these are the images of the shadow, the anima, and the animus.

The first is one that appears at one time or another in the dreams of every person. As might be expected, the shadow is a dark and threatening figure, usually someone unknown to the dreamer.

---

[11] Quoted by Jung, *Collected Works*, Vol. 9, Part 1, p. 4; from Migne, *Patrologiae Latinae*, Vol. 40, Col. 30.

For instance, people often dream of Negroes at such a time as sickness, when they have no contact with a Negro at all. In fairy tales the "trickster" shows the original nature of this figure, doing all sorts of mischief for which man must take the blame. What the shadow represents is that inferior or undeveloped side of man that has been left behind in our attempt to become as completely rational and moral as possible. It is the uncivilized part of us, the primitive, which is also an essential part. Jung never tired of reminding us that this figure is usually 90 per cent pure gold when one no longer projects it out upon other people. But its real value cannot be found until one looks at these elements objectively, instead of seeing them in some other person who is hated and feared.

The other two principal figures are counterparts in the dreams of men and women. In the psyche of every man there is an identifiable female figure, which Jung called by the ancient name of the "anima," and in a woman's psyche it is matched by the male figure, which he termed the "animus." In the same way that the shadow is a reality based on the instincts, these two dream-images come from something equally real and insistent in men and women. The unconscious feminine within a man and the masculine traits in women are rooted in our physical structure and are carried by our genes and chromosomes, as well as by our psychological structure and our culture. Generally this figure seems to carry all that is most foreign to the conscious personality—in a man his moods, his vanity, his touchiness, and also his belief in the good and beautiful, his knowledge of the divine, and his ability to love and make love work; and in a woman the worst of her opinionated, argumentative side, and also her ability to relate the ideal, the perfect, the true (even unwanted truth), to the hard facts of being.

Unquestionably it is difficult for people to face and to come to terms with these realities within themselves. It seems far more agreeable to cloak the anima and animus in a cult of romantic love than to set these conflicting impulses loose within ourselves. Nor is the shadow a burden many of us want to bear; it is not pleasant to realize that our own lives contain primitive and destructive elements that cannot be escaped. We much prefer to see these things in other people. Unfortunately these images do not stay put when they are unconscious and only projected. The man who only searches for an appropriate person to carry his psychic counterpart finds sooner or later that this kind of love turns sour. The shadow that is hidden from the outside world can burst forth and make the kindest of men into a tyrant within his own family, and we have seen what happens to an educated, hard-working nation like Germany when these unconscious shadow elements break out and transform a whole people into demonic destroyers.

But these are the penalties of unconsciousness. Through dream experiences these elements can come into consciousness within a man, so that he finds the very creative springs of life in them instead of conflict and turmoil. Of course, this is never automatic, never simple or easy. It is sure to cost whatever we have, and to be worth it. As the shadow and the ego with its awareness come to form a harmonious team, one finds that much of the zest and creativeness in ordinary daily living originate from these rejected parts of himself. The images of the shadow often change from dark, distasteful figures to pure gold. The man who comes to terms with his inner feminine qualities finds even deeper values; he finds his very soul and the peace of wholeness and detachment, along with a new level of creativity and relationship. Similarly, a woman, in finding her inner masculine function, will find her life inwardly fructified and made whole and satisfying.

The importance of dreams and of the proper understanding of dreams in these processes cannot be overemphasized. Through dreams these inner functions appear in images that come alive for us and can be dealt with. Otherwise they remain unconscious and man falls into projection. When he does not deal inwardly with the shadow and the anima-animus, he is led by one into the cult of war, from the iron curtain within his own home on up to global war, which our time has brought to such awful perfection; or by the other into the cult of love, the idolatry that destroys the very foundation of life and society. And this at the cost of his birthright of finding himself, which has its beginning in the creative imagery of the dream.

The three figures we have discussed only begin to suggest the variety of forms that can appear. There are as many archetypes as there are typical situations in life, and these three happen to be the most common, the ones everyone must meet in one way or another. Jung went on to draw quite detailed pictures of others, such as the child archetype, the wise old man, the maiden, the Self (or inner redeemer), the holy marriage; and he once remarked that it took so much research material to be sure what the symbols meant that he learned not to lecture about it. He risked putting some people to sleep if he offered enough explanation of such symbols to make valid comparisons with the way people react today.[12] Most of us, in fact, are a little afraid to imagine that we are connected with the great symbols we see moving in history, in art and religion and poetry.

In addition he outlined the meaning of many non-human images that are important in understanding dreams. For instance, the sea often symbolizes the vast unconscious out of which man's conscious life emerged and from which much of its sustenance still comes. Many people dream of the house that is their personal dwelling, or the automobile in which they get around in life, representing one's conscious life and his ego, as against images of hotels, or of trains and railway stations, which speak of group life and mores. These are fairly easy to comprehend, as is the realization that animals often stand as symbols for the instinctive life within us. But there are many, many images, like the rock, the fountain, the bird, vessels of many kinds, even the father, which leave the dreamer cold until their original, usually religious meaning can be found and brought to life. The journeys that are made in dreams frequently represent one's inner, spiritual quest, while earthquake or disaster may signify that a great, perhaps overwhelming change is taking place in the psychic structure of one's life. Going back to childhood experience, say to a school classroom, usually represents the process of psychological reorientation and learning again, of growth. Indeed, there are too many such figures and images to ignore the fact that dreams speak a basic general language that can be understood.

It must be made perfectly clear, however, that *these symbols can NEVER be studied from a book to give an easy, shorthand method of understanding dreams.* Like any living language, they must be read in context, in connection with the personal associations they hold for the dreamer. In fact, as Jung often pointed out, dream interpretation is never a static process, but always an evolving one. Before any attempt at interpretation can be made, one must know the dreamer and the general state of his psyche, as well as all the facts that relate to the particular dream. It was the failure to see

12 Ibid., p. 50. Jung wrote two entire books, *Aion* and *Mysterium Coniunctionis*, on the last two of these symbols, the self and the holy marriage. These are among his most complex and interesting works.

dreams in this light that kept the ancient dream interpreters from catching the full significance of the material that went into their dream books. They seemed to be seeking an eternal, dependable language rather than the parable of an inner life, and so they missed the meaning of many dreams. And yet, like Synesius, they did realize that no dream is meaningless.

## The ways of expressing meaning

There are several different ways in which dreams express meaning. Primarily because they picture what is *not* present in consciousness, they bring a person memories, experiences, images that can reveal the unconscious element in his relationships. Simply because they do not depend upon consciousness, but bring up the images and associations as they occur, dreams often reveal dormant qualities in the personality. In fact, Jung observed that they very often stand in glaring opposition to conscious intentions, particularly if a person's attitude toward life is very one-sided.

In such cases there are sometimes striking examples of the compensatory behavior or function of dreams; a dream may speak directly to the person's situation, calling attention to qualities of life which he has forgotten or ignored. One dream like this that I will never forget was told me by a very sweet old lady, who confessed with horror shortly before she died that she had a recurrent dream of strangling her mother. Yet nothing could have been further from possibility; and that was just the trouble. This woman would have had good reason for anger at her mother, who had ruined her life. But she was too nice to face such horrid thoughts, and so her dream reminded her that she was not being honest with herself. This same principle of compensation can also act with opposite force, like the instances in which criminals have been known to dream of acts of kindness and generosity which they would never think to do consciously.

This principle also accounts for many of the dreams that were seen by the early Christians as the work of the devil or demons. Since many of these men actually were one-sided, both in the way they lived and in the way they looked at life, they had dreams that simply seemed evil to them. It did not occur to them that these dreams represented a function of compensating for one's view of life. But when the hermit dreamed of his voluptuous women, something deep within him, whether we call it the devil or not, presented him with this fare. A part of his own deepest self was offering him a reminder of what he was denying and sacrificing. And if the sacrifice is not conscious, is it indeed a sacrifice?

At the other extreme, there are dreams that simply emphasize the conscious attitude, or only introduce variations in it, and these also suggest the process of compensation. These dreams suggest that an individual's conscious attitude is "adequate" toward the psychic forces within him; it takes in enough of the unconscious to be in balance with it, at least for the moment. These dreams are very often abstract; they deal with images and figures that symbolize the complex situation within the person, but they often stress form and relationship by putting the emphasis on geometric, numerical, or even color arrangements. One example of this is certainly found in Ezekiel's vision of the wheels (1:15ff.) and in several places Jung discussed such dreams.[13]

Once in a while these dreams may take the form of clear, direct statements, although this does not happen very frequently. The unconscious, however, out of which consciousness has arisen, is quite capable of speaking consciously as well as symbolically. The dream we have described that came to Dr. A. J. Gordon in his Boston church was one of these. In it the setting, the people who were members of his church, and the words they spoke were all perfectly clear and familiar. Only the figure of Jesus, appearing as an ordinary churchgoer, had to be identified for him. It was dreams of this kind which were so highly valued in ancient times, undoubtedly because so many people hoped for specific guidance in this way.

Dreams of somewhat the same quality have also been reported by scientists at times when they were wholly engrossed in some problem. A story of this kind was told over television not long ago, of a physiologist who had been concentrating on a problem without reaching the solution. One night he was awakened by a dream that described the solution to a T, and he wrote it out and went back to sleep. In the morning his memory was not exact and his notes were undecipherable, but they were identified three nights later when he dreamed the same dream all over again.

Between these two extremes are all the "ordinary" dreams that take up bits of yesterday's experience and play them out as a strange

13 Particularly Vol. 11, pp. 65ff., and Vol. 9, Part 2, pp. 290ff.

new drama. These dreams are often profoundly symbolic, and it is my experience that they generally offer greater help and guidance than those that are clear and direct. Just because of their compensatory behavior an understanding of them can disclose new ways of approaching the day's problems. But this is not all. Over a longer period something far more important can be observed.

Where attention is given to dreams over a long period of time, as in the analytical situation, a vital process of development appears in the personality itself. Age-old dream symbols appear which represent a new center of personality, a higher center. In the isolated dream this process remains hidden in the compensation of the moment. But "with deeper insight and experience, these apparently separate acts of compensation arrange themselves into a kind of plan. They seem to hang together and in the deepest sense to be subordinated to a common goal."[14] This is what Jung described as the process of *individuation*, by which a man becomes at one with his own individuality, and at the same time with mankind, with the humanity of which he is a part. The process that Jung has described may well be the most important reason for paying attention to dreams. It is an inner way that is quite natural in man, but as is very obvious in today's world, it is by no means automatic. To bring together both the dream world within one and the outer world of real people and things is a living process that is demanding and difficult and can easily be sidetracked. Jung stressed the religious nature of this process in many ways, particularly in his discussions of the dream symbols that move men toward this goal.[15]

In addition, there is the clairvoyant or telepathic dream that sometimes brings spontaneous knowledge of something in the future or at a distance. This is abundantly clear from the numerous examples in the literature on dreams, although it is not understood. Jung has suggested that the constraining forces of time and space do not limit the unconscious as they do the conscious mind. It appears that, while the conscious mind is limited and circumscribed, the unconscious is not contained within the boundaries of either time or

---

[14] C. G. Jung, *Collected Works*, Vol. 8, p. 289.

[15] Some of the most fascinating of this material was presented in the seminars on dream analysis given by Dr. Jung in 1928, 1929, and 1930, in which he turned for comparative material to many experiences and stories described by Christians, often from old and neglected sources. The printed reports of these seminars are available in the library of the Jung Institute in Zurich for study by qualified persons.

space. The recent controlled experiments at Maimonides Hospital in New York[16] leave no doubt about the ability of the unconscious mind to receive information in some way other than by sense experience, and then to represent it in dreams.

We do not have any explanation of how these dreams occur, however, nor any real insight into the reason for them, even though there are many proven instances. For this reason it is probably wise, as we have already suggested, to value the occurrence of such dreams without making them an end in themselves. Jung suggested the basic nature of this problem in his excellent discussion of "A Psychological View of Conscience."[17] There is no question that such dreams come from a wisdom beyond our own. But we will wait a long time for our consciousness to start catching up with the wisdom of God if we ignore the dream that has personal religious significance and sit around waiting for an ESP experience. Many of the men who come the closest to a real understanding of dreams, and who have themselves experienced fruitful dream lives, have never once had a dream of a telepathic or prophetic nature.

Last of all, there are experiences of the numinous dream, the dream that is lightened by a special light and power and quality. These dreams tell us that we stand in a holy place. There rises within one a holy fear and awe, the very foundations of life tremble, and one finds himself in the very presence of God. It may be possible to understand certain attributes of these numinous contents, as Jung suggested in several places, but when it comes to the total effect one can only say as Jung did that a light has burst forth in the darkness which the dark cannot catch up with.[18] Something incomprehensible, which has all the quality of a religious experience, has taken over. Such dreams are as meaningful as a waking religious experience and, like any other divine encounter, are valuable in themselves. The symbols of the unconscious may even slip away and we know the one who gives us our dreams, the one who has fashioned life, the one toward whom our lives turn as the lodestone toward the magnetic pole.

[16] Montague Ullman, M.D., Stanley Krippner, Ph.D., and Sol Feldstein, B.E.E., "Experimentally-induced Telepathic Dreams: Two Studies Using EEG-REM Monitoring Technique," *International Journal of Neuropsychiatry*, Vol. 2, No. 5, October 1966, pp. 420ff.
[17] C. G. Jung, *Collected Works*, Vol. 10, pp. 450ff.
[18] C. G. Jung, *Collected Works*, Vol. 14, p. 255.

## The skill to understand dreams

It takes skill to understand and interpret dreams. There will probably not be much argument about this as a general proposition, but it is a subject on which Jung was quite specific, and one which emphasizes the difference of his whole approach. It is also a subject he continued to write about. At least once he even recommended it to the Protestant clergy because of the great and unique opportunity he felt was given them in the world today.[19]

About the only hard and fast rule Jung made, however, was to listen to the unconscious, to approach it without deciding beforehand what it has to say. If one reminds himself first of all, "I have no idea what this dream means," then he is forced to let the dream and the associations around it tell him what he wants to know. Once the memories and experiences associated with the dream are known, then the exacting task of actual interpretation can begin. And this "needs psychological empathy, ability to coordinate, intuition, knowledge of the world and of men, and above all a special 'canniness' which depends on wide understanding as well as on a certain *'intelligence du coeur.'* "[20] One is reminded of the church's own words in the Renaissance, the recipe phrased by Pererius for an interpreter, "who, as it were, grasps the very pulse of man's social and individual activity . . . [who is] divinely inspired and instructed."

Where, then, does one get the ability, let alone the courage, to attempt this? There are five ways, each of them indispensable. In the first place, there is no substitute for practice. By listening, by asking and offering explanations, one gains experience. He watches to see which thought clicks, both in the person's mind and in his life, and also which interpretations misfire, and gradually an instinct develops, a feeling for the meaning of one dream and also of many dreams. There is no other way but to try.

Next, one must come to know a great deal about the other person, about his conscious life, his convictions. Dream-images can only be truly understood as they are seen rising out of a total life; in this sense Jung calls them "true symbols . . . expressions of a content not yet consciously recognized or conceptually formu-

[19] C. G. Jung, *Collected Works*, Vol. 11, pp. 348ff.
[20] C. G. Jung, *Collected Works*, Vol. 8, p. 286.

lated."[21] They come into focus in the perspective of a man's life, and the more that is known of his life, the clearer these symbols become. Even during the hour that I am able to spend with most people I find that my understanding of the dreams they bring grows rapidly. Indeed, it is quite foolish to attempt more than very general interpretations of a person's dreams until we do know him fairly well. To interpret the dreams of those we do not know comes closer to magic than to a legitimate art.

The third requirement is even more important. One must listen to his own dreams if he is to help other people understand theirs. There is no easy way around this; it is the only way to reach the heights and depths, the far corners of the soul's life. Only by paying attention to the unconscious, by listening to the contents that are still unknown in oneself, can he encourage these depths in himself and others to speak. In addition, he must know where these experiences lead; our dreams often bring us into dangerous and forbidden territory where there is conflict and struggle and pain, and one needs the confidence of another person who knows the way. Besides this, it is amazing how much more someone else can tell me about the meaning of *my* dreams than I can ever figure out by myself. After all, they speak of what is not conscious in me, and it is simpler for me to see the meaning in another person's dreams which *his* inner blindness hides from his eyes. Thus I doubt if anyone can help another person understand dreams unless he himself has been counseled, guided, enlightened by someone wise in the ways of men and God.

Then there is a requirement that is easy to put into words but is the most difficult to put into action. In order to understand dreams one must first of all seek wisdom; he must be conversant with life. According to Jung it takes a "special canniness," or in the medieval words of Pererius, "a complete and perfect knowledge, confirmed by many tests of human character, interests, customs, and persuasions." This is a large order. To understand dreams one must live *widely* and *well*.

And finally, one must know God if he is to recognize the divine significance in dreams. These meanings are not often discovered by men who are driven just by natural impulses and imprisoned in the commonplace. Yet there have always been expressions of the

[21] C. G. Jung, *Collected Works*, Vol. 16, p. 156.

numinous or divine in dreams, and one who is open to the voice of God, whose consciousness and powers of reflection are developed, will recognize them. He must also know the religious and mythological traditions of mankind, and know them well enough to bring life to the symbols in dreams and amplify their meaning. This is a truly religious task, as our own tradition certainly shows. From Paul on through the Middle Ages the church was never without men who used the gifts of wisdom and interpretation to understand dreams. Paul was only the first of many who made a conscientious effort to understand his dreams and, to a great extent, to govern his life by them.

## The importance of Jung

Indeed, Jung calls modern Christians back to the consideration of life from a point of view that was once the Christian way. For those who know what it is to be lost in the rationalism of this modern era, he has something to say that hardly anyone else is trying to express. Jung's approach to the psyche, to human experience, offers men a way by which they can find the lively religious meaning that once welled up in Christian life. Through the symbolic, the religious approach to men's experience they can know that God still speaks out of the depth of the human soul, and sometimes his voice will be heard clearly. Through this quite different view of life, Christians can reach once again a real understanding of their religious heritage, making it real and vital for themselves and others, and keeping in touch with the source of revelation that God is constantly providing through the depth of man's being. Jung's theory of dream interpretation has significance far beyond the practice of psychotherapy.

If Jung is so important, then why is it that more clergy have not realized his significant contribution? Why has it not been more readily seized upon in religious circles? The answer is at the same time both simple and difficult. In the first place, Jung often wrote badly from the standpoint of most readers. It takes fortitude to wade through his writings unless one is already interested in Jung. For decades the only work by which he was generally known among English-speaking peoples was his first book, *The Psychology of the Unconscious*, which he himself referred to as one of the "sins

of my youth." Even in the revised form as *Symbols of Transformation*, it took many years of acquaintance with Jung before
I could get through it.

Then, Jung's writings are based upon experience, and unless one
has investigated such experiences in himself or in others, it is not
too likely that he will be open to believing that such things happen.
Jung's studies, which were based directly upon his own experiences
and those of his patients, have appeared esoteric and farfetched to
many people. The facts he presented are not generally accepted in
our society, since they are derived from experiences to which few
people have exposed themselves. This involves a major philosophical
question, which will be discussed in the next chapter.

The last reason is the most difficult and disturbing. Jung himself
underwent a direct confrontation with God in his own life journey.
Those who would understand or use the Jungian method must make
a similar confrontation and journey. Jung's method must be lived.
It cannot just be understood. Jung wrote in his autobiography:
"These talks with the 'Other' were my profoundest experiences: on
the one hand a bloody struggle, on the other supreme ecstasy . . ."
and "God alone was real—an annihilating fire and an indescribable
grace."[22] Most modern Christianity has forgotten the reality of such
encounters, which are very painful, and it does not choose to be
reminded.

Instead, the reminder that dream experience is very real is still
coming from the scientific and medical world. In fact, there is much
in the present medical work on dreaming which backs up the things
we have been discussing.

## A third state of existence

It is surprising how fast our ideas can change today. Ten years
ago most people held the idea that dreams were fleeting experiences
that happened once in a while, just by chance. Then the reports on
the new research began to be published. Using the electroenceph-
alograph to study eye movements as well as brain waves in sleep,
the investigators have discovered periods of dreaming so universal
and so different from either waking or non-dreaming sleep that today these are considered a third state of existence. According to

[22] *Memories, Dreams, Reflections*, pp. 48 and 56.

Dr. Charles Fisher, who has summarized this research for the American Psychoanalytic Association, the recent findings suggest that

> . . . dreaming is a predictable, universal, and basic psycho-biological process, occurring in a special organismic *third* state, and associated with such distinctive physiological events that it has to be considered as very different from both non-dreaming sleep and waking, although it has some characteristics of both.[23]

A great deal has been learned about this state of dreaming, which takes up nearly 20 to 25 per cent of the sleeping time of every one of us. At regular intervals it breaks "the monotonously impassive mask of sleep," and a whole set of physiological reactions begin which are tuned to a dream. The sleeper's eyelids begin to ripple, indicating that his eyes are moving rapidly, and his brain waves have changed from the random zigzag of sleep to a flattened, low-voltage pattern almost like attentive waking. At the same time metabolism rises; heart action, blood pressure, and breathing are all roused from the slow, even rhythms of sleep and suddenly speed up or slow down unaccountably. In men there is almost always full or partial penile erection. Although skin resistance and arousal thresholds are noticeably higher, the chemicals that normally prepare for arousal are released in abundance. Even the fine muscles of the ear respond as they do in waking attention, and in many regions of the brain spontaneous firing of nerve cells increases well beyond the waking level. This "uniquely intense condition of nervous excitation"[24] is even called by the name *rapid eye movement period*, or REMP, which is one of several outward, muscular reactions.

[23] Charles Fisher, M.D., "Psychoanalytic Implications of Recent Research on Sleep and Dreaming," *Journal of the American Psychoanalytic Association*, Vol. 13, No. 2, April 1965, p. 198. A visit to a sleep laboratory is invaluable in understanding the fascinating discoveries that keep coming from this new science. Here—where one can see the sleepers, the wires taped about their heads, and actually watch the electronic machines tracing out the individual rhythms of brain waves and various muscular movements in co-ordinated patterns—he begins to comprehend the possibilities of dream research. Even the inexperienced eye can quickly detect the distinctive difference between the waking tracing and the various stages of sleep. My own initiation was under the skillful direction of Dr. Paul Naitoh at the Naval Medical Research facility at Point Loma, California, where sleep deprivation is studied. In most aspects, however, the apparatus and methods here are essentially the same as those used in many other laboratories where the content and varied significance of dreams are being studied.

[24] Frederick Snyder, M.D., "Toward an Evolutionary Theory of Dreaming," *The American Journal of Psychiatry*, Vol. 123, No. 2, August 1966, pp. 122f.

Yet for all practical purposes the motor system is switched off; the elementary reflexes no longer function, and there is loss of muscle tone. Even things like sleepwalking and enuresis, which were always considered a part of dreaming, never occur during REMPs, or only rarely, as in the case of sleep talking. At the same time there is actually more body movement and movement of the fine muscles than there is in the rest of sleep, non-REM sleep, when muscle tone and reflexes are both in working order. In effect, the body is allowed certain expression and yet is protected from acting out its dream. It is no wonder that dreaming or REM sleep is sometimes called "paradoxical sleep."

Dreaming periods alternate with non-REM periods in regular cycles occurring on an average of four or five times a night. The REMPs last from a few minutes to over an hour,[25] increasing successively in length during the night, while the non-REM periods become progressively shorter. The first rapid eye movements appear only after a prolonged period of non-REM sleep, although at sleep onset there is a brief period when hypnagogic images are appearing that is unique. It is the only time when the typical dreaming pattern of the EEG (electroencephalogram) occurs without the presence of REMs.

All people dream, whether this surprises them or not. Ninety per cent of the time, persons wakened from REM sleep remember a dream. Besides this, some kind of mental activity seems to go on all of the time. When a sleeper is awakened in any period and asked what was going through his mind, there is almost always recall of something specific. Usually it is less distinct in non-REM sleep and is less visual, more connected with the events of the day and more like "thinking" than the vivid, spontaneous memory of a dream. Yet images and even full-length dreams have been reported from non-REM sleep, and it appears very difficult to confine dreaming to just one period of sleep or to one particular kind of mental activity.[26] Sometimes, in fact, a pattern seems to run through all the dreams of a night, as if these various periods were all working to-

---

[25] The original study by Dement and Kleitman showed that, for persons dreaming four times a night, the mean duration of the first REMP was nine minutes, the second nineteen, the third twenty-four, and the fourth twenty-eight minutes. Fisher, op. cit., p. 201.

[26] Ibid., pp. 213ff. Also, W. David Foulkes, "Dream Reports from Different Stages of Sleep," Journal of Abnormal and Social Psychology, Vol. 65, No. 1, January 1962, pp. 15 and 21ff.

gether to produce one final, very important product—man's conscious being.

No one doubts the direct effect of the physical body in this process. REMPs are triggered in one of the most remote and primitive parts of the brain, the pontile limbic formation, which is probably tied to instinctual drives and emotions, including penile erection. They have also been studied in babies and in many different animals that cannot be questioned about a dream and yet show all the physical reactions that go with dreaming.[27] But on the other hand, it appears equally certain that dreams have specific effect on the body, perhaps many of them. The best-known is the rapid eye movement that reflects almost exactly what is happening in a dream. For instance, one of the experimenters who discovered this was watching some horizontal eye movements of a subject and predicted a dream about a tennis match; when the sleeper awoke, he reported that he had been watching two men throw tomatoes at each other across a fence. On top of this, sudden changes in heart rate, respiration, and blood pressure often dovetail so exactly with changes in eye movement that these functions, as well as other movements, appear to reflect the psychic experience of dreaming. Indeed, it is difficult to ignore the inter-play of body and psyche that is being revealed by these studies. Some heart attacks may quite possibly be the direct result of psychic stimulation and excitement during dreaming.

The studies are also revealing a great deal about the need to dream. Subjects who were deprived of most of their REM sleep made inordinate attempts to dream during the experiments, as many as thirty by the fifth night, and then proceeded to make up for the deprivation on the first "recovery" nights. Various effects on the personality were observed, ranging from moderate anxiety and disturbance of motor control, memory, concentration, to almost psychotic manifestations when deprivation was prolonged. In one case of a person who stayed awake for two hundred hours, psychotic episodes occurred that looked "for all the world like dream episodes

[27] REMPs seem to be present at birth in all mammals, and there is good reason to suspect that they go on before birth. (Synder, op. cit., p. 125.) Perhaps Lovejoy is right in his ideas, and the brain of the newborn infant already houses images that are active and ready to be worked on. Arthur O. Lovejoy, *The Revolt Against Dualism*, New York, W. W. Norton & Company, Inc., 1930.

during sleep,"[28] and seemed to reflect the same basic rhythms. Alcohol and also certain drugs like Dexadrine and the barbiturates have been found to suppress dreaming, and it is suggested that dream deprivation may play a part in delirium tremens. On the other hand, certain drugs, notably LSD, have a striking effect of lengthening REM periods.

At any rate one thing is perfectly clear from these studies. The human organism has a need to dream. This need was originally based on certain physiological mechanisms. But sometime in early development, as Dr. Fisher puts it, "these physiological mechanisms are taken over by the psychological process of dreaming and a new function emerges, namely, the regulation of instinctual drive discharge processes through hallucinatory wish fulfillment, as opposed to physiological discharge through motor patterns."[29] In short, the human animal begins to dream its way to becoming a man.

Thus the scientific world continues to pile up evidence that shows the importance of dreaming in men's lives. From the beginning of Freud's revealing discoveries, the medical interest in dreams has gradually grown. Jung's findings in particular offer support for the traditional religious view, and the most recent research suggests that dreams may be as important in the development of man as they have been in religious practice.

[28] Fisher, op. cit., p. 247.
[29] Ibid., p. 280.

# *nine*      A Return to the Christian Interpretation of Dreams

We have seen the importance of dream interpretation in Christian tradition, and also in modern medical practice and research. In Christian theology the belief that God was able to speak to man through dreams and visions persisted until Aquinas began to be so universally accepted. In practice the belief still continues here and there. Medically the importance of dreams has been appreciated since earliest times. Physicians have used them in various ways in practice; and now that scientific methods of interpretation have been developed, these methods are in use by psychiatrists all over the world. The most recent research shows the extraordinary significance of dreaming to human life. It is even suggested that without this function, and the ability to know the choices presented in sleep, man might not have developed at all.

In addition, one important group of psychiatrists and psychologists, following the direction of Dr. C. G. Jung, has come full circle to a renewed and very deep appreciation of the dream from the religious point of view. Jung in particular came to the realization that dreams offer contact with a realm that seems to be the same as the spiritual realm described by the church, and that it is a realm of being with uncommon power for good as well as for evil in the lives of people.

In spite of all this, dreams are either ignored or strangely in disfavor in the modern church. What is the reason? Just what is the theology of the Christian church today?

## Where are we today?

There have probably been several reasons for paying less, or a different attention to dreams. But today the Christian neglect comes from one main reason. There is no place for the dream in the Aristotelian world view that has almost completely replaced the original thinking and philosophy of Christianity. This Aristotelian view, as proposed by Aquinas and refined by Descartes, states quite simply that there are only two realities. There is material reality and there is rational consciousness, and beyond this there is nothing else for man to know. This is just about as far as one can get from the traditional Christian view.

Yet matter and reason are all that exist for the modern student of religious philosophy. This is the point of view of every one of these men, from F. R. Tennant through MacIntosh to John Baillie. It is also the point of view of existentialism and logical positivism. And these are the philosophies that seem to attract modern theologians. Bultmann, Bonhoeffer, Robinson, Pike—none of them find any outlook from existence as they see it but some kind of positivism or existentialism. When it is even admitted that forms of being can exist apart from their expression in physical matter, such "modes" or "forms" are not really thought of in relation to man; they are considered unknowable, existing in some kind of metaphysical space that has no perceptible reality.

This thinking today stems from the philosophy of Husserl (phenomenology), which limits the experience of phenomena to those consciously received. Husserl quite explicitly considered Freud and found his "notion" of the unconscious mind a contradiction in terms, thus rejecting any such dimension of personality or any consideration of dreams or other forms of "divine madness." Jaspers, Heidegger, Marcel, and Sartre all follow suite. The European theologians who are the authorities for religious thinking today have taken this same line, and Bultmann and Barth in particular have been closely associated with the leaders of this school of thought. Its epistemology does not differ very much from Aristotelian, except that reason as a means of knowledge has been dropped out. Indeed, existentialism is the last dying gasp of Aristotelianism. It was only with Merleau-Ponty that the unconscious has been reconsidered among existentialists, and his untimely death in 1962 kept him from working out the implications of his thought and seeing its effect upon theology.[1]

Thus the idea of a realm of non-physical, non-rational reality that makes contact with men is simply ruled out to begin with. There is no place for the dream to come from. Since dreams are certainly neither material nor rational, they must be merely the undigested bits of yesterday's physical sensations and thoughts, a rehash—and garbled at that. The fact that most dreams have quite a different aspect from this makes no difference. This is the only possible view of reality, and so the dream is rejected before it is allowed to speak.

This rejection of the religious and philosophic significance of dreams is stated very clearly by one of the editors of the recent symposium, *The Dream and Human Societies.* In his introductory article on the cultural function of the dream, based on examples from classical Islam, Dr. von Grunebaum starts off by saying:

> For our purpose, we designate Descartes as the first fully self-conscious spokesman of the recent West, and we term all civilizations before his time, Eastern or Western, "medieval" or, more blandly, "premodern."[2]

And he goes on to show that the theory of knowledge held by previous cultures and religions, the older theories of revelation in dreams, can no longer be taken seriously by modern man. The irony of all this is that Descartes, the first "modern" man, received the inspiration for his method and his point of view from a dream experience. It was a dream that would eventually put an end to dreaming.[3]

---

[1] *Existential Philosophers: Kierkegaard to Merleau-Ponty*, ed. by George Alfred Schrader, Jr., New York, McGraw-Hill Book Co., Inc., 1967, pp. 423ff.

[2] Von Grunebaum and Caillois, eds., op. cit., p. 5.

[3] The very idea that rational consciousness provides the only method to understand life was given birth in a triple dream experience that occupied Descartes as he slept during the night of November 10, 1619, and brought him from chaos to clarity. L. L. Whyte notes that Descartes as a thinker considered that dreams "expressed a movement of the organs of the sleeper, that they constituted a language translating a desire. But to Descartes as a person the dreams were, as he said, a divine command to devote his inner life to the search for truth."

This experience, which Whyte describes in some detail, "marked out the path for the rest of his life. After a few days Descartes regained his normal composure and began to write. Descartes tells us that the triple dream was associated with the supreme question, 'What way of life shall I follow?' and that the dream brought him the answer as a compelling command from Heaven or Olympus: Search for the truth, by applying the mathematical method (analytical geometry,

Not only Descartes but the whole of Western civilization has been given direction by Descartes' dream. It would seem logical to pay attention to the man Descartes as well as to his thinking. If we do so, we find a belief in a higher power expressing itself through a dream. The same kind of experience also happened to both Aquinas and John Baillie, but at the end of their lives, giving them a direct relationship with that higher purpose. To be logical, we moderns must consider the source from which the "modern" philosophical method has arisen, as well as the method itself. Otherwise we limit ourselves like the followers of Islam, who revere the dreams of the Prophet but find no truth in their own.

If Rudolf Bultmann is correct in holding that theology cannot challenge the prevailing world view, but must adjust to it, then revelation and inspiration through dreams is a dead issue for Christians in our time. We would have to agree that Christianity must adjust itself, altering its traditional understanding and interpretation. If, however, it is possible to question the rational materialism of our time, it is then possible to consider a kind of philosophy like the Platonism that made Christianity a world religion, a religion that worked. This would require the individual to seek a view of the world very different from the prevailing one. He would need a point of view that has a place for non-physical reality and a method of knowing it.

## Which view?

As we turn to this question, it is worth noting the direction that scientific thinking is taking today, and how far, as Korzybski shows in *Science and Sanity*, the older thinking of Aristotle has been overthrown. Men who deal with the science of relativity have had to free themselves from the strict Aristotelian materialism of today's point of view in order to grasp a new conception of time and space and matter. It is interesting how these great minds see the source of their inspiration. When Einstein and Jung were together once, Jung asked the scientist if it took a great deal of strict discipline and

in the main) to all other studies. This twin experience, the dream and the discovery of his method, did in fact put an end to his emotional and intellectual confusions and gave a decisive direction to his subsequent life. Olympus had spoken through his unconscious, and Descartes had been lifted out of his past self to acquire a new vision of truth." Whyte, op. cit., pp. 87 and 89f.

mental concentration to come to his conclusions. And Einstein replied, "Oh, no. I meditate and the numbers dance before me."

These men know how difficult it is to reach through the things they discover and come to any final, objective knowledge about the real nature of this world around us. But as they have given up, first the Aristotelian idea of a Prime Mover apart from all things, and then the Cartesian idea of a cosmology based on mechanical principles, they have found new ways flooding in to deal with this reality they seek. These are new symbolic ways of thinking, imaginative almost beyond the dreams of an older science. Indeed, far from clinging only to the established methods of working with matter itself, these new scientists have turned to the symbol and image from within. Besides the results we have seen, the scientist finds that there is more to know than he thought. And he goes on seeking in an unspoken faith that objective truth exists ·and is waiting to be revealed.

In doing so, these scientists have approached a Platonic theory of reality as few have done in recent centuries. Eddington, Whitehead, and others show the importance of the Platonic way of thinking. Yet it remains for others to see this from the Christian standpoint. For one, Teilhard de Chardin has postulated the reality of non-physical existence in accounting for the facts of evolution. Jung, although he was first and foremost a medical doctor, postulated the same reality in order to account for the facts that he uncovered in the empirical study of man's psyche—facts that he had to understand and deal with in order to bring health to his patients. I myself have seen this same reality at work in the lives of many who have regained health and meaning as they learned to listen to the depth of themselves through dreams and then tried to live more in harmony with this depth and purpose.

The reality of men's experiences of the non-physical is supported by a basic religious theory of knowledge. This is a philosophic approach to man's experience, the way he comes to know the world around him, which springs from Plato's ultimate forms of reality. It sees the soul or psyche of man as being in contact with typical forms of experience that Augustine described as "contained in the divine understanding." In simplest terms, this theory sees the "form" —which is quite real even apart from any material expression— as already in existence before man's senses can grasp it in physical form and take it directly into rational consciousness; and at this deeper level of his being the Christian has traditionally held that God, through his ability to speak directly to man, has the power to offer or impose new relationships, or even new forms. These can then be pictured in dreams or spoken of prophetically. This branch of philosophy, which is called epistemology, goes on to show the reasons for understanding men's actual behavior in this way.

In my book *Tongue Speaking* I have sketched such a philosophy and epistemology, in which both dreams and the other charismata are meaningful. The Reverend John A. Sanford, has also written a work on this religious theory of knowledge; his manuscript, which has not yet found a publisher, describes clearly the foundation for the reality of the non-physical world. This is not the place for us, however, to get into detailed discussion of theories of knowledge.

As Tillich has shown so explicitly in his study of theology, every theory of knowledge contains an implicit theory about the nature of being, the nature of the universe and of God. This can be discussed in several volumes, as Tillich has done so well from a somewhat different point of view from the one we suggest, or it can be discovered and understood in actual experience. If one can concede the possibility that an essentially Platonic view of the world may be valid, then it is possible to discover the nature of spiritual reality in experiences like dreams. The dream can then become meaningful, a source of self-knowledge and revelation.

The actual fact of finding inspiration in dreams gives substance to the hypothesis that such a level of reality does exist. Once one has accepted this hypothesis, and then listens carefully to his dreams, he will find, as so many others have, that he is presented with a consistent body of impressive and powerful materials. He finds a reality of many layers and levels, apart from the physical world. He finds that it contains everything from yesterday's memories and forgotten faces to terrifying encounters with destructive and demonic darkness, and numinous experiences of the divine. It may come as a single image, or in the form of a poetic story, or like an allegory, or directly as a command; or one may find endless tales and images that he must struggle to understand. Occasionally a dream breaks over the barriers of time and space and brings telepathic knowledge or some precognition. But unless a person takes time to record and consider his dreams, he usually remembers only a few that were different enough to be startling or just goofy. Dreams move from one level to another of this inexhaustible reservoir of non-physical reality, but in the long run with a consistency and direction that is difficult to believe until one has experienced it.

Once one knows this reality, it makes very little difference what name he gives to it. Call it the "unconscious" or the "spiritual world," the "objective psyche" or "heaven and hell," the "collective unconscious" or the "realm of gods and demons," or even *"ʿālam al-mithāl"*—these are all merely names to describe what man finds as he listens to the reality that comes through the depth of himself. In the last of Jung's writings, in which he spoke simply as a man rather than as a scientist, he suggested that what he had described as the objective psyche was the same reality that had been called the spiritual world by religious people from the dawn of time. He wrote:

> I have, therefore, even hazarded the postulate that the phenomenon of archetypal configurations—which are psychic events *par excellence*—may be founded . . . upon an only partially psychic and possibly altogether different form of being. For lack of empirical data I have neither knowledge nor understanding of such forms of being, which are commonly called spiritual. From the point of view of science, it is immaterial what I may *believe* on that score, and I must accept my ignorance. . . . Nevertheless, we have good reason to suppose that behind this veil there exists the uncomprehended absolute object which affects and influences us—and to suppose it even, or particularly, in the case of psychic phenomena about which no verifiable statements can be made.[4]

What is the modern Christian to make of dreams, then, when he has opened his mind in this way to the possibility that they may speak to him of something beyond or different from his conscious ego?

## Possibilities of meaning

Whatever else a dream is, once one has admitted the possibility of meaning, it at least mirrors what goes on in one man's psyche or personality. About this there is agreement among medical men who work with dreams, psychologists who study them, and also other modern students of dreams. A great deal of literature expresses this

[4] C. G. Jung, *Memories, Dreams, Reflections*, New York, Pantheon Books, Inc., 1963, pp. 351f.

same point of view.[5] In one way or another, then, dreams reveal the condition of a man's psychic being. They show the things a man is hiding from, often as graphically as Freud described these elements; and sometimes they reveal what he really wants. When either kind is properly understood, it can guide the direction of a man's life. Dreams can be precise guideposts through trouble, direction signs toward meaning and fulfillment. Thus they are the concern of those who would help people out of confusion and difficulty, who want to help men grow and mature psychologically and spiritually. In most cases the pastor who is interested in helping his flock in this way can make good use of dreams. They offer a key to much that is going on in the personality that is hard to get at and understand in other ways.

The history I have presented also makes it very clear that modern psychoanalysis has no exclusive on the use of dream material or its interpretation. In fact, it was an analyst who once suggested to me that the New Testament is undoubtedly the best guidebook known for anyone who is seeking maturity and integration of the personality. Christian dream interpretation is a legitimate individual Christian undertaking, and an excellent Christian pastoral exercise. Indeed, most Christian pastors should know how to interpret and understand this material, which so often reveals the state of a man's personality.

This brings us to a second and even more important point. From the Christian point of view, and also that of other religions, God is in intimate relationship with the total human psyche or personality. In fact, from a religious point of view nothing is more important to the health of the personality than its relation to God, to that center of non-physical, creative meaning that is at the heart of things. Since dreams mirror and reveal the personality's innermost condition, they inevitably speak of man's relationship to God, as

[5] Literature from the Renaissance to the present abounds in dreams, which are seen as either a reflection of the state of man's personality, or an intrusion from beyond or from a deeper level of his being. Dante, Chaucer, Shakespeare, Rabelais, Milton, Tolstoy, Goethe, Dickens are but a few who based incidents or whole stories on dreams. *Dr. Jekyll and Mr. Hyde* came from a dream of Stevenson's; Mary Shelley wrote *Frankenstein* on the inspiration of a dream. The influence of dreams and the unconscious in the theater today is the subject of a whole book, the interesting work by W. David Sievers, *Freud on Broadway*. In *Demian* Hermann Hesse wrote of dreams as a profound and integral part of his own life story. This subject alone deserves a whole book.

well as of other relationships. Thus God is able to speak to men through them. Sometimes dreams that speak of the soul's religious health are shot through with a numinous quality, mingled with the commonplace. Sometimes it even seems that God speaks directly and with overpowering force, but these seem to be rare dreams.

At other times dreams that tell a man of his relationship with God replay the ancient symbols of myth or the stories of Jesus. When they speak symbolically, one has to track down the meaning of the symbols and relate them to his own life in order to understand the deep significance of their content. For some people dreams of this kind are almost nightly occurrences, but those that appear sketchy or irrelevant also may mirror the dreamer's inner condition and speak of God's relationship, for God is deeply related to man's inner condition. If God is real at all, and if there is a non-physical realm in which he has life and power to move the unlimited realities of the spirit, then dreams have unquestionable importance for men.

## Some dreams that were important

Dreams that lead men to the depth of metaphysical meaning are often heard by those who take the time to listen. One of the most impressive dreams of this kind occurred to a friend of mine just before he died; it is recorded in his son's book, *Gottes Vergessene Sprache*. This dreamer was a priest of the Episcopal church, a fine pastor and the author of a book on healing, *God's Healing Power*, but he had never been interested in dreams. The last five years of his life were plagued by mounting physical illness and by increasing depression and anxiety about death. On several occasions he discussed this with his wife and son. Then during the week before his death he had the following experience, which he described immediately to his wife, who recorded it:

> In the dream [she wrote] he awakened in his living room. But then the room changed, and he was back in his room in the old house in Vermont as a child. Again the room changed: To Connecticut (where he had his first job), to China, to Pennsylvania (where he often visited), to New Jersey, and then back to the living room. In each scene after China, I . . . was present, in each instance being of a different age in accordance with the time represented. Finally he sees himself lying on the couch back in the living room. I am descending

the stairs and the doctor is in the room. The doctor says, "Oh, he's gone." Then, as the others fade in the dream, he sees the clock on the mantelpiece: The hands have been moving, but now they stop! As they stop, a window opens behind the mantelpiece clock and a bright light shines through. The opening widens into a door, and the light becomes a brilliant path. He walks out on the path of light and disappears.

"My father knew, of course," the son's book goes on, "that this was a dream of his approaching death, but no longer did he have any anxiety. When he died a week later it was in complete peace; he fell asleep at home and 'forgot' to awaken. We had a special stone marker made for his grave, which has etched into it the 'path of light' down which he went."[6]

This was indeed one of those numinous experiences that can bring meaning and focus to a whole life. It gathered up the dreamer's life in retrospect, then pointed to the clock, which represents time and time that has run out. Behind the clock was light, a common symbol for divine life and radiance—"the light of the world." It appeared as a path on which he walked out. He had found his God in the last telling moment of life and saw his continued existence with the God of light.

Two other dreams have come up rather recently in counseling, each of which brought the dreamer to a new experience of God. The first of these came to a young man of nineteen who was overwhelmed by doubts and deep inner insecurity. He was potentially an excellent student, with a bent for philosophy, but he had lost his way and could not meet his classmates, with all their own doubts, on their own ground. One night he dreamed that he was watching a movie that started, he wrote to me,

> . . . with a whole group of children in a bicycle race. They are about nine years old and are riding like mad. There is a narrator off-scene who points out that the children are all racing, trying as hard as they can. He seems to be talking about running the race in life. One little redheaded child, who is racing furiously, has another child on his handle bar. The race goes over a hill and when they start down, the camera looks up, and there on a mountain side like the rock of Gibraltar is a diagram with the letters L O V E engraved in the stone. And the narrator continues: "If you can remember that love

[6] John A. Sanford, op. cit., pp. 45f.

is not being loved or saved, but is more of a giving, then you will see how this diagram illustrates the concept of love's being—inside, outside, and all around."

The meaning of the dream was quite clear; he was in the race of life, but he had forgotten where he was racing and what was the object of his race. When we talked later, he brought up the words of the New Testament, the commandment: *that you love one another as I have loved you.* He also remembered Plato's belief that it was only through love that one came into relation with the forms, and he saw how this fits in with the religious understanding of love as the only entrance to the eternal world of images.

He realized that he had been trying to live his life only intellectually, and out of this dream experience he came to terms with his own capacity to love, which had been much repressed. As he overcame the fear of himself and of the world around him, his fear of meaninglessness and emptiness began to disappear. The experience of God became real for him once again.

Another young man came to me even more recently whose religious life had come to a dead halt. Where it had once been very powerful and real, he found only an aching void. He had wanted to enter the ministry, but decided that this was impossible without conviction. In the spring of 1967 he had heard a series of lectures on dreams, and now he decided in desperation to listen to his own dreams. In one of them he heard the instruction to make a long journey like Abraham and visit the person who suggested that dreams were a way to know God; and he followed through on it.

The night before he arrived here he had a dream in which he saw himself standing like the rich young ruler in the Bible, listening to be told the one thing that he lacked. During the days that followed he *was* told, through the depth of himself, the one thing that he lacked. And this young man, seizing it, found that his faith in God, his sense of meaning, the reality of God as a burning fire in his life have all returned, with interest as if to pay for his trouble.

Again, only a few months ago, a close friend in my church was warned in a startling, precognitive dream of the death of his newborn grandchild. The baby, born that day, a Friday, was in critical condition. In the night my friend dreamed of a woman's voice telling him that the child was dead. The next morning he shared the dream with his wife, and during the day he could not rid himself of the oppression it had caused. On Sunday morning the phone rang and he answered it; the same voice, using the same words he had heard in his dream, informed him that the child was dead. In this strange, inexplicable way they had been prepared to accept the tragedy.

There are many, many such experiences today, involving people of all ages. Dreams do still speak—how, then, do we understand them?

## Understanding symbols

When men forget how to think symbolically, the symbols of dreams become a closed book. Men forget that these images describe realities that influence the human psyche. Thinking in this way is very different from the rational, analytical thinking that Descartes helped to define for the modern world. Symbolic thinking is thinking through images, through imagination. It has its own meanings, its own direction and way, which can be understood by the rational, conscious mind. Thus it is the basis of many great scientific discoveries, as well as being the language of literature and art. It is symbolic thinking that also produces religious writings and is used in the practice of Christian meditation and meditative reading. When men learn to think symbolically again, they will not only understand the language of dreams, of art and literature, but they will also understand the Bible quite a bit better than they do now.

Each of these ways of using symbolic thinking is valuable to the individual who is trying to follow the Christian way of living. The life and teachings of Jesus, who lived and spoke symbolically, first of all require an understanding of this language. Then there are the great religious writers, from Augustine to Charles Williams and T. S. Eliot. These and other devotional writers offer the general instructions for Christian life, while the dream speaks specifically to the individual. None of us can really afford to neglect these sources of God's direction, or to be ignorant of the way in which they communicate it to us.

Beyond this, can we actually afford to neglect the theological foundations of our church? It never occurred to the early Christian fathers to doubt the validity and value of dream experiences as expressions of God's providence and as a way of communicating with the more-than-human world. In ignoring the value and significance of dreams, the church today is denying not only the biblical and Greek tradition, but also the sophisticated thinking of several centuries of hard-fought pioneering. These men, writing in the period of the church's greatest vitality, recognized the deep and mysterious communication of God with man. Dreams and visions were an important part of that communication. Is it possible to believe that these men simply suffered from an illusion common to their age and not, in the same breath, cast doubts upon the entire theological formulation of Christianity?

Jesus, the Bible, the early church—all speak from essentially the same point of view. They all say essentially the same thing. And what they say simply does not get across in a purely Aristotelian hookup. If Jesus speaks to the whole of life, as the church still says that he does, then it is worth trying his whole point of view, and dreams are an important part of that whole point of view. What concrete suggestions, then, can be offered for taking these experiences seriously?

## Four practical suggestions

We offer four of them. In the first place, one must stretch his mind to entertain the hypothesis that there might exist a non-physical reality that can interact with men. Until one has consciously decided to take this hypothesis seriously, his investigation of dreams will be only a curiosity or a toying with the occult. Anyone who has been overwhelmed by neurosis knows that something outside of ordinary experience can stop him in his tracks. Fortunately there is another way of approaching this possibility which works better than being forced to by neurosis. A conscious decision is the best—really the only—beginning for serious consideration of dreams.

The next step is to keep a written record of one's own dreams, and to make it a part of a personal spiritual journal. If it is important to relate to whatever reality there is beyond the human ego, if religion is important, it is also important to keep a record of one's contact and confrontation with spiritual reality. Almost every Christian who has gone very far upon a spiritual way of life has kept such a journal, and an essential part of it is a record of dreams, as recommended by Synesius of Cyrene so long ago.

This has to be done immediately upon awakening. Unless a dream is written down almost immediately, hardly anything but the outline of a few strikingly vivid dreams can ever be recalled. Within a few minutes the rest is irretrievably gone. And this has to be done even when one awakens in the middle of the night from a dream. Too hard? Not when one becomes interested in what is happening. A notebook and pencil on the nightstand help, and soon the ability comes to recall even fragments and isolated images from the depth of sleep. These are sometimes even more important than longer dreams. It was upon such images in visions that the prophets Amos, Ezekiel, and Jeremiah based whole prophecies to their people.

People who keep such a spiritual journal usually find that they dream far more frequently than they had realized. In the beginning one may seem to be immersed in almost endless variety without much order or meaning. Repetitions of ordinary scenes or figures one knows almost too well may seem to predominate. But as a person begins to notice even slight variations from a daytime event, and to realize the compensatory meaning in many of the familiar images, he begins to recognize recurring themes, patterns that suggest that something is trying to come through. The more attention that is given, the more fluently dreams seem to speak. One begins to feel a life trying to communicate behind the dream.

There are people, it is true, who find it almost impossible to remember dreams, probably because of personality type. For them it is important to value the effort of the dreamer (and equally for the dreamer to value other ways of finding this reality), and to try some other approach, such as meditative reading, or perhaps some creative artistic or social activity. Ultimately one's own myth will find expression.[7]

Then, third, comes the work of interpreting dreams. The most basic and sometimes the hardest thing to realize is the fact that the figures who appear in dreams usually refer to aspects of ourselves. They represent something that is going on in the depth of one's own being that is different from the way he acts in the everyday world. They sometimes tell a great deal more besides, but not until one has come to this most profound realization.

[7] The understanding of myth as a religious language, expressing the spiritual reality within and from beyond man, is not very much known today. Most people still seem to look for some prescientific cosmology, some historical or social meaning, or a limited artistic value in myth. This subject, again, deserves treatment in a separate work.

And this can only be found as one comes to understand the dream symbolically and imaginatively, as one learns to think intuitively in symbols.

The art of dream interpretation is the art of intuition. It is the same faculty that understands and appreciates the great works of pictorial art, literature, and drama. Through the dream, as in these other ways, one receives the symbol as a message (not necessarily a moral) that is given. One listens to the non-rational symbol because it speaks to him, communicates with him. One comes to understand a great painting, drama, or religious work as he lets it sink in, just looking or listening or meditating. In much the same way the dream is understood as one looks at it and listens to it, allowing his fancy and imagination to brood over it.

As Hugh Lynn Cayce has suggested, it takes as much time and effort to learn the language of dreams as to learn a foreign language. But the kind of effort is quite different. If Jung's theory of types is correct, some people are simply more literal while others are more intuitively-minded, and it should be natural for some to become more adept at understanding dreams. Still, there is no one who really tries who cannot develop some skill and so learn a great deal about the world of spirit that can be learned in no other way.

It is the attempt to understand and interpret dreams solely by analytical and rational methods that falls into absurdity. The dream book, from ancient Assyria to the present, is only the ultimate of this absurdity, which tries to make a matter of science out of something that is really a matter of art and intuition. This was the error into which Islamic dream interpretation fell. It applied Aristotelian logic to the dream and came up with nonsense.

On the other hand, one's own intuition and understanding of symbolism is rarely enough to get very deep into the meaning of most dreams. There is a great deal of help in the studies that Jung has published. The most basic of these, *Modern Man in Search of a Soul*, *Two Essays on Analytical Psychology*, and *Memories, Dreams, Reflections*, offer a general background for getting at this meaning, and for some people *Man and his Symbols*, written by Jung and several co-workers, is a helpful beginning because of the pictorial approach. Then there are Jung's more difficult works, such as *Symbols of Transformation*, *Psychology and Alchemy*, and *Psychology and Religion: West and East*, which deal for the most part with dreams and visionary materials. There are also the specific articles on dream interpretation to which we have already referred. In addition, many of Jung's interpretations of particular dream symbols can be found by checking the excellent indexes in his collected works. These often offer hints about the meaning when a dream seems obscure, particularly if it has arisen out of the spiritual world and not just the personal unconscious.

After gaining some of this insight, it is much easier to understand the materials presented in the appendix that follows. One realizes that, with growth in maturity and spirituality, he can be open to the same kind of experience that is described by the great men of Christianity from the time of the New Testament on. Augustine, Synesius, Tertullian, and others of the fathers can be read to great advantage. Clearly the Jungian return to the dream is not in opposition to Christian tradition and practice. It is rather a return to the orthodox practice and understanding of earlier Christians. It is a renewal of the early Christian way of looking at life and spirituality. When one finds that real insight and wisdom can come through an understanding of his own dreams, his whole appreciation of the Christian way becomes deepened and enriched.

My final suggestion is to find another person to talk with about these experiences. It is very difficult to understand dreams alone. They are the products of one's own unconsciousness, and so the very simplest symbols sometimes elude a person simply because they are so close, and yet his ordinary life seems so different. The other person need not be a trained analyst. Of course, there are professional analysts who can help, and there are Christian ministers in some places who are becoming trained in this art. But any person who is deeply interested in the spiritual way, who is open to the possibility of meaning in dreams, will be able to help. And it is my experience that the individual who is truly interested in understanding his dreams, who actually looks for another to help him, will find someone. God seldom keeps these avenues closed to those who are seeking.

Neither Jung nor psychology is the last word in the matter of dreams. They have carried the ball as far as they can in a secular environment, and it is time for the church to get back to its traditional job of dealing with the human psyche.

## A job for the church

Tragically, the church as a whole does not yet see that it has a job to do. There is hostility to psychology, and a deep-rooted fear. Both are based on the completely un-Christian idea that there *is* no reality like the one Jesus talked about. The church is deeply afraid of the psychologist because he has the power to open this realm to people, and when he does, they will be able to find out one of two things: either the church was right in the beginning, and it has to admit this now (which in itself is painful) and get back to the real job; or people may find out that there is no reality behind the church's words, and one has to forget the foolishness about a religious approach to life.

It was an astute psychologist who once remarked to me that she believed there was a place for religion in the church as well as in the psychologist's office. But, she added, it would be a long time before the church found this out if people went on using the same old words without seeing that they needed to know more about the experiences the words describe. Those who have taken this way of experience find, instead of hostility to the psychologist, a deep appreciation of what he has done to remind us of man's inexplicable roots. Behind just such experiences as the dream there is reality to discover, and they go on extending these discoveries.

The church with all of its faults offers a stability and a consciousness of historical norms and values that are most important when one deals with anything as potent as the dream and the deep powers of the spiritual world that it expresses. The very conservatism of the church is our safeguard when we deal with dreams and the realm they express. On the other hand, the church that fails to come into contact with this living reality is left with little but a shell of outworn forms and dead morals and ritual. Instead of helping the serious Christian to reach the deepest levels of his own, indigenous religious experience, it has little to offer him but a pattern of behavior. It has no way to help him bring life and power into his religious practice when it overlooks the basic experiences that are the business of religion.

The youth today are facing this need head-on and in ever larger numbers. Their revolt itself, their use of marijuana, of LSD and other mind-expanding drugs, their interest in Maharishi and Hindu meditation, their turning toward the fellowship of the ingroup are all obvious attempts to find some meaning beyond the rationalism and materialism in which their parents have encased them. In other days these young people would have turned to some Christian way of seeking, but finding a religion as rational and comprehensible as that of the modern theologians and modern churches, they turn away today. I have heard the complaint of dozens of these young men and women who are seeking seriously, cries in anguish and anger against the sterility of ordinary Christianity. And once they take the dream seriously from a religious point of view, they find a whole new realm of religious experience and interest opened to them through contact with something beyond the bounds of the ordinary church practice they have known.

The church at the present is saddled with the prejudice of modern culture that only the material and the rational are real and significant. Consideration of the dream will help us break out of this prejudice and realize that there is another realm of being, a realm in which the ancient church was a specialist, as the modern church needs to be now. Troxler, a German-Swiss physician writing a century or so ago, put the problem well: "Life has married the unconscious and involuntary to the reasonable and spontaneous— and so man should not separate what heaven has joined."[8] The purpose of considering dreams is to prevent this divorce.

Many will say, as they have of other things: "But isn't this dangerous—this consideration of the murky, irrational, unconscious depths of man?" And I can only reply again that it is most certainly dangerous. But which is more dangerous—a dead religion or a dangerous one; neurotic, unconscious people or those dealing with the depths of themselves? When religion is dead, the involuntary and unconscious forces are either projected out upon others, invoking the cult of war and hate, or else they break forth in the individual in depression and anxiety and psychosomatic illness.

Naturally dealing with the depths of one's self is dangerous and may well lead to disaster. Jung himself witnessed just how close his confrontation with this reality brought him to the edge of psychic illness and dissociation. Many, like Nietzsche, Hölderlin, Van Gogh, have gone over the brink into psychosis. But if we do not deal creatively with the non-physical powers with which we

[8] Quoted by L. L. Whyte, op. cit., p. 139.

are in such intimate contact, we can well be destroyed, both as individuals and as a culture. On the other hand, those who do withstand the dark night of the soul find their lives filled with creativity and meaning and power. There is no easy way to find or live with God.

# Appendix

# TERTULLIAN
## A *Treatise on the Soul*
## CHAPTERS XLIV–XLIX

*Chap. XLIV.*—*The story of Hermotimus, and the sleeplessness of the emperor Nero. No separation of the soul from the body until death.*

With regard to the case of Hermotimus, they say that he used to be deprived of his soul in his sleep, as if it wandered away from his body like a person on a holiday trip. His wife betrayed the strange peculiarity. His enemies, finding him asleep, burnt his body, as if it were a corpse: when his soul returned too late, it appropriated (I suppose) to itself the guilt of the murder. However the good citizens of Clazomenae consoled poor Hermotimus with a temple, into which no woman ever enters, because of the infamy of this wife. Now why this story? In order that, since the vulgar belief so readily holds sleep to be the separation of the soul from the body, credulity should not be encouraged by this case of Hermotimus. It must certainly have been a much heavier sort of slumber: one would presume it was the nightmare, or perhaps that diseased languor which Soranus suggests in opposition to the nightmare, or else some such malady as that which the fable has fastened upon Epimenides, who slept on some fifty years or so. Suetonius, however, informs us that Nero never dreamt, and Theopompus says the same thing about Thrasymedes; but Nero at the close of his life did with some difficulty dream after some excessive alarm. What indeed would be said, if the case of Hermotimus were believed to be such that the repose of his soul was a state of actual idleness during sleep, and a positive separation from his body? You may conjecture it to be anything but such a licence of the soul as admits of flights away from the body without death, and that by continual recurrence, as if habitual to its state and constitution. If indeed such a thing were told me to have happened at any time to the soul—resembling a total eclipse of the sun or the moon—I should verily suppose that the occurrence had been caused by God's own inter-position, for it would not be unreasonable for a man to receive admonition from the Divine Being either in the way of warning or of alarm, as by a flash of lightning, or by a sudden stroke of death; only it would be much the more natural conclusion to believe that this process should be by a dream, because if it must be supposed to be, (as the hypothesis we are resisting assumes it to be,) not a dream, the occurrence ought rather to happen to a man whilst he is wide awake.

*Chap. XLV.—Dreams an incidental effect of the soul's activity. Ecstasy.*

We are bound to expound at this point what is the opinion of Christians respecting dreams, as incidents of sleep, and as no slight or trifling excitements of the soul, which we have declared to be always occupied and active owing to its perpetual movement, which again is a proof and evidence of its divine quality and immortality. When, therefore, rest accrues to human bodies, it being their own especial comfort, the soul, disdaining a repose which is not natural to it, never rests; and since it receives no help from the limbs of the body, it uses its own. Imagine a gladiator without his instruments or arms, and a charioteer without his team, but still gesticulating the entire course and exertion of their respective employments: there is the fight, there is the struggle; but the effort is a vain one. Nevertheless the whole procedure seems to be gone through, although it evidently has not been really effected. There is the act, but not the effect. This power we call *ecstasy*, in which the sensuous soul stands out of itself, in a way which even resembles madness.* Thus in the very beginning sleep was inaugurated by ecstasy: "And God sent an ecstasy upon Adam, and he slept" [Genesis 2:21]. The sleep came on his body to cause it to rest, but the ecstasy fell on his soul to remove rest: from that very circumstance it still happens ordinarily (and from the order results the nature of the case) that sleep is combined with ecstasy. In fact, with what real feeling, and anxiety, and suffering do we experience joy, and sorrow, and alarm in our dreams! Whereas we should not be moved by any such emotions, by what would be the merest fantasies of course, if when we dream we were masters of ourselves, (unaffected by ecstasy). In these dreams, indeed, good actions are useless, and crimes harmless; for we shall no more be condemned for visionary acts of sin, than we shall be crowned for imaginary martyrdom. But how, you will ask, can the soul remember its dreams, when it is said to be without any mastery over its own operations? This memory must be an especial gift of the ecstatic condition of which we are treating, since it arises not from any failure of healthy action, but entirely from natural process; nor does it expel mental function —it withdraws it for a time. It is one thing to shake, it is another thing to move; one thing to destroy, another thing to agitate. That, therefore, which memory supplies betokens soundness of mind; and that which a sound mind ecstatically experiences whilst the memory remains un-

* We had better give Tertullian's own succinct definition: *Excessus sensus et amentiae instar.*

checked, is a kind of madness. We are accordingly not said to be mad, but to dream, in that state; to be in the full possession also of our mental faculties [*prudentes*], if we are at any time. For although the power to exercise these faculties [*sapere*] may be dimmed in us, it is still not extinguished; except that it may seem to be itself absent at the very time that the ecstasy is energizing in us in its special manner, in such wise as to bring before us images of a sound mind and of wisdom, even as it does those of aberration.

*Chap.* XLVI.—*Diversity of dreams and visions. Epicurus thought lightly of them, though generally most highly valued. Instances of dreams.*

We now find ourselves constrained to express an opinion about the character of the dreams by which the soul is excited. And when shall we arrive at the subject of death? And on such a question I would say, When God shall permit: that admits of no long delay which must needs happen at all events. Epicurus has given it as his opinion that dreams are altogether vain things; (but he says this) when liberating the Deity from all sort of care, and dissolving the entire order of the world, and giving to all things the aspect of merest chance, casual in their issues, fortuitous in their nature. Well, now, if such be the nature of things, there must be some chance even for truth, because it is impossible for it to be the only thing to be exempted from the fortune which is due to all things. Homer has assigned two gates to dreams,— the *horny* one of truth, the *ivory* one of error and delusion [*Odyssey*, XIX.562ff.; *Aeneid*, VI.894]. For, they say, it is possible to see through horn, whereas ivory is untransparent. Aristotle, while expressing his opinion that dreams are in most cases untrue, yet acknowledges that there is some truth in them. The people of Telmessus will not admit that dreams are in any case unmeaning, but they blame their own weakness when unable to conjecture their signification. Now, who is such a stranger to human experience as not sometimes to have perceived some truth in dreams? I shall force a blush from Epicurus, if I only glance at some few of the more remarkable instances. Herodotus [I.107,ff.] relates how that Astyages, king of the Medes, saw in a dream issuing from the womb of his virgin daughter a flood which inundated Asia; and again, in the year which followed her marriage, he saw a vine growing out from the same part of her person, which overspread the whole of Asia. The same story is told prior to Herodotus by Charon of Lampsacus. Now they who interpreted these visions did not deceive the mother when they destined her son for so great an enterprise, for Cyrus both inundated and overspread Asia. Philip of Macedon, before he became a father, had seen imprinted on the pudenda of his consort Olympias the form of a small ring, with a lion as a seal. He had concluded that an offspring from her was out of the question (I suppose because the lion only becomes once a father), when Aristodemus or Aristophon happened to conjecture that nothing of an unmeaning or empty import lay under that seal, but that a son of very illustrious character was portended. They who know anything of Alexander recognise in him the lion of that small ring. Ephorus writes to this effect. Again, Heraclides has told us, that a certain woman of Himera beheld in a dream Dionysius' tyranny over Sicily. Euphorion has publicly recorded as a fact, that, previous to giving birth to Seleucus, his mother Laodice foresaw that he was destined for the empire of Asia. I find again from Strabo, that it was owing to a dream that even Mithridates took possession of Pontus; and I further learn from Callisthenes that it was from the indication of a dream that Baraliris the Illyrian stretched his dominion from the Molossi to the frontiers of Macedon. The Romans, too, were acquainted with dreams of this kind. From a dream Marcus Tullius (Cicero) had learnt how that one, who was yet only a little boy, and in a private station, who was also plain Julius Octavius, and personally unknown to (Cicero) himself, was the destined Augustus, and the suppressor and destroyer of (Rome's) civil discords. This is recorded in the Commentaries of Vitellius. But visions of this prophetic kind were not confined to predictions of supreme power; for they indicated perils also, and catastrophes: as, for instance, when Caesar was absent from the battle of Philippi through illness, and thereby escaped the sword of Brutus and Cassius, and then although he expected to encounter greater danger still from the enemy in the field, he quitted his tent for it, in obedience to a vision of Artorius, and so escaped (the capture by the enemy, who shortly after took possession of the tent); as, again, when the daughter of Polycrates of Samos foresaw the crucifixion which awaited him from the anointing of the sun and the bath of Jupiter.* So likewise in sleep revelations are made of high honours and eminent talents; remedies are also discovered, thefts brought to light, and treasures indicated. Thus Cicero's eminence, whilst he was still a little boy, was foreseen by his nurse. The swan from the breast of Socrates soothing men, is his disciple Plato. The boxer Leonymus is cured by Achilles in his dreams. Sophocles the tragic poet discovers, as he was dreaming, the golden crown, which had been lost from the citadel of Athens. Neoptolemus the tragic actor, through intimations in his sleep from Ajax himself, saves from destruction the hero's tomb on the Rhoetean shore before Troy; and as he removes the decayed stones, he returns enriched with gold. How many commentators and chroniclers vouch for this phenomenon? There are Artemon, Antiphon, Strato, Philochorus, Epicharmus Serapion, Cratippus, and Dionysius of Rhodes, and Hermippus—the entire literature of the age. I shall only laugh at all, if indeed I ought to laugh at the man who fancied that he was going to persuade us that Saturn dreamt before anybody else; which we can only believe if Aristotle, (who would fain help us to such an opinion,) lived prior to any other person. Pray forgive me for laughing. Epicharmus, indeed, as well as Philochorus the Athenian, assigned the

* See an account of her vision and its interpretation in Herodotus III.124.

very highest place among divinations to dreams. The whole world is full of oracles of this description: there are the oracles of Amphiaraus at Oropus, of Amphilochus at Mallus, of Sarpedon in the Troad, of Trophonius in Boeotia, of Mopsus in Cilicia, of Hermione in Macedon, of Pasiphäe in Laconia. Then, again, there are others, which with their original foundations, rites, and historians, together with the entire literature of dreams, Hermippus of Berytus in five portly volumes will give you all the account of, even to satiety. But the Stoics are very fond of saying that God, in his most watchful providence over every institution, gave us dreams amongst other preservatives of the arts and sciences of divination, as the especial support of the natural oracle. So much for the dreams to which credit has to be ascribed even by ourselves, although we must interpret them in another sense. As for all other oracles, at which no one ever dreams, what else must we declare concerning them, than that they are the diabolical contrivance of those spirits who even at that time dwelt in the eminent persons themselves, or aimed at reviving the memory of them as the mere stage of their evil purposes, going so far as to counterfeit a divine power under their shape and form, and, with equal persistence in evil, deceiving men by their very boons of remedies, warnings, and forecasts,—the only effect of which was to injure their victims the more they helped them; while the means whereby they rendered the help withdrew them from all search after the true God, by insinuating into their minds ideas of the false one? And of course so pernicious an influence as this is not shut up nor limited within the boundaries of shrines and temples: it roams abroad, it flies through the air, and all the while is free and unchecked. So that nobody can doubt that our very homes lie open to these diabolical spirits, who beset their human prey with their fantasies not only in their chapels but also in their chambers.

*Chap. XLVII.—Dreams variously classified. Some are God-sent, as the dreams of Nebuchadnezzar; others simply products of nature.*

We declare, then, that dreams are inflicted on us mainly by demons, although they sometimes turn out true and favourable to us. When, however, with the deliberate aim after evil, of which we have just spoken, they assume a flattering and captivating style, they show themselves proportionately vain, and deceitful, and obscure, and wanton, and impure. And no wonder that the images partake of the character of the realities. But from God—who has promised, indeed, "to pour out the grace of the Holy Spirit upon all flesh, and has ordained that His servants and His handmaids should see visions as well as utter prophecies" [Joel 2:28]—must all those visions be regarded as emanating, which may be compared to the actual grace of God, as being honest, holy, prophetic, inspired, instructive, inviting to virtue, the bountiful nature of which causes them to overflow even to the profane, since God, with grand impartiality, "sends His showers and sunshine on

the just and on the unjust" [Matthew 5:45]. It was, indeed by an inspiration from God that Nebuchadnezzar dreamt his dreams [Daniel
2:1ff.]; and almost the greater part of mankind get their knowledge of
God from dreams. Thus it is that, as the mercy of God super-
abounds to the heathen, so the temptation of the evil one encounters
the saints, from whom he never withdraws his malignant efforts to steal
over them as best he may in their very sleep, if unable to assault them
when they are awake. The third class of dreams will consist of those
which the soul itself apparently creates for itself from an intense application to special circumstances. Now, inasmuch as the soul cannot
dream of its own accord (for even Epicharmus is of this opinion),
how can it become to itself the cause of any vision? Then must this
class of dreams be abandoned to the action of nature, reserving for the
soul, even when in the ecstatic condition, the power of enduring whatever incidents befall it? Those, moreover, which evidently proceed
neither from God, nor from diabolical inspiration, nor from the soul,
being beyond the reach as well of ordinary expectation, usual interpretation, or the possibility of being intelligibly related, will have to
be ascribed in a separate category to what is purely and simply the
ecstatic state and its peculiar conditions.

*Chap. XLVIII.—Causes and circumstances of dreams. What best con-
tributes to efficient dreaming.*

They say that dreams are more sure and clear when they happen
towards the end of the night, because then the vigour of the soul
emerges, and heavy sleep departs. As to the seasons of the year, dreams
are calmer in spring, since summer relaxes, and winter somehow
hardens, the soul; while autumn, which in other respects is trying to
health, is apt to enervate the soul by the lusciousness of its fruits. Then,
again, as regards the position of one's body during sleep, one ought
not to lie on his back, nor on his right side, nor so as to wrench his
intestines, as if their cavity were reversely stretched: a palpitation of
the heart would ensue, or else a pressure on the liver would produce a
painful disturbance of the mind. But however this be, I take it that it
all amounts to ingenious conjecture rather than certain proof (although
the author of the conjecture be no less a man than Plato [*Timaeus* 71]);
and possibly all may be no other than the result of chance. But, generally speaking, dreams will be under control of a man's will, if they
be capable of direction at all; for we must not examine what *opinion*
on the one hand, and *superstition* on the other, have to prescribe for
the treatment of dreams, in the matter of distinguishing and modifying
different sorts of food. As for the *superstition*, we have an instance
when fasting is prescribed for such persons as mean to submit to the
sleep which is necessary for receiving the oracle, in order that such
abstinence may produce the required purity; while we find an instance

of the *opinion* when the disciples of Pythagoras, in order to attain the same end, reject the bean as an aliment which would load the stomach, and produce indigestion. But the three brethren, who were the companions of Daniel, being content with pulse alone, to escape the contamination of the royal dishes [Daniel 1:8ff.], received from God, besides other wisdom, the gift especially of penetrating and explaining the sense of dreams. For my own part, I hardly know whether fasting would not simply make me dream so profoundly, that I should not be aware whether I had in fact dreamt at all. Well, then, you ask, has not sobriety something to do in this matter? Certainly it is as much concerned in this as it is in the entire subject: if it contributes some good service to superstition, much more does it to religion. For even demons require such discipline from their dreamers as a gratification to their divinity, because they know that it is acceptable to God, since Daniel (to quote him again) "ate no pleasant bread" for the space of three weeks [10:2ff.]. This abstinence, however, he used in order to please God by humiliation, and not for the purpose of producing a sensibility and wisdom for his soul previous to receiving communication by dreams and visions, as if it were not rather to effect such action in an ecstatic state. This *sobriety*, then, (in which our question arises,) will have nothing to do with exciting ecstasy, but will rather serve to recommend its being wrought by God.

## Chap. XLIX.—No soul naturally exempt from dreams.

As for those persons who suppose that infants do not dream, on the ground that all the functions of the soul throughout life are accomplished according to the capacity of age, they ought to observe attentively their tremors, and nods, and bright smiles as they sleep, and from such facts understand that they are the emotions of their soul as it dreams, which so readily escape to the surface through the delicate tenderness of their infantine body. The fact, however, that the African nation of the Atlantes are said to pass through the night in a deep lethargic sleep, brings down on them the censure that something is wrong in the constitution of their soul. Now either report, which is occasionally calumnious against barbarians, deceived Herodotus [IV, 184], or else a large force of demons of this sort domineers in those barbarous regions. Since, indeed, Aristotle remarks of a certain hero of Sardinia that he used to withhold the power of visions and dreams from such as resorted to his shrine for inspiration, it must lie at the will and caprice of the demons to take away as well as to confer the faculty of dreams; and from this circumstance may have arisen the remarkable fact (which we have mentioned) of Nero and Thrasymedes only dreaming so late in life. We, however, derive dreams from God. Why, then, did not the Atlantes receive the dreaming faculty from God, because there is really no nation which is now a stranger to God, since the gospel flashes its glorious light through the world to the ends of the earth? Could it then be that rumour deceived Aristotle, or is this caprice still the way of demons? (Let us take any view of the case), only do not let it be imagined that any soul is by its natural constitution exempt from dreams.

# ORIGEN
## *Against Celsus*
## BOOK I, CHAPTER XLVIII

*Chap.* XLVIII.

Although the Jew, then, may offer no defence for himself in the
instances of Ezekiel and Isaiah, when we compare the opening of the
heavens to Jesus, and the voice that was heard by Him, to the similar
cases which we find recorded in Ezekiel and Isaiah, or any other of the
prophets, we nevertheless, so far as we can, shall support our position,
maintaining that, as it is a matter of belief that in a *dream* impressions have been brought before the minds of many, some relating
to divine things, and others to future events of this life, and this either
with clearness or in an enigmatic manner,—a fact which is manifest to
all who accept the doctrine of providence; so how is it absurd to say
that the mind which could receive impressions in a *dream* should be
impressed also in a waking vision, for the benefit either of him on whom
the impressions are made, or of those who are to hear the account of
them from him? And as in a dream we fancy that we hear, and that
the organs of hearing are actually impressed, and that we see with our
eyes—although neither the bodily organs of sight nor hearing are
affected, but it is the mind alone which has these sensations—so there
is no absurdity in believing that similar things occurred to the prophets,
when it is recorded that they witnessed occurrences of a rather wonderful kind, as when they either heard the words of the Lord or beheld
the heavens opened. For I do not suppose that the visible heaven was
actually opened, and its physical structure divided, in order that Ezekiel
might be able to record such an occurrence. Should not, therefore, the
same be believed of the Saviour by every intelligent hearer of the
Gospels?—although such an occurrence may be a stumbling-block to
the simple, who in their simplicity would set the whole world in movement, and split in sunder the compact and mighty body of the whole
heavens. But he who examines such matters more profoundly will say,
that there being, as the Scripture calls it, a kind of general divine

perception which the blessed man alone knows how to discover, according to the saying of Solomon, "Thou shalt find the knowledge of God;" and as there are various forms of this perceptive power, such as a faculty of vision which can naturally see things that are better than bodies, among which are ranked the cherubim and seraphim; and a faculty of hearing which can perceive voices which have not their being in the air; and a sense of taste which can make use of living bread that has come down from heaven, and that giveth life unto the world; and so also a sense of smelling, which scents such things as leads Paul to say that he is a sweet savour of Christ unto God; and a sense of touch by which John says that he "handled with his hands of the Word of life;"—the blessed prophets having discovered this divine perception, and seeing and hearing in this divine manner, and tasting likewise, and smelling, so to speak, with no sensible organs of perception, and laying hold on the Logos by faith, so that a healing effluence from it comes upon them, saw in this manner what they record as having seen, and heard what they say they heard, and were affected in a similar manner to what they describe when eating the roll of a book that was given them. And so also Isaac smelled the savour of his son's divine garments, and added to the spiritual blessing these words: "See, the savour of my son is as the savour of a full field which the Lord blessed." And similarly to this, and more as a matter to be understood by the mind than to be perceived by the senses, Jesus touched the leper, to cleanse him, as I think, in a twofold sense,—freeing him not only, as the multitude heard, from the visible leprosy by visible contact, but also from that other leprosy, by His truly divine touch. It is in this way, accordingly, that John testifies when he says, "I beheld the Spirit descending from heaven like a dove, and it abode upon Him. And I knew Him not; but He that sent me to baptize with water, the same said to me, Upon whom you will see the Spirit descending, and abiding on Him, the same is He that baptizeth with the Holy Ghost. And I saw, and bear witness, that this is the Son of God." Now it was to Jesus that the heavens were opened; and on that occasion no one except John is recorded to have seen them opened. But with respect to this opening of the heavens, the Saviour, foretelling to His disciples that it would happen, and that they would see it, says, "Verily, verily, I say unto you, Ye shall see the heavens opened, and the angels of God ascending and descending upon the Son of man." And so Paul was carried away into the third heaven, having previously seen it opened, since he was a disciple of Jesus. It does not, however, belong to our present object to explain why Paul says, "Whether in the body, I know not; or whether out of the body, I know not: God knoweth." But I shall add to my argument even those very points which Celsus imagines, viz., that Jesus Himself related the account of the opening of the heavens, and the descent of the Holy Spirit upon Him at the Jordan in the form of a dove, although the Scripture does not assert that He said that He saw it. For this great man did not perceive that it was not in keeping with Him who commanded His disciples on the occasion of the vision on the mount, "Tell what ye have seen to no man, until the Son of man be risen from the dead," to have related to His disciples what was seen and heard by John at the Jordan. For it may be observed as a trait of the character of Jesus, that He on all occasions avoided unnecessary talk about Himself; and on that account said, "If I speak of Myself, My witness is not true." And since He avoided unnecessary talk about Himself, and preferred to show by acts rather than words that He was the Christ, the Jews for that reason said to Him, "If Thou art the Christ, tell us plainly." And as it is a Jew who, in the work of Celsus, uses the language to Jesus regarding the appearance of the Holy Spirit in the form of a dove, "This is your own testimony, unsupported save by one of those who were sharers of your punishment, whom you adduce," it is necessary for us to show him that such a statement is not appropriately placed in the mouth of a Jew. For the Jews do not connect John with Jesus, nor the punishment of John with that of Christ. And by this instance, this man who boasts of universal knowledge is convicted of not knowing what words he ought to ascribe to a Jew engaged in a disputation with Jesus.

[References: Proverbs 2:5, II Corinthians 2:15, I John 1:1, Ezekiel 3:1ff., Genesis 27:27, Matthew 8:3, John 1:32ff., John 1:51, II Corinthians 12:2, Matthew 17:9, John 5:31, and John 10:24.]

# GREGORY OF NYSSA
## On the Making of Man
## CHAPTER XIII

*XIII. A rationale of sleep, of yawning, and of dreams.*

1. This life of our bodies, material and subject to flux, always advancing by way of motion, finds the power of its being in this, that it never rests from its motion: and as some river, flowing on by its own impulse, keeps the channel in which it runs well filled, yet is not seen in the same water always at the same place, but part of it glides away while part comes flowing on, so, too, the material element of our life here suffers change in the continuity of its succession of opposites by way of motion and flux, so that it never can desist from change, but in its inability to rest keeps up unceasingly its motion alternating by like ways: and if it should ever cease moving it will assuredly have cessation also of its being.

2. For instance, emptying succeeds fulness, and on the other hand after emptiness comes in turn a process of filling: sleep relaxes the strain of waking, and, again, awakening braces up what had become slack: and neither of these abides continually, but both give way, each at the other's coming; nature thus by their inter-change so renewing herself as, while partaking of each in turn, to pass from the one to the other without break. For that the living creature should always be exerting itself in its operations produces a certain rupture and severance of the overstrained part; and continual quiescence of the body brings about a certain dissolution and laxity in its frame: but to be in touch with each of these at the proper times in a moderate degree is a staying-power of nature, which, by continual transference to the opposed states, gives herself in each of them rest from the other. Thus she finds the body on the strain through wakefulness, and devises relaxation for the strain by means of sleep, giving the perceptive faculties rest for the time from their operations, loosing them like horses from the chariots after the race.

3. Further, rest at proper times is necessary for the framework of the

body, that the nutriment may be diffused over the whole body through the passages which it contains, without any strain to hinder its progress. For just as certain misty vapours are drawn up from the recesses of the earth when soaked with rain, whenever the sun heats it with rays of any considerable warmth, so a similar result happens in the earth that is in us, when the nutriment within is heated up by natural warmth; and the vapours, being naturally of upward tendency and airy nature, and aspiring to that which is above them, come to be in the region of the head like smoke penetrating the joints of a wall: then they are dispersed thence by exhalation to the passages of the organs of sense, and by them the senses are of course rendered inactive, giving way to the transit of these vapours. For the eyes are pressed upon by the eyelids when some leaden instrument, as it were (I mean such a weight as that I have spoken of), lets down the eyelid upon the eyes; and the hearing, being dulled by these same vapours, as though a door were placed upon the acoustic organs, rests from its natural operation: and such a condition is sleep, when the sense is at rest in the body, and altogether ceases from the operation of its natural motion, so that the digestive processes of nutriment may have free course for transmission by the vapours through each of the passages.

4. And for this reason, if the apparatus of the organs of sense should be closed and sleep hindered by some occupation, the nervous system, becoming filled with the vapours, is naturally and spontaneously extended so that the part which has had its density increased by the vapours is rarefied by the process of extension, just as those do who squeeze the water out of clothes by vehement wringing: and, seeing that the parts about the pharynx are somewhat circular, and nervous tissue abounds there, whenever there is need for the expulsion from that part of the density of the vapours—since it is impossible that the part which is circular in shape should be separated directly, but only by being distended in the outline of its circumference—for this reason, by checking the breath in a yawn the chin is moved downwards so as to leave a hollow to the uvula, and all the interior parts being arranged in the figure of a circle, that smoky denseness which had been detained in the neighbouring parts is emitted together with the exit of the breath. And often the like may happen even after sleep when any portion of those vapours remains in the region spoken of undigested and unexhaled.

5. Hence the mind of man clearly proves its claim to connection with his nature, itself also co-operating and moving with the nature in its sound and waking state, but remaining unmoved when it is abandoned to sleep, unless any one supposes that the imagery of dreams is a motion of the mind exercised in sleep. We for our part say that it is only the conscious and sound action of the intellect which we ought to refer to mind; and as to the fantastic nonsense which occurs to us in sleep, we suppose that some appearances of the operations of the mind are accidentally moulded in the less rational part of the soul; for the soul, being by sleep dissociated from the senses, is also of necessity out-

side the range of the operations of the mind; for it is through the senses that the union of mind with man takes place; therefore when the senses are at rest, the intellect also must needs be inactive; and an evidence of this is the fact that the dreamer often seems to be in absurd and impossible situations, which would not happen if the soul were then guided by reason and intellect.

6. It seems to me, however, that when the soul is at rest so far as concerns its more excellent faculties (so far, I mean, as concerns the operations of mind and sense), the nutritive part of it alone is operative during sleep, and that some shadows and echoes of those things which happen in our waking moments—of the operations both of sense and of intellect—which are impressed upon it by that part of the soul which is capable of memory, that these, I say, are pictured as chance will have it, some echo of memory still lingering in this division of the soul.

7. With these, then, the man is beguiled, not led to acquaintance with the things that present themselves by any train of thought, but wandering among confused and inconsequent delusions. But just as in his bodily operations, while each of the parts individually acts in some way according to the power which naturally resides in it, there arises also in the limb that is at rest a state sympathetic with that which is in motion, similarly in the case of the soul, even if one part is at rest and another in motion, the whole is affected in sympathy with the part; for it is not possible that the natural unity should be in any way severed, though one of the faculties included in it is in turn supreme in virtue of its active operation. But as, when men are awake and busy, the mind is supreme, and sense ministers to it, yet the faculty which regulates the body is not dissociated from them (for the mind furnishes the food for its wants, the sense receives what is furnished, and the nutritive faculty of the body appropriates to itself that which is given to it), so in sleep the supremacy of these faculties is in some way reversed in us, and while the less rational becomes supreme, the operation of the other ceases indeed, yet is not absolutely extinguished; but while the nutritive faculty is then busied with digestion during sleep, and keeps all our nature occupied with itself, the faculty of sense is neither entirely severed from it (for that cannot be separated which has once been naturally joined), nor yet can its activity revive, as it is hindered by the inaction during sleep of the organs of sense; and by the same reasoning (the mind also being united to the sensitive part of the soul) it would follow that we should say that the mind moves with the latter when it is in motion, and rests with it when it is quiescent.

8. As naturally happens with fire when it is heaped over with chaff, and no breath fans the flame—it neither consumes what lies beside it, nor is entirely quenched, but instead of flame it rises to the air through the chaff in the form of smoke; yet if it should obtain any breath of air, it turns the smoke to flame—in the same way the mind when hidden by the inaction of the senses in sleep is neither able to shine out through them, nor yet is quite extinguished, but has, so to

say, a smouldering activity, operating to a certain extent, but unable to operate farther.

9. Again, as a musician, when he touches with the plectrum the slackened strings of a lyre, brings out no orderly melody (for that which is not stretched will not sound), but his hand frequently moves skilfully, bringing the plectrum to the position of the notes so far as place is concerned, yet there is no sound, except that he produces by the vibration of the strings a sort of uncertain and indistinct hum; so in sleep the mechanism of the senses being relaxed, the artist is either quite inactive, if the instrument is completely relaxed by satiety or heaviness; or will act slackly and faintly, if the instrument of the senses does not fully admit of the exercise of its art.

10. For this cause memory is confused, and foreknowledge, though rendered doubtful by uncertain veils, is imaged in shadows of our waking pursuits, and often indicates to us something of what is going to happen: for by its subtlety of nature the mind has some advantage, in ability to behold things, over mere corporeal grossness; yet it cannot make its meaning clear by direct methods, so that the information of the matter in hand should be plain and evident, but its declaration of the future is ambiguous and doubtful,—what those who interpret such things call an "enigma."

11. So the butler presses the cluster for Pharaoh's cup: so the baker seemed to carry his baskets; each supposing himself in sleep to be engaged in those services with which he was busied when awake: for the images of their customary occupations imprinted on the prescient element of their soul, gave them for a time the power of foretelling, by this sort of prophecy on the part of the mind, what should come to pass.

12. But if Daniel and Joseph and others like them were instructed by Divine power, without any confusion of perception, in the knowledge of things to come, this is nothing to the present statement; for no one would ascribe this to the power of dreams, since he will be constrained as a consequence to suppose that those Divine appearances also which took place in wakefulness were not a miraculous vision but a result of nature brought about spontaneously. As then, while all men are guided by their own minds, there are some few who are deemed worthy of evident Divine communication; so, while the imagination of sleep naturally occurs in a like and equivalent manner for all, some, not all, share by means of their dreams in some more Divine manifestation: but to all the rest, even if a foreknowledge of anything does occur as a result of dreams, it occurs in the way we have spoken of.

13. And again, if the Egyptian and the Assyrian king were guided by God to the knowledge of the future, the dispensation wrought by their means is a different thing: for it was necessary that the hidden wisdom of the holy men should be made known, that each of them might not pass his life without profit to the state. For how could Daniel have been known for what he was, if the soothsayers and magicians had not been unequal to the task of discovering the dream? And how could

Egypt have been preserved while Joseph was shut up in prison, if his interpretation of the dream had not brought him to notice? Thus we must reckon these cases as exceptional, and not class them with common dreams.

14. But this ordinary seeing of dreams is common to all men, and arises in our fancies in different modes and forms: for either there remain, as we have said, in the reminiscent part of the soul, the echoes of daily occupations; or, as often happens, the constitution of dreams is framed with regard to such and such a condition of the body: for thus the thirsty man seems to be among springs, the man who is in need of food to be at a feast, and the young man in the heat of youthful vigour is beset by fancies corresponding to his passion.

15. I also knew another cause of the fancies of sleep, when attending one of my relations attacked by frenzy; who being annoyed by food being given him in too great quantity for his strength, kept crying out and finding fault with those who were about him for filling intestines with dung and putting them upon him: and when his body was rapidly tending to perspire he blamed those who were with him for having water ready to wet him with as he lay: and he did not cease calling out till the result showed the meaning of these complaints: for all at once a copious sweat broke out over his body, and a relaxation of the bowels explained the weight in the intestines. The same condition then which, while his sober judgment was dulled by disease, his nature underwent, being sympathetically affected by the condition of the body—not being without perception of what was amiss, but being unable clearly to express its pain, by reason of the distraction resulting from the disease— this, probably, if the intelligent principle of the soul were lulled to rest, not from infirmity but by natural sleep, might appear as a dream to one similarly situated, the breaking out of perspiration being expressed by water, and the pain occasioned by the food, by the weight of intestines.

16. This view also is taken by those skilled in medicine, that according to the differences of complaints the visions of dreams appear differently to the patients: that the visions of those of weak stomach are of one kind, those of persons suffering from injury to the cerebral membrane of another, those of persons in fevers of yet another, that those of patients suffering from bilious and from phlegmatic affections are diverse, and those again of plethoric patients, and of patients in wasting disease, are different; whence we may see that the nutritive and vegetative faculty of the soul has in it by commixture some seed of the intelligent element, which is in some sense brought into likeness to the particular state of the body, being adapted in its fancies according to the complaint which has seized upon it.

17. Moreover, most men's dreams are conformed to the state of their character: the brave man's fancies are of one kind, the coward's of another; the wanton man's dreams of one kind, the continent man's of another; the liberal man and the avaricious man are subject to dif-

ferent fancies; while these fancies are nowhere framed by the intellect, but by the less rational disposition of the soul, which forms even in dreams the semblances of those things to which each is accustomed by the practice of his waking hours.

# ST. AUGUSTINE
## LETTER IX
### (A.D. 389)

Nebridius, who was a very close friend of Augustine, had written him asking:

When at any time it pleases higher (by which I mean heavenly) powers to reveal anything to us by dreams in our sleep, how is this done, my dear Augustin, or what is the method which they use? What, I say, is their method, i.e. by what art or magic, by what agency or enchantments, do they accomplish this?

Augustine replied:

1. Although you know my mind well, you are perhaps not aware how much I long to enjoy your society. This great blessing, however, God will some day bestow on me. I have read your letter, so genuine in its utterances, in which you complain of your being in solitude, and, as it were, forsaken by your friends, in whose society you found the sweetest charm of life. But what else can I suggest to you than that which I am persuaded is already your exercise? Commune with your own soul, and raise it up, as far as you are able, unto God. For in Him you hold us also by a firmer bond, not by means of bodily images, which we must meanwhile be content to use in remembering each other, but by means of that faculty of thought through which we realize the fact of our separation from each other.

2. In considering your letters, in answering all of which I have certainly had to answer questions of no small difficulty and importance, I was not a little stunned by the one in which you ask me by what means certain thoughts and dreams are put into our minds by higher powers or by superhuman agents. The question is a great one, and, as your own prudence must convince you, would require, in order to its being satisfactorily answered, not a mere letter, but a full oral discussion or a whole treatise. I shall try, however, knowing as I do your tal-

ents, to throw out a few germs of thought which may shed light on this question, in order that you may either complete the exhaustive treatment of the subject by your own efforts, or at least not despair of the possibility of this important matter being investigated with satisfactory results.

3. It is my opinion that every movement of the mind affects in some degree the body. We know that this is patent even to our senses, dull and sluggish though they are, when the movements of the mind are somewhat vehement, as when we are angry, or sad, or joyful. Whence we may conjecture that, in like manner, when thought is busy, although no bodily effect of the mental act is discernible by us, there may be some such effect discernible by beings of äerial or etherial essence whose perceptive faculty is in the highest degree acute,—so much so, that, in comparison with it, our faculties are scarcely worthy to be called perceptive. Therefore these footprints of its motion, so to speak, which the mind impresses on the body, may perchance not only remain, but remain as it were with the force of a habit; and it may be that when these are secretly stirred and played upon, they bear thoughts and dreams into our minds, according to the pleasure of the person moving or touching them: and this is done with marvellous facility. For if, as is manifest, the attainments of our earthborn and sluggish bodies in the department of exercise, e.g. in the playing of musical instruments, dancing on the tightrope, etc., are almost incredible, it is by no means unreasonable to suppose that beings which act with the powers of an äerial or etherial body upon our bodies, and are by the constitution of their natures able to pass unhindered through these bodies, should be capable of much greater quickness in moving whatever they wish, while we, though not perceiving what they do, are nevertheless affected by the results of their activity. We have a somewhat parallel instance in the fact that we do not perceive how it is that superfluity of bile impels us to more frequent outbursts of passionate feeling; and yet it does produce this effect, while this superfluity of bile is itself an effect of our yielding to such passionate feeling.

4. If, however, you hesitate to accept this example as a parallel one, when it is thus cursorily stated by me, turn it over in your thoughts as fully as you can. The mind, if it be continually obstructed by some difficulty in the way of doing and accomplishing what it desires, is thereby made continually angry. For anger, so far as I can judge of its nature, seems to me to be a tumultuous eagerness to take out of the way those things which restrict our freedom of action. Hence it is that usually we vent our anger not only on men, but on such a thing, for example, as the pen with which we write, bruising or breaking it in our passion; and so does the gambler with his dice, the artist with his pencil, and every man with the instrument which he may be using, if he thinks that he is in some way thwarted by it. Now medical men themselves tell us that by these frequent fits of anger bile is increased. But, on the other hand, when the bile is increased, we are easily, and almost without any provocation whatever, made angry. Thus the

effect which the mind has by its movement produced upon the body, is capable in its turn of moving the mind again.

5. These things might be treated at very great length, and our knowledge of the subject might be brought to greater certainty and fulness by a large induction from relevant facts. But take along with this letter the one which I sent you lately concerning images and memory, and study it somewhat more carefully; for it was manifest to me, from your reply, that it had not been fully understood. When to the statements now before you, you add the portion of that letter in which I spoke of a certain natural faculty whereby the mind does in thought add to or take from any object as it pleases, you will see that it is possible for us both in dreams and in waking thoughts to conceive the images of bodily forms which we have never seen.

# ST. AUGUSTINE
## LETTER CLIX
### (A.D. 415)

The Bishop of Uzala, Evodius, was one of Augustine's early friends. In the year 414 he wrote to Augustine (Letter CLVIII), describing certain dreams and visions which made him ask; What are we after death? He went on to say:

9. These dreams suggest another question. I do not at this moment concern myself about the mere creations of fancy, which are formed by the emotions of the uneducated. I speak of visitations in sleep, such as the apparition to Joseph in a dream, in the manner experienced in most cases of the kind. In the same manner, therefore, our own friends also who have departed this life before us sometimes come and appear to us in dreams, and speak to us. For I myself remember that Profuturus, and Privatus, and Servilius, holy men who within my recollection were removed by death from our monastery, spoke to me, and that the events of which they spoke came to pass according to their words. Or if it be some other higher spirit that assumes their form and visits our minds, I leave this to the all-seeing eye of Him before whom everything from the highest to the lowest is uncovered. If, therefore, the Lord be pleased to speak through reason to your Holiness on all these questions, I beg you to be so kind as make me partaker of the knowledge which you have received. There is another thing which I have resolved not to omit mentioning, for perhaps it bears upon the matter now under investigation:

10. This same youth, in connection with whom these questions are brought forward, departed this life after having received what may be called a summons at the time when he was dying. For one who had been a companion of his as a student, and reader, and shorthand writer to my dictation, who had died eight months before, was seen by a person in a dream coming towards him. When he was asked by the person who then distinctly saw him why he had come, he said, "I have come to take this friend away"; and so it proved. For in the house itself, also,

there appeared to a certain old man, who was almost awake, a man bearing in his hand a laurel branch on which something was written. Nay, more, when this one was seen, it is further reported that after the death of the young man, his father the presbyter had begun to reside along with the aged Theasius in the monastery, in order to find consolation there, but lo! on the third day after his death, the young man is seen entering the monastery, and is asked by one of the brethren in a dream of some kind whether he knew himself to be dead. He replied that he knew he was. The other asked whether he had been welcomed by God. This also he answered with great expressions of joy. And when questioned as to the reason why he had come, he answered, "I have been sent to summon my father." The person to whom these things were shown awakes, and relates what had passed. It comes to the ear of Bishop Theasius. He, being alarmed, sharply admonished the person who told him, lest the matter should come, as it might easily do, to the ear of the presbyter himself, and he should be disturbed by such tidings. But why prolong the narration? Within about four days from this visitation he was saying (for he had suffered from a moderate feverishness) that he was now out of danger, and that the physician had given up attending him, having assured him that there was no cause whatever for anxiety; but that very day this presbyter expired after he had lain down on his couch. Nor should I forbear mentioning, that on the same day on which the youth died, he asked his father three times to forgive him anything in which he might have offended, and every time that he kissed his father he said to him, "Let us give thanks to God, father," and insisted upon his father saying the words along with him, as if he were exhorting one who was to be his companion in going forth from this world. And in fact only seven days elapsed between the two deaths. What shall we say of things so wonderful? Who shall be a thoroughly reliable teacher as to these mysterious dispensations? To you in the hour of perplexity my agitated heart unburdens itself. . . .

[Evodius went on to tell one of his own dreams and ask urgently about the soul's existence after death, and what is meant by wisdom, such as the gift given to Solomon. In answer Augustine wrote:]

*Letter CLIX* (A.D. 415) *To Evodius, my lord most blessed, my venerable and beloved brother and partner in the priestly office, and to the brethren who are with him, Augustin and the brethren who are with him send greeting in the Lord.*

1. Our brother Barbarus, the bearer of this letter, is a servant of God, who has now for a long time been settled at Hippo, and has been an eager and diligent hearer of the word of God. He requested from us this letter to your Holiness, whereby we commend him to you in the Lord, and convey to you through him the salutations which it is our duty to

offer. To reply to those letters of your Holiness, in which you have inter-woven questions of great difficulty, would be a most laborious task, even for men who are at leisure, and who are endowed with much greater abil-ity in discussing and acuteness in apprehending any subject than we pos-sess. One, indeed, of the two letters in which you ask many great ques-tions has gone amissing, I know not how, and though long sought for cannot be found; the other, which has been found, contains a very pleasing account of a servant of God, a good and chaste young man, stating how he departed from this life, and by what testimonies, communicated through visions of the brethren, his merits were, as you state, made known to you. Taking occasion from this young man's case, you propose and discuss an extremely obscure question concern-ing the soul,—whether it is associated when it goes forth from this body with some other kind of body, by means of which it can be carried to or confined in places having material boundaries? The investigation of this question, if indeed it admits of satisfactory investigation by beings such as we are, demands the most diligent care and labour, and therefore a mind absolutely at leisure from such occupations as en-gross my time. My opinion, however, if you are willing to hear it, summed up in a sentence, is, that I by no means believe that the soul in departing from the body is accompanied by another body of any kind.

2. As to the question how these visions and predictions of future events are produced, let him attempt to explain them who understands by what power we are to account for the great wonders which are wrought in the mind of every man when his thoughts are busy. For we see, and we plainly perceive, that within the mind innumerable images of many objects discernible by the eye or by our other senses are produced,—whether they are produced in regular order or in con-fusion matters not to us at present: all that we say is, that since such images are beyond all dispute produced, the man who is found able to state by what power and in what way these phenomena of daily and perpetual experience are to be accounted for is the only man who may warrantably venture to conjecture or propound any explanation of these visions, which are of exceedingly rare occurrence. For my part, as I discover more plainly my inability to account for the ordinary facts of our experience, when awake or asleep, throughout the whole course of our lives, the more do I shrink from venturing to explain what is extraordinary. For while I have been dictating this epistle to you, I have been contemplating your person in my mind,—you being, of course, absent all the while, and knowing nothing of my thoughts,— and I have been imagining from my knowledge of what is in you how you will be affected by my words; and I have been unable to apprehend, either by observation or by inquiry, how this process was accomplished in my mind. Of one thing, however, I am certain, that although the mental image was very like something material, it was not produced either by masses of matter or by qualities of matter. Accept this in the meantime from one writing under pressure of other duties, and in haste. In the twelfth of the books which I have written on Genesis this

question is discussed with great care, and that dissertation is enriched with a forest of examples from actual experience or from trustworthy report. How far I have been competent to handle the question, and what I have accomplished in it, you will judge when you have read that work; if indeed the Lord shall be pleased in His kindness to permit me now to publish those books systematically corrected to the best of my ability, and thus to meet the expectation of many brethren, instead of deferring their hope by continuing further the discussion of a subject which has already engaged me for a long time.

3. I will narrate briefly, however, one fact which I commend to your meditation. You know our brother Gennadius, a physician, known to almost every one, and very dear to us, who now lives at Carthage, and was in other years eminent as a medical practitioner at Rome. You know him as a man of religious character and of very great benevolence, actively compassionate and promptly liberal in his care of the poor. Nevertheless, even he, when still a young man, and most zealous in these charitable acts, had sometimes, as he himself told me, doubts as to whether there was any life after death. Forasmuch, therefore, as God would in no wise forsake a man so merciful in his disposition and conduct, there appeared to him in sleep a youth of remarkable appearance and commanding presence, who said to him: "Follow me." Following him, he came to a city where he began to hear on the right hand sounds of a melody so exquisitely sweet as to surpass anything he had ever heard. When he inquired what it was, his guide said: "It is the hymn of the blessed and the holy." What he reported himself to have seen on the left hand escapes my remembrance. He awoke; the dream vanished, and he thought of it as only a dream.

4. On a second night, however, the same youth appeared to Gennadius, and asked whether he recognised him, to which he replied that he knew him well, without the slightest uncertainty. Thereupon he asked Gennadius where he had become acquainted with him. There also his memory failed him not as to the proper reply: he narrated the whole vision, and the hymns of the saints which, under his guidance, he had been taken to hear, with all the readiness natural to recollection of some very recent experience. On this the youth inquired whether it was in sleep or when awake that he had seen what he had just narrated. Gennadius answered: "In sleep." The youth then said: "You remember it well; it is true that you saw these things in sleep, but I would have you know that even now you are seeing in sleep." Hearing this, Gennadius was persuaded of its truth, and in his reply declared that he believed it. Then his teacher went on to say: "Where is your body now?" He answered: "In my bed." "Do you know," said the youth, "that the eyes in this body of yours are now bound and closed, and at rest, and that with these eyes you are seeing nothing?" He answered: "I know it." "What, then," said the youth, "are the eyes with which you see me?" He, unable to discover what to answer to this, was silent. While he hesitated, the youth unfolded to him what he was endeavoring to teach him by these questions, and forthwith said: "As

while you are asleep and lying on your bed these eyes of your body are now unemployed and doing nothing, and yet you have eyes with which you behold me, and enjoy this vision, so, after your death, while your bodily eyes shall be wholly inactive, there shall be in you a life by which you shall still live, and a faculty of perception by which you shall still perceive. Beware, therefore, after this of harbouring doubts as to whether the life of man shall continue after death." This believer says that by this means all doubts as to this matter were removed from him. By whom was he taught this but by the merciful, providential care of God?

5. Some one may say that by this narrative I have not solved but complicated the question. Nevertheless, while it is free to every one to believe or disbelieve these statements, every man has his own consciousness at hand as a teacher by whose help he may apply himself to this most profound question. Every day man wakes, and sleeps, and thinks; let any man, therefore, answer whence proceed these things which, while not material bodies, do nevertheless resemble the forms, properties, and motions of material bodies: let him, I say, answer this if he can. But if he cannot do this, why is he in such haste to pronounce a definite opinion on things which occur very rarely, or are beyond the range of his experience, when he is unable to explain matters of daily and perpetual observation? For my part, although I am wholly unable to explain in words how those semblances of material bodies, without any real body, are produced, I may say that I wish that, with the same certainty with which I know that these things are not produced by the body, I could know by what means those things are perceived which are occasionally seen by the spirit, and are supposed to be seen by the bodily senses; or by what distinctive marks we may know the visions of men who have been misguided by delusion, or, most commonly, by impiety, since the examples of such visions closely resembling the visions of pious and holy men are so numerous, that if I wished to quote them, time, rather than abundance of examples, would fail me.

May you, through the mercy of the Lord, grow in grace, most blessed lord and venerable and beloved brother!

# EXCERPTS FROM
## SYNESIUS OF CYRENE
### Concerning Dreams
### Translated by Augustine Fitzgerald*

1. If dreams are prophets, and if the visions seen in dreams are riddles of their future fortunes to anxious men, they would in that case be full of wisdom, though certainly not clear. In sooth their lack of clearness is their wisdom.

> 'For the gods keep man's life concealed.'

To obtain the greatest things without labour is a divine prerogative, whereas for men, not merely 'in front of virtue' but of all fair things,

> 'The gods have set sweat.'

Now divination must be the greatest of all good things, for it is in knowledge and, in a word, in the cognitional part of his faculties that God differs from man, as does man from the brute. But whereas the nature of God is sufficient unto Himself for knowledge, man through divination attains to much more than belongs to our human nature. For the mass of mankind can know only the present . . .

but not the affairs of the gods, which the common language of poetry shows are ruled by Zeus, the oldest in time and in knowledge. Philosophy confirms that the gods are nothing else but minds, intelligences, and one who is worthy to rule over gods does so because of the superior force of wisdom. For this reason also the wise man is akin to God.

2. Let the foregoing be proof that divinations are amongst the best of the vocations of man; and if all things are signs appearing through

* *The Essays and Hymns of Synesius of Cyrene*, London, Oxford University Press, 1930.

all things, inasmuch as they are brothers in a single living creature, the cosmos, so also they are written characters of every kind, just as of those in a book some are Phoenician, some Egyptian, and others Assyrian. . . .

Just as men learn to read books—each in his own way, some only a phrase, others the whole story—so they learn to read signs in the universe, signals of the relationship between the parts of a great whole. What is called magic is actually the attraction of one thing through the agency of another. The wise man knows that he has present with him the pledges of things which are for the most part far away.

Men learn to use this magic, and to find what binds the parts together, just as the musicians learn which notes come next in a particular harmonic series, or as the mathematician manipulates the parts of a problem from outside of it. But there is also discord in the cosmos, parts of the universe which agree and yet battle with other parts, and this struggle contributes to the unity of the whole. The unity resulting from opposites is the harmony of the cosmos. The man who places himself outside of it can no longer make any use of his wisdom, but uses the universe against itself.

The diversity of things in the universe and their relationship furnish the bulk of the subject-matter in the initiations and prophecies. And while it is not lawful to discuss initiations, there is no offense in explaining divination.

3. The whole of this art has already been praised as much as possible, but now it is time to appropriate the best part that is in it, and to linger over its speculative side. . . .

Obscurity is common to all forms of divination. Dreams should not be dismissed for this reason. Rather we should seek this branch of knowledge which is within us and is the special possession of the soul of each of us. For the soul holds the forms of things that come into being, only producing what is befitting, and reflecting as in a mirror the image by which a person grasps those things that remain there.

Therefore, as we do not understand the activities of the mind before the controlling force has announced them to the multitude, and whatever has not come to that controlling force is hidden from the living being; so then we shall not have a perception even of the forms in the first soul, before the impress of them comes to the imagination. And this very imagination seems to be a sort of life in itself, a little lower down in the scale, and having its basis in a peculiar property of nature. It has even its own sense-perceptions, for we see colours and we hear sounds, and we have an overpowering sense of touch, at times when the organic parts of the body are at rest. Perhaps this form of sense-perception is the more hallowed. In this way we constantly enter into relationship with gods who give us counsel and answer us in oracles, and take care of us in other ways. So then, if any one, in his dreams, receives the present of a treasure, I shall not be at all surprised; or if a man quite uncultured should fall asleep and, meeting the Muses in his dream and exchanging question and answer with them, should become a cunning bard. This has happened in our own time and does not seem to me very astounding. I pass over plots that have been revealed, and the number of people whom the dream in the guise of a physician has cured of illness. But whenever a dream opens up to the soul a path conducting it to the most perfect points from which to view existing things, a soul that has never yet aspired, nor has given its mind to the ascent, it would be indeed the climax of the occult force in existing things that this dream should override nature and unite to the realm of mind the man who has wandered so far from it that he knows not whence he has come.

And if any one deems the way upward a great undertaking, but disbelieves in the imagination, for that even by its means the happy union may ne'er be gained, let him listen to the sacred oracles which tell of the diverging paths, after hearing, of course, the whole list of the available resources for the ascent, in virtue of which it is possible to make the seed within us grow:

> 'To some,' it is written, 'he gave the revelation of the
>     light to be a lesson,
> Others even in their dreams, He made fruitful with his
>     courage.'

Do you see? He makes a distinction between the happy possession of knowledge and its acquirement. One man learns, he means, while awake, another while asleep. But in the waking state man is the teacher, whereas it is God who makes the dreamer fruitful with His own courage, so that learning and attaining are one and the same. Now to make fruitful is even more than to teach.

Synesius then turns to the relation of man's psyche to the total universe, depicting in great depth and detail the role of the imagination, of spirit in the life of the soul. Aside from the studies of Augustine, this is about the most sophisticated discussion of human psychology which has come down to us from antiquity. It goes beyond our present study, and we summarize only the necessary points.

Some men despise dreams and seek an art of divination above the common herd. But is not a man wise, precisely because he gains a greater share out of things common to all? It is the greatest good to look upon God by the imagination, for the imaginative spirit is the most widely shared organ of sensation, the first body of the soul. About it nature has constructed all of the functions of the brain. Sense-perception through the outer organs remains only animal in character, no perception at all, until it comes into contact with the imagination. This is the divine faculty which sees with its whole spirit and has power over all the remaining senses.

The man who thinks he knows best what he has seen with his own eyes has no way of knowing which images he sees are distorted. Then the imaginative spirit becomes diseased, and the extraneous bodies which have entered in must be purged and purified if the man is to see clearly again.

The imagination comprehends our spiritual nature, because it moves on the border between reason and unreason, between matter and that which has no body, between the divine and the demonic. It borrows from each extreme, thus imaging in one nature things that dwell far apart. This is difficult for philosophy to comprehend.

The imaginings of dreams, however, are similar to the other life for which our soul prepares. The envelope of soul-matter is in turn god, demon of every sort, and phantom. Within it the soul enters a struggle to fulfill its own contract with the life of the universe, to descend to the regions ruled by the elements of matter, and to bring back up to the spheres what it has snatched from the extremes of fire and air. The imaginative spirit lives in all this enormous interval of space, and is able to accompany the soul as it rises, even until it reaches the highest point.

Thus, man's imaginative spirit obtains true impressions of the life of the soul. It also influences that life, and can even draw the soul towards God; or, if the imagination is empty and inactive, it leaves a vacuum into which an evil spirit enters. To investigate the state of the soul and the spirit around it, we must pay attention to the visions which the imaginative spirit emits, particularly in sleep.

7. We, therefore, have set ourselves to speak of divination through dreams, that men should not despise it, but rather cultivate it, seeing that it fulfils a service to life; and it is to this end that we have so much occupied ourselves with the imaginative nature. The immediate need of it here below has been perhaps less clearly shown by our discourse, but a better fruit of a sane spirit is the uplifting of the soul, a really sacred gain; so that it becomes a sort of cult of piety to endeavour that this form of divination should be ours. Nay, some men already through some such motive, enticed by their passion for knowledge of the future, have had set before them, instead of a groaning board a sacred and modest one, and have hailed the joys of a couch pure and undefiled. For as to the man who would consult his bed as he does the tripod of the Pythian deity, far be it from him to make the nights spent in it witnesses of unbridled passion. Rather does he bow before God and pray to Him. What is collected little by little becomes much in the end, and that which happens through quite another cause terminates in a greater one. Thus those who did not set out at first with this object have come, in their advance, to love God and one day to be united to Him. We must not therefore disregard a prophetic art which journeys to divine things, and has, dependent on it, the most precious of all things which are in the power of man. Nor indeed has the soul that is united with God less need here because of the fact that it has been deemed worthy to handle better things. Nor is it heedless of the animal in us.

Nay, from its vantage ground it has a steady and much more distinct view of things below than when it is with them and is mingled with the inferior elements. Remaining unmoved, it will give to the animal in us the appearances of things that come into existence. This is, according to the proverb, 'to descend without descending', where the better takes unchallenged mastery of the worse. This art of divination I resolve to possess for myself and to bequeath to my children. In order to enter upon this no man need pack up for a long journey or voyage beyond the frontiers, as to Pytho or to Hammon. It is enough to wash one's hands, to keep a holy silence, and to sleep.

> 'Then did she make all ablutions, and dressing in purified
> raiment Prayed she long time to Athene . . .'

8. We shall pray for a dream, even as Homer, perchance, prayed. And if you are worthy, the god far away is present with you. Nay, even what time the god sets little store on these matters, he comes to your side if only you are asleep; and this is the whole system of the initiation. In it no one has ever yet lamented his poverty, on the ground that thus he had less possessions than the rich. On the other hand, some of the ceremonies which deal with foreknowledge choose their priests from the most heavily assessed as the Athenians chose their trierarchs. And great expense there must needs be, and, no less, happy opportunity, if

we are to obtain a Cretan herb, an Egyptian feather, an Iberian bone, and, by Zeus, some prodigy begotten and nourished in a hidden corner of earth or sea,

> 'Where that the sun god sinks neath the earth and where
>     he arises.'

For surely this and much like it is said of those who practise external divination, and what ordinary person would be rich enough for this out of his own resources? But the dream is visible to the man who is worth five hundred *medimni*, and equally to the possessor of three hundred, to the teamster no less than to the peasant who tills the boundary land for a livelihood, to the galleyslave and the common labourer alike, to the exempted and to the payer of taxes.

It makes no difference to the god whether a man is an *eteoboutades* or a newly-bought slave. And this accessibility to all makes divination very humane; for its simple and artless character is worthy of a philosopher, and its freedom from violence gives it sanctity. . . .

Almost with tongue in cheek, Synesius discusses the fantastic complications of other forms of divination or foreknowledge, compared with the great simplicity of the really divine work. If we give ourselves up to these other things, we not only need trunk-loads of equipment, but we have to be content if they make some concession to the remaining needs of life. And, seriously, these other practices are base, and hateful to God. For not to await voluntarily any one's coming, but to set him moving by pressure and leverage, is even punished by law when it happens among men.

Of divination by dreams, each one of us is perforce his own instrument, so much so that it is not possible to desert our oracle there even if we so desired. Nay, even if we remain at home, she dwells with us; if we go abroad she accompanies us; she is with us on the field of battle, she is at our side in the life of the city; she labours with us in the fields and barters with us in the market place. The laws of a malicious government do not forbid her, nor would they have the power to do so, even if they wished it, for they have no proof against those who invoke her. For how then? Should we be violating the law by sleeping? A tyrant could never enjoin us not to gaze into dreams, at least not unless he actually banished sleep from his kingdom; and it would be the act of a fool to wish for that which is impossible of fulfilment, and of an impious man to make laws which should be contrary to nature and to God. To her then we must go, woman and man of us, young and old, poor and rich alike, the private citizen and the ruler, the town dweller and the rustic, the artisan and the orator. She repudiates neither race, nor age, nor condition, nor calling. She is present to every one, everywhere, this zealous prophetess, this wise counsellor, who holdeth her peace. She herself is alike initiator and initiated, to announce to us good tidings; in such wise as to prolong our pleasure by seizing joy beforehand; to inform against the worst so as to guard against and to repel it beforehand. . . .

For whatever use and sweetness there is in hope, and whatever reality fear controls, all are found in dreams. In fact, there is nothing else that so entices men towards hope. This element is so abundant and so healing in dreams that men who have been bound by fear, when they awaken to dreams of hope, find themselves straightway unbound. Furthermore, it is not well to despair of dreams, when so often one is only confusing the weakness of the interpreter with the nature of the visions themselves. And since we have a pledge from the divinity in the promise of our dreams, we profit twice if we prepare to enjoy these greater things which the dream state can hold out to us. Not only do we have the pleasure of anticipation, but we can profit from the chance to examine them beforehand and prepare wisely for what we shall do.

9. Yet I have narrowly missed incurring a charge of ingratitude; for while I explained just now that it (i.e., divination by dreams) is a good thing wherewith to journey or stay at home, to trade or command troops, and that it helps all men and all things, yet I have never made public what it has done for me personally. Certainly no other thing is so well calculated to join in man's pursuit of wisdom; and of many of the things which present difficulties to us awake, some of these it makes completely clear while we are asleep, and others it helps us to explain. And something of this sort happens. At one moment one seems like a man asking questions, at another the same man discovering and in process of thought. It has frequently helped me to write books, for it has prepared the mind and made the diction appropriate to the thought. Here it cuts out something, there it brings in new matter instead. It has befallen me already to be admonished by it also in respect of the whole style of my language, when it runs riot and flames up with novel forms of diction, in emulation of the archaic Attic, which is foreign to us, and this by the agency of a god who, at one moment tells me something, and again what something means, and at another shows me how to smooth down the excrescences growing out of my language. Thus it has restored my diction to a state of sobriety, and has castigated my inflated style. Moreover when I am engaged in the chase, it has suggested to me stratagems of the hunter's art against those wild beasts who show skill alike in running and hiding; and when in weariness I have been on the point of abandoning the quest, the dream has enjoined upon me a blockade of the quarry, and has

promised me fortune on an appointed day, so that we have slept in the open more happily and with confidence. And when the day appointed has come and fortune is with us at last, it has shown us swarms of netted game and of wild beasts that have fallen to our spears.

My life has been one of books and of the chase, except what time I spent as an ambassador. Would that I had not been compelled to see three unspeakable years lost to my life! But even in them I derived the greatest profit from divination, and that on many occasions. For plots directed against me it made ineffective, plots of ghost-raising sorcerers. It exposed these to me, saved me from them all, and helped me in the management of public office in the best interest of the cities, and it finally placed me, more undaunted than was ever any Greek, on terms of intimacy with the emperor.

One man may prefer one, another man another (system of divination), but dream divination is present to all, the good genius to every man, and one that contrives something for the minds of the awakened also. In this way is a soul a wise possession, that it is free from a whole flood of vulgar sensations which attract to it extraneous matter of every sort. Whatever ideas it has, and however many things it receives from the mind, all these, when left to itself, it makes over to those who are inclined towards that which is within, and it ferries across to them whatsoe'er comes from the godhead. For as it is itself of such a character, a cosmic god is also associated with it, from the fact that its nature comes from the same source.

10. Such categories of dreams, then, are more divine, and are either quite clear and obvious, or nearly so, and in no wise stand in need of the diviner's science. But they may come to the help only of such men as live according to virtue, whether that be acquired by wisdom or engrained by habit, and if at a given moment they should come to any other, it would be with difficulty, though they might so come.

It is not for some trifling purpose that a dream of this higher order will come to the chance recipient. Further, a frequent and a very widely shared class will be the enigmatic. To this the science of divination must be applied, for its genesis was, so to speak, strange and portentous, and as it has sprung from such sources, its development is most obscure. Now its character is as follows. From all that nature possesses, all things that are, that have come into being and that shall be (since this too is a phase of existence), from all these things, I say, images flow and rebound from their substance. For if each perceptible thing is form coupled with matter, and if we discover an escape of matter in the combination, reasoning shows that the nature of the images also is canalized, so that in both cases perceptible things renounce the dignity of real being. Now the imaginative *pneuma* is a powerful reflecting mirror of all the images that flow off in this way. For, wandering in vain and slipping from their base, on account of the indefiniteness of their nature, and because they are recognized by no being of real existence, whenever these fall in with psychical *pneumata*, the which are images indeed, and have a seat fixed in nature, then they lean upon them and take their rest as though at their own hearth-stone. Of those things, therefore, which have come into being, inasmuch as they have already passed into the activity of existence, the images sent forth are distinct, until in the fullness of time they become faint and evanescent. Of existing things, inasmuch as they are still standing, the images are more tenacious of life and more distinct, but those of future events are more indefinite and indistinguishable. For they are the advanced waves of things not yet present, efflorescences of unful-filled nature, as it were, riddles of closely stored seeds, skipping away and darting out.

Thus also art is needed with a view to coming events, for the images which proceed from them are only shadowed, and the symbols are not as clear as in the case of already existing things. Nevertheless they are of a wonderful nature, even as they stand, wonderful in that they have come into existence from things that have not yet existed.

11. But it is high time that we should say of this art how it may help us. The best way is to prepare the divine *pneuma* in such wise that it may be worthy of the direction of mind and of God, and not be a recipient of obscure energies. And the best culture is the one leading through philosophy, which brings a calm from passions, for when once disturbed by these the *pneuma* is occupied, as it were a territory; and through a wise and temperate life, one that least maddens the animal nature and that has least tendency to bring it into the last body. For turmoil would reach even to the first body, but this ought to be kept unperturbed and unmoved. But since this is an easy prayer for every one to join in, but is of all things the most difficult to co-operate in attaining, then as we wish sleep to be unprofitable to none, come now, let us seek a definition even for indefinable things; in a word, let us put together an art of divining dream-images. Now it is something in this wise. When mariners sailing the sea come suddenly upon a rock, and presently disembarking see a city of men, as often as they see the same rock, they will take it as a sign of the city. And just as when, in the case of generals, we know from the scouts that they themselves will appear, though we do not see them (for that from the same indication they have always in the past appeared on the scene); so on each occasion we obtain from the dream-images a signal of the activity of coming events.

For these are forerunners of those same things, and like things are forerunners of like. Therefore it is the skipper's fault if, when the same rock becomes visible, he fails to recognize it, or is unable to say to what land the ship is moving. . . .

But understanding dreams is not this simple. Aristotle and reason have asserted that in every case sense-perception creates memory, memory experience, experience in turn science. And there are many dream books which follow exactly this reasoning. But these are to be laughed at, because they are little use. This standard conforms to the nature of bodies, but it is not the case with the imaginative spirit. The imagination does not act like matter, putting together one body after another out of elements which one logically expects to find associated together. Instead the imaginative spirit associates the most dissimilar things.

How then can completely dissimilar things be revealed by the same images? Obviously this is impossible. Some difference must exist, and if it does, let us ask first if we should naturally except a plane mirror, a concave one, and a distorted one to reflect exactly the same images. It is even more difficult in an individual character to capture that which is like a general image.

12. For this reason we must dismiss the idea that all men are under the same laws; rather must each man hold himself as material for the art. Let him inscribe on his memory the affairs in which he has been involved, and the nature of the visions which have preceded them.

. . . It would be a wise proceeding even to publish our waking and sleeping visions and their attendant circumstances; the wise thing to do, I say, unless the culture of the city is like to be too rustic for so novel an enterprise. We shall therefore see fit to add to what are called 'day books' what we term 'night books,' so as to have records to remind us of the character of each of the two lives concerned; for our argument already laid it down that a certain life exists in imagination, at one moment better, at another worse than the intermediate, according to the relation of the *pneuma* to health and disease. If in this way, therefore, we make profitable the observation by which the art is developed, and if nothing slips our memory, in other respects also the result will be a refined pastime; it will be paying oneself the compliment of a history of one's waking and sleeping moments. . . .

Any one can see how great the work is, on attempting to fit language to visions, visions in which those things which are united in nature are separated, and things separated in nature are united, and he is obliged to show in speech what has not been revealed. It is no mean achievement to pass on to another something of a strange nature that has stirred in one's own soul, for whenever by this phantasy (of dreaming) things which are expelled from the order of being, and things which never in any possible way existed, are brought instead into being—nay, even things which have not a nature capable of existence, what contrivance is there for presenting a nameless nature to things which are *per se* inconceivable? Again, it (the phantasy) neither makes these forms appear numerous and all present at the same moment, nor yet does it present them after an interval, but exactly as the dream itself might have them and pass them on to us; for we believe whatever it wills us to believe. To survive at all and without cutting a sorry figure amidst all this, would be proof of a masterly rhetoric. It conducts itself wantonly even against our understanding itself, becoming the cause of something more than thought. For we are not indeed insensible to the visions; rather are our approbations and partialities strong, and not least our detestations. And the many trickeries that are bound up with this, attack us in our sleep. Pleasure is at that moment most of all a thing full of charm, such as to impart to our souls loves or hatreds even in the waking state. If any one were to utter no lifeless words, but rather to accomplish that for the sake of which the discourse was seriously undertaken, he would need stirring language to put his auditor into the same condition and amidst the same thoughts as himself.

Now in dreams one conquers, walks, or flies simultaneously, and the imagination has room for it all; but how shall mere speech find room for it? So a man sleeps and dreams; he sees a dream, and arises from it still sleeping, as he thinks, and shakes off his dream while still recumbent. He philosophizes a little on the vision that has appeared to him, according to his knowledge; and this is a dream, but the other is a double dream. Accordingly he believes it not, and thinks that now he is awake and that what appears to him is really alive. Forthwith a fierce struggle ensues, and a man dreams that an attack is made on himself, then that he has left all behind and is waking up, again that he has made trial of himself and has discovered the deception. In some such way must the sons of Aloeus be suffering punishment for piling up the mountains of Thessaly against the gods.* But there is no law of Adrastea in the way of the sleeper, to forbid him from rising from earth more happily than Icarus, from soaring above the eagles, or reaching a point above the loftiest spheres themselves. So one looks steadily upon the earth from afar, and discovers a land not visible even to the moon. It is also in his power to hold converse with the stars and to meet the unseen gods of the universe. That which is difficult to describe then takes place easily, namely that the gods are visibly manifest, nor do the gods feel even a particle of jealousy. The dreamer has not even descended to the earth after a short interval; he is already there. Nothing is so characteristic of dreams as to steal space and to create without time. Then the sleeper converses with sheep and fancies their bleating to be speech, and he understands their talk. So new and so extensive a wealth of subjects is there for one who has the courage to let loose his language upon them.

13. I even think that myths take their authority from dreams, as those in which peacock, fox, and sea hold converse. But these are small things compared with the independence of dreams. And although myths are a very small part of dreams, nevertheless they were approved by the sophists as a preparation for the work of eloquence. And for these men to whom the myth is the beginning of their art, the dream ought to be its appropriate end. And there is this in addition, that one has not worked the tongue in vain, as in the case of myths, but that he has become wiser in judgement. Let every man, then, with leisure and ease proceed to write a narrative of whatsoe'er happens in his waking

* Otus and Ephialtes, who attempted to pile Ossa on Olympus and Pelion on Ossa. *Odyssey*, XI.315.

and sleeping states. Let him spend some of his time on this. Of the time so spent the greatest help will be found in his knowledge of letters. Let him put together the art of divination which we have extolled, than which nothing could be of more varied service to him.

## NOTE

Nicephorus Gregoras, in the early part of the fourteenth century in Constantinople, wrote a Commentary on this treatise of Synesius. In a letter to Joannes Cantacuzenus (Ep. 23), the substance of which is repeated in one addressed to Demetrios Cavasilas many years later (Ep. 155), he extols this work in the following terms: 'You know, I think, that I wrote a book long ago inspired by my profound gratitude towards the great Synesius. He wrote, as you are aware, a most remarkable work on Dreams. Just as nature made every effort, and with great success, to show in him a man of the highest order among the Greeks, in like manner this work is the best of all that he has written, and he made every effort that it should appear so. . . . He gives us his own personal evidence in the matter. God inspired him, and he had no recourse to his forces as a man, he tells us, in this work. He simply lent his pen to it. God did all. Thus the work is the production, so he writes, of a man possessed by a prophetic inspiration, and full of the Divinity. For this reason the greater part of the book has been composed in an obscure style, as were the oracles that the Delphic Tripod gave forth, and that were, as you know, full of prophetic phrases sedulously concealed and unintelligible to the ignorant, phrases which screened them as if behind a curtain of heavy obscurity. Yielding to numerous requests, we have sought to elucidate this work, to what extent it was possible, by the help of a varied Commentary.' (Nic. Greg. *Ep.*, ed. Guilland, Paris, 1927.)

There is nothing in this passage from the Letters of Nicephorus that is not contained in the text of *De Insomniis*, and a Letter to Hypatia (Ep. 154), concerning the manner in which it was written. But it is interesting as showing to what an extent the works of Synesius were admired by the erudite of the fourteenth century, and also as indicating that at this time the work on dreams, which has been regarded by modern commentators with less favour than the other essays, was esteemed as the most important. One of the friends who urged Nicephorus to write a

Commentary on it was Theodorus Metochites, the Prime Minister of the Emperor Andronicus II, who was the most learned man of the fourteenth century, and had instructed Nicephorus in Greek philosophy as well as astronomy, and had become his patron at the Court. Nicephorus, like Synesius, was an astronomer as well as a rhetorician, and wrote a work on the construction of an astrolabe, which, he tells his correspondent Cavasilas (Ep. 155), he laboured over with the same ardour that he put into his study of Synesius. It seems that Byzantium in the fourteenth century was not so far off in point of culture from Athens and Alexandria of the fourth and fifth.

BENEDICT PERERIUS

DE MAGIA

*Concerning the Investigation of Dreams
and Concerning Astrological Divinations.
Three books.
Against the false and superstitious arts.*

Translated by Elizabeth Shedd, 1961

*BOOK II. Concerning the Investigation of Dreams.*

There is no one class of dreams nor one explanation for
them. Therefore, the cause of all of them is not the
same, so that they should not all be either confirmed
or rejected on the same grounds. Indeed, sacred works
deride many dreams and even condemn them; but
certain dreams they praise and highly respect. For the
majority of them are groundless; but more than a few
are natural, arising from definite causes in nature.
Others, moreover, are thrust upon mortals by the
cunning and malice of the devil. Finally, some are
given to men by divine inspiration. Further diligent
examination of dreams produces a most felicitous
knowledge of them, very fine in itself, and serves im-
mensely to illuminate several obscure passages in the
Holy Scripture. It can, in truth, be most useful in
regulating and tempering the lives of men. But first,
it is of great assistance to refute the ignorance (more
accurately, I should say, the foolishness and stupidity)
of certain men who examine dreams too carefully,

[MS p. 115]     anxiously and superstitiously. Thus encouraged by
these considerations about the nature, variety and
validity of dreams, I have engaged in several useful
inquiries exacting the utmost skill, and have attempted
to explain them in this book.

## INDEX OF INQUIRIES OF BOOK II.
## CONCERNING DREAMS.

[MS p. 116]

## FIRST INQUIRY: CAN ONE HAVE ANY FAITH IN DREAMS?

The opinions of the vulgar and the wise on this matter are drawn in various directions. However, this inquiry may in one sentence be able to sort out the facts through the classification of dreams. For without doubt, a few dreams are to be trusted, though most should be entirely discredited. To be sure, it is equally foolish to believe either in all dreams or in none, and either belief seems to be a mark of extreme stupidity or stubbornness. But assuredly, that adage of Cicero is both clever and true: nothing can be said which is so absurd that it might not be said by some philosopher. For what can be more *irrational* (ἄλογον) and *impossible* (ἀδύνατον) than to think that all dreams are true and must be believed? For yourself see how Protagoras, clearly one of that group of ancient and venerable philosophers, claims faith in all dreams and, examining them with great authority, claims to establish their veracity or fallaciousness not by the very nature of things but only by the opinion of men. Man is the measure of all things, and each and everything is such as it seems to man, be he sober or drunk, in good or poor health, awake or sleeping. Close to this type of error are certain Stoics, far too superstitious and almost fanatical philosophers, who rejected no dreams and maintained that in all there is power to

*Margin notes:*

Cicero, *On Divinations*

Opinion of Protagoras, the Stoics: all dreams are true

[MS p. 117]

Xenophanes
& the Epi-
cureans:
all dreams
are with-
out value

indicate and signify something. Nevertheless they say that certain dreams are thought to be meaningless and misleading (1) in so far as they are tenuously expressed and for this reason obscure and difficult to understand; (2) because, on account of their ambiguity, they seem to be applicable to various subjects and therefore able to confirm nothing certain for us through observation of them; but (3) especially since cleverness and wisdom equal to discerning the force of these dreams will not easily be found among men. In contrast, Xenophanes of Colophon—a memorable philosopher even by virtue of his very age, for he was nearly contemporary with the birth of philosophy in Greece—and also the advocates of the gentle and attractive Epicurean discipline held views contrary to these and denied the authority and the validity of all dreams. "Moreover, one must not believe in any dreams," so they would argue. Nature is the one and the same force behind all dreams; thus, there ought to be a constant criterion for believing either in all dreams or in none. But in most dreams it is not possible to believe; therefore, there is no reason why, when most dreams have been discredited, we ought to believe in any in particular. In addition, if certain dreams are trustworthy and definite, it is necessary that there be some definite efficient cause of them. But what are the causes? Nature, people say, and God. Yet nature, indeed, is a friend of order and constancy; and in dreams there is no order, but inconstancy full of accident. Moreover, it seems beneath God and foreign to his majesty, that He should approach the couches of sleeping men, rush to their bedsides and interrupt their snoring with dreams which they would not remember, not understand, or even contemn upon awakening. Or, should they think the dreams were important to them, they would be filled with foolish superstition; for days and nights their minds would hang either paralyzed with inane fear of impending evils or elated with the false expectation of future blessings. Yet how much more suitable it would have been to the purpose of God, how much more worthy of his superiority and advantageous to the interest of men, to give visions not to the base and uneducated,

[MS p. 118]

but to the excellent and wise, not to the sleeping but to those awake, in truth, to those more fitted to understand; and that God give signs—not through riddles and devious, intricate ways—but directly, openly,

clearly because he would wish to be understood by
man.

The right
approach to
dreams

In this fashion those philosophers ramble on about
dreams, in sum either accrediting or condemning
them, but wandering manifestly very far astray from
the paths of truth. But the proper attitude, standing
as a middle road so to speak, distinguishes different
classes of dreams. Of these dreams it flatly denounces
and rejects most as being groundless, empty of all

The majority
of dreams
are without
value

rational basis and meriting no confidence. It is superfluous to argue this, since it is clearer than the light
of the sun. For everyday experience, as each day we
dream the whole night through, teaches how many
and what dreams we have. Out of so many dreams
does truth emerge? Indeed occasionally some truth
does emerge, but since this is extremely rare and
occurs without any logical pattern, nothing can be
adduced as to why it should not be thought to have
happened by chance and fortuitously. Reason herself
also compels that the same thing be admitted. For
what other cause of such dreams—those meriting no
confidence—is there unless it be spirits, servants of

The cause
of dreams

the conscious, sensing mind, and more especially of
fantasy which characteristically fashions dreams in
which fragments and traces of impressions received
in the waking hours—fragments which in the schools
we call "species," and thus I term "spirits"—settle
and entrench themselves and are agitated during sleep
by vapors of food and drink stealing into the head.
And tossed about from here to there, these spirits give
rise to various dreams and visions, but on account of
the disorderly tossing of these spirits the dreams are
exceedingly confused, frequently even turbulent and
distorted, and ultimately such that they can have no
power to signify anything. So then are dreams as they
variously take shape in cloudy forms; images and likenesses of living things or of other objects which for a

[MS p. 119]

very brief moment we watch changing into other
images and again into others; and soon all are dispersed and vanish into the deep. He who would think
that these images bear a definite meaning of anything should be regarded as dull and fatuous. But it
seems no less a sign of ignorance to attribute to dreams
definite indications and signs of symbolic meaning
(*significandarum rerum*). If we ignore the visions of
the drunk, the crazed and the insane and do not take
them into consideration, assuredly dreams must be

equally ridiculed and contested—rather even more so, because generally they are themselves more jumbled, confused and bizarre. Wittily indeed, but nevertheless truthfully, people have said that if it had been arranged by nature that sleeping men should do what they dream, it would be absolutely necessary that all men who went to bed should be bound, on the ground that they were about to do things more ridiculous, absurd and incredible than the insane do.

Testimony of divine Scriptures as to the emptiness of dreams

The Holy Scriptures also confirm this opinion in declaiming the levity and superficiality of those who by believing in dreams—that is, in most vain and deceptive things—show themselves worthy to be jibed at by the mockery of all. Thus in Ecclesiastes, Chapter V, it is written, "*Where there are many dreams, there are a maximum of vanities and countless words.*" Similarly, in Ecclesiasticus, Chapter XXXIV, we read this: "*The imprudent extol dreams; just as he who catches a shadow and runs after the wind, so is he who heeds dreams; dreams have made many men stray and have ruined those who have hope in them.*" Finally, whenever the Scriptures wish to point out something vain, tenuous, elusive and fallacious, they express it most frequently through comparison and similarity to dreams.

Many dreams are true

[MS p. 120]

On the other hand, as it must not be denied that truth and validity are absent in most dreams, so it must be admitted that certain dreams are true and sure. For if there were nothing truthful and sure in any dreams, the most renowned of physicians would be acting quite naively and superstitiously when with such painstaking care they study the dreams which often come over the sick in order to diagnose their ills and to cure them. The natural philosophers (*physiologi*), likewise, would spend themselves in futile labor, hunting down and investigating with so great zeal into the causes, powers and significance of dreams. Besides, so many of the stories of former times, attested to by well known men, confirmed and substantiated by records and by examples of truthful dreams which amazingly conformed to the very word with the actual outcome of the situation, would be false. How many dreams are mentioned in sacred writings, dreams not only valid and truthful, but also very full of divine mysteries. Let the reader recall to his memory the dreams of Abraham, Abimelech, Jacob, Laban, Joseph, Pharaoh, Solomon, King Nebuchadnezzar, Daniel, Mor-

Matthew 1
and 27
Acts 16

decai (*Mardochaeus*), and Judas Maccabaeus; and in addition to these the dreams in the New Testament of blessed Joseph, the Magi and the wife of Pilate; and finally the dream of St. Paul, which is told by Luke in the Acts of the Apostles. Even Homer noted this distinction among dreams, though it was veiled, in the poetic tradition, in the garments of fable, when he fashioned two gates, one of horn through which truthful dreams are sent out to men and the other of ivory through which false dreams are released. Vergil, imitating Homer, as indeed he was accustomed to do, expressed the same sentiment in the Aeneid, Book VI, with these words:

Remark of
Homer dis-
tinguishing
the meaning
of true and
false dreams

> There are twin gates of sleep: one of them is wrought of horn, through which easy exit is given to true visions; the other is made of gleaming ivory and shines brightly but through it the shades send false dreams toward heaven.

[MS p. 121]

Macrobius
Book I,
Chapter 3

But why did the poet assign the gate of horn to truthful dreams and the gate of ivory to false ones? Macrobius in that Commentary in which he explains the dream of Scipio sets forth the reason for this.

## SECOND INQUIRY: CONCERNING THE CAUSES OF TRUE DREAMS

It has been said that some dreams are false and others true. Since we have rejected the false ones, therefore, let us consider the true ones. But since what dreams are true and by what sign and peculiar mark they are recognized from the false cannot be clearly understood unless we investigate and discover all the causes of truthful dreams, it is quite fitting at this time to discuss what has been believed and advanced by others concerning causes of this sort. Hippocrates in his book on dreams (*de insomniis*) established two types of truthful dreams: one he calls divine, the other natural. Divine dreams, he says, are sent by God and always presage memorable occurrences and events marked by joy or sorrow, good fortune or misery, be they private or public affairs. Moreover, he says that the explanation of these dreams must be sought from soothsayers and interpreters of divine meanings. The dream of Cyrus the Great who founded the monarchy of the Persians is said to have been of this nature. The sun was seen at his feet

The various
views of the
authorities
as to the
causes of
dreams:
Hippocrates

Cyrus' dream

while he was sleeping, and three times he reached out for it with his hands, and three times turning it slipped away. The wise, learned magi of the Persians answered that this dream signified that he would hold imperial power for thirty years, and so indeed it happened. Hippocrates thinks that natural dreams arise nearly always out of causes latent within the body of the

[MS p. 122] person sleeping and that they indicate good or bad states of the body itself, i.e., abundance and excess or, on the other hand, insufficiency and absence of those humors which exist in the body, or the presence of any one of them that may be spoiled by motion in its own place or wildly and turbulently agitated. Indeed, the observation and conjectural interpretation of these dreams for medical purposes to devise and establish cures is thought to be of very great value.

Plato     Plato in the Symposium thinks that truthful dreams and portents of the future originate with demons; for demons are the medium between God, who is immortal and incorporeal, and man who is both corporeal and mortal, especially since they themselves are also corporeal like us and immortal like God. For

The nature & function of demons according to Plato     Plato thinks that God does not meddle in human affairs nor have any intimate association or intercourse with men, but rather that contacts and colloquies between God and men, either awake or sleeping, are initiated and accomplished by means of demons. Doubtless, he says, it is the function and duty of demons to convey the prayers and offerings of men to God and to bear God's assistance and blessings down to men. Through them, prophecies, sorcery, magic, every method of divination and the practice of interpreting omens reach men. Thus demons are the heralds, mediators and agents of God; but they act also as the patrons of men, their defenders and masters and, as I should say using the word coined by Apuleius, their "guardian angels" (salutigerulos, literally "greeting carriers"). These are the opinions not only of Plato but of Empedocles and Pythagoras before him. Augustine discusses and argues learnedly and incisively against them in Book VIII, Chapters 20–21

Aristotle     and Book IX of the City of God. Aristotle in the tract which he wrote On Divination through Dreams denies that any dreams are given to men by God. On

[MS p. 123] the contrary truthful dreams are either certain natural signs that have proceeded from natural causes, which skillful philosophers and physicians actually examine to good advantage, or else they are in a certain measure the origins of those things which one will do later upon awakening. For sometimes during sleep certain things occur which seem able to lead us toward some action and which afterward when awakened we appropriately utilize and in taking proper action we are pleased. The Stoics have established three causes of dreams. The first is God Who, since He is supremely omniscient and provident of all things and the benevolent patron of mankind, by Whom man becomes the more discrete (*cautior*), gives him dreams which are tokens of the future and warnings of those things which he must act upon and guard against. The second cause which they establish is fate, by which things are linked in a kind of eternal chain and fixed in a knot, since the Stoics think that antecedent causes and forewarning signs of all future occurrences are sent ahead both through other media and also through dreams themselves. They make the third cause the nature of our soul which is divine. For the soul of man, when his outward senses have been numbed by sleep and are void of all activity and the soul is itself free and delivered of all cares and preoccupations, becomes more vigorous and apt to understand, since at that time it more vividly remembers the past, is alert to the present and foresees the future. Porphyry traces the validity of dreams in part to the innate conceptions in the souls of men, which he takes as meaningful hints of all things that the soul has retained from another life as it enters this body. But the soul, forcibly overcome and suppressed here, cannot apprehend them when the senses are awake; in sleep, however, they manifest themselves to it more clearly and become known. In part he traces dreams to demons: the good and true dreams to good demons, and to evil demons, the perverse, deceptive and false dreams. Synesius discourses at length on the "phantastical spirit" (*phantasticus spiritus*), which is the vehicle of the life-giving principle (*animae*). For by this medium which acts as a chain that principle is attached and linked to this earthly body. Likewise the soul when released from the body moves from one place to another through it, and through it the souls of evildoers suffer the punishments of hell; without its presence in the body no one is able to perceive or understand. Furthermore, reflections of all things which are, were and will be are impressed upon this spirit, and on it they shine as in a mirror, those of the present clearer than those of the past—for the older they

The Stoics

Porphyry: concerning the truth of dreams

[MS p. 124] Synesius on the phantastical spirit

are the less brilliant—and still less clear, reflections of future things which obviously are not, nor ever have been, in existence. But since future events are constrained within the power of causes, they have certain antecedents and forerunners which are the less distinct as the signs are far away and it is in this class that he thinks dreams must be placed. Thus through dreams things are indicated in almost imperceptible images and likenesses—not evenly, however, but according to the varying makeup and plan of that phantastical spirit, as with the action in mirrors and because of the differentiation in matter and form, images are reflected as varied and unlike one another. Synesius further advises us sufficiently to condition and well prepare this phantastical spirit to receive calm and veracious visions in sleep by moderate nourishment, upright actions and pursuits, and by settling the anxieties of the mind. So it was that Pythagoras, when he was about to go to bed, would make himself sleepy by the song and verses of the lyre and this way prepare himself to have good and happy dreams; for the same reason he forbade his servants to eat beans because this food undergoes a great inflation aggravating to the tranquility of a mind seeking truth. But these notions concerning a phantastical spirit which have been handed down by Synesius are nonsense as are the fancies of Pythagoreans and Platonists more void of truth and more incredible even than the tales of the poets.

But so that we may also enjoy something from the ecclesiastical authorities, St. Gregory in the *Dialogues*, Book IV, Chapter 48, lists six causes of dreams. For dreams exist, he says, either (1) from the plenitude or emptiness of the body, or (2) from preceding daily thoughts and cares, or (3) from illusion created by the devil, or (4) out of thought of man together with illusion of the devil, or (5) out of the revelation of God, or (6) finally out of the thought of man together with the revelation of God. When Gregory has recalled the same six causes of dreams in his *Moralia*, Book 8, Chapter 13, he then illustrates them with pertinent opinions in the Holy Scriptures and confirms them with examples.

*The first two types which we have advanced we all know from experience. Four, however, we find in sacred literature. For if dreams did not very often take shape through illusions created by a*

Pythagoras

[MS p. 125]

St. Gregory gives six causes of dreams

*concealed enemy, the Scriptures, Ecclesiasticus 34, would never have said: "Dreams and empty illusions lead many men astray" and certainly it would not have been written in Leviticus 19, "You shall not practice augury nor shall you analyze dreams." With these words, which form part of an execration, it is clearly demonstrated what attitudes are associated with augurs. Again, if at times dreams did not arise from reflection together with illusion, Solomon would not declare in Ecclesiastes, Chapter 5: "Dreams follow upon many cares." And if dreams did not sometimes originate in the mystery of a revelation, why would Joseph have seen himself in a dream appointed to be advanced above his brethren, or the espoused of Mary have been warned by the Angel in a dream to take the Child and fly into Egypt? Again unless dreams did not upon occasion proceed from reflections combined with revelation, Daniel in explaining the vision of Nebuchadnezzar would not have begun his interpretation by saying, "O king, the thoughts which came into your head upon the bed are those which will come to pass hereafter."*

Matthew 2
[MS p. 126]

Daniel 2

This is what Gregory wrote in the *Moralia*, and the foregoing is what others have advanced on the causes of dreams.

I have personally diligently scrutinized the causes of dreams which are of value for signifying something and worthy of observation and I have noted four causes in particular that can be recalled.

**Four causes of true dreams**

The first cause concerns any effect upon the body which is dominant and overpowering within the body itself—that is, if, for example, yellow or black bile, the phlegmatic humor, or the blood should be in excess, or if any other vitiating and noxious substance should be lying inordinately within the body. Galen in *On Prophecies Drawn from Dreams*, Book 5, relates that a certain man dreamed that a second shinbone was made for him out of stone; soon, however, he began to become paralyzed in that very part of his body. Furthermore, those who are about to sweat profusely in an incipient crisis often dream that they are sweating, being sprinkled with hot water in a bath or swimming in a lake or river. It also comes to pass not infrequently that we toss about while sleeping or that we suffer even though only dreaming, like those

**The first cause: any effect upon the body**

who sweat in their sleep or are seized by fever and dream that they are so affected. It has been related by Pliny in the *Natural Histories,* Book VII, Chapter 50, that Publius Cornelius Ruffinus (sic) lost his sight while he was sleeping and that he himself dreamed it as it was happening.

The second cause of dreams attests to any strong disturbance or aroused state of mind. I mean love, hope, fear, or hate. For those who love ardently often dream of their amours; those who are afraid are frequently troubled in sleep by threatening and fearful visions. Here also the ingrained habits and experiences of the life we lead are pertinent. For a fisherman nearly always dreams of seas, lakes, rivers, nets, fish; a hunter, of forests, ravines, mountains, and wild animals; a soldier, of the calls of the trumpet, the clashing of armor, wounds, blood, slaughter. A certain fisherman in Theocritus drolely says, *"Every dog dreams of bread and I dream of fish."* This same cause includes the cares and anxieties of our preceding waking hours and whatever preys upon our minds and preoccupies us; very often visions similar to those anxieties come to us in sleep. Thus in the Book of Ecclesiastes, Chapter V, it is written *"Dreams follow upon cares."* I would certainly place Hannibal's dream, which has been transmitted and believed by many, in this class of dreams. Hannibal was burning with an insatiable hate of the Roman name, aflame with utter passion to exterminate Roman rule. In order that this might be accomplished more easily he was anxious to transfer the war from Spain to Italy so that he might seek out the Roman seat of power. Since, therefore, he was extremely perturbed by various thoughts and considerations about this matter, he had a vision in his sleep which miraculously answered his question and prayer. He saw a youth of super-human nature, who said that he had been sent to him by Jove as a leader of his invasion into Italy and bade him not glance around at what would take place behind his back. At first Hannibal was terrified and did not dare divert his eyes in any direction from that boy. But as human nature is inclined toward the forbidden, he was unable to constrain his eyes, and looking back, he saw a portent awful not only to see but even to describe, a huge monster with many serpents coiled about him, which trampled down and crashed through everything whichever way he charged. At the same time

---

The second cause:
[MS p. 127]
violent turbulation of the soul

Hannibal's dream foretelling the devastation of Italy

[MS p. 128]

he saw heaven darken with deep black clouds everywhere he looked, and dense clouds shot through with lightning rushing over. Hannibal was stunned and asked his guardian what was the significance of this monster and portent. He answered that it was the devastation of Italy, that he (Hannibal) should continue to push forward toward whatever place he intended and that he should not inquire anything further, but rather allow the fates to remain veiled. And certainly, this dream did take shape out of Hannibal's previous reflections and concerns while he was awake. But nevertheless, the outcome of the situation well enough confirmed the verity of his dream, for Hannibal brought even more evil into Italy than had been foretold by that vision.

**The third cause: the cunning of the devil**

The third cause of dreams I attribute to the power and cunning of the devil. For he breathes many things into the sleeping and suggests dreams, always in an insidious and malicious way, obviously so that by whatever method he can, he may be troublesome and do injury to many. The devil, then, is the architect and agent of certain dreams, and here is apparent what is clearly understood in sacred writings: the analysis (*observationem*) of dreams is so despised by God that when practised by magicians and augurs, it, together with other evil works of the sorcerers is condemned to dire punishments. This is not at all surprising for any other reason, as blessed Gregory explains in the *Dialogues*, Book IV, Chapter 48, since the devil is most always implicated in dreams, filling the minds of men with poisonous superstition and not only uselessly

**Certain dreams are [MS p. 129] sent by the devil**

deluding but perniciously deceiving them. The stories about Aesculapius, Serapis, and Amphiaraus confirm the fact that the devil at one time was wont in many instances to sport with the mortal races, blinded by impiety, with this kind of dreams. For it is written in Philostratus, Pausanias and Strabo that the three former men, highly esteemed by the people, were accustomed, like God, to prescribe cures for individual diseases through the medium of dreams to those who entered their temples afflicted by various diseases. In

**Dream of Alexander the Great**

this classification, I think, belongs that noble dream of Alexander the Great, according to the authority of the writings which have passed on the affairs of his life and merit confidence among many people. For when, in a certain battle, Ptolemy, who was the first king of Egypt after Alexander, had been struck by a poison spear and lay dying in extreme agony from this wound, Alexander, sitting next to him, fell asleep and saw in his sleep a dragon carrying a small root in his mouth at the same time indicating where that root would grow which would assuredly have immediate power to cure Ptolemy and many soldiers wounded by the same weapon. The herbs were sought, found and put to use, and soon followed the promised effect.

**Two kinds of dreams sent by the devil**

There are, however, two particular types of dreams initiated by the devil, one of which pertains to the disclosure and manifestation of occult secrets. For the devil can know and indicate to men through dreams the natural effects which will necessarily arise at any moment from certain causes, whatever he himself is about to do, and what things, both present and past, are hidden from men. The second type of dream has the power of exciting confusion in the mind so that when the humors and vapors which are in the body have been agitated and thrown off balance, men are excessively aroused, either to sensual pleasure, or to hate and vindictiveness, or to other perverse states of mind.

**[MS p. 130] How dreams of the devil may be distinguished from other dreams**

Furthermore, it can be conjectured in two ways quite probably enough which are the dreams sent by the devil. First, indeed, if dreams take place frequently which are significant of future events or occult matters, knowledge of which does not contribute to a constructive end, either for oneself or for others, but to a wrong or idle display of curious knowledge, it will be considered, and not rashly, that the initiator of these dreams is the devil, that it is he who by this method attempts to infuse the minds of men with vain superstition, if not even ensnare them in criminal impiety. Second, if dreams that are obscene, repulsive and full of cruelty and impiety come so very often to sober, upright and religious men, it is not unjustly held that these dreams proceed from the devil. For the devil tries to pollute the bodies of sleeping men with impure dreams and defile them so that he may make their minds, when they awaken, somehow partners in his foulness. But if he cannot accomplish this, he at least attends to one thing, that by grieving, disturbing and afflicting pious men with such sights, he may render them slower and more indolent for prayer, for the offices of charity, and for the taking of the holy sacraments. Cassian in his twenty-second *Collation*, Chapter 6, gives a most enlightening example of diabolic cunning and maliciousness. Indeed, Justin Martyr in response to the twenty-first question of the

Orthodox, lucidly and skillfully expresses his position on this matter. For when these questions were put to him, he replied to the interrogation in the manner we have here indicated. There remains the fourth and

**The fourth cause of dreams is divine**

last cause of dreams which we can rightly call divine. This entire discussion of ours was instituted above all for the sake of stating and elucidating this cause. What has been said up to now serves this end. However, examples of dreams which have been sent by God

**[MS p. 131]**

are encountered at random in the divine books; above we have lifted some examples from sacred books and more can be added if anyone wishes to assemble all of them. For the rest, so that the force and nature of divine dreams may be fully and clearly understood, I shall, in the scholastic tradition, take up several questions, lucidly to be sure, but briefly and concisely, and still observing brevity, I shall also refer to many examples, complete and undiminished for the consideration of the reader.

## THIRD INQUIRY: BY WHAT SIGNS MAY IT BE KNOWN WHETHER A DREAM HAS BEEN SENT BY GOD OR NOT?

**The method of recognizing divine dreams is twofold**

As it now occurs to me, one can determine whether a dream has been sent by God in two ways. First, certainly, the excellence of the thing signified in the dream: if things, of which certain knowledge can only reach man by the will and grant of God, become known to a man through a dream, they are of such kinds as are called "future contingencies" (*futura contingentia*) in the schools of theologians. Indeed, they are the heart's secrets which, enclosed within the soul's deepest recesses, completely conceal themselves from all intellectual perception of mortals; and, finally, they are the principal mysteries of our faith, made manifest to no one except by the instruction of God. A dream, therefore, which contains this sort of knowledge and revelation may be considered divine. Second, the divinely inspired dream is powerfully conveyed by a certain interior illumination and stir

**[MS p. 132]**

ring of souls whereby God thus enlightens the mind, influences the will, and convinces man of the trustworthiness and validity of this dream in order that he may clearly recognize that God is its author and freely decide that without any doubt he both wants to and ought to believe in it. On this point that memo

**Memorable opinion of St. Gregory**

rable opinion of Gregory in the *Dialogues*, Book IV, Chapter 48, is, as Gregory says,

*Saints at times distinguish between illusions and revelations, the real voices and images of visions, with penetrating delicacy, so that they know what they may receive from good inspiration and what they may suffer from illusion. For if the mind of man, which does occasionally utter many truths that it might serve in the end to free the soul from some misconception, were not alerted against these things, it would plunge itself through the agency of the deceiving spirit into many futile pursuits.*

This is as far as Gregory goes here. In his works, the reader will find this same position more extensively and lucidly treated in the *Moralia*, Book VIII, Chapter 13. Thus, just as the natural light of the mind makes us clearly perceive the truth of first principles and embrace it with our approval immediately before the introduction of any proof, so indeed, when dreams have been given by God, the divine light flooding into our souls has effect with the result that we recognize these dreams as being both true and divine and are confirmed in our faith. Correctly, therefore, it is told in Ecclesiasticus 34 that *"If the visitation were not sent by the Lord, you would not open your heart to dreams,"* which means that a few dreams are given to men by God, through his miraculous visitation of their souls.

God affects men in various ways through dreams [MS p. 133]

However, according to sacred writings, this visitation of God through dreams often comes about in many different ways. For sometimes God troubles and frightens men through dreams, as it is related of Abimelech and Laban in Genesis. In Job 4 and 7 it says: *"You will make me afraid by dreams and visions and you will strike me with terror."* Sometimes during sleep God arouses man and incites him to undertake some great and difficult task by disclosing the definite prospect of a favorable outcome, just as it happened in the dreams of Gideon and Judas Maccabaeus. Often He warns and advises what a man ought to do or whether he ought to flee: such were the dreams of blessed Joseph and the Magi. The words which are written in Job 33 attest to this: *"When men are sleeping in bed, He opens their ears and, enlightening them, provides them with knowledge."* And it was also at one time the practice of God to bestow prophetic inspiration upon some men. For in Numbers 12 God says: *"If there be a prophet of the Lord among you, I shall appear to him in a*

Judges 7
2 Maccabees 11
Matthew 2

*vision or I shall speak to him in a dream."* And in
Joel 2 dreams are included among other gifts of the
Holy Spirit. We also read in I Kings 3 that the gift
of wisdom and knowledge was promised by God to
Solomon during his sleep. The future brilliance of
some men's honor and glory is also revealed from time
to time through a dream, as we read in the Scriptures
happened to the young Joseph and to Mordecai. To
certain ones, moreover, divine mysteries were disclosed
in sleep: Jacob's dream of the mystic ladder and
Daniel's concerning the kingdom of Christ were of this
nature. Finally, at times God has prefigured and revealed beforehand the future event of human affairs:
such were the dreams of Abraham in Genesis 15, of
Pharaoh in Genesis 41 and of Nebuchadnezzar in
Daniel 2 and 4.

Divine dreams reach men in different ways, sometimes accompanied by terror and a great upheaval of
body and soul, as happened to Abraham and Nebuchadnezzar. Occasionally a dream has been given to someone who has not been permitted to apprehend the
meaning, as in the dreams of Pharaoh and Nebuchadnezzar. To Daniel, however, and to other prophets, comprehension was divinely conveyed at the
same time as the dreams themselves. On the other
hand, understanding of the two dreams through which
Joseph's future dignity and power over his brothers
was foretold to him was given to no one at the time;
but, later, the truth of these dreams was made known
and understood by the very outcome of the situation.
That variety too is seen in divine dreams; for some
dreams are clear and lucid, obviously denoting the
actual things themselves, as were the dreams of
blessed Joseph, the three Magi, and St. Paul, whereas
others are obscure and involved, actually making implications through metaphors (*similtudines*). Of this
kind were the dreams of Pharaoh about the seven
ears of corn and the seven oxen, of Nebuchadnezzar
about the statue and the tree, and not least those of
Pharaoh's butler and baker. In addition, it seems
that upon occasion either God himself speaks with
men in sleep, as in the dreams of Jacob and Solomon;
or an angel, as in the dreams of blessed Joseph; or
some man, as in the dream of St. Paul. Moreover,
when He has been repeatedly asked, God often
sends dreams as an interpretation of a dream: thus
He entrusted to Daniel in sleep, who had so fervently
prayed to Him while awake, the interpretation of the

I Kings 3

Genesis 37
Esther 11

Genesis 28
Daniel 7

Genesis 15
Ways divine
dreams are
conveyed
[MS p. 134]
Genesis 41
Daniel 2

Genesis 37

Matthew 1 & 2
Acts 16
Genesis 41
Daniel 2
Genesis 40

Genesis 28
I Kings 3
Matthew 1 & 2
Acts 16

Daniel 2

dreams which Nebuchadnezzar had had. Indeed, it is seen in I Samuel, Chapter 28, that there was once among the Hebrews a certain admirable procedure and custom of taking counsel with God in extremely uncertain, critical matters, so that He would indicate through dreams what was true or what needed to be done. Last, certain divinely inspired dreams answer to the preceding reflections and cares of men's waking hours. Among this kind ought to be included the first dream of Nebuchadnezzar, told in Daniel 2, and similarly the first dream of blessed Joseph which St. Matthew relates in his first chapter, the above mentioned dream of Hannibal, and also that of Scipio Aemilianus, concisely composed and most eloquently narrated by Cicero.

[MS p. 135]

## FOURTH INQUIRY: WHY SHOULD GOD CONVEY HIS SECRETS TO MEN IN SLEEP?

Since the soul of a man in sleep would seem to be the least receptive and the least capable of understanding divine matters, it definitely seems fitting to inquire why God has wished not infrequently to instruct men both in the secrets of His providence and in the mysteries of heavenly affairs through dreams. But actually, we can bring forth varied reasons for this occurrence. Hippocrates touches upon the first reason at the beginning of his book on dreams: the soul is cut off by men while awake in various pre-occupations. It is held apart by serious business, and distracted by cares; moreover, it is called toward things outside itself by those matters which are exterior to it, and because of the different impressions of the senses, it is led astray and hindered by the multiplicity of noises of human activity; it is drawn away from contemplation of itself and of things celestial. In addition, it vacillates in uncertain deliberations; it is aroused by different interests and emotions which do not allow it to see clearly or judge impartially that which is true and valid. On the other hand, in rest and sleep the mind is free and delivered of all disturbances and hindrances of this kind; it is entirely present and conscious of its own being; it attends to itself, and all of its own powers are with it; it holds its faculties collected together and joined; keen, prepared to understand, it is fully and utterly capable of all things which should be placed before it from without. One may set down the second reason for the

Five reasons why so many things are divinely revealed to the sleeping

[MS p. 136]
The soul is better able to grasp divine revelations in sleep

same thing. What we receive when awake we are accustomed to discuss and examine with subtle analysis and to recall to calculation and to weighing upon the balance of human reason, for we demand that all things conform to the rule of reason. If what has been presented to us meets this standard, we approve; if there is discrepancy, it is renounced and rejected. In sleep, however, the mind of man accepts without examination things which have been cast before it; it is more prepared and conditioned to trust and follow divinely inspired visions. Moreover, all men who have written on divine matters agree that it is more conducive to understanding these things—not only intellectually but also emotionally, so to speak, and with a sort of spiritual sensitivity and with taste—for a man to be directed and ruled from without rather than governing himself, for him to be a listener rather than an arbitrator and judge, and, last, for him to have a simple faith rather than to investigate and ponder the reasons for believing. The third reason, which lies in dreams itself, has been treated in

Aristotle

Aristotle's tract *On Divination*. He says:

> *Whatever impulse by which the mind of a sleeping person is kept activated and stirring from without, however slight and nominal, has nevertheless a great power to motivate the mind, is firmly grounded in it and cleaves to it tenaciously. This occurs, moreover, because of the stillness of the night, the calm and idleness of the sense organs and the absence of all things to which minds normally direct their attention. For at that*

[MS p. 137]

> *time when the senses have been lulled to sleep and the body languishes, what is exterior is not perceived.*

For at that propitious moment, God instructs man without any disturbance, without the observation of other men, finally without the interruption of anything. Particularly, moreover, since the further our mind is drawn away from association with the senses and contact with the body, the more readily it seems to be influenced and the keener it is for understanding the divine messages. Too, during sleep, which is a kind of likeness or imitation of death, the mind somehow seems to be separated from participation in the body and the body's chains, and to a certain extent unquestionably relaxes. The fourth reason is, in my opinion, how much more influential is God than any man in teaching and enlightening man. Certainly man can teach man, but not unless he is awake, listening, and attentive. God, however, can even instruct him very effectively when he is sleeping and dreaming. Thus he rightfully proclaims that he holds supreme power and influence over all the forces and faculties of the human mind. And then I shall suggest a fifth reason, evidently so that no one may think that death takes away from man all knowledge and that there is no other method of organizing knowledge except through consciousness, discursive reasoning, and preliminary understanding of other things. Averroes in his own

**Against Averroes**

commentary on Aristotle, *On Divination through Dreams*, does not dare to deny that prophecy can come to man either through sleep or through revelation. Yet, he denies that the arts or speculative sciences are available to anyone by this process. He says:

**[MS p. 138]**

*The nature of man is one: just one, therefore, will be the mode of learning and teaching, namely, through the intermediary senses, so through the various experiences received and careful rational analysis of them. For if, in addition to the common and usual means of learning, there were yet this other one through dreams or revelation, which would be much easier and far superior, the former method would be the more difficult and trying, thus the more superfluous, and therefore would not be given to man. For God and nature do not act fruitlessly, and God would not act on things of which I am capable of doing very well and securely.*

And so he writes. Indeed, this argument would not be obviously groundless if anyone should say (though no one among us does) that this way of learning through dreams or revelations were either natural to man or frequent and customary. But that these comments of Averroes, like others of his on the knowledge, power and providence of God and the nature of the human soul are unscholarly, dull and fallacious and arise from an overflowing fountain of impiety and ignorance of things divine, is clear enough alone from the

**Genesis 2
I Kings 3**

**Exodus 31**

examples noted in the Scriptures of Adam, Solomon, Daniel and many of the prophets, to whom knowledge of numerous things was suddenly given by God; but in addition from those of Bezaleel and Aholiab who, it is narrated in the Book of Exodus, were suddenly informed by divine inspiration that Moses had completed the tabernacle together with all its appurtenances and adornments with perfect skill.

[MS p. 139]

## FIFTH INQUIRY: WHY SHOULD DREAMS BE GIVEN BY GOD TO OBSCURE AND UNEDUCATED MEN BUT NOT TO THE LEARNED?

The error
of Aristotle
and Cicero

Aristotle and Cicero thought that by just this one reckoning of all dreams which are believed to be divine, their trustworthiness and validity could be disparaged and disregarded. For if these dreams, they say, were given to men by God, it is reasonable that they would not be given to humble and uneducated men, but to those individuals excelling in knowledge and wisdom. In this they erred because they obviously ignored the distinction between divine dreams, those which I say are truly divine, and those which are not divine but erroneously regarded as such. Witness the gods of the pagans who, there is absolutely no doubt, were demons as far as we Christians are concerned. They were somehow unable to foresee with certainty and to know the future occurrences and the consequences of human affairs, for this is the province of God alone, and so they could not predict or reveal in advance these events with definite words or signs. This is why they did not give dreams through which the future was unveiled to educated and wise men clearly so that these men, recognizing the vanity and fallaciousness of those dreams, would not shatter the authority of the very gods in the eyes of others and publicly expose their oracles which were void of supposed divinity and the inanities of their "truth" to the derision and contempt of the masses. Therefore, they gave such dreams to the uneducated and to those unskilled at differentiating between truth and deception, but most particularly to the superstitious who for this reason are within themselves quite prepared and inclined to believe anything whatsoever. On the other hand, dreams which are sent by the true God of which we read are generally given to men of piety preeminent in their wisdom, such as Abraham, Jacob, Solomon and Daniel. Nevertheless, a few dreams are also given to men not so learned in this way but still of strong faith and renowned for their exceptional purity. Outstanding virtue and piety, moreover, render the soul of a

Why demons
were at one
time accus-
tomed to
give dreams
not to
learned and
discreet men
but to uned-
ucated and
base men

[MS p. 140]

Why certain
dreams have
been granted
by God even
to impious
men

man more docile and more fit for the comprehension
of things divine than do either human wisdom or
knowledge. For those who excel in worldly capacities
or learning are nearly always either impious or proud
or twisted by the iniquitous sins, and these qualities
completely cut off the souls of men from spiritual doctrines or divine enlightenment. It does not escape me
that certain divinely inspired dreams have come to
wicked and impious men such as Pharaoh and Nebuchadnezzar. But these dreams were not given to them
primarily for their own sakes nor were they bestowed
along with understanding of them. As a result, when
those men could not find an interpretation of those
dreams among their own seers, they were compelled
to seek it from worshippers of the true God and by
this way came to know the true God and to venerate
Him and hold His servants in admiration and respect.
This is what the dreams of Pharaoh and Nebuchadnezzar, which were interpreted by Joseph and Daniel,
manifestly illustrate.

## SIXTH INQUIRY: WHY ARE DIVINELY IN-
SPIRED DREAMS SOMETIMES OBSCURE
AND PERPLEXING?

[MS p. 141]

Cleverness
of demons
in giving
dreams fore-
shadowing
the future

But let us investigate and discover the reason why
divinely inspired dreams are not always clear and
open but rather perplexing, shadowed and obscured
by images and likenesses of other things and not only
hidden in meaning to others but least perceptible
even to those to whom they are given. Although the
gods of the pagans, i.e., the demons, could not have
certain knowledge of future events, they quite often
gave dreams to indicate the future, but obscure and
ambiguous ones which could easily be distorted and
applied to different, even conflicting consequences; this
way the dream would seem to conform to whatever
happened. But if the dreams did not correspond to the
outcome, this was attributed not to their falsity
but to the ignorance of the interpreters who, because
of the dreams' obscurity and ambiguity, had not correctly interpreted them. However, dreams whose origin
we know from the Scriptures to have been God's are
most often given distinctly and explicitly; such, we
read, were the dreams of Abimelech, Laban, Judas
Maccabaeus, Solomon, blessed Joseph and the three
Magi. Nevertheless, it must not be denied that certain

Four reasons
why divine
dreams some-
times may
be extremely
obscure

dreams have been sent in a covered, obscure manner
to refined men also and clearly for this end: that they
acquire an understanding of these dreams which they
could get from no others but holy men, and that
they should honor those servants of God and seek after
God with the highest reverence and veneration. Indeed, if these obscure dreams have also been given to
the servants of God, it is for that purpose that in en-
treating God in extreme earnestness with many tears
and ardent prayers, they should at last gain insight
and understanding of these dreams and, on account of
the difficulty in gaining this, have more esteem for
Him and hold Him dearer. Besides the vagueness of
the dreams themselves, that of the things they signify
is also clarified. In addition, most of the more sublime
mysteries are conveyed more quickly through images
and representations than if they had been expressed

[MS p. 142]

in words clear and exact. For many and varied and
profound as the mysteries are, one statue seen by
Nebuchadnezzar in his sleep was able to foreshadow
them, whereas had it been necessary to impart them
through words proper, they could hardly have been
declared in the longest discourse. Finally, God sometimes intends that dreams be hidden and incomprehensible for a while so that their truth may be the
more firmly recognized and acknowledged through the
consequences itself and the succession of events. This
is clearly seen in Joseph's two dreams which prefigured
his ascent to supreme rank and power.

## SEVENTH INQUIRY: IS A CHRISTIAN PER- MITTED TO EXAMINE DREAMS?

Two difficulties are touched upon in these words,
the first of which is whether divine law permits Christians to examine dreams inquisitively. The answer to
this is easy and immediate, for they are permitted to
examine certain dreams but not others. First, dreams
which indicate good or bad states of the body and the
maladies of both body and soul are observed and ex-
ploited to full advantage by physicians of the soul and
body. Second, it is allowed to take note of the causes
from which arise the dreams which infect our brain,
frighten, confuse and unnerve us so that either we
may by observing effects study the causes unknown
to us and grasp them, or we may discover some way
of repelling this nuisance from us. And this privilege
has often been utilized by holy men. Indeed, we read

Four kinds
of dreams
may be ob-
served and
attended
without sin

[MS p. 143]

in Cassian's twenty-second *Collation* that the ancient masters and tutors of the monks were carefully versed in investigating and ferreting out the causes of certain dreams. Third, the observation of dreams, in so far as some truth pertaining to the speculative sciences or giving counsel as to what should be done is thus made known to man, ought not to be condemned either as superstitious or vain. Finally, dreams which often arouse us and provoke us to crime are forced upon us for consideration by the devil just as, conversely, those by which we are moved and encouraged toward good acts, such as celibacy, generosity, compassion, and espousal of religion, are sent by God to be pondered, not by the superstitious of spirit, but by the religious man, wise, cautious and mindful of his own well-being.

However, it is characteristic of the foolish—that I may not say stupid—to think that an account must be made and concern taken for any dream whatsoever, regardless of how it reaches us, be it rarely, without purpose and by accident. For as has been illustrated above, the majority of dreams possess nothing true or certain but are pervaded by deception and chance. Moreover, it has not only been permitted to regard dreams as though there were invariably something divine in them as the pagans evidently believed there to be in the chatter, flight and feeding of birds and in the entrails of animals so that they thought to derive foreknowledge from them and divined the future. But this practice has been utterly censured, condemned and forbidden in the Scriptures, as even no less than the sins of magic and spells. This is clearly understood in Leviticus 19 and Deuteronomy 18, and the last book of the Paralipomenon, ("leftovers," II Chronicles), Chapter 33,* and in other passages of the Holy Scriptures. And actually, to wish to know the future, which God has placed in His power alone, is arrogant, impious curiosity. To think, moreover, that sure signs of the future are contained in dreams which have no connection or relationship with future things is foolish. Too little have I stressed that this is plainly impious and stupid, for the following proves that those who regard dreams in such a way have been infected and depraved by foolish, profane and absurd opinions. Either those people think that all

[MS p. 144]

* The three places in which Jerome translated "soothsaying" as "to observe dreams." See note, p. 159.

future happenings depend upon natural causes, and
this is false; or they think that these things can be
indicated by any dreams whatsoever, which is obviously ridiculous; or they think that all future events
are accurately foreseen and known by the devil, which
is blatant impiety; or else they think that the future is
revealed by God at random and indifferently through
any dreams to any men, which is absurd. There is no
one who does not see it. And in the end, to place so
much importance on dreams and to depend upon
them to such an extent that one directs the whole
rationale of his life toward their standard, as it were,
and either undertakes or declines action and personal
affairs out of habitual consideration of dreams, is not
only beneath the excellence of man, but also smells of
that fatal necessity of the Stoics, which has been so
many times damned in the Church and exploded and
rejected by better philosophers. So if the astrologers,
who think that human affairs hang upon the stars,
suspended so to speak and entirely removed, are de-
servedly censured and refuted by scholars, then assuredly so much the more ought the superstitious ob-
servers of dreams to be reprehended, especially since
the stars are superior to dreams in their stature in
nature, stability of motion, constancy of order, am-
plitude of power and superior efficacy.

*There is
greater
futility
in the ob-
serving of
dreams than
of stars*

[MS p. 145]   EIGHTH INQUIRY: WHAT MAN MAY RIGHT-
              FULLY INTERPRET DREAMS?

We answer the foregoing question which is asked
as to which man may rightfully interpret dreams in
the following manner. Not just any man may interpret
those of the dreams which have the power to indicate
something and which merit examination and interpretation. Three classes of dreams of this nature can
be distinguished: many are natural, certain ones human and still a few are divine. There is no doubt
that interpretation of the natural dreams should be
properly left to skilled and learned natural philosophers
(*physici*) and physicians, especially to those who know
how to compare the images presented in dreams with
one another and discern what they represent and from
what causes they customarily arise; similar to him who,
taking in hand any fragmented patterns and images
and successfully fitting together their scattered parts,
accurately perceives what the likenesses concern, be

it men, horses, or other things, and he correctly evaluates them. However, the shrewdest appraiser of human dreams, the most apt and accurate interpreter, will be naturally he who is most thoroughly versed in human affairs and likewise one who, as an extremely experienced man, has attained to a complete and perfect knowledge, confirmed by many tests of human character, interests, customs and persuasions, which also assume great variety in different men; one who, as it were, grasps the very pulse of man's social and individual activity. Yet again, it is up to him to explicate divine dreams who stands in readiness to apprehend them, since it is clear that no one can interpret them unless he be divinely inspired and instructed. *"For no one has known what is of God,"* says Paul in Chapter 2 of the First Epistle to the Corinthians, *"except the spirit of God."* But this is especially so since the symbols of divine dreams are ordained through the plan and will of God alone and for this reason can be made known to men only through the revelation of God. Wherefore Daniel thus addressed King Nebuchadnezzar who was anxious and distraught about his dream by which he had been utterly terrified because he could learn its meaning from none of his wise men: *"Neither magicians nor seers, nor augurs nor wise men can explain to the King the mystery about which he asks; but it is God in heaven revealing his mysteries."*

Iamblichus thinks that divine dreams almost never come to men, except at the beginning or end of sleep, clearly because at the former time the mind of man is not yet possessed and stultified by vapors of food and drink and at the latter time when, with sleep fleeting, the fog of the vapors has been dispersed and the mind has emerged from those baser considerations, it is purer and more keyed to receiving divine messages. Therefore, it was the custom of seers and interpreters of dreams to inquire of those referring dreams to them at what time they occurred. For if they happened in deep sleep, the seers flatly rejected them since it was not consistent with any logic that dreams should be divinely bestowed upon a mind sunk in heavy sleep. But, if, however, the dreams occurred at the end of sleep when the mind was now almost awakened to its proper functions, then the seers, deciding that these dreams were divinely inspired and worthy of God as their author, accepted their obligation to consider and

[MS p. 146]

Daniel 2

Iamblichus refuted: as to time when divine dreams come to men interpret them. Philostratus' *Life of Apollonius,* Book 2, Chapter 24, should also be read. Yet actually Iamblichus' teachings of which this one is the most scholarly were chronicled from the superstitious observations, or more accurately, I should say, figments of Egyptian priests. In truth, God has not been bound in that way to the laws of time, nor does He need the moment of time to act. For wherever, whenever and whomever He wishes He inspires with His dreams. He can at any time, and indeed even without time, suddenly calm the nervous agitation of human beings, still the tumult of their animal souls, purge them of phantasy, enlighten their minds and properly ready their spirits to receive divine dreams.

[MS p. 147]

## NINTH INQUIRY: CAN THERE BE FREE USE OF REASON AND WILL IN SLEEP?

*Often in dreams there is free use of reason*

Very often in dreams, especially in those which come to the learned, wise and saintly, the soul of man, because it is related to the use of reason and the activity of the mind, is unfettered, extricated and free. For sometimes the reasoning power of a sleeping person lucidly understands simple things and either places them in proper context or distinguishes them, analyzes, evaluates, and marvels at them, and often it makes new discoveries. The very soul also turns inward upon itself to review its own actions and appraise its keenness. It reflects upon its strength, waits, hangs back, hesitates, debates within itself whether or not the man is sleeping at that time. These things moreover, clearly demonstrate the free exercise of reason during this period. Nevertheless, it must not therefore be concluded that, since the power of reason is sometimes liberated in sleep, the exercise of free will is likewise implemented. For perfect liberty of a man is necessary for complete and perfect exercise of free will: that is, it is imperative that there be liberation of all the senses and powers so that it is the man himself who then acts and is in no way acted upon, that he is the master of himself and of all his own actions, and that during that time it is in his power either to act in a particular way or not to act at all. This never occurs in sleep.

*Never in sleep is use of free will accomplished*

[MS p. 148]

## TENTH INQUIRY: ON THE DREAM OF SOLOMON IN WHICH GOD PROMISED AND GRANTED TO HIM THE GIFT OF WISDOM

There remains a slight problem which is found in I Kings Chapter 3. While sleeping, Solomon saw God and He bade him request whatever of all things Solomon longed for most. Solomon, thereupon, asked for wisdom and understanding to rule over his people for whom he was responsible and had sacrificed all of his other possessions, riches which still seem to be sought after and coveted above all things by the princes of this world. Solomon's request so pleased God that He promised to give Solomon supreme wisdom, in addition to the wealth which he had not asked for, and to bestow them both in overflowing abundance. From this account in the very Scriptures it seems to be well enough established that in this dream Solomon was exercising freely and without impediment not only reason but also volition: for that entreaty made in sleep would not have been able to please God so much and to elicit such a great gift of wisdom had it not been made by his own free will. This difficulty can be handled and solved in three ways. First certainly, it can be replied that Solomon's petition during sleep pleased God not in itself, but on account of a certain similar request made previously in waking hours and from which the one in sleep unquestionably derived. For Solomon had most ardently entreated and beseeched of God the gift of knowledge and wisdom. God expressed through that dream that this request had been most gratifying to Him and that it would have the desired effect. But perhaps this answer will seem more than slightly awkward and contrived to some. Therefore, let me submit another solution; for it could be said that this was a dream in the beginning but then by the miraculous working of God was converted into an ecstatic or rapturous experience, such as actually often occurred to St. Paul or the prophets. In this state the spirit of Solomon, as permitted by the body, was deflected from consciousness of external things like the spirit of sleeping people; though here it was done through the power of God so that, delivered and free then to exercise the functions of both reason and free will, Solomon voluntarily sought of God what he wished, and by asking things which were pleasing to God, was all worthy to receive them from him. But this answer is not satisfactory. Now I submit for

Threefold
solution
[MS p. 149]

consideration whether a perfect use of free will can
exist in rapture and ecstacy. I firmly maintain that the
Holy Scriptures do not support the foregoing explanation. At least in the above mentioned passages where
they are about to describe that vision of Solomon,
they declare that God appeared to Solomon in a

I Kings 3

dream; and then, having related the vision, they add
*"Thereupon Solomon awoke and understood that it
was a dream,"* whereby it is specifically indicated that
this vision was in no way a rapturous transport or
ecstacy, but entirely a dream, albeit a divine dream,
obviously given by God to enlighten and to instruct
Solomon. St. Thomas gives these two solutions to the

[MS p. 150]

proposed question in I, 2. Question 113, article 3, to 2.

Therefore, unless I am mistaken, there will yet be a
third more likely and suitable answer, which has been
highly praised even by Tostadus in his twelfth inquiry
concerning the First Book of Kings, Chapter 3. We

Why that
dream was
given to
Solomon

maintain that since Solomon was then truly sleeping
and his vision was a dream just as the Scriptures
attest, anything that is said to have been accomplished
thereupon, as a consequence enacted at that time, was
done not in reality, but rather through the imaginary
vision of the sleeping person. Thus Solomon at that
moment seemed to himself to be seeking knowledge
from God and God also seemed to him to assent to
his request, while in reality, however, there was no
petition, no desire on Solomon's part and likewise
no response and no promise from God. Why therefore,
you ask, was that dream given to Solomon by God?
Evidently, unless my conjecture is wrong, He did it
for three reasons: first, that it might be recognized
that the author and bestower of all blessings is God
and that all benefits must be sought and requested
from Him. Second, that it might be made clear which
choice and petition of blessings is pleasing and wel-
come to God: those which are spiritual are far preferred to the corporeal, the celestial blessings to the
terrestrial, and finally those concerning the coming
interest and well-being of others to those which are
vain and fruitless. And last, so that it might be open
and manifest from the example of Solomon how great
is the benignity and munificence of God toward his
servants, whose prayers and entreaties He not only
answers but far surpasses and over abundantly ful-
fills. Consider, then, Solomon: he sought only knowledge from God, having renounced all other goods beyond this, which are the most precious and dear to

men. But God generously granted both knowledge above Solomon's hope and other blessings beyond Solomon's prayer.

[MS p. 151]  Now let our discussion on dreams terminate here, as I fear it would become painful and boring to the reader should it be protracted. For even as sleep sweetly revives the limbs and restores strength because it is quiet and peaceful, if dreams which are too long, serious and oppressive occur in sleep, they will tire and weaken the body and soul alike. Thus we have had to be extremely cautious that this discussion of ours on dreams not become long beyond usefulness, lose the appreciation of the readers and turn the pleasure which they have perhaps derived into criticism and hostility.

# Bibliography

Arthur M. Abell, *Talks with Great Composers*. New York, Philosophical Library, Inc., 1955.

*Aeschylus* (Plays), trans. Lewis Campbell. London, Oxford University Press (Humphrey Milford), 1912.

*The Anchor Bible*. Garden City, New York, Doubleday & Company, Inc., various dates.

*The Ante-Nicene Fathers*. Grand Rapids, Michigan, Wm. B. Eerdmans Publishing Company, various dates.

Apuleius, *The Golden Ass*, trans. Robert Graves. New York, Pocket Books, Inc., 1958.

St. Thomas Aquinas, *The "Summa Theologica,"* trans. The Fathers of the English Dominican Province. New York, Benziger Bros., Inc., various dates.

*Five Comedies of Aristophanes*, trans. Benjamin Bickley Rogers. Garden City, New York, Doubleday & Company, Inc., 1955.

*The Basic Works of Aristotle*, ed. Richard McKeon. New York, Random House, Inc., 1941.

——————*On the Soul, Parva Naturalia, and On Breath*, trans. W. S. Hett. Cambridge, Harvard University Press, 1957.

W. F. Arndt and F. W. Gingrich, *A Greek-English Lexicon of the New Testament*. Chicago, The University of Chicago Press, 1952.

Artemidorus (Artemidorus Daldianus), *The Interpretation of Dreams*, trans. Robert Wood. London, Tenth Edition, 1690.

Saint Augustine, *Treatises on Marriage and Other Subjects*, trans. Ruth Wentworth Brown. New York, Fathers of the Church, Inc., 1955.

*Babylonian Talmud*, trans. Michael L. Rodkinson. New York, New Talmud Publishing Company, Second Edition, 1901.

Baedae, *Opera Historica* (The Venerable Bede, *Ecclesiastical History of the English Nation*), trans, J. E. King. Cambridge, Harvard University Press, 1954.

John Baillie, *Christian Devotion*. New York, Charles Scribner's Sons, 1962.

——————*Our Knowledge of God*. New York, Charles Scribner's Sons, 1939.

Henri Bergson, *The World of Dreams*. New York, Philosophical Library, Inc., 1958.

Joseph Breuer and Sigmund Freud, *Studies in Hysteria*. Boston, Beacon Press, Inc., 1961.

Francis Brown, S. R. Driver, and Charles A. Briggs, *A Hebrew and English Lexicon of the Old Testament*. Oxford, The Clarendon Press, 1907.

*The Works of Sir Thomas Browne*, ed. Charles Sayle. Edinburgh, John Grant, 1912.

Edwin A. Burtt, *Types of Religious Philosophy*. New York, Harper & Brothers, 1951.

Karl Gustav Carus, *Psyche: zur Entwicklungsgeschichte der Seele*. Pforzheim, Flammer und Hoffman, 1846.

Hugh Lynn Cayce, *Venture Inward*. New York, Harper & Row, 1964.

Hugh Lynn Cayce, Tom C. Clark, and Shane Miller, *Dreams: The Language of the Unconscious*. Virginia Beach, Va., A.R.E. Press, 1966.

Cicero, *De Senectute, De Amicitia, De Divinatione*, trans. William Armistead Falconer. Cambridge, Harvard University Press, 1964.

F. C. Copleston, *Aquinas*. Baltimore, Penguin Books, Inc., 1961.

Alexander Cruden, *Cruden's Complete Concordance to the Old and New Testaments*. New York, Holt, Rinehart & Winston, Inc., 1949.

Walter Clyde Curry, *Chaucer and the Mediaeval Sciences*. New York, Barnes & Noble, Inc., 1960.

George Barton Cutten, *The Psychological Phenomena of Christianity*. New York, Charles Scribner's Sons, 1908.

Emile Dermenghem, *Muhammad and the Islamic Tradition*, trans. Jean M. Watt. New York, Harper & Brothers, 1958.

E. R. Dodds, *The Greeks and the Irrational*. Boston, Beacon Press, Inc., 1957.

——————*Pagan and Christian in an Age of Anxiety*. Cambridge (Eng.), The University Press, 1965.

Robert Donington, *Wagner's "Ring" and Its Symbols*. New York, St. Martin's Press, Inc., 1963.

*Dreams: A Key to Your Secret Self*. New York, Dell Publishing Company, Inc., 1965.

Monsignor Louis Duchesne, *Early History of the Christian Church*. London, John Murray Ltd., Vol. II (1931), Vol. III (1938).

J. W. Dunne, *An Experiment with Time*. New York, The Macmillan Company, 1938.

Mircea Eliade, *Myths, Dreams and Mysteries*. New York, Harper & Brothers, 1960.

Havelock Ellis, *The World of Dreams*. London, Constable and Company Ltd., 1915.

*The Plays of Euripides*, trans. from the text of Paley by Edw. P. Coleridge. London, G. Bell & Sons Ltd., 1913.

*Existential Philosophers: Kierkegaard to Merleau-Ponty*, ed. George Alfred Schrader, Jr. New York, McGraw-Hill Book Co., Inc., 1967.

Ladislas Farago, *Patton: Ordeal and Triumph*. New York, Dell Publishing Company, Inc., 1965.

G. P. Fedotov, *A Treasury of Russian Spirituality*. New York, Sheed & Ward, Inc., 1948.

Charles Fisher, M.D., "Psychoanalytic Implications of Recent Research on

Sleep and Dreaming," *Journal of the American Psychoanalytic Association*, Vol. 13, No. 2, April 1965, pp. 197–303.

Augustine Fitzgerald, *The Essays and Hymns of Synesius of Cyrene*. London, Oxford University Press (H. Milford), 1930.

W. David Foulkes, "Dream Reports from Different Stages of Sleep," *Journal of Abnormal and Social Psychology*, Vol. 65, No. 1, January 1962, pp. 14–25.

Sigmund Freud, *Collected Papers*. New York, Basic Books, Inc., 1959.

————A *General Introduction to Psychoanalysis*. New York, Washington Square Press, Inc., 1960.

————*The Interpretation of Dreams*. New York, Basic Books, Inc., 1955.

Paul Friedländer, *Plato: An Introduction*, trans. Hans Meyerhoff. New York, Harper & Row, for the Bollingen Foundation, 1964.

Brewster Ghiselin, ed., *The Creative Process: A Symposium*. Berkeley, University of California Press, 1952.

A. J. Gordon, D.D., *How Christ Came to Church: A Spiritual Autobiography*. New York, Fleming H. Revell Company, 1895.

*Great Books of the Western World*. Chicago, Encyclopaedia Britannica, Inc., 1952.

Saint Gregory the Great, *Dialogues*, trans. Odo John Zimmerman, O.S.B. New York, Fathers of the Church, Inc., 1959.

————*Morals: On the Book of Job*. Oxford, John Henry Parker, 1844.

Mary Hamilton, *Incubation (or the Cure of Disease in Pagan Temples and Christian Churches)*. London, Simpkin, Marshall, Hamilton, Kent & Company, 1906.

M. Esther Harding, *Journey Into Self*. New York, David McKay Company, Inc., 1956.

Adolf Harnack, *History of Dogma*, trans. James Miller. London, Williams & Norgate, 1912.

Jane Harrison, *Prolegomena to the Study of Greek Religion*. New York, Meridian Books, Inc., 1960.

James Hastings, *Dictionary of the Bible*. New York, Charles Scribner's Sons, 1943.

Edwin Hatch, *The Influence of Greek Ideas on Christianity*. New York, Harper & Brothers, 1957.

Alexander Heidel, *The Gilgamesh Epic and Old Testament Parallels*. Chicago, The University of Chicago Press, 1949.

Herodotus, *Histories*, trans. A. D. Godley. London, William Heinemann, 1921–28.

Hesiod, *Works*, trans. Hugh G. Evelyn-White. Cambridge, Harvard University Press, 1950.

*Hippocrates* (Works), trans. W. H. S. Jones. Cambridge, Harvard University Press, 1957.

*Iliad of Homer*, trans. Theodore Alois Buckley. Philadelphia, David McKay, Publisher, 1896.

*The Odyssey of Homer*, trans. George Herbert Palmer. Boston, Houghton Mifflin Company, 1921.

*The Interlinear Greek New Testament*. Chicago, Follett Publishing Company, 1960.

*The Interpreter's Bible*. New York, Abingdon Press, 1951–57.

*The Interpreter's Dictionary of the Bible*. New York, Abingdon Press, 1962.

William James, *The Varieties of Religious Experience*. New York, Longmans, Green & Company, 1925.

Morris Jastrow, *A Gentle Cynic: Being a Translation of the Book of Koheleth, Commonly Known as Ecclesiastes*. Philadelphia, J. B. Lippincott Company, 1919.

Saint Jerome, *Dogmatic and Polemical Works*, trans. John N. Hritzu, Washington, D.C., The Catholic University of America Press, 1965.

*The Jewish Encyclopedia*. New York, Funk and Wagnalls, 1925.

Joannis Saresberiensis (John of Salisbury), *Opera Omnia*, (Vol. III, *Polycratici Libri*). Oxonii, Apud J. H. Parker, 1848.

*The Works of Flavius Josephus*, trans. William Whiston. Philadelphia, Porter & Coates, no date.

*Josephus* (Works), Vol. I, *The Life, Against Apion*, trans. H. St. J. Thackeray. Cambridge, Harvard University Press, 1956.

C. G. Jung, *Collected Works*. New York, Pantheon Books, Inc. (Random House, Inc.), for the Bollingen Foundation.

Vol. 4, *Freud and Psychoanalysis*, 1961;
Vol. 5, *Symbols of Transformation*, 1956;
Vol. 7, *Two Essays on Analytical Psychology*, 1953;
Vol. 8, *The Structure and Dynamics of the Psyche*, 1960;
Vol. 9, Part 1, *The Archetypes and the Collective Unconscious*, 1959;
Vol. 9, Part 2, *Aion: Researches into the Phenomenology of the Self*, 1959;
Vol. 10, *Civilization in Transition*, 1964;
Vol. 11, *Psychology and Religion: West and East*, 1958;
Vol. 12, *Psychology and Alchemy*, 1953;
Vol. 14, *Mysterium Coniunctionis*, 1963;
Vol. 16, *The Practice of Psychotherapy*, 1954;
Vol. 17, *The Development of Personality*, 1954.

——————*Memories, Dreams, Reflections*, recorded and edited by Aniela Jaffé. New York, Pantheon Books, Inc., 1963.

——————*Psychological Types*. London, Routledge & Kegan Paul Ltd., 1953.

Erhart Kaestner, *Mount Athos: The Call from Sleep*. London, Faber & Faber Ltd., 1961.

C. Kerényi, *Asklepios: Archetypal Image of the Physician's Existence*. New York, Pantheon Books, Inc., for the Bollingen Foundation, 1959.

H. D. F. Kitto, *The Greeks*. Baltimore, Md., Penguin Books, Inc., 1958.

Nathaniel Kleitman, *Sleep and Wakefulness*. Chicago, The University of Chicago Press, 1963.

Joseph J. Kockelmans, ed., *Phenomenology: The Philosophy of Edmund Husserl and its Interpretation*. Garden City, New York, Doubleday & Company, Inc., 1967.

*The Koran* (commonly called the Alkoran of Mohammed). London, Frederick Warne and Co., no date.

Alfred Korzybski, *Science and Sanity: An Introduction to Non-Aristotelian Systems and General Semantics*. Lakeville, Conn., The International Non-Aristotelian Library Publishing Company, 1958.

Lawrence S. Kubie, "Blocks to Creativity," *International Science and Technology*, No. 42, June 1965, pp. 74 ff.

William Langland, *Piers The Ploughman*, trans. J. F. Goodridge. Harmondsworth, Middlesex (Eng.), Penguin Books Ltd., 1959.

Nikolai Leskov, *Selected Tales*. New York, Farrar, Straus & Cudahy, Inc., 1961.

Lloyd Lewis, *Myths after Lincoln*. New York, Grosset & Dunlap, Inc., 1957.

Hans Lietzmann, *A History of the Early Church*. Cleveland, The World Publishing Company, 1961.

William Lorris and J. Clopinel (Jean de Meun), *Roman de la Rose*, trans. J. S. Ellis. London, J. M. Dent and Co., 1890.

Authur O. Lovejoy, *The Revolt Against Dualism*. New York, W. W. Norton & Company, Inc., 1930.

Norman MacKenzie, *Dreams and Dreaming*. London, Aldus Books Ltd., 1965.

Moses Maimonides, *The Guide for the Perplexed*, trans. M. Friedländer. London, Routledge & Kegan Paul Ltd., 1951.

Raissa Maritain, *St. Thomas Aquinas: The Angel of the Schools*. New York, Sheed & Ward, Inc., 1955.

*MD* Cover Story, "Dreams and History," *MD Medical Newsmagazine*, Vol. 9, No. 12, December 1965, pp. 167 ff.

Pedro Meseguer, S. J., *The Secret of Dreams*. London, Burns & Oates Ltd., 1960.

*The Life of the Rev. John Newton*. Oradell, New Jersey, American Tract Society, no date.

*A Select Library of the Nicene and Post-Nicene Fathers of the Christian Church* (First and Second Series). Grand Rapids, Michigan, Wm. B. Eerdmans Publishing Company, various dates.

Philip Mason Palmer and Robert Pattison More, *The Sources of the Faust Tradition: From Simon Magus to Lessing*. New York, Oxford University Press, 1936.

*Patrologiae: Cursus Completus (Latinae et Graecae)*. Parisiis, Apud Garnier Fratres, Editores, et J.-P. Migne, Successores, various dates (translations by Gerald F. Penny).

Benedictus Pererius, *De Magia: Concerning the Investigation of Dreams and Concerning Astrological Divinations. Three Books. Against the False and Superstitious Arts*. 1598. (Translation by Elizabeth Shedd.)

Gaspar Peucer, *Les Devins, ou commentaire des principales sortes de divination*. Anvers, 1584.

Philo (Works), Vol. V (*On Dreams: That They are God-Sent*), trans. F. H. Colson and the Rev. G. H. Whitaker. Cambridge, Harvard University Press, 1949.

*Writings from the Philokalia on Prayer of the Heart*, E. Kadloubovsky and G. E. H. Palmer, trans. London, Faber & Faber Ltd., 1954.

Mohammed Marmaduke Pickthall, *The Meaning of the Glorious Koran*. New York, The New American Library of World Literature, Inc., 1960.

Josef Pieper, *Love and Inspiration: A Study of Plato's Phaedrus*. London, Faber & Faber Ltd., 1965.

*The Dialogues of Plato*, trans. B. Jowett. London, The Clarendon Press, Fourth Edition rev., 1953.

*Plutarch's Lives* (the translation commonly called Dryden's), rev. by A. H. Clough. Boston, Little, Brown & Company, 1872.

A. Poulain, S. J., *The Graces of Interior Prayer: A Treatise on Mystical Theology*, trans. Leonora L. Yorke Smith. London, Routledge & Kegan Paul Ltd., 1957.

Helen Walker Puner, *Freud: His Life and His Mind*. New York, Dell Publishing Company, Inc., 1959.

A. J. J. Ratcliff, *A History of Dreams*. London, Grant Richards Ltd., 1923.

Kenneth Rexroth, "Classics Revisited—LV: The Works of Herodotus," *Saturday Review*, Vol. L, No. 48, December 2, 1967, p. 23.

Erwin Rohde, *Psyche: The Cult of Souls and Belief in Immortality among the Greeks*. London, Kegan Paul, Trench, Truebner & Co., 1925.

Albert Rosenfeld, "10,000-to-1 Payoff," *Life*, Vol. 63, No. 13, September 29, 1967, pp. 121–28.

Sir David Ross, *Aristotle*. New York, Barnes & Noble, Inc., 1966.

John A. Sanford, *Gottes Vergessene Sprache*. Zurich, Rascher Verlag, 1966.

Robert Haven Schauffler, *Florestan: The Life and Work of Robert Schumann*. New York, Henry Holt & Company, Inc., 1945.

W. David Sievers, *Freud on Broadway*. New York, Hermitage House, Inc., 1955.

David Simpson, *A Discourse on Dreams and Night-Visions*. Macclesfield (Eng.), Edw. Bayley, 1791.

Frederick Snyder, M.D., "Toward an Evolutionary Theory of Dreaming," Discussion by William C. Dement, M.D., *The American Journal of Psychiatry*, Vol. 123, No. 2, August 1966, pp. 122–42.

Society for Psychical Research, *Proceedings*, Vol. 10, 1894; *Journal*, Vol. 34, 1948.

Society for Psychical Research, *Proceedings*, Vols. 10 and 34, 1894, 1948.

*The Tragedies of Sophocles*, trans. Sir Richard C. Jebb. Cambridge (Eng.), University Press, 1917.

Sources Orientales, *Les Songes et Leur Interprétation*. Paris, Editions du Seuil, 1959.

William Harris Stahl, *Macrobius: Commentary on the Dream of Scipio*. New York, Columbia University Press, 1952.

Berthold Strauss, *The Rosenbaums of Zell: A Study of a Family*. London, Hamakrik Book and Binding Co., 1962.

Burnett Hillman Streeter, *Reality*. New York, The Macmillan Company, 1927.

Suetonius, *Lives of the Caesars*, trans. J. C. Rolfe, Cambridge, Harvard University Press, 1928.

Modeste Tchaikovsky, *The Life and Letters of Peter Illich Tchaikovsky*. New York, John Lane Company, 1906.

Thérèse of Lisieux, *Autobiography of a Saint*, trans. Ronald Knox. London, Fontana Books, 1960.

Calvin Trillin, "A Third State of Existence," *The New Yorker* (A Reporter at Large), Vol. 41, No. 31, September 18, 1965, pp. 58–125.

Montague Ullman, M.D., Stanley Krippner, Ph.D., and Sol Feldstein, B.E.E., "Experimentally-induced Telepathic Dreams: Two Studies Using EEG-REM Monitoring Technique," *International Journal of Neuropsychiatry*, Vol. 2, No. 5, October 1966, pp. 420–37.

U. S. Public Health Service, *Current Research on Sleep and Dreams* (Publication No. 1389). Washington D.C., U. S. Government Printing Office, 1966.

Laurens van der Post, *The Heart of the Hunter*, New York, William Morrow & Company, Inc., 1961.

G. E. von Grunebaum and Roger Caillois, eds., *The Dream and Human Societies*. Berkeley, University of California Press, 1966.

Eduard von Hartmann, *Philosophy of the Unconscious*. New York, Harcourt, Brace & Company, Inc., 1931.

Joseph Walsh, M.D., "Galen's Writings and Influences Inspiring Them," *Annals of Medical History*, Vol. 6 (New Series), No. 1, January 1934, pp. 1–30.

Victor White, O.P., *God and the Unconscious*. Cleveland, The World Publishing Company, 1961.

Thomas Whittaker, *Macrobius: or Philosophy, Science and Letters in the Year 400*. Cambridge (Eng.), The University Press, 1923.

Lancelot Law Whyte, *The Unconscious Before Freud*. New York, Basic Books, Inc., 1960.

John Wild, *Plato's Theory of Man: An Introduction to the Realistic Philosophy of Culture*. New York, Octagon Books, Inc., 1964.

John R. Willis, S. J., ed., *The Teachings of the Church Fathers*. New York, Herder & Herder, Inc., 1966.

Werner Wolff, *The Dream—Mirror of Conscience*. New York, Grune & Stratton, Inc., 1952.

Ralph L. Woods, ed., *The World of Dreams*. New York, Random House, Inc., 1947.

Xenephon, *The Anabasis*, trans. the Rev. J. S. Watson. New York, Harper & Brothers, 1894.

*Zolar's Encyclopedia and Dictionary of Dreams*. Garden City, New York, Doubleday & Company, Inc., 1963.

*Biblical quotations from:*

*The Holy Bible*, Revised Standard Version 1952. New York, Thomas Nelson & Sons.

*The New English Bible: New Testament*. London, Oxford University Press and Cambridge University Press.

*The Complete Bible: An American Translation*. Chicago, The University of Chicago Press.

Grateful acknowledgment is made to the following for the use of material included in this book:

ABINGDON PRESS  Excerpts from articles by Samuel Terrien, Charles L. Taylor, Jr., and R. H. Charles from *The Interpreter's Bible*. Reprinted by permission.

BASIC BOOKS, INC.  Excerpts from *The Unconscious Before Freud*, by Lancelot Law Whyte, Basic Books, Inc., Publishers, New York, 1960. Reprinted by permission.

BENZIGER BROTHERS, INC.  Excerpts from St. Thomas Aquinas, *The "Summa Theologica,"* translated by the Fathers of the English Dominican Province, Vol. 1 and Vol. 4. Reprinted by permission.

BOLLINGEN FOUNDATION AND ROUTLEDGE & KEGAN PAUL LTD. Excerpts from *The Collected Works of C. G. Jung*, translated by R. F. C. Hull. Bollingen Series XX. Copyright by Bollingen Foundation, New York. Distributed by Princeton University Press. Volume 4, *Freud and Psychoanalysis*, 1961. Volume 8, *The Structure and Dynamics of the Psyche*, 1960. Volume 9, i, *The Archetypes and the Collective Unconscious*, 1959. Volume 10, *Civilization in Transition*, 1964. Volume 16, *The Practice of Psychotherapy*, 1954. Reprinted by permission.

THE CATHOLIC UNIVERSITY OF AMERICA PRESS Excerpts from Saint Augustine, *Treatises on Marriage and Other Subjects*, and Saint Jerome, *Dogmatic and Polemical Works*. Reprinted by permission.

WILLIAM B. EERDMANS, JR. Excerpts from *The Ante-Nicene Fathers*, and *A Select Library of the Nicene and Post-Nicene Fathers of the Christian Church*. Reprinted by permission.

THE CLARENDON PRESS Excerpts from *The Dialogues of Plato*, translated by Benjamin Jowett, and *The Essays and Hymns of Synesius of Cyrene*, by Augustine Fitzgerald. Reprinted by permission.

HARVARD UNIVERSITY PRESS AND THE LOEB CLASSICAL LIBRARY Excerpts from *Hippocrates*, translated by W. H. S. Jones. Vol. IX. Reprinted by permission.

RANDOM HOUSE, INC. Excerpts from *Memories, Dreams, Reflections*, by C. G. Jung. Reprinted by permission.

UNIVERSITY OF CALIFORNIA PRESS Excerpts from *The Dream and Human Societies*, edited by G. E. von Grunebaum, and *The Greeks and the Irrational*, by E. R. Dodds. Reprinted by permission.

# Index